THE COMING OF THE AMERICAN AGE, 1945–1946
VOLUME I

THE COMING OF THE AMERICAN AGE, 1945–1946

DUBIOUS VICTORY

The United States and the

End of World War II

Lisle A. Rose

THE KENT STATE UNIVERSITY PRESS

Publication of this book was assisted by the American Council of Learned Societies under a grant from the Andrew W. Mellon Foundation.

ISBN: 0-87338-136-x.
Library of Congress Catalog Card Number 72-619702.
Manufactured in the United States of America
at the Press of the Oberlin Printing Company.
Designed by Harold Stevens.

First printing.

FOR MARIBETH, MILDRED, JULIE,
SHEILA AND JOHN

Contents

Introduction   ix

1. The Edge of Victory   1
2. Inside U.S.A.   37
3. "A Farmer Boy from Jackson County"   84
4. The April Crisis over Eastern Europe   91
5. Countervailing Influences in Washington and Europe—
    April, May, and June   111
6. The Riddle of the Far East—April and May   127
7. Toward a Rapprochement—
    San Francisco and Central Europe, May and June   164
8. Healing the Breach—The Hopkins Mission   182
9. The Decision to Invade Japan—June and July   204
10. The Emergence of Jimmy Byrnes   244
11. Potsdam—The European Issues   270
12. Potsdam—The Atomic Bomb and the Far East   305
13. Hiroshima   356

    A Note on Sources   369
    Index   373

vii

★

___

Introduction

___

The drama of the Cold War that has enveloped and shaped our lives since shortly after the end of World War II has tended to obscure what is truly the central fact of our time—America's indisputable possession of the balance of global power. Whether we in the United States will admit it or not, Washington's actions and reactions, Washington's willingness or unwillingness to initiate policies and programs, Washington's determination or lack thereof to exert all or a fraction of the national power at its disposal has largely molded the contours of world politics over the past quarter of a century. This fact is implicit, indeed, in much of the recent flood of writing about the origins and course of the Cold War. Whether America's ultimate stewardship over the affairs of the world in the past quarter-century has been "good" or "bad" will preoccupy scholars for years to come. But that it has existed there can be little doubt.

How has American pre-eminence been chiefly expressed and defined? A growing number of scholars have emphasized the economic factor. They have argued with greater or lesser intensity that aggressive American plans to shape the postwar international economic structure along the lines of free trade and capitalistic supremacy led to attempts to create a global American empire, and this, in turn, caused the estrangement of Communist Russia and the beginnings of cold war between East and West. Certainly there is ample evidence to show that a number of American policymakers between 1942 and 1945 thought long, if not always deeply or wisely, about the kind of postwar international economic order that they wished to see established.[1] But the fact remains that it was not until December of 1945, when the promise of a postwar loan to Russia at last petered out, or until May of 1946, when United States officials ceased reparations shipments from their zone to the Soviet zone in Germany, that America employed its economic preponderance in a negative way in world affairs. And it was not until 1947 that the United States employed this preponderance in a positive fashion. Moreover, American economic policy since 1947, with the exception of the very early Marshall Plan years in Europe, has been demonstrably tied primarily and increasingly to military aid to those governments concerned with containing, repelling, or protecting themselves from "Communist aggression." In Asia, for example, prior to the Communist triumph in China and the Korean War that swiftly followed, private American investment was limited and declining in comparison to the pre-World War II era. A roughly similar pattern has prevailed in Latin America.[2]

Militarily, however, the United States first revealed and exerted its global supremacy in the form of atomic weaponry as early as the summer of 1945 as it sought to bring the war against Japan to an abrupt conclusion. Washington's subsequent decision to retain the atomic monopoly and then, after the Russian breakthrough, to maintain nuclear supremacy, has been the salient factor defining

---

[1] Much of this thinking is summed up in the 1946 report of the Colmer Committee of the United States House of Representatives, 79th Cong., 2nd Sess., *Postwar Economic Policy and Planning* (Washington: U.S. Government Printing Office, 1946), *passim*; and United States Department of State, *Postwar Foreign Policy Preparation, 1939–1945* (Washington: Department of State, 1949), *passim*.

[2] Guy Wint, *Spotlight on Asia*, 2d ed., rev. (Middlesex, England: Penguin Books, 1959), pp. 165, 190; David Green, "The Cold War Comes to Latin America," in Barton J. Bernstein, ed., *Politics and Policies of the Truman Administration* (Chicago: Quadrangle Books, 1970), pp. 149–190.

America's global pre-eminence and the nature of the Russian and later Chinese challenge to that pre-eminence during the past twenty-five years. And American responses to conceived "Communist aggression" and "probes" since 1945 have led this country into two massive demonstrations of conventional military power—in Korea in the early nineteen-fifties and in Indochina in the nineteen-sixties. While the world has said comparatively little until recently about America's dominant influence over the tides of international trade and finance, it has never ceased to be impressed and obsessed, as have Americans themselves, by their predominant military power—ultimately defined always in nuclear terms. The fact is plain: the American Age has been one defined largely in military terms—by the predominant military might of the United States and by Washington's willingness to use a portion of that might to protect vital national interests. It was Hiroshima, not the failure to implement the Russian loan, not the Truman Doctrine, not the Marshall Plan, and not Point Four, which ushered in the American Age and the bitter peace between East and West that soon followed.

It is doubtless true that even with the atomic shield intact and conventional military power substantially unimpaired the American era is coming to a close as Russia at long last achieves nuclear parity while the new Afro-Asian world and the fully revived economies of Europe and Japan generate problems and pressures too great for any nation to contain or control. Public revulsion over Vietnam may also breed a kind of neo-isolationism that will sharply inhibit future unilateral American exercises of power. Whatever the merits or demerits of these contentions, certainly enough time has now elapsed since the inception of the American Age in 1945–1946 to permit a careful and detailed analysis of its origins.

This is what I have tried to accomplish in the following pages and in a subsequent volume, which hopefully will appear in the not distant future. Both volumes are devoted to two interrelated questions. These, in turn, may be subsumed under the general query as to why the American government and people acted as they did during the first year of Harry Truman's Presidency when the United States emerged from the position of partner in the wartime Grand Alliance to undoubted leadership of the industrial "free" world of the West and of its crumbling colonial enclaves in Africa and Asia. The first question relates to decision-making within the highest echelons of the Truman administration during its first year. Did the American government actively seek the preeminent global role which it clearly possessed no later than the spring of 1946? Or did the Truman administration unwittingly stumble into the position of world leadership? Was there, in other words, a conscious, well-defined, grand design animating American foreign policy during the final months of World War II and the first months of peace, or not? The second question deals with the dynamic interplay between foreign policy-making on the one hand and domestic politics and public opinion on the other. To what extent did domestic cleavages, conflicts, and aspirations prey upon American diplomacy and direct its course? What influence did a divided and turbulent people have upon the conduct and content of American foreign policy during the crucial twelve months between the spring of 1945 and the spring of 1946?

No doubt some readers will be offended by my assumptions and conclusions. It might be well at the outset, therefore, to state that the American response to the agony and passion of World War II strikes me as intensely human and readily understandable. Few if any other people in a similar situation could have summoned any greater wisdom or magnanimity to the task of waging world war while seeking global peace. Nor should the ferocious brutality with which Stalin and his cohorts frequently pursued their essentially limited aims be forgotten or dismissed. But the fact remains that war destroys compassion as well as understanding, that mass participation in a righteous crusade obliterates intellectual clarity as well as tolerance, that exposure to battle, however remote, develops a taste for power and dominance in even the most generous of hearts. That this should have happened to the Americans, as well as the French, the Germans, the British, the Japanese, and the Russians, during the terrible years 1939–1945 should come as no surprise. But in the Americans' case the shock of recognition is inevitably more poignant. From the early days of Puritan New England until well into this century the idea that distance and institutions protected the American people from the corruptions that burdened the rest of mankind has been nothing less than a national creed. We have always believed that we were a chosen folk, set above most of the errors and follies which soiled the public life and private virtues of human beings elsewhere. If the upheavals of the recent years in this country have tended to obliterate this comfortable myth and to make us hypercritical of ourselves and our past, we may at least rejoice that a balance between thoughtless condemnation and self-adulation is in some measure finally being struck in this country. I have undertaken and carried through this project in the hope that it may contribute somewhat to the development of a dialogue of civility about our recent past. If it does so it will have been well worth whatever energy and emotion was expended on its behalf.

ACKNOWLEDGEMENTS

Many people have contributed in one way or another to the making of this volume. Professors Lawrence Kaplan and Robert Ferrell have provided constant encouragement and intelligent criticism. I have had the good fortune of being able to talk over many of my ideas on the end of the Second World War and the origins of the Cold War and the American Age with Theodore Wilson and Richard McKinzie of the Truman Library Institute and with Giora Kulka currently of the American Studies Department, Hebrew University, Jerusalem. Needless to say, they are in no way responsible for whatever errors of fact and interpretation that may appear in the following pages. I am also greatly indebted to the gracious and helpful staffs in all of the libraries in which I worked. I would like to pay particular acknowledgement to Philip Lagerquist and his staff at the Truman Library and especially to Mrs. Laura Heller and Mrs. Cathy Abernathy who put me on to valuable materials I might otherwise have missed. Mrs. Bernice Holt, curator of the Byrnes Collection at the Robert Muldrow Cooper Library of Clemson University shared her great knowledge of the Byrnes papers and Byrnes' career with me and helped expand and enrich my knowledge of this fascinating public servant during his time of greatest influence on national affairs. And, finally, a good friend, John Knowlton of the Library of Congress extended valuable aid and comfort during my stay at the Manuscript Division.

No book is easy to write, and possibly I encountered greater obstacles in completing this one than do most authors. The dedication is insufficient tribute to those who never let me down—and never let me forget where my true interests lay.

1

The Edge of Victory

Early springtime 1945. Under seasonal rains and a slowly warming sun Europe lay in ruins after nearly six years of unremitting world war. Conflict had not yet ceased, but it had narrowed to isolated pinpricks here and there in central Germany and within the smoldering rubble of Berlin. Elsewhere, in a broad swath from the Volga to the Channel, the Continent was a desert of shattered, silent cities, decaying countrysides, and slowly emptying concentration camps. Tens of millions had perished; several millions more wandered famished, homeless, and despairing through ravaged lands.[1] The vanquished lived from day to day in a greater or lesser degree of morbid apathy, awaiting the pleasure and programs of their conquerors. The victors peered into the future with

[1] James A. Stilwell, "Civilian Supply Problems in Europe," U.S. Department of State *Bulletin*, XII (May 20, 1945), 917–923, 927; Acting Secretary of State (Grew) to Secretary of War (Stimson), June 8, 1945, in *Foreign Relations of the United States, 1945; Conference of Berlin*, 2 vols. (Washington: U.S. Government Printing Office, 1960), I: 524n.; "Report of Earl G. Harrison, United States Representative on Intergovernmental Committee on Refugees, August 1945," copy in Samuel I. Rosenman Papers, 1945, Box 1, Harry S. Truman Library, Independence, Mo.; Gordon Wright, *The Ordeal of Total War, 1939–1945* (New York: Harper & Row, 1968), pp. 243–254.

trepidation or determination, depending upon their relative powers and appetites.

Bitterness and recrimination flowed through the western tier of nations, where four years of Nazi occupation had bred a spirit of mean suspicion. Nowhere was this mood blacker than in France, where "physical privation and moral humiliation" had left an indelible mark upon the national mentality. The Allies—Britain and America—were blamed for not providing massive amounts of food, shelter, capital goods, and weapons to the prostrate nation in order to assure instant recovery. General deGaulle and his followers angrily fastened upon long years of insult from Franklin Roosevelt, upon their narrow margin of power, and upon their exclusion from current great power politics, and plotted ways to disconcert the Allies with shows of French independence.[2]

The liberated peoples of Western Europe were not alone in their anxieties for the future. Mounting unease gripped the leaders and people of the Grand Alliance as well as they contemplated divergences in policies and goals, mingled with growing disparities in power and influence. The resultant tensions were becoming ever more obvious week by week and even day by day. Britain was in a state of palpable decline; Soviet Russia and the United States, both on the periphery of Europe, were clearly on an ascendant course. No one could predict the outcome of such momentous developments.

War had fallen upon Britain with cruel impact in 1940, and for the next five years the English people struggled to survive and conquer. They could spare little thought or energy to any other task. During the fourth year of the war, however, their Prime Minister momentarily raised his eyes from battle and diplomacy to ponder somberly the consequences of a steady and tremendous effusion of British blood, sweat, and tears upon the future of the nation and its empire across the seas. "A dangerous optimism is growing up about the conditions it will be possible to establish here after the

---

[2] Ambassador in France (Caffery) to Secretary of State (Stettinius), January 3, February 21, 1945, in *Foreign Relations of the United States, 1945; Diplomatic Papers*, 9 vols. (Washington: U.S. Government Printing Office, 1967–1969), IV: 661–664, 672–673; Anthony Eden, *The Reckoning; Memoirs of the Earl of Avon* (Boston: Houghton, Mifflin & Co., 1967), pp. 531, 574.

war," Winston Churchill wrote in January 1943 in response to the proposed Beveridge plan for comprehensive social insurance in the postwar era.

> Our foreign investments have almost disappeared. The United States will be a strong competitor with British shipping. We shall have great difficulties in placing our necessary exports profitably. Meanwhile, in order to help Europe, we are to subject ourselves to a prolonged period of rationing and distribute a large part of our existing stocks. We are to develop the tropical Colonies and raise the condition of their inhabitants. We must clearly keep a large Air Force and Navy, so as not to be set upon again by the Germans, . . .

"The question steals across the mind," Churchill continued, "whether we are not committing our forty-five million people to tasks beyond their compass, and laying on them burdens beyond their capacity to bear."[3]

By the spring of 1945 the answer was already beyond doubt. For six long years Great Britain had strained every sinew in the elemental struggle for survival. Now, on the eve of victory, her industrial economy had been severely taxed, her foreign trade enormously reduced, and her financial structure critically weakened. The popular living standard, it was later estimated, had fallen fifteen to twenty percent, whereas in wartime America and Canada it had actually risen by nearly the same amount.[4]

A prime factor in the decline of British power at war's end was the exhaustion of the English people themselves. Late in June 1944 with the light of peace clearly visible down the dark tunnel of violence, England was abruptly forced to endure what might well be called a second Battle of Britain. For in that month Hitler commenced his wild and desperate rocket offensive against the island. Between June 13 and early September Nazi V-1 and V-2 missiles

[3] Quoted in Winston S. Churchill, *The Hinge of Fate* (New York: Bantam Books, 1962), pp. 838–839.

[4] "A Record of British War Production Compiled by the *Times* [of London] 1945," copy in author's possession; "Address by Walter N. Thayer before the Bond Club of New Jersey, February 27, 1946," William L. Clayton Papers, Box 41, Harry S. Truman Library, Independence, Mo.; *Business Week*, October 27, 1945, p. 46; William Hardy McNeill, *America, Britain, and Russia* (London: Oxford University Press, 1953), pp. 439–440.

killed or injured 21,000 people and destroyed or damaged over a million dwellings in a frightening reign of terror from the skies. By November the casualty figures alone had risen to 29,000. The silent nature of the V-2 attacks was peculiarly horrifying. Homes and humans died in a sudden eruption of flame. Morale plummetted. Lord Beaverbrook told Harry Hopkins that summer with typical British understatement: "For the first time, the English are not absolutely sure of themselves. . . . Here we are somewhat in the doldrums. . . . The slogan of 'London can take it' will prevail. But there may be quite a lot to take."[5]

Exhausted and battered at home, weary beyond measure, the British people, strain as they might, were unable to give their leaders the military weapons and forces necessary to maintain power parity *vis-à-vis* Russia and America within the Grand Alliance. By March of 1945 American military preponderance on the western front in Europe had far surpassed that of Great Britain and was steadily growing. At sea the situation was even worse. In the midst of the Potsdam Conference Churchill saw fit to remind his allies that during the war Britain "had built only one capital ship and had lost ten or twelve." The Prime Minister later added, "We have no possibility of regaining naval equality with the United States."[6]

Sea power, of course, had been the traditional cornerstone of empire. As Britain's fleet strength was whittled down in European waters during the first two years of the war, her response in Asia to the Japanese onslaught of 1941–1942 was feeble in the extreme. As early as January of 1942, therefore, the Pacific Dominions commenced a public policy of drift toward the United States. "Without any inhibitions of any kind," to quote the words of the Australian Prime Minister, they now looked "to America, free of any pangs as to our traditional links with the United Kingdom." Canada, long

[5] British Information Services, New York, "Report on the Flying Bomb," September 1944 (copy in author's possession), *passim*; *Newsweek*, XXV (January 8, 1945), 51; Robert E. Sherwood, *Roosevelt and Hopkins; An Intimate History*, 2 vols. (New York: Bantam Books, 1950), II: 473–474; A. J. P. Taylor, *English History, 1914–1945* (New York: Oxford University Press, 1965), pp. 583–584.

[6] Stephen E. Ambrose, *Eisenhower and Berlin, 1945; The Decision to Halt at the Elbe* (New York: W. W. Norton & Company, Inc., 1967), p. 53; John Ehrman, *Grand Strategy*, vol. VI of *History of the Second World War*, ed. J. R. M. Butler (London: Her Majesty's Stationery Office, 1956), pp. 19–21; *Foreign Relations, 1945; Conference of Berlin*, II: 254, 265.

a simultaneous member of the American economic sphere and the British political system, maintained and strengthened this dual relationship throughout the war to the overall detriment of the Empire.[7]

Thus by the time of Germany's collapse in early May of 1945, the British government and people found their great power responsibilities to be of almost impossible weight. Yet at the other end of Europe another power, traditionally feared and only recently embraced in an atmosphere of wary friendship and expediency, was swiftly emerging to a position of undeniable dominance. Whether Soviet Russia and her ideology could be contained within the traditional European framework of balance of power politics was at this time highly problematical. Consequently the conservative gentlemen of the Churchill government in London gazed longingly across the grey waters of the Atlantic, hoping once again, despite the anti-imperialist atmosphere in Washington, to entice the New World to redress the balance of the Old.

The Russian regime and economy had, of course, been grievously shaken by the Second World War. Indeed, in terms of sheer physical destruction and loss of life, Russia's wounds were much deeper than those sustained by Great Britain. Figures vary, but it is certain that Russia lost seven million of her people between 1941 and 1945, the figure divided in rough equality between soldiers and civilians. Some respectable accounts place the figure as high as twenty million.[8]

Material losses were also enormous as the Soviet and German armies swayed to and fro across the vast steppes and plains. The Russians in their retreats pursued a scorched earth policy. The Germans in their withdrawals sought to demolish everything in sight.

[7] Churchill, *Hinge of Fate*, pp. 6–7; McNeill, *America, Britain, and Russia*, pp. 39–40.

[8] Nicholas V. Riasanovsky, *A History of Russia* (New York: Oxford University Press, 1963), p. 585; Alexander Werth, *Russia at War, 1941–1945* (New York: Avon Books, 1964), p. 904. Harrison E. Salisbury contends that the Russian "death toll was minimized for political and security reasons. The Soviet Government for years deliberately understated the military and civilian death toll of World War II. The real totals were of such magnitude that Stalin, obviously, felt they would produce political repercussions inside the country. To the outside world a realistic statement of Soviet losses (total population losses are now estimated at well above 25 million lives) would have revealed the true weakness of Russia at the end of the war." *The 900 Days; The Siege of Leningrad* (New York: Avon Books, 1969), p. 595.

Broad areas were thus devastated twice or more. After making due allowance for propagandistic exaggeration, Soviet figures on Russian capital losses during the war remain staggering in scope and scale: 1,700 towns and 70,000 villages totally or partially destroyed; six million buildings, including 84,000 schools, 43,000 libraries, and 31,000 factories, and 1,300 bridges damaged or obliterated; the loss of 137,000 tractors, seven million horses, and seventeen million head of cattle. The melancholy statistics march on and on.[9] "The whole industrial situation was little short of disastrous by the end of the war."[10]

Despite such terrible losses the Soviet Union had emerged by 1945 as the major power in Europe, and her Red Army cast a long and, to many, a baleful shadow over the whole of the Continent. Its leadership initially decimated and demoralized by the great purges of the mid- and late-1930s, the Red Army by 1944–1945 was the largest, most experienced, and possibly the finest fighting force in being. If the Soviet industrial system of 1945 was in a condition "little short of disastrous," it had nonetheless, with the aid of generous American lend-lease assistance, powerfully equipped a superb army before lapsing into exhaustion. In the last six months of 1944 Soviet tank strength increased from 9,300 to 13,400 vehicles. The number of Soviet divisions jumped from 513 to 527 and that of armored and mechanized brigades from 290 to 302. Total Soviet strength on the eastern front on the eve of the final drive to Berlin was 5,300,000 men, supported by no less than 16,600 front line aircraft.[11] Marching through Eastern Europe that last spring of the war, the Red Army gave observers the impression of an enormous and malignant horde.

> First came the Soviet armoured divisions, "well disciplined, well armed and trained . . . the columns of guns and lorries, the parachute divisions, motor cyclists, technical units. . . ." They were followed by "columns of marching soldiers, dirty, tired, clad in ragged uniforms— tens and hundreds of thousands of columns . . . columns of women

[9] Riasanovsky, *loc. cit.*
[10] Werth, *Russia at War*, p. 905.
[11] Field-Marshal Erich von Manstein, "The Development of the Red Army, 1942–1945," in *The Red Army*, ed. B. H. Liddell Hart (New York: Harcourt Brace & Co., 1956), p. 148.

and girls in military grey-green uniforms, high boots and tight blouses, with long hair greased with goose-fat . . . children, mainly small boys; the *bez prizorni* from burned-out villages and towns. . . . Behind the first spearheads drive the staff; they drive in German luxury cars . . . cars with their secretaries and secretary-girl friends and secretary companions . . . cars with war-booty, cases of china, kilometres of textile materials, fur coats, carpets, silver. . . . Cars of the Agitprop Brigade with broadcasting apparatus and theatrical properties . . . lorries belonging to the Political Commissariat, the staffs and motorised units of NKVD . . . lorries with tons of Russian delicacies, caviar, sturgeon, salami, hectolitres of vodka and Crimean wine. . . . Behind the staffs more marching columns, without a beginning and without an end . . . finally the rearguard; miles and miles of small light carts drawn by low Cossak horses . . . a flood from the Steppes, spreading across Europe."[12]

Any attempt to defeat, to neutralize, or to intimidate this vast and ferocious[13] military machine would have been an act of incredible folly. The Red Army was a brute fact—and quite probably the most potent brute fact—of immediate postwar European political life.

Security and recovery nonetheless obsessed Stalin and his fellow masters of Soviet Russia during the final months of the war. And their single-minded pursuit of these goals, coupled with the increasing power which they could bring to bear to achieve them, largely defined the internal problems and politics of the Grand Alliance at this time.

Soviet determination to erect a *cordon sanitaire* of pliable satellite states in Eastern Europe became known to Western statesmen very early in the war. In December of 1941, when British Foreign Secretary Anthony Eden visited Moscow, he was asked by the Russians for "an explicit recognition of their occupation of the Baltic States and of their new frontier with Finland." Some months later Vyacheslav Molotov, in London for talks with Churchill, pressed for Anglo-American recognition of the 1939 Soviet claims to Poland east of the Curzon Line as well as Russian "claims on Rumania."

---

[12] J. Stransky, *East Wind over Prague* (1950), pp. 22–25, quoted in David Rees, *The Age of Containment; The Cold War, 1945–1965* (New York: St. Martin's Press, 1967), pp. 16–17.

[13] For an account of the Red Army's drive through and behavior in eastern Germany at the beginning of 1945, see Juergen Thorwald, *Defeat in the East* (New York: Ballantine Books, 1959), *passim*.

In both instances the British refused to discuss the matter, having already pledged to the United States "not to enter into any secret agreement for territorial revision during the course of the war."[14]

Yet neither the British nor the Americans could long suppress an instinctive sympathy for the Soviet drive for security. Russia, after all, had been the pariah of the European world between the wars. When collective security had been belatedly attempted to contain Nazi Germany, the Russians had steadfastly upheld their end of the agreements, despite exclusion from the last great prewar settlement at Munich. Although the Munich sellout probably cost the Soviets very little,[15] it did give Stalin an opportunity to express righteous and heartfelt anger over the collapse of collective security in Europe—and especially Eastern Europe—against Nazi Germany.[16] Henceforth, if Russia chose to go it alone, who could honestly fault her?

Surely not Winston Churchill. A year later, with the Nazi and Soviet division of Poland an accomplished fact and World War II already a month old, the then First Lord of the Admiralty stated in a public broadcast: "Russia has pursued a cold policy of self-interest. We could have wished that the Russian armies should be standing on their present line as the friends and allies of Poland instead of as invaders. But that the Russian armies should stand on this line was clearly necessary for the safety of Russia against the Nazi menace."[17]

British—and American—sympathies for the Russian cause were further stimulated by events after 1941, most notably by the twin facts that, as Churchill said, it was the Red Army which "tore the guts out of the Wehrmacht," and that Anglo-American forces were unable significantly to draw off German pressure on the Russians until the final year of the war. Indeed, the persistent issue of the Second Front in 1942–1943 clearly generated much mistrust and antagonism in the minds and hearts of Stalin and his colleagues. In

---

[14] Churchill, *Hinge of Fate*, pp. 284, 289.

[15] Cf. George F. Kennan's discussion in *Russia and the West under Lenin and Stalin* (New York: Mentor Books, 1962), pp. 303–305.

[16] Werth, *Russia at War*, p. 62.

[17] Quoted in Winston S. Churchill, *The Gathering Storm* (New York: Bantam Books, 1961), p. 399.

May of 1942, surely against his better judgment, Roosevelt told Molotov: "we are preparing a second front."[18] The Russian seems naturally to have assumed the President was speaking of Western Europe; in fact the Allied blow, when it fell several months later, was aimed at North Africa. Stalin's reaction when Churchill and the American envoy Averell Harriman visited him the following August was to take issue with every one of the Prime Minister's excuses "with a degree of bluntness," Harriman later said, "amounting almost to insult." Stalin "made such remarks as—you cannot win wars if you are afraid of the Germans and unwilling to take risks." Churchill defended the Anglo-American position with care and tact, and a "glum" Stalin finally mustered sufficient appreciation of the North African possibilities so as not to create an open rift.[19]

Such a breach very nearly appeared the following year, however. After the Casablanca Conference Stalin cabled Roosevelt and Churchill his "understanding that by the decisions you have taken, you have set yourselves the task of crushing Germany by the opening of a Second Front in Europe in 1943." When all hope that that event should materialize once again evaporated at mid-year, American missions in Stockholm, Berne, and Helsinki were filled with rumors that Stalin might well be ready to turn to his German enemies to see if they would not guarantee him the security that his Western Allies seemingly refused to grant. Whether such rumors had any foundation in fact cannot now be known. What is certain is that at the end of June Stalin cabled Churchill a long review of all the assurances that Russia had been given over the past thirteen months concerning a second front, "and concluded with words which could be interpreted only as charges of deliberate bad faith by the Western Allies."[20]

[18] Sherwood, *Roosevelt and Hopkins*, II: 147.
[19] *Ibid.*, p. 208; Churchill, *Hinge of Fate*, pp. 416–421.
[20] Sherwood, *Roosevelt and Hopkins*, II: 306, 346; Churchill, *Hinge of Fate*, pp. 238, 289–292, 297–298, 416–421, 427–429, 431–432; Stalin to Roosevelt, June 11, 1943, Stalin to Churchill, June 24, 1943, in *Stalin's Correspondence with Churchill and Attlee, 1941–1945* (New York: Capricorn Books, 1965), pp. 131–132, 136–138; B. H. Liddell Hart, *History of the Second World War* (New York: G. P. Putnam's Sons, 1970), p. 488. Vojtech Mastny, "Stalin and the Prospects of a Separate Peace in World War II," *The American Historical Review*, LXXVII (December 1972), 1365–1388; *Foreign Relations of the United States, 1943; Diplomatic*

Yet despite their sympathy for Russia's quest for security, and despite their discomfiture over their inability to mount a second front in 1942 or 1943, the British steadfastly refused to abandon Poland wholly to Soviet designs. Britain, after all, had gone to war with Nazi Germany in 1939 in defense of the prewar Polish state and government. Indeed, the Polish government fleeing into exile had found shelter and succor in London. Any changes in postwar Poland's territorial or political *status quo* would at least have to be gravely weighed and quite possibly resisted by the British. Since Stalin and the Russians were determined to have a friendly— which almost surely meant Communist-dominated—postwar Polish government on their border, plus a major territorial revision of the Polish state—which would incorporate into the Soviet Union that part of eastern Poland beyond the Curzon Line—the deepest divisions within the Grand Alliance were bound to converge on this issue. The rigid intransigence of the Polish government in exile in London only served to make matters worse. Thus throughout the war British policy oscillated between reluctant support and guilty rejection of Polish demands for meaningful independence.

By the end of 1944, however, the relative positions of the Allied armies and the disparities of power between Britain and Russia within the Grand Alliance had foreclosed whatever opportunities there might have been for any significant British or London Polish influence over events in Eastern Europe. The Red Army stood on the Vistula, gasping after its first triumphant leap westward from the Soviet border toward Berlin. Other Soviet divisions had already penetrated deeply into the Balkans. Soon the entire great mass would gather its energies once more for the final swift leap toward the Nazi capital. Behind the army, in Poland, Stalin had first given powers of civil control and was now preparing to extend recognition to a Communist-laden Committee of National Liberation, which at the close of the year would become known as the Lublin

Papers, 6 vols. (Washington: U. S. Government Printing Office, 1963–1965), III: 621–622, 667–668, 682–686. American correspondents in Russia in 1942 and 1943 were frequently accosted by angry citizens, who accused London and Washington of waging a deliberate policy of peripheral warfare in Europe, leaving the Soviet Union to battle Hitler's legions to mutual exhaustion so that the West could "control the world" after victory. Maurice Hindus, *Mother Russia* (Garden City, N.Y.: Doubleday, Doran & Co., 1943), p. 376.

Provisional Government. Moreover, Stalin had already taken steps to assure the destruction of as many non-Communist elements inside Poland as possible. Those members of the Polish Resistance who had heeded London's call to identify themselves to the advancing Russian Liberation quickly found themselves arrested, and some were summarily executed. When, in August of 1944, Warsaw had revolted against its German garrison, certain that the nearby Red Army would come to its aid, Stalin simply stopped his forces and unshakably refused to allow the Anglo-American air forces to render aid to the city through use of Russian airfields. The subsequent extirpation of the rebels by the withdrawing Germans generated bitterness and rage everywhere and clearly indicated Stalin's iron determination to resolve the Polish issue his way.[21]

Meanwhile the Anglo-American forces, which had at last invaded the Continent in June, were—and were to remain throughout the year—bogged down on the far side of the Rhine. What could the British, in their own weakened condition, have done other than what they did do? In October of 1944 Churchill flew to Moscow to make his famous deal with Stalin, wherein Britain agreed to renounce significant influence in the Balkans in return for Soviet pledges to refrain from direct aid to the Communist rebels in Greece. While there the Prime Minister summoned London Polish Premier Stanislaw Mikolajczyk and once again, as he had so often done in the past, urged him and his government to accept the Curzon Line and thus accept the forceful wrench of the Polish state westward. In return Stalin had hinted to Churchill that Mikolajczyk himself might be tapped to head a reorganized Polish provisional government. Mikolajczyk, as *he* had so often done in the past, stubbornly responded that all such political and territorial decisions could only be made by the Polish people themselves. Lurking behind Mikolajczyk's intransigence was the devout hope, scarcely kindled by Roosevelt, that the Americans, the third factor in the

---

[21] Hugh Seton-Watson, *The East European Revolution*, 3d ed. (New York: Frederick A. Praeger, Inc., 1956), pp. 154–155; Winston S. Churchill, *Triumph and Tragedy* (New York: Bantam Books, 1962), pp. 110–124, gives the fullest account. Cf. also Eden, *The Reckoning*, pp. 548–549; George F. Kennan, *Memoirs (1925–1950)* (New York: Bantam Books, 1969), p. 221; Edward J. Rozek, *Allied Wartime Diplomacy; A Pattern in Poland* (New York: John A. Wiley and Sons, 1958), pp. 248–259.

power equation composing the Grand Alliance, might be induced to intervene decisively on behalf of the London Poles. Poor Mikolajczyk. To his utter horror—"shocked surprise" was his public reaction—he was soon informed by Molotov, with American Ambassador Harriman present and silent, that at the Tehran Conference the year before Roosevelt had already approved the territorial transfer to Russia east of the Curzon Line. The shattered Premier returned to London to urge his colleagues to accept the line with minor revisions. Their stout refusal forced him to step aside at the end of the year and threw control of the London Polish government into the hands of the extreme anti-Soviet intransigents.[22]

In truth, whatever British or Polish hopes existed that America might risk further strain within the Big Three Alliance in order to project her influence into Eastern Europe were wholly chimerical. As we shall see, American officials conceived that their major interests lay elsewhere, in Asia and the Pacific, and they accordingly threw the bulk of their power and attention in that direction. Moreover, to achieve their aims in this region, Soviet aid was deemed of prime importance. The essential disinterest of the United States in Eastern Europe and the subversion of European interests generally to affairs in the Far East clearly appeared in a secret conversation which Roosevelt and Harriman had had with Stalin and Molotov at Tehran in December of 1943. It was this conversation to which the Soviet Foreign Minister correctly alluded at Moscow a year later when he told Mikolajczyk that Roosevelt had already accepted the Russian demand for the Curzon boundary.

In the hot stillness of a Middle Eastern afternoon in his quarters at the Soviet Embassy in Tehran, the President first told Stalin that he had summoned him "to discuss a matter briefly and frankly." Roosevelt "said it referred to internal American politics" and, according to the record, began by saying

---

[22] Churchill, *Triumph and Tragedy*, pp. 196–197, 204, 205; Seton-Watson, *East European Revolution*, pp. 155–156; Rozek, *Allied Wartime Diplomacy*, pp. 267–293, 313–318. The bitter remembrances of the London Polish Ambassador to Washington during the war years are set forth in Jan Ciechanowski, *Defeat in Victory* (New York: Doubleday & Company, Inc., 1947). See esp. pp. 167–356 for an account of the evasive American attitude toward the London Poles.

that we had an election in 1944 and that while personally he did not wish to run again, if the war was still in progress, he might have to.

He added that there were in the United States from six to seven million Americans of Polish extraction, and as a practical man, he did not wish to lose their vote. He said personally he agreed with the views of Marshal Stalin as to the necessity of the restoration of a Polish state but would like to see the Eastern border [of Poland] moved further to the west [*i.e.*, to the Curzon Line] and the Western border moved even to the River Oder [thereby completely supporting Stalin's demands]. He hoped, however, that the Marshal would understand that for political reasons outlined above, he could not participate in any decision here in Tehran or even next winter [1944–1945] on this subject and that he could not publicly take part in any such arrangement at the present time.

MARSHAL STALIN replied that now the President explained, he had understood.

THE PRESIDENT went on to say that there were a number of persons of Lithuanian, Latvian, and Estonian origin, in that order, in the United States. He said that he fully realized the three Baltic Republics had in history and again more recently been a part of Russia and added jokingly that when the Soviet armies re-occupied these areas, he did not intend to go to war with the Soviet Union on this point.

He went on to say that the big issue in the United States, insofar as public opinion went, would be the question of referendum and the right of self-determination. *He said he thought world opinion would want some expression of the will of the people, perhaps not immediately after their re-occupation by Soviet forces, but some day,* and that he personally was confident that the people would vote to join the Soviet Union.

After some little conversation on the matter Roosevelt begged Stalin for "some public declaration in regard to . . . future elections." Stalin replied that there would be "plenty of opportunities for such an expression of the will of the people," and the interview ended.[23]

As the Yalta accords of February 1945 on Poland and liberated Europe clearly attest, Roosevelt never deviated significantly from this fundamentally disinterested view of Eastern Europe. Fully sympathetic to the Russian quest for security, he at no time sought

[23] *Foreign Relations of the United States, Diplomatic Papers; The Conferences at Cairo and Tehran, 1943* (Washington: U.S. Government Printing Office, 1961), pp. 594–595. Italics added.

to contest significantly Soviet control over the region east of the Elbe.

However, geographic security was inseparable from material recovery in the minds of Russian officials as the European war reached its climax. A prostrate Soviet Union would ultimately be incapable of resisting future German aggression no matter how deep or secure the buffer zone of satellite states might be. Russia demanded not only physical separation from future German power, but also superior strength *vis-à-vis* that power. From the Soviet perspective the only way to attain both revenge and incontestable superiority over Germany was to rule and ruin her at the same time. The Russians at Yalta quickly accepted the rather vaguely conceived, four-zone joint-occupational arrangement initially worked up at British initiative in the European Advisory Commission. Beyond that Stalin and Molotov insisted that ravaged Germany be compelled to supply massive amounts of "first aid" through vast reparations payments, which would allow the Soviet economy to rebuild itself. The removal of eighty percent of *all* German industry and the sum total of twenty billion dollars, half of which would go to Russia, were the reparations figures advanced by Soviet officials at the Crimean meeting.[24]

This draconian solution to the problem of postwar Germany struck a responsive chord in most hearts. "The vast emotions of an outraged and quivering world,"[25] to quote Churchill, were currently riveted on the Master Race. Yet already many in the West were pondering the question of how badly the Germans should be defeated. The issue increasingly divided men and governments as the war drew to a close and nowhere more so than in Washington, where passion clashed with reason and self-interest. The result was a paralysis in policy-making.

[24] Lucius D. Clay, *Decision in Germany* (New York: Doubleday & Company, Inc., 1950), pp. 11, 13–15; Philip E. Mosely, "The Occupation of Germany; New Light on How the Zones Were Drawn," reprinted in *The Kremlin and World Politics* (New York: Vintage Books, 1960), pp. 155–188, esp. p. 169; John L. Snell *et al., The Meaning of Yalta; Big Three Diplomacy and the New Balance of Power* (Baton Rouge: Louisiana State University Press, 1956), pp. 53–57; James F. Byrnes, *Speaking Frankly* (New York: Harper & Brothers, 1947), pp. 26, 81; Michael Balfour and John Mair, *Four Power Control in Germany and Austria, 1945–1946* (London: Oxford University Press, 1956), p. 40.

[25] Cited in Balfour and Mair, *Four Power Control*, p. 31.

Serious planning for the postwar disposition of Germany had commenced within the State Department as early as January of 1944. By the spring of that year a policy of "stern peace with reconciliation" began to emerge in the Department's planning committee, headed by Philip Mosely, Dean Acheson, and Leo Pasvolsky, the latter a professional economist. This committee renounced both the partitioning of Germany and a harsh peace, though zones of occupation—tentatively agreed upon by Churchill, Stalin, and Roosevelt at Tehran—were approved. Instead, in a memorandum of August 4, the committee advocated "a limited control of the German economy and the elimination of Germany's economic domination of Europe, but the eventual reabsorption of Germany into the world economy." The maintenance of German production at a level sufficient to maintain a tolerable standard of living was also urged. As a matter of bureaucratic routine the State Department committee had included a number of delegates from Treasury, chief among whom was Harry Dexter White. Knowing his own sentiments and those of his chief, Secretary Henry Morgenthau, Jr., White reserved judgment and had the issue brought to Morgenthau's attention during the latter's trip to Europe. It was a portentous journey, for Morgenthau arrived in England at the height of the Nazi rocket attacks to learn that the European Advisory Committee was drawing its own plans for postwar Germany on the basis of unity and not dismemberment. From that point on Morgenthau fought to reverse the emerging Anglo-American policy of generosity in favor of far more drastic measures.[26]

The chief motive behind Morgenthau's initiative seems to have been the hatred of a sensitive man for Nazi barbarities. His proposed solution to the German menace was to plan extreme measures to insure its utter disappearance. Some days after his return, for example, the Secretary asked his more moderate counterpart in the War Department, Henry L. Stimson, "if you let the young children of today be brought up by SS Troopers who are indoctrinated with Hitlerism, aren't you simply going to raise another gen-

[26] John Morton Blum, *From the Morgenthau Diaries*, 3 vols. (Boston: Houghton, Mifflin & Co., 1967), III:*Years of War, 1941–1945*, pp. 331–332, 334, 339–342.

eration of Germans who will want to wage war?" Morgenthau urged that the Allies "take a leaf from Hitler's book and completely remove these children from their parents and make them wards of the state, and have ex-US Army officers, English Army officers and Russian Army officers run these schools and have these children learn the true spirit of democracy."[27] Morgenthau was convinced that, as he later wrote, "Germany Has The Will to Try it Again." She also had the industrial means, and those means, as well as the will, had to be destroyed.

> We know that the most advanced metallurgical industry in Europe made possible the Panzer divisions which crushed a dozen peaceful people. We know that the electrical industry made possible the Luftwaffe and its career of destruction and terror. We know that the chemical industries made possible the lethal chambers of Maidenack. We cannot afford to say, therefore, that we deplore Maidenack, that we condemn the Luftwaffe, that we abhor the Panzers, but that we are perfectly willing to have the German industries which created them remain to do it again.[28]

Morgenthau's moral fervor informed and suffused the drastic counterplan which he submitted to Roosevelt on the eve of the second Quebec Conference in September and which soon bore his name. In essence the Morgenthau Plan proposed to "pastoralize" postwar Germany through a forced return of the great majority of her citizens to agricultural pursuits. This would be accomplished by depriving her of all but the lightest industries. All of the heavy industrial foundations of modern warmaking would be stripped from the German people. Only those industries necessary to support and service an agrarian economy and society would be permitted to remain. At the same time Germany would be dismembered—partitioned into northern and southern states with the industrial Ruhr region internationalized and the coal-rich Saar Valley given to France and portions of industrial Silesia and East Prussia turned over to Poland. Thus Morgenthau sought to solve conclusively the delicate question as to whether zones of occupation were or were

---

[27] *Ibid.*, p. 344.
[28] Henry Morgenthau, Jr., *Germany Is Our Problem* (New York: Harper & Brothers, 1945), Chapter VIII; p. 127.

not to be the basis of a *de facto*, permanent dismemberment of the German state. In his determination to banish Germany forever from the circle of great industrial and military powers, Morgenthau provided an unequivocal and attractive solution.[29]

It was attractive on at least two counts. First, it satisfied the popular aspiration for a "hard" peace which then existed in both America and Britain. In 1944–1945 "relatively few people could think rationally and without emotion about a post-Hitlerian Germany," one scholar later recalled. Despite Noel Coward's tongue-in-cheek plea not to "be beastly to the Germans," in the month of Yalta a public opinion poll in England revealed that fifty-four percent of those queried "either hated or had no use for the German people, not simply the Nazi Government." A similar poll conducted in the United States in the summer of 1944 indicated near unanimous —eighty-one percent—support of the policy of unconditional surrender. Half a year later sixty percent of those polled believed that Germany would begin planning another war as soon as she was defeated.[30] Under the Morgenthau Plan such anxieties could be checked, if not dissipated.

The plan was appealing to internationalists in another way. It might well alleviate the "desperate economic problems which would face Britain after the war." At the second Quebec Conference, where Morgenthau's influence with Roosevelt and Churchill was strongest, agreement was reached providing for an American credit of $6,500 million to Britain, in large part to enable her to take over the postwar markets which German heavy industry, under Morgenthau's plan, would no longer be able to serve. "Morgenthau's response to those critics who claimed that German industry was essential to European prosperity was that Britain would fill the gap."[31]

The Morgenthau Plan represented the closest that American policy ever came to matching Russian designs on postwar Germany.

[29] Balfour and Mair, *Four Power Control*, p. 20; Philip E. Mosely, "Dismemberment of Germany; The Allied Negotiations from Yalta to Potsdam," in *Kremlin and World Politics*, pp. 132–154.

[30] Snell, *et al.*, *Meaning of Yalta*, p. 38; Blum, *Morgenthau Diaries*, III: 328.

[31] Balfour and Mair, *Four Power Control*, p. 21; Blum, *Morgenthau Diaries*, III: 356–359.

But in one crucial respect even the Morgenthau Plan conflicted with emerging Soviet intentions. This was in the area of reparations. Morgenthau's long message outlining his plan to Roosevelt and Churchill at Quebec flatly stated that "Reparations, in the form of future payments and deliveries, should not be demanded."[32] Months later Morgenthau defended his position in a somewhat tedious and obscure chapter. The gist of his argument, however, was simply that in order for Germany to make reparations year after year it would be necessary for the Allies either to allow her to rebuild her industrial plant in order to produce and sell the goods needed to make the payments, or to subsidize her payments themselves, as had occurred after World War I. In the one instance the whole point of the Morgenthau Plan would be defeated; in the other the American taxpayer, who uneasily sensed a coming postwar depression, would be forced to pay the bills of the defeated Master Race.[33] Either way the attempt to create a peaceful, democratic, postwar Germany, which suffused Morgenthau's thinking, would be defeated.

In any event the plan never became official American policy. Neither the State Department, save momentarily for Cordell Hull, the War Department, nor even certain elements in the Treasury felt that the plan was either workable or desirable.[34] Secretary of War Stimson summed up much of the opposition to the plan when, in a "polite but vehement" memo to Roosevelt in early September, he stressed the essentially destructive orientation of Morgenthau's proposal. "War is destruction. This war more than any previous war has caused gigantic destruction," Stimson wrote. "The need for the recuperative benefits of productivity is more evident now than ever before. . . . Moreover speed of reconstruction is of great importance if we hope to avoid dangerous convulsions in Europe." Thus, "the recuperative benefits of productivity" outweighed all other considerations. Europe must be put back on her feet, and the

---

[32] The Memorandum is reprinted in full as the frontispiece to Morgenthau, *Germany Is Our Problem*.

[33] *Ibid.*, pp. 76–88.

[34] Blum, *Morgenthau Diaries*, III: 345, 359; Henry L. Stimson and McGeorge Bundy, *On Active Service in Peace and War* (New York: Harper & Brothers, 1948), p. 570.

heavy industries of Silesia, East Prussia, and the Ruhr were essential to that end. Moreover, to reduce the German population to a total or near subsistence level would "mean condemning the German people to a condition of servitude in which, no matter how hard or how effectively a man worked, he could not materially increase his economic condition in the world." Behind such reasoning, of course, lay the usually unspoken American capitalistic assumption that "democracy" was more than a political process. It was also a way of life, in which the promises of upward economic and social mobility joined with political freedom to keep society at once stable and fluid. Morgenthau could not hope to democratize the descendants of Hitler's storm troopers by keeping them in economic bondage at a near subsistence level.[35]

By the time of the Yalta Conference, "it was clear that Mr. Roosevelt had never really intended to carry out the Morgenthau Plan, . . ." though as late as January the Treasury Secretary continued to press his case on the President with vigor and clarity.[36] Just what plan the President and the Departments of State and War did wish to carry out in Germany never became very clear. At the Crimea the United States steadfastly refused to be pinned down by the Russians to any set reparations figure, and the zonal agreements and arrangements were vague in regard to detail.[37] The one piece of American planning for Germany which did emerge in the winter of 1944–1945 and which actually controlled occupation policy in its early phase was JCS 1067, a document shot through with contradictions and ambiguities. "Almost every statement was followed by a qualification": Germany was an enemy nation and was to be occupied under that concept. However, she was also to be treated as an embryonic democracy. No steps looking toward the economic rehabilitation of the country should be taken, save those that might be necessary for eventual reconstruction on a democratic basis "or to prevent disease and unrest."[38] And so on and so on. In

---

[35] Blum, *Morgenthau Diaries*, III: 361–362; Stimson and Bundy, *On Active Service*, pp. 566–582.

[36] Stimson and Bundy, *On Active Service*, p. 582; "Memo by Secretary of the Treasury Morgenthau to President Roosevelt, January 10, 1945, *Foreign Relations, 1945; Diplomatic Papers*, III: 389–392.

[37] Byrnes, *Speaking Frankly*, p. 81.

[38] Balfour and Mair, *Four Power Control*, pp. 23–24.

truth, Morgenthau had driven his cause home too well. The administration had once, for a time, accepted the notion of a hard peace. Planners could never be certain that it might not do so again. An oscillating and uncertain policy was the result. And such a policy never conclusively ran counter to Soviet aspirations—at least prior to Potsdam.

Viewed from the perspective of the immediate post-Yalta period, then, Soviet-American relations, while containing the seeds of potential discord over the future of Germany and the issue of possible free elections in Eastern Europe nonetheless were far more harmonious than were relations between the Soviets and the British. To be sure, there was a very perceptible hardening of State Department attitudes toward the Soviets as the final year of the war opened. But the fact remained that England and Russia entertained deep and divergent interests in Europe, especially in the region east of the Elbe, which most United States officials, including Roosevelt and Hopkins, simply did not at that time share. American insistence that no *final* political or territorial settlements be made on the Continent prior to a final postwar peace conference on the scale of Versailles[39] certainly did serve to keep open the possibility that the United States might in the near future reverse herself and project her influence abruptly and deeply into the European cockpit. Yet the basic disinterest in Eastern Europe consistently shown by Roosevelt and his unofficial but very real foreign minister, Harry Hopkins, coupled with the hesitation and vagueness of thought revealed in all the planning about postwar Germany, save that undertaken by Morgenthau, were significant reflections of the fact that American policy-makers were basically preoccupied with other problems. Stabilization of the peacetime European political and economic structure in concert with Britain and Russia were *important American goals* throughout the war. But *vital American interests* in the early spring of 1945 revolved around military triumph in the Pacific and the postwar future of Asia.

By the autumn of 1944 many Americans had come to the conclusion that Germany was beaten and indeed might surrender in

[39] Cf. Churchill, *Triumph and Tragedy*, pp. 198, 200.

a matter of weeks. Fears that the Normandy invasion might soon become bogged down in the kind of static trench warfare that had so hideously sapped Allied strength between 1915 and 1917 were dissipated in the magnificent sweep of the Anglo-American armies through France and the low countries in August and early September.[40] But in the Pacific the wave of conflict was just approaching its crest. Japan's total defeat in the near future was still very much in doubt. It was to this theater during the final year of World War II that leading American officials thrust the preponderant weight of national power and devoted the preponderant amount of their personal interest. The Pacific war and Asian affairs, not Europe, shaped official thinking about Russia and the Grand Alliance in the months between the Anglo-American breakout across France and Hiroshima.

The history of the Pacific war between the autumn of 1944 and the spring of 1945 was one of unbroken Allied successes paid for at a spiraling cost in casualties. By the time the Okinawa campaign commenced on April 1, Japan had clearly lost the war. A predominantly maritime power as befitted her island status, Japan had lost the last major operative elements of her fleet in a fruitless defense of the Philippines the previous autumn.[41] Although still possessed of many thousands of aircraft, the Japanese air force had long since lost its best pilots in combat over the Pacific or China. Although the home army remained largely intact, the island empire was wide open to assault from the sea and the sky. Indeed, the battle of Japan proper may be said to have begun as early as mid-February, when elements of the United States fleet had launched the first large-scale carrier strikes against the home islands from positions near the Japanese coast.[42] And in subsequent weeks, while the Americans successfully conquered Iwo Jima and prepared to launch their invasion of Okinawa, only 350 miles south of Kyushu, the United States Army Air Force initiated the first of its horrendous fire bomb

[40] Sherwood, *Roosevelt and Hopkins*, II: 451; Winston S. Churchill, *Closing the Ring* (New York: Bantam Books, 1962), pp. 499–500; Fleet Admiral William D. Leahy, *I Was There* (New York: Whittlesey House, 1950), p. 219; David E. Lilienthal, *Journals of David E. Lilienthal; The TVA Years* (New York: Harper & Row, 1964), p. 653.

[41] C. Vann Woodward, *The Battle for Leyte Gulf* (New York: The Macmillan Co., 1947), *passim*; Leahy, *I Was There*, p. 286.

[42] *Newsweek*, XXV (February 26, 1945), 27.

raids against Japan's cities. Rising at dusk from their airfields in the Marianas, vast armadas of B-29s streamed northward through the Pacific night, unhindered by the carefully husbanded remnants of the Japanese air force, to spread huge swaths of flame, destruction, and death across the crowded urban areas of the home islands. The first fire bomb raid on Tokyo on the night of March 9–10 was hideously effective. Over 83,000 civilian Japanese perished in a vast conflagration which left nearly five square miles of the capital reduced to a charnel house of cinders, ashes, and corpses. In the following weeks and months no major and few minor Japanese cities were spared the torch. Although these attacks were justified primarily in terms of the wide dispersal of Japanese light industry into private homes and backyard shops, the terrorist aspects of the policy of "area" bombing were never denied. That the raids did spread fear and panic, that they did hasten the demoralization of the Japanese population, there can be no doubt. Japan's cities were reduced to "limitless acres of ruin." Bombing, coupled with the ever-tightening noose of surface and subsurface naval blockade, reduced the average citizen of Japan to life "on a hand to mouth basis that made a mockery of the modern industrial civilization he had believed he was establishing. He was at best shabby, and usually he was ragged. Nearly always he was personally unclean . . . one sign of the social corruption that had set in. . . . People stood in long lines to obtain the simplest articles of a simple diet . . . the food situation was critical throughout the latter part of the war and was becoming desperate at the end."[43]

Nonetheless, despite mounting misery among the civilian population, Japan's military leadership determined to fight on. For over two years a quiet, behind-the-scenes struggle had raged between

[43] Wesley Frank Craven and James Lea Cate, *The Army Air Forces in World War II; The Pacific: Matterhorn to Nagasaki, June 1944 to August 1945* (Chicago: University of Chicago Press, 1953), pp. 608–658 *passim*; Martin Caidin, *A Torch to the Enemy* (New York: Ballantine Books, 1960), *passim*; Henry L. Stimson Diary, June 1, 1945, Stimson Papers, Sterling Memorial Library, Yale University (hereinafter cited Stimson Diary); Masuo Kato, *The Lost War; A Japanese Reporter's Inside Story* (New York: Alfred A. Knopf, 1946), pp. 3–10; *New York Times*, March 10, 1945, p. 1:9; *Newsweek*, XXV (May 7, 1945), 49. John Toland has estimated the Japanese death toll in the March Tokyo fire bomb raid at 130,000. *The Rising Sun; The Decline and Fall of the Japanese Empire, 1936–1945* (New York: Random House, 1970), pp. 671–677.

soldiers and statesmen within the Japanese government over the issue of war or peace. But by the spring of 1945 the always slim chance for a negotiated settlement of the Pacific war was rapidly fading, in large part because of the rising tide of zealotry within Japan itself. Repeated defeat had tragically served only to rigidify the fanaticism of most of Japan's ruling militarists. "The mind, the soul, the spirit" of Japan, they preached to their civilian colleagues and the public at large, would at last overcome the material and strategic advantages of the invaders during the ultimate military contest for the homeland. And should defeat come, death in defense of the Emperor and the existing political system—the "national polity"—was preferable to surrender and participation in the end of the national polity. " 'One Hundred Million Die Together' " was no empty promise on the part of the military, which brooked no public opposition to its propaganda. In 1945, as in 1942, Japan was a police state, and the punishments for any deviation from the norm, as prescribed by the militarists and enforced by the secret police, were always severe and increasingly fatal.[44]

Japan's capacity for bitter resistance had been demonstrated time and time again in the long, agonizing, and bloody American march across the Pacific.[45] At Okinawa it was to be demonstrated once again. On Easter Sunday 1945, a dozen days before Franklin Roosevelt's death, the largest invasion and support armada in history, numbering more than 1,500 vessels of every size and kind from patrol boats to battleships and aircraft carriers, began landing 182,000 assault troops on the last major defensive barrier before the home islands. Within a week the struggle for possession of the island was proving to be a faithful reflection of the fanaticism of Japan's military leadership. It also seemed a chilling foretaste of what the Americans could expect to experience in far greater

[44] Robert J. C. Butow, *Japan's Decision to Surrender* (Stanford, Calif.: Stanford University Press, 1954), pp. 1–57 esp. pp. 8, 12; Toland, *Rising Sun*, pp. 739–870 *passim*.

[45] A few of the many contemporary accounts of the Pacific fighting which reflect its consistent frightfulness are: Howard Handleman, *Bridge to Victory*; *The Story of the Reconquest of the Aleutians* (New York: Random House, 1943); Robert Sherrod, *On to Westward*; *War in the Central Pacific* (New York: Duell, Sloan and Pearce, 1945); General Holland M. Smith, *Coral and Brass* (New York: Charles Scribner's Sons, 1948); Five Official Marine Combat Writers, *The U.S. Marines on Iwo Jima* (Washington: The Infantry Journal, 1945).

severity as they fought their way into Japan proper. Offshore the support force was incessantly terrorized day and night by the suicide planes of Japan's kamikaze force. On April 12 alone 175 suicide planes reached the Okinawa area, half a dozen warships were struck, and one was sunk outright. By the end of the month damaged American ships clogged the nearby anchorage of Kerama-Retto, while on the radar picket lines and among the mass of ships offshore, the strain of waiting for the next attack, "the anticipated terror made vivid from past experience, sends some men into insanity, hysteria, breakdown." On the island itself the invasion, which it had been hoped might prove a quick operation, ground to a halt before the escarpment and ravine-studded Shuri Line, and a bloody struggle in the mud, blow for blow "a savage killing match," ensued.

> The Japanese strategy is now painfully clear. The Japanese Army ashore is to fight to the death, protracting the battle to the utmost, to pin the U.S. Fleet to close support of the land forces. Intensive conventional air attacks, kamikaze assaults, suicide boat raids, naval surface and submarine sorties [by the few remaining units of the Japanese fleet] and all the desperation measures which can be envisaged by a militaristic nation facing certain defeat are invoked against the U.S. support ships, transports and men-of-war.

Between April 1 and June 22, when Japanese resistance was at last subdued, 75,000 Americans were killed, wounded, or missing on Okinawa and its adjacent waters.[46]

Okinawa merely reconfirmed what the American government, military, and people had long known. Every inch of soil torn from Japanese hands was paid for in blood. Because of their fervent devotion to a root and branch extirpation of Japanese militarism, Americans had become reconciled to the ultimate necessity of an

---

[46] Hanson W. Baldwin, *Battles Lost and Won* (New York: Avon Books, 1968), pp. 463–478; Samuel Eliot Morison, *Victory in the Pacific, 1945*, Vol. XIV of *History of United States Naval Operations in World War II* (Boston: Little Brown and Company, 1961), pp. 152–282; A. Russell Buchanan, *The United States and World War II*, 2 vols. (New York: Harper & Row, 1964), II: 559–567; Rikihei Inoguchi, Tadashi Nakajima and Roger Pineau, *The Divine Wind; Japan's Kamikaze Force in World War II* (New York: Ballantine Books, 1968), pp. 123–133; William Craig, *The Fall of Japan* (New York: Dell Publishing Co., Inc., 1967), pp. 9–14.

invasion of the home islands.[47] But they viewed the enterprise with the profoundest dread. The United States, it is true, was relatively unscathed by World War II. Her metropolitan area never experienced an important attack, her civil population was secure from assault, and her armed forces suffered by far the lightest proportion of casualties of all of the major combatants. But as the war in both Europe and the Pacific reached its climax and American forces became fully engaged with the enemy, casualty figures had begun to rise alarmingly. In the year ending December 31, 1942, the period of greatest reverses and initial victories, including Pearl Harbor, Bataan, Corregidor, Guadalcanal, and the North African landings, the United States Army suffered 37,000 casualties, of whom 2,300 were listed as killed in action. For the three-month period, December 30, 1944, to March 31, 1945, the army suffered 802,000 casualties, of whom 159,000 were listed as killed in action. Some estimates of American casualties to be suffered in the proposed invasion of Japan alone ran close to the one million mark out of a total national population of around 140 million.[48]

The appalling price of final victory decisively molded much of public and official thinking in the United States toward the Soviet Union in the spring and summer of 1945. Active Russian participation in the final stages of the Japanese war, along with American use of Soviet air and naval bases in Siberia, seemed to promise a dramatic diminution of American bloodletting when the awful moment of invasion at last came.[49]

The decision to seek Soviet military aid in the Far East was itself a confession of the failure of American policy toward China. Singlehandedly the Americans in late 1943, led by Secretary of

---

[47] Ehrman, *Grand Strategy*, pp. 203–211; Leslie R. Groves, *Now It Can Be Told; The Story of the Manhattan Project* (New York: Harper & Brothers, 1962), p. 264.

[48] "Memorandum for the Office of the Secretary of War, April 16, 1945, Casualty Figures of the United States Army and Navy," Stimson Papers.

[49] Walter Lippmann, conversing with Assistant Secretary of State Archibald MacLeish in late May 1945 remarked "that Okinawa has taught us that we need the Russians in the Pacific war, since an attempt to storm the Japanese home islands from the sea would cost us a generation of young men." Lippmann was evidently hoping that a mere Soviet declaration of war would shock Tokyo into surrender. "Memorandum of Conversation Between Walter Lippmann and Archibald MacLeish, May 23, 1945," Records of the Department of State, decimal file 711.61/5-2345, National Archives, Washington, D.C.

State Cordell Hull, had foisted Chiang Kai-shek's already exhausted nation upon the reluctant British and Russians as a co-equal great power and prime stabilizing element in postwar East Asian politics.[50] As much to cover this commitment as to prosecute fully the Pacific war, the United States had sought to strengthen Chiang's Kuomintang party government in China through heavy amounts of military aid including advisers at the highest echelons. Strategically, the object of American policy was simply to keep China in the war and to strengthen her sufficiently so that "she might exact a constantly growing price from the Japanese invader." Had this policy succeeded, the Chinese army by 1945 would have been in a position to either wipe out or pin down the Japanese army on the Asian continent so as to preclude its withdrawal to the home islands to strengthen defenses there against an American invasion.[51]

No later than 1944, however, "the devitalizing effects of six years of war" in China "became pronounced to an alarming degree." A series of disheartening military reverses late that year, at a time when the Allies were on the offensive everywhere else, pitilessly revealed Nationalist China's military impotence. Until very late in the war "Chiang Kai-shek's authority was confined to the southwest corner, with the rest of South China and East China occupied by the Japanese. North China was controlled by the Communists. . . ." In the summer of that unhappy year one observer found that the Kuomintang capital at Chungking "reeked of corruption, and Chungking's officials were drenched in cynicism."[52] By the spring of 1945 the Nationalist Chinese war effort and economy were in a shambles; morale had nearly collapsed. Many of the

[50] Herbert Feis, *The China Tangle; The American Effort in China from Pearl Harbor to the Marshall Mission* (New York: Atheneum Press, 1965), pp. 96–100.

[51] United States Department of State, *United States Relations with China with Special Reference to the Period 1944–1949*, reprinted and hereinafter cited as *China White Paper*, 2 vols. (Stanford, Calif.: Stanford University Press, 1967), I: 28–30; Stimson and Bundy, *On Active Service*, p. 528; *Newsweek*, XXV (April 23, 1945), 60–61.

[52] Theodore H. White, editorial notes to Chapter 11 of *The Stilwell Papers* (New York: William Sloane and Associates, 1948), p. 323; Harry S. Truman, *Memoirs*, 2 vols. (New York: Signet Books, 1965), II: *Years of Trial and Hope, 1946–1952*, p. 80; "Report by the Secretary of Embassy in China (Service)," Yenan, March 17, 1945, *Foreign Relations, 1945; Diplomatic Papers*, VII: 287–289.

most productive areas of China had long been in Japanese hands and had only recently been liberated. Ruinous inflation had burgeoned, "and the new Chinese middle class which had been the backbone of Kuomintang liberalism found itself increasingly beggarized. In this situation the extreme right wing and reactionary elements in the Kuomintang came to exercise increasing power and authority." Chiang himself was aware that enthusiasm for his regime was waning in American circles both in China and at the State Department in Washington. But there seemed little prospect that he could reverse the flow of incipient disaster.[53]

Late in April Harold R. Isaacs cabled the gloomiest portrait yet of Chiang's Kuomintang China. Dictatorship, corruption, venality, outright thievery, and inefficiency were all about. "Criminal ignorance and cupidity" defined the senior commanders of the Nationalist Chinese Army. And to the north, occupying and operating "in vast regions around and behind the Japanese lines of communication," carrying on "a constant, fluid guerrilla warfare," lay Mao Tse-Tung's Chinese Communist forces with a claimed strength of 600,000 men.[54] The Communists had come a long way in the eleven years since their banishment by Chiang to remote Shensi province. As with so many other fanatical revolutionary groups of the twentieth century, theirs had been a triumph of tenacity and good fortune over immediate circumstance. Now, in the final spring of the war, they could claim control over wide areas of North China and a record of military activity against the Japanese as honorable or more so than the Kuomintang. Three times during the course of the war Chiang and Mao's deputy, Chou En-lai, met to discuss prospects of an end to civil discord for the sake of victory over a common enemy. All three times, the last only in February of 1945, when the talks were initiated and presided over by the "blandly confi-

[53] Charles F. Romanus and Riley Sunderland, *Time Runs Out in CBI* (Washington: Department of the Army, 1959), p. 254; *China White Paper*, I: 59; "Memo from John Carter Vincent to Mr. Ballantine and Mr. Grew, March 1, 1945, Subject, 'Situation in China,'" Records of the Department of State, decimal file 893.00/3-145; Consul General William R. Langdon, Kunming, Yunan, China, to Secretary of State, April 6, 1945, *ibid.*, decimal file 893.20/4-645, National Archives, Washington, D.C. A recent popular account of America's failing effort in China, which disdains source citation, is Barbara W. Tuchman, *Stilwell and the American Experience in China, 1911–1945* (New York: The Macmillan Company, 1971).

[54] *Newsweek*, XXV (April 23, 1945), 60–61.

dent" American Ambassador, Major General Patrick J. Hurley, negotiations had broken down. At the final meeting Chiang had simply wanted the Communists to end their determined opposition to his regime and incorporate themselves within it. "The Communists wanted an immediate end to the present one-party rule of Chiang Kai-shek and the creation of a coalition government to serve during the transition to a constitutional regime."[55] Stalemate was one result; the other was an increasing frequence of armed clashes between Kuomintang and Communist forces in those areas where their spheres of operations or governance overlapped. As early as January of 1945 worried American observers commented upon "the fact that neither the Chinese Government nor the Chinese Communists were directing their main efforts against Japan," but rather against each other. Outright civil war between the two forces appeared in the making, especially after the collapse of the third round of negotiations in February.[56]

It was against this background of growing exhaustion and chaos in China that American officials began to explore the possibilities of bringing Russia in to help during the final phases of the Pacific war. With China virtually prostrate, some help against the Japanese in Northeast Asia, especially in Manchuria, was necessary.

As early as August of 1942 American officials had begun to appreciate the value of future Soviet aid in the Pacific war. In that month Harriman raised the subject with Stalin, who replied "that it was his intention to come into the Pacific war when he was in a position to do so." Of course this remark could in no way be construed as a commitment, but Harriman subsequently testified that "Because of their ambitions in the East, there was never any doubt in my mind that the Soviets would attack the Japanese in Manchuria in their own due time. The question was whether they could come in early enough to be of any help to us and to save American lives."[57] Thus at an early stage resignation and hope

[55] *Ibid.* (February 26, 1945), 47.

[56] *China White Paper*, I: 61; Feis, *China Tangle*, p. 223. For logical and chronological reasons I have chosen to defer to Volume II discussion of the vitally important conflict between Ambassador Hurley and members of the Chungking Embassy staff over support of the Chinese Communists in 1944 and 1945.

[57] Harriman testimony, August 17, 1951, in *Military Situation in the Far East, August 1951, Part 5* (Hearings Before the Committee on Armed Services and the

mingled in the minds of American officials when they thought of Soviet entry into the war against Japan. Such an attitude inevitably disposed them toward accommodation on a *quid pro quo* basis such as was to result at Yalta. Two months after the initial Harriman-Stalin conversations, Harry Hopkins stressed the importance of securing air bases in the Soviet maritime provinces from which to bring Japan under early air attack. By August of 1943 the Joint Chiefs of Staff began pressing the President to seek direct Russian military support in prosecuting the Japanese war, and they cited such aid as "the most important factor the United States has to consider in relation to Russia." In Moscow two months later Stalin surprised and delighted Secretary of State Cordell Hull with the abrupt and unsolicited announcement that Russia expected to enter the war against Japan at some unspecified date.[58]

From that moment on preoccupation with the coming entry of the Soviet Union into the war against Japan was intensive in official American circles. At Tehran in November Stalin reaffirmed Russia's intentions to fight the Japanese. Returning to Moscow, Ambassador Harriman and Major General John Deane, head of the American military mission to Russia, agreed "that our primary long range objective was to obtain Soviet participation in the war against Japan."[59]

That Soviet entry into the Pacific war decisively shaped American attitudes toward the Russians can be clearly seen from the outcome of the Yalta Conference of early February 1945. "Voluminous intelligence material and evaluations thereof," which Roosevelt took with him to the Crimea, "indicated a long and hard war" in the Pacific. "Imbued with this feeling, President Roosevelt went to Yalta with one major purpose in his mind," a critic has written, "to obtain Russian participation in the war against Japan in order to bring the struggle to a more rapid conclusion even at the price we should have to pay for Soviet intervention."[60]

Committee on Foreign Relations, United States Senate, 82nd Cong., 1st Sess.), p. 3329.

[58] Sherwood, *Roosevelt and Hopkins*, II: 237, 364; Ehrman, *Grand Strategy*, p. 211; Feis, *China Tangle*, pp. 100–102.

[59] Major General John Deane, *The Strange Alliance; The Story of Our Wartime Relations with the Russians* (New York: The Viking Press, 1947), p. 47; *Foreign Relations; Conferences at Cairo and Tehran*, pp. 489, 499–500.

[60] Ellis M. Zacharias, *Secret Missions; The Story of an Intelligence Officer* (New

This contention is fully supported by the agreements reached at Yalta between Roosevelt and Stalin, save that it neglects Roosevelt's equally strong—and ultimately successful—determination to secure agreements binding the Russians fully and irrevocably into the emerging structure of the United Nations organization.[61] At the Crimean meeting Roosevelt and Stalin, along with Churchill, reached agreements on the future political structure of both Europe and Asia—agreements which in their full sweep perfectly reflected the pre-eminent influence which the Far East exerted on American diplomacy during the many months of the Second World War. The agreements pertaining to Europe were vague—so vague, in fact, that they could be and subsequently were almost diametrically interpreted.

The Declaration on Liberated Europe, brought forward at American initiative,[62] is a case in point. Churchill and the State Department obviously sought through this document to undo in desultory fashion the famous Anglo-Soviet spheres of influence agreement respecting the Balkans and Greece reached by the Prime Minister and Stalin at Moscow four months earlier. The new agreement simply stated that all three powers would join "in assisting the peoples liberated from the domination of Nazi Germany and the peoples of the former Axis satellite states of Europe to solve by democratic means their pressing political and economic problems." "The establishment of order in Europe and the re-building of national economic life," the document continued, "must be achieved by processes which will enable the liberated peoples to destroy the last vestiges of Nazism and Fascism and to create democratic institutions of their own choice." Such processes would include the estab-

York: G. P. Putnam's Sons, 1946), pp. 332–333. This view has been recently corroborated by Forrest C. Pogue, *George C. Marshall: Organizer for Victory, 1943–1945* (New York: The Viking Press, 1973), pp. 533–534. Pogue, however, stresses the fact that the Joint Chiefs simply "assumed" an eventual Soviet entry into the Pacific war and did not urge a "deal" on Roosevelt. It was Harriman who suggested that Stalin would almost certainly demand a price for Soviet sacrifices. Pogue's excellent biography, like its subject, eschews interest in the politics and diplomacy of the Grand Alliance.

[61] Cf. Frank McNaughton Report, "Vandenberg," January 13, 1945, Frank McNaughton Papers, Box 6, Harry S. Truman Library, Independence, Mo.; Sherwood, *Roosevelt and Hopkins*, II: 495–500.

[62] Eden, *The Reckoning*, p. 599.

lishment and maintenance of internal peace if and where required, the relief of economic and physical distress among the peoples concerned, establishment of "broadly representative" interim governments, and finally, the facilitation, where necessary, of free elections.[63] While seemingly providing a clear-cut, step-by-step process of de-Nazification and "democratization" in each of the formerly Fascist or Nazi-oriented nations of Europe, the Declaration was in fact a flat failure. The need to maintain internal "order," as defined by any one of the three powers, for instance, might well preclude formation of a "broadly representative" interim government or, even later, of free elections. Such would soon be the case, in fact, in a number of East European countries.

That the President, if not the State Department, recognized the inherent weaknesses of the Declaration and placed little faith in it as an effective expression of national diplomatic intent may be seen from Washington's formal reaction to supplementary French proposals to expand the practical scope and scale of the document. The British, Soviet, and American ambassadors presented the Yalta agreements to the French government at the close of the conference. Paris responded to the vaguely worded Declaration with that exquisite combination of condescension and cupidity which has ever been the hallmark of Gallic diplomacy. The Declaration as it stood was a poorly written state paper that meant nothing, the French implied. But if given formal institutional teeth, it might serve as the basis of a postwar four-power trusteeship over much of Europe. Was this what "the Three" had in mind? Washington's response was an embarrassed no. Establishment of occasional *ad hoc* consultative machinery at best, and informal discussions in general would be the most that Washington would expect to obtain from implementation of the Declaration.[64]

The Polish agreement was, if possible, even more opaque. Just precisely what *was* meant by the "reorganization" of that Lublin

[63] The Declaration on Liberated Europe is published in United States Department of State, *Foreign Relations of the United States, Diplomatic Papers; The Conferences at Malta and Yalta, 1945* (Washington: U. S. Government Printing Office, 1955), pp. 971–973.

[64] State Department Memorandum with enclosures to Officer in Charge of the American Mission, Paris, February 27, 1945, Records of the Department of State, 1945, decimal file 740.0011EW/2-1945, National Archives.

government which the Russians insisted was "at the head of the Polish people"? Reorganization was to be on "a broader democratic basis," according to the Polish Declaration, "with the inclusion of democratic leaders from Poland itself and from Poles abroad."[65] But how many? In what proportion? Roosevelt's personal chief of staff, Admiral Leahy, was astounded at the wording of the Polish agreement. "Mr. President," he said, "this is so elastic the Russians can stretch it all the way from Yalta to Washington without ever technically breaking it." "I know Bill—I know it," Roosevelt replied. "But it's the best I can do for Poland at this time."[66] Here again was a major source of future vexation, but, as with the Declaration on Liberated Europe, it was not one which unduly disturbed or even interested the Americans. And for a very good reason. For they had made it quite clear at the first session that they planned an early military exit from postwar Europe. At the initial session "Mr. Roosevelt had made a momentous statement. He had said that the United States would take all reasonable steps to preserve peace, but not at the expense of keeping a large army in Europe, three thousand miles away from home. The American occupation would therefore be limited to two years."[67] Preservation of future stability and the expansion of political democracy—where possible—in Europe would therefore constitute an important American goal; it would *not* constitute a vital American interest.[68]

---

[65] The Yalta Polish Declaration may be found in Churchill, *Triumph and Tragedy*, p. 331.

[66] Leahy, *I Was There*, pp. 315–316. With respect to the Polish boundary issue, Jan Ciechanowski, the London Polish Ambassador to Washington, was informed by Secretary of State Stettinius upon the latter's return from the Crimea that at Yalta Roosevelt had "been prepared 'to fight for the Polish cause.'" However, the President found the initial atmosphere "so tense" and Stalin so "stubbornly resolved" to carry out his designs on Poland that the President "could not insist on rejecting the Soviet territorial demands." Ciechanowski, *Defeat in Victory*, p. 302.

[67] Churchill, *Triumph and Tragedy*, p. 303. Churchill understandably thought these remarks "the highlight" of the first Yalta session. Arthur Bryant, *Triumph in the West, 1943–1946; A History of the War Years Based on the Diaries of Field Marshal Lord Alanbrooke, Chief of the Imperial General Staff* (New York: Doubleday & Company, Inc., 1959), p. 309.

[68] Secretary of State Edward R. Stettinius later commented with respect to the Yalta Polish accords: "*As a result of the current military situation* [at the time of Yalta] *it was not a question of what Great Britain and the United States would permit Russia to do in Poland, but what the two countries could persuade the Soviet Union to accept.* This was the essential *American* spirit of Yalta." Italics his. Edward

The Yalta Far Eastern agreements, on the other hand, by their very detail and precision revealed where the felt vital interests of the United States lay at the time. Prior to his discussions with Stalin on Far Eastern matters, Roosevelt had been told "that the surrender of Japan might not occur until 1947, and some [advisers] predicted even later. The President was told that without Russia it might cost the United States a million casualties to conquer Japan." At the beginning of discussions Stalin bluntly told Roosevelt "that if his conditions were not met it would be very difficult to explain to the Russian people why they must go to war against Japan." It was an impressive point. Devastated Russia, with a fatigued population, needed peace, not further war. Moreover, the three-month hiatus between the close of the German conflict and the sudden commencement of operations against Japan was almost certain to condition the Russian people to a sense of final victory. If they were to be roused once more to what at the time seemed certain to be a further prolonged effort, the promise of some future tangible results would have to be extended. Roosevelt obviously sensed this, for according to Sherwood, "there was not much discussion." Indeed, it was strictly a two-man agreement between the President and the Generalissimo, for not even Stettinius was present when the deal was made. Of equal significance was the total exclusion of the British from the conversations. "The Far East played no part in our formal discussions at Yalta," Churchill later remarked. The successful drive to win subsequent Soviet aid against Japan "was regarded as an American affair . . . we were not consulted but only asked to approve. This we did. . . . To us the problem was remote and secondary." The British would soon change their opinion on this final point.[69]

Stalin's part of the bargain was brief and to the point. At some future date, but before the initial American invasion of Japan (three months after the end of the war in Europe was the tentative

R. Stettinius, *Roosevelt and the Russians; The Yalta Conference* (New York: Doubleday & Company, Inc., 1949), p. 301.

   [69] Stettinius, *Roosevelt and the Russians*, p. 304; *Military Situation in the Far East, August 1951, Part 5*, pp. 3332–3333; Sherwood, *Roosevelt and Hopkins*, II: 512; Hindus, *Mother Russia*, p. 376; Eden, *The Reckoning*, pp. 593–594; *China White Paper*, I: 115; Churchill, *Triumph and Tragedy*, p. 335.

time fixed upon), Russia would enter the Pacific war "in order to contain Japanese forces in Manchuria and prevent their transfer to the Japanese home islands."[70] In return Roosevelt and Churchill formally agreed first to retain the *status quo* in Outer Mongolia. They next agreed that "the former rights of Russia violated by the treacherous attack of Japan in 1904 shall be restored." Specifically this meant Russian reoccupation of southern Sakhalin, the lease of Port Arthur from China as a naval base, and the internationalization of the port of Dairen with Russian interests paramount. To consummate this agreement Roosevelt and Churchill had to grant Russia the right to form a joint company with the Chinese in order to run the two railroads across Manchuria, which would link Dairen with Soviet territory. Soviet interests in this company would be "pre-eminent," but existing Chinese claims to sovereignty over Manchuria were guaranteed. Finally, it was baldly stated that "The Kurile islands shall be handed over to the Soviet Union."[71]

The fourth party to these agreements, China, was neither invited to Yalta nor consulted about her wishes in the matter. Chungking, it was rationalized, was a hotbed of intrigue. Should the Chinese be informed of the Yalta Far East agreements, the word would swiftly fly to Tokyo, and the Japanese might strike the Russians first. Roosevelt, Stalin, and Churchill stipulated, however, that at some unspecified date the concurrence of Chiang Kai-shek would have to be secured to the agreements "concerning Outer Mongolia and the ports and railroads referred to." Stalin then specifically committed Russia to "conclude with the National Government of China a pact of friendship and alliance between the U.S.S.R. and China in order to render assistance to China with its armed forces for the purpose of liberating China from the Japanese yoke."[72] This latter provision was interpreted to mean that a Sino-Soviet treaty incorporating the Yalta territorial agreements would have to be concluded *before* Soviet entry into the Pacific war and resultant Russian aid to China would be forthcoming.

[70] *China White Paper*, I: 115.
[71] The Yalta Far Eastern Agreements are republished in *ibid.*, pp. 113–114.
[72] *Ibid.*; *Military Situation in the Far East, August 1951, Part 5*, p. 3334.

Roosevelt, of course, gave away a great deal to Stalin at Yalta. At a stroke he helped to restore Russia as a great power in the Far East, and in giving in to Soviet demands for southern Sakhalin and the Kuriles he paved the way as well for the possible future rise of Russia as a great Pacific naval power rivalling that of the United States. And yet the need for Soviet aid in the war against Japan seemed of overriding importance. In actuality, Stalinist Russia was to obtain little more in terms of territory and power than Czarist Russia had enjoyed half a century before. In return, thousands of American lives might be spared.

It seemed a comparatively cheap price. Years later Admiral Leahy recalled that Roosevelt had returned from Yalta not only with a high heart but with a clean conscience. "He had no regrets about what the Russians were to get," Leahy said. "He thought they were valid claims."[73]

Thus at Yalta the Americans and Soviets momentarily seemed to have bridged the enormous gaps of ideology, temperament, conflicting histories, and rival political systems that had for so long separated them in mutual suspicion and antagonism. To the British, of course, the Crimean accords on Europe, and especially Poland, represented but fragile and temporary agreements that might not lead to satisfactory permanent solutions. The Far East was irrelevant. Consequently they were irritated at the American euphoria, which was grounded in the naïve belief that Yalta represented not simply one more round of hard Big Three diplomacy but rather generated important final decisions "that must influence the future of the world." "Harry Hopkins, lying on his sick-bed, is firmly convinced that a new Utopia has dawned," Churchill's physician and confidant caustically remarked.[74] "We really believed in our hearts that this was the dawn of the new day we had all been praying for and talking about for so many years," Hopkins later added in agreement. "We were absolutely certain that we had won the first great

[73] "George M. Elsey Memorandum for the Yalta File," June 27, 1951, George M. Elsey Papers, Box 47, Yalta File, Harry S. Truman Library, Independence, Mo.
[74] Sir Charles Wilson [Lord Moran], *Churchill, Taken from the Diaries of Lord Moran; The Struggle for Survival, 1940–1965* (Boston: Houghton Mifflin Co., 1966), p. 249.

victory of the peace. . . . The Russians had proved that they could be reasonable and far seeing and there wasn't any doubt in the minds of the President or any of us that we could live with them and get along with them peacefully for as far into the future as any of us could imagine."[75]

The millennium thus beckoned tantalizingly; the war appeared to promise some transcendant purpose after all. A shattered world, assaulted by barbarism, could be reconstructed and reconstituted on foundations of harmony between East and West, Communism and capitalism. Critics were momentarily silenced or abashed.

Events of the coming months would swiftly shake this confidence and darken this spirit. There would be renewed calls within and beyond the American government for a reassessment of policy, looking toward a harder line with the Russians. Yet the spirit of Yalta was far from eclipsed by these unhappy developments. As a result, the final days of Roosevelt's Presidency and of World War II in Europe were to be filled with the clash between mounting dis illusion and lingering hope within the Grand Alliance.

[75] Sherwood, *Roosevelt and Hopkins,* II: 516.

2

Inside U. S. A.

Seldom during their turbulent history had the American people faced the future in such a bewildering mood of anticipation and insecurity as they did in the spring of 1945. All were conscious of "the immense problems besetting us . . . the immense forces battering us." Yet there was hope that "the violence could be harnessed, the issues talked out."[1]

At home three and one-half years of war had completely altered the American economy. The Great Depression of the thirties had disappeared under a flood of government contracts. Despite increasingly stringent controls, the American standard of living between 1941 and 1945 had risen markedly, and the pool of popular purchasing power had grown ever wider and deeper. Beneath the crust of affluence, however, lurked unease, division, and recrimination, which frequently boiled to the surface. Roosevelt and Congress were in total opposition on almost every piece of legislation not directly connected with the prosecution of the war and many bills that were.[2] Within the ruling Democratic Party itself, the traditionally

[1] Chester Rowell in the *San Francisco Chronicle*, April 25, 1945, p. 1:3.
[2] Cf. *Lilienthal Journals*, pp. 559–560, 626–627, 629–643; Allen Drury, *A Sen-*

dominant and arch-conservative old guard of southern rural Tories and their handful of northern business allies was being increasingly challenged for power and influence by organized labor, which had itself become a self-conscious political interest only with Roosevelt's New Deal policies of the previous decade.

Labor's determination to wrest control of the democracy from the South in the name and for the sake of New Deal liberalism was dramatized in July of 1943. In that month Sidney Hillman, former president of the Amalgamated Clothing Workers and associate director-general of the Office of Production Management early in the war, formed the Political Action Committee of the CIO. The PAC was committed to fight for every kind of liberal New Deal proposal that the southern ruling gentry abhorred, including a postwar full-employment bill, unemployment compensation, a guaranteed minimum wage, and a Fair Employment Practices Commission to assure racial justice in government hiring. Hillman and PAC soon flexed their political muscle. In 1944 Hillman was one of those who decisively rejected the Vice Presidential candidacy of former Senator and Supreme Court Justice James F. Byrnes of South Carolina. Thereafter the PAC moved into the South as well as broad areas of the North in support of liberal New Deal candidates and in quest of increased voter registration lists. Conservative southern politicians were bitter. "By 1944 . . . it seemed that labor was beginning to replace the South as the principal source of support of the administration Democrats." The "Roosevelt Revolution" that had begun in 1936 with the massive shift of the northern cities to the Democrats was now reaching the highest levels of the party as urban liberals and labor figures shouldered their way into party councils. "Southern Democrats, resentful of the new alliance, hoped that after the war, with the expected diminution of government bureaus, the base of power would return to Congress," and labor's influence within the administration and party would ebb.[3]

ate Journal, 1943–1945 (New York: McGraw-Hill Book Co., 1963), pp. 8–410 *passim*; Roland Young, *Congressional Politics in the Second World War* (New York: Columbia University Press, 1956), *passim*.

[3] Robert A. Garson, "The Alienation of the South; A Crisis for Harry S. Truman and the Democratic Party, 1945–1948," *Missouri Historical Review*, LXIV (July 1970), 448–452.

Conservative fears of emergent labor influence within the Democratic Party were merely a part of a much larger pattern of wartime concern. Labor and corporate enterprise had both stengthened their prestige and power immeasurably in the months after Pearl Harbor as, in uneasy partnership, they generated the production miracle that underlay Allied success. But the price had been high. "Wages, profits, products and conditions of work were all subject to directives and decrees by the Federal Government," a later Secretary of Labor recalled. "Management sacrificed the right to produce what it pleased and subjected itself to wartime profit levies. Labor surrendered the right to strike and permitted its wages to be controlled by formulas and directives."[4] Now with the end of the war in sight, at least in Europe, both labor and corporate enterprise prepared to continue their depression-spawned struggle to control the national price and market system.

During the mid-war period the few strikes that had been carried out, notably by John L. Lewis of the United Mine Workers, had brought angry public reaction against the "Labor bosses" and "Labor gangsters."[5] Representatives of corporate enterprise, however, feared organized labor more for the solid gains it had apparently made under wartime duress than for the few strikes real or proposed. Addressing a general meeting of the Business Advisory Council for the Department of Commerce in January of 1945, James Tanham, who was then chairman of the industry section of the National War Labor Board, deplored "the gradual impingement of unions on the rights of management, such as their demand to negotiate job and production standards, joint wage reviews, individual promotions, and joint disciplinary action." At roughly the same time young George Romney bluntly charged in an Automotive Council Statement to the Senate Manpower Investigating Committee that the "principal objective of the CIO postwar plan drive is usurpation of the authority and functions of management." Rom-

[4] Lewis Schwellenbach, "The Labor Situation; Remarks by Secretary of Labor L. B. Schwellenbach before the [New York] *Herald Tribune* Forum, Oct. 31, 1945," Lewis B. Schwellenbach Papers, Box 2, Library of Congress.
[5] J. N. Beasley to Connally, January 19, 1943, H. T. Bibb to Connally, January 20, 1943, W. N. Beard to Connally, January 22, 1943, and other letters in "Tom Connally, 1943 Folder," Tom Connally Papers, Box 26, Library of Congress.

ney bitterly complained that under wartime government labor policy "unions and union representatives have been exempt from laws with which every other American or American organization must comply. They have been granted special privileges which justify the statement 'Unions can do no wrong.' "[6]

Businessmen were proud—one might venture to say arrogantly so—of the role they had played in shaping and meeting wartime production decisions. Driven into a decade-long crisis of confidence by the Great Depression and real or fancied "anti-business" New Deal legislation and rhetoric, corporate spokesmen by 1944 felt a sufficient revival of assurance to plead "that industry should take the initiative" in postwar planning. They begged government officials "for open encouragement" of business and asked the administration to "leave industry to its own devices and ingenuity" in the postwar world. Only in that way, they argued, could economic growth and stability be assured. Any real or threatened diminution of corporate industry's power in the economy was fervently resented. Business spokesmen thus hurried to condemn such apparent government favoritism to labor as the National Labor Relations Board's decision in late March of 1945 to allow plant foremen, the "traditional base of the management pyramid," to be eligible for unionization.[7]

Militant labor, on the other hand, felt that despite, or possibly because of, wartime gains, the end of world conflict should be the time to push for total, long-term job and wage security. In his last days Franklin Roosevelt had hinted broadly that the federal government should underwrite a plan for a guaranteed annual wage. By the final weeks of the war the CIO had determined to incorporate such a demand into its broad package, which already included, as we have seen, further wage increases, unemployment compensation, and a full employment bill.[8]

[6] Copies of these two addresses are in the Clayton Papers, Box 28.

[7] B. C. Black to Harry S. Truman, with enclosure, May 3, 1945, Harry S. Truman Papers, Office File, Box 172, Harry S. Truman Library, Independence, Mo.; "Speech Delivered by Thomas McCabe, President of Scott Tissue Company, July 13, 1944," Clayton Papers, Box 17; *Business Week*, March 31, 1945, p. 15.

[8] *Newsweek*, XXV (April 12, 1945), 70; "Abstract of Proceedings, Conference of State Industrial Union Councils on Full Production," June 28, 29, 30, 1945, John W. Gibson Papers, Harry S. Truman Library, Independence, Mo.

The stage was set, then, for a major, postwar, domestic confrontation between big business and organized labor, spearheaded by the CIO. Only the federal government possessed the power and resources to attempt to head off such a confrontation, and the chaotic history of the war years did not encourage optimism. The attempt itself, furthermore, was certain to take time and patience and would inevitably divert a substantial proportion of the President's time and attention and that of his key advisers from pressing global concerns.

Divisions within the Democratic Party and between labor and management certainly did not exhaust the list of major domestic problems confronting the American government at the close of World War II. For there were also critical conflicts of interest within the federal bureaucracy itself. The epic and frequent battles between the "war lords of Washington" may well have been the inevitable outcome of Roosevelt's humane and democratic determination to establish federal production agencies in such a fashion that no single bureaucratic empire nor any single interest group would unduly benefit from the war effort.[9] But the effect was to further that public distrust of government officials as well as labor bosses and businessmen which was already present as an unhappy legacy of the depression decade.

The great mass of Americans, of course, were not government bureaucrats, corporate executives, or union members. They were the people who, as consumers, wage earners, and taxpayers, struggled through the grim thirties only to become accustomed after 1941 "to ceiling prices and the alphabetic complexities of ration books," and to "higher [tax] rates, pay as you go and many new tax forms." All of them "conserved paper and fats, bought billions of dollars in bonds and did all we could to achieve victory on the home front,"[10] while overseas the vast citizen armies and navies also worried about the future in the long stretches of boredom or in the brief respites from combat. To nearly every American the Great

---

[9] The best account to date of the wartime economy, and one that stresses and applauds Roosevelt's policy of planned bureaucratic chaos, is Eliot Janeway, *The Struggle for Survival; A Chronicle of Economic Mobilization in World War II* (New Haven: Yale University Press, 1951), *passim*, esp. pp. 1–44.

[10] Schwellenbach, "The Labor Situation," Schwellenbach Papers.

Depression was an immediate and raw experience in which the margin of security had been paper thin if not nonexistent. It must be avoided again, if possible, at all costs.

Aboard a troopship to England in 1943, the novelist John Steinbeck caught the mood of wartime America with pungent fidelity. "Ours is not a naïve army," he wrote.

> Common people have learned a great deal in the last twenty-five years, and the old magical words do not fool them any more. They do not believe the golden future made of words. . . . They remember the foreclosed farms, the slaughtered pigs to keep the prices up, the plowing under of crops, because there was not intelligence enough in the leaders to devise a means of distributing an oversupply of food. They remember that every plan for general good life is dashed to pieces on the wall of necessary profits. These things cannot be overstated. . . . They would like freedom from want. That means the little farm in Connecticut is safe from foreclosure. That means the job left when the soldier joined the Army is there waiting, and not only waiting but will continue while the children grow up. That means there will be schools, and either savings to take care of illness in the family or medicine available without savings.

"Talking to many soldiers, it is the worry that comes out of them that is impressive," Steinbeck continued.

> Is the country to be taken over by the special interests through the medium of special pleaders? Is inflation to be permitted because a few people will grow rich through it? Are fortunes being made while the men get $50 a month? Will they go home to a country destroyed by greed? . . . What do the soldiers hear? —that Mr. Jones is calling Mr. Wallace names; that Mr. Jeffers is fighting with Mr. Ickes; Czars of this and that are fighting for more power and more jurisdiction.[11]

The soldiers, of course, merely reflected the anxieties of those left behind who had conveyed their emotions through the nearest Army or Fleet Post Office.

While the servicemen overseas worried about affairs at home, those left behind in the quiet villages, the great cities, and the fe-

[11] John Steinbeck, *Once There Was a War* (New York: The Viking Press, 1958), pp. 76–78.

verishly active wartime boomtowns, such as Willow Run, Mobile, San Diego, Oak Ridge, and a dozen others across the country, were no less concerned about the unfolding of events abroad and the emerging configuration of the postwar world. Public influence, exercised chiefly through the press and Congress, came to play a notable and vibrant role in American foreign policy-making during World War II.

The "public mood," if such can ever be said to exist, is extraordinarily difficult to fathom at any moment in time, and especially so in modern America. But the war, as a collective experience in emergency, did crystallize and standardize certain feelings. Above all else the generation of the 1940s searched longingly for belief amidst chaos. In 1935 Sherwood Anderson had written:

> "We are people who passed through the World War and its aftermath. We saw the up-flaring of prosperity, lived through the Harding and Coolidge times. We got the hard-boiled boys and the wise-crackers. We got, oh, so many new millionaires. As a people now we are fed up on it all.
> "We do not want cynicism. We want belief. . . ."[12]

A decade later, in the midst of world war, the yearning remained as strong as ever.

At the apex of wartime emotionalism burned the promise that global war would transform the world for the better, that through naked conflict with evil aggression the disillusionments generated by a decade of depression and appeasement would be forever destroyed. This was the central theme embedded in the flood of books, articles, and especially films, which sought to capture even as they reflected the mind of wartime America. Barbara Deming in her admirable and disturbing essay on the films of the forties demonstrates time and again how thoroughly millions of Americans were exposed to the message that national involvement in World War II was in itself a transcendant act of faith. Democracy and decency were at last on the verge of total triumph over dictatorship and degradation. Participation in the war was a cathartic act that would

---

[12] Sherwood Anderson, *Puzzled America*, quoted in Alan Barth, *The Loyalty of Free Men* (New York: Pocket Books, Inc., 1952), p. 27.

sweep away the sense of shame and guilt and futility that had so gripped the United States throughout the depression decade. Global war, it was promised, would give the lost individual of the thirties a renewed sense of place and purpose. It was an incomplete and unsatisfactory message. Perceptive Americans then and later sensed how essentially cheap and false the promise was. The lost individual remained; the moral vacuum endured. But in the feverish atmosphere of commitment to the prosecution of total war the message satisfied popular wants for the time being and gave to battle the attributes of a crusade.[13]

Russia and China were the great allies. Britain was fighting the good fight too, but her imperial system had to be modified to conform to the brave new democratic world of the coming peace. Germany and especially Japan, with Pearl Harbor a living mark for revenge, were the hated enemies that must not only be defeated but destroyed. With war's end the United Nations, the living embodiment of American postwar hopes as expressed in the Atlantic Charter, would lead the way into the desperately hoped for world of peace and plenty. A kind of moral imperialism, then, was the hallmark of American thinking as the war in Europe came to a close and the war in the Pacific reached its climax in the early months of 1945.

The wartime mood of comradeship and folk solidarity felt toward Russia was greatly furthered by the abrupt commitment to internationalism, which the attack on Pearl Harbor induced in the minds of a majority of Americans. In its most tangible form this commitment was embodied in the impulse to re-create in stronger fashion an international security organization to replace the moribund League of Nations. As Robert Divine has shown, it was largely public pressure, and not official leadership, which generated this American initiative in the field of international politics.[14] Public receptivity to official and unofficial propaganda promoting a cult of Russia swiftly followed. But just *why* it followed is a tantaliz-

---

[13] Barbara Deming, *Running Away from Myself; A Dream Portrait of America Drawn from the Films of the Forties* (New York: Grossman Publishers, 1969), *passim*, esp. pp. 1–71. Cf. also John William Corrington's superb novel, *The Bombardier* (New York: G. P. Putnam's Sons, 1970); Rollo May, *Man's Search for Himself* (New York: W. W. Norton & Company, Inc., 1953).

[14] Robert A. Divine, *Second Chance; The Triumph of Internationalism in America during World War II* (New York: Atheneum Press, 1967), pp. 52–68.

ing question that fascinated contemporaries fully as much as it has the historian.

From 1942 on a barrage of books, magazine articles, and motion pictures depicted with varying degrees of emphasis a peace-loving Russia, filled with simple folk who were "just like us" and led by a regime whose undoubted tyranny was either carefully ignored or explained away as irrelevant in the building of a harmonious postwar order. Stalin and the Russians were hailed as our most powerful and glorious allies in a "people's war" whose crusading aim was to build a stable, secure, and open world for the betterment of all. Those who fought democracy's battles, no matter who they were, must be democrats either in being or in embryo. According to this vision, all the common people of the earth, and especially the Russians, shared a fundamental desire to achieve what the American way of life had already attained: freedom, political equality, and comparative affluence. Political systems might differ, but common aspirations and temperament could not be suppressed. The coming world of peace would be an American and a Russian world, and therefore—it was hoped and preached—it could be, with luck and tolerance, a secure world warmly wrapped in the bonds of mutual good will between East and West.[15] After the war, cries one of the characters in the film, *Three Russian Girls*, " 'the people of the whole world will meet together at one big table,' and there the whole world will come to know the taste of— 'What did you call it?' the Russian girl asks the American aviator. 'Pumpkin pie!' he tells her again." Everyone will partake of America's pumpkin pie, "and everybody gets an equal share. 'One big family—that is America,' someone sums up."[16]

[15] The most forceful and widely read reflections of this optimism were: Wendell L. Willkie, *One World* (New York: Simon & Schuster, 1943); and David E. Lilienthal, *TVA: Democracy on the March* (New York: Harper & Brothers, 1944), esp. Chapter 20. Joseph E. Davies, *Mission to Moscow* (New York: Simon & Schuster, 1941) was and is in a class by itself. Some popular elaborations on the theme were: John Scott, "Valiant Russia's Industrial Might," *National Geographic Magazine*, LXXXIII (May 1943), 525–549; Quentin Reynolds, "A Russian Family," *Colliers*, CXII (August 7, 1943), 28 ff.; "It Happens in Moscow," *Colliers*, CXII (August 21, 1943), 19 ff.; Eddie Gilmore, "I Learn about the Russians," *National Geographic Magazine*, LXXXIV (November 1943), 619–640; Edward C. Carter, "Soviet Russia's Contribution to Peace," *The Annals of the American Academy of Political and Social Science*, CCXXXIV (July 1944), 47–53; Nila Magidoff, "Americans and Russians Are So Alike," *American Magazine*, CXXXVIII (December 1944), 17 ff.

[16] Quoted in Deming, *Running Away from Myself*, p. 9.

The idea that "the Russians are just like us" became quite popular in the middle years of the war. Ironically, this sentimentalization of the Soviet government and people occasionally led to the kind of hard-headed appreciation of Russian problems, anxieties, and expansionist appetites, which subsequent disillusion destroyed.[17] More often than not romanticism simply resulted in puerility. In June of 1943, for example, former Ambassador to Russia Joseph E. Davies returned to Moscow at Roosevelt's behest to lay the groundwork for an upcoming foreign minister's conference there and the subsequent meeting of the three heads of state at Tehran. Davies' blatant apologia of the Stalinist purges of the thirties—*Mission to Moscow*—had just been filmed, and he proudly showed it to Stalin and his colleagues in the Kremlin one night after dinner. According to one correspondent, "Apparently even the members of the politburo snickered when they saw themselves represented in this ridiculous picture."[18]

So great was the yearning of most Americans for a postwar world of peace and plenty, however, that even the most sober among them could not resist the temptation from time to time to see Stalin's Russia as other than it was. As late as January of 1945, in the course of an issue devoted to postwar world trade and the prospect of opening up Russian markets to American business, the editors of *Fortune* asked if everything in the Soviet way of life was so different from America. "Maybe Russia is in many ways not so very different from the U.S. under the New Deal. Is the typical manager of a Russian factory a Marxian doctrinaire? Sometimes he looks like a midwestern earthmover."[19]

The Roosevelt administration, of course, welcomed words such as these even as it disseminated its own propaganda through the Office of War Information. And Roosevelt's own positive attitude toward the Russians and "Uncle Joe" Stalin, his buoyant faith in the harmonious future of Soviet-American relations, served to further the work that public commitment to internationalism

[17] Cf., for example, Richard E. Lauterbach, *These Are the Russians* (New York: Harper & Brothers, 1944, 1945), pp. 329–347, 358.

[18] C. L. Sulzberger, *A Long Row of Candles* (New York: The Macmillan Co., 1969), p. 213.

[19] *Fortune*, XXXI (January 1945), 146–147.

and the wartime propaganda cult of Russia had begun. Millions of his fellow countrymen took to heart the President's admonition upon his return from Yalta that "There can be no middle ground here. We shall have to take the responsibility for world collaboration, or we shall have to bear the responsibility for another world conflict."[20] And as Roosevelt spoke, it seemed for this brief moment that all might be well. The euphoria of the Americans as they left the Crimea was grounded in an appreciation that for once propaganda and reality had seemingly merged. The personal wishes and emotions of politicians and statesmen appeared to correspond to public aspirations. As late as Roosevelt's death there remained a tremendous reservoir of support for Russia, as the President's successor swiftly discovered. Jews, of course, were understandably in the vanguard of the pro-Soviet movement, for it had been Russia more than any other nation that had not only borne the brunt of the Nazi onslaught, but had blunted and broken it. The Jewish Council formed one of the largest groups within Russian War Relief, Inc., the biggest such organization of its size at the time.[21] But hundreds of other Americans wrote to Harry Truman during his early weeks in office to plead that Roosevelt's policies not be changed. Press sources close to the Democratic National Committee incessantly played on this theme. As late as March of the following year such pleas continued to find their way into the White House mailroom.[22]

The above factors in themselves certainly explain much of the pro-Soviet sentiment which permeated large areas of American life in the mid- and even late war years. Roosevelt's charisma and the romantic propaganda of wartime comradeship surely appealed to millions of politically uneducated and intellectually malleable souls. But what of the hard-headed businessman whose undeniable

[20] Address to Congress, March 1, 1945, quoted in Basil Rauch, ed., *Franklin D. Roosevelt; Selected Speeches, Messages, Press Conferences and Letters* (New York: Rinehart and Co., 1960), p. 387.
[21] Louis Levine to Harry S. Truman, April 16, 1945, Max Kitzer to Harry S. Truman, May 24, 1945, Truman Papers, Office File 220.
[22] Louis Gould to Harry Truman, May 8, 1945, Robert P. Wilson to Truman, May 21, 1945, E. E. Ward to Truman, May 24, 1945, Press Research, Inc., Washington, D.C., Release, "The Polish Lobby," June 4, 1945, p. 2, Thomas H. Garves to Truman, June 6, 1945, Mrs. Ruth K. Siegel to Truman, March 2, 1946, *ibid.*

commitment to the capitalistic system should have made him profoundly wary of such sentimental blandishments? What forces induced him, or his public spokesmen, to ever assume that beneath the skin of a Soviet factory manager was beating the heart of a midwestern earthmover? In 1944 a brilliant New Dealer pondered this question and came up with an intriguing suggestion which contemporary opinion and immediate events seemed to bear out: In effect, the American businessman admired the Russians because both held and exercised a commensurate amount of power. The American businessman was essentially an authoritarian and no democrat at heart and neither were the Russians. "It is what one *does* that affects his thinking ... and not the things he *says*," David Lilienthal wrote. "A man can't have a democratic spirit if he must *do a job* that is anti-democratic. Does this explain why American industrialists come back as full of praise for Russia; find them so much like ourselves (this Batt and [Donald] Nelson have said to me; and even [Eddie] Rickenbacker said much the same things with trimmings)?"[23]

This attitude was brilliantly exemplified in a letter sent to Assistant Secretary of State Will Clayton in January 1945 by one of his former business partners in a Houston cotton brokerage firm. In essence Lamar Fleming wrote a short essay warning his former colleague against too close an American postwar association with Britain. The Empire was practically finished, and England's influence on the Continent was rapidly diminishing to "the zero point," Fleming argued. "The British Empire and British international influence is a myth already." Fleming then added that the only proper course for the United States was a return to "isolationism in the politico-military sense," and he prayed that "we will determine wisely that part of the World that wants our protection and influence, limited strictly to the part which we reasonably can be sure we can protect. ... If we do that," he concluded, "I do not think it means foregoing economic and social cooperation with the rest of the world."

It was in this context that Fleming viewed the Russians and their rise to power. "I think it is evident and inevitable that Russia will

---

[23] *Lilienthal Journals*, July 12, 1944 entry, p. 645.

establish a tight sphere of influence considerably beyond her erst-while European borders and doubtless beyond her Asiatic borders. I don't think we can affect this much, except to the extent that we may encourage some nations to pursue policies for which they do not have the strength, with the possible result that exhaustion would add them to the Russian orbit." The inevitability of power and deference to its expansion so long as that expansion does not affect vital national interests—this was the heart of Fleming's mes-sage to the Assistant Secretary of State. Significantly, Clayton swift-ly passed the letter on to his fellow assistant secretaries.[24] This, after all, was what Roosevelt had been implicitly saying for months —in private to the Poles and in public to everyone who would lis-ten. It suffused American policy toward the Soviets and Eastern Europe. On the issue of Soviet expansion Roosevelt and a signifi-cant proportion of the American business interests were in near perfect agreement.

How intimate this agreement was was dramatized by the issue of the Russian loan. As early as 1943 Stalin's determination to rebuild his country's devastated economy as rapidly as possible met with an appreciative response among American officials—particularly those with strong ties to the national industrial corporate structure. Sweeping fiscal concessions to debtor nations through an interna-tional monetary fund and bank were one thing, but extension of needed aid to our great wartime ally and future partner in the policing of the peacetime world was something else. While the first policy might find us drained by the weaker and economically declining nations of the world, the second would strengthen the prospects for a stable and harmonious postwar international peace.

It was precisely this point that War Production Board Chairman Donald M. Nelson grasped in early 1943. Stalin had just dissolved the Comintern and had reestablished the Orthodox churches in Russia, and pondering the future at this sunny juncture, "Nelson arrived at the conviction that an expansion of postwar trade with

---

[24] Lamar Fleming to Will Clayton, January 4, 1945, Clayton to Assistant Secre-tary of State James Dunn, January 11, 1945, Box 17, Clayton Papers. A subse-quent letter by Fleming was devoted to his distinctly melancholy view of the pos-sibility that with the fall of the British Empire we might be pushed willy-nilly into assuming England's imperial and Continental burdens and thus come face to face with Russia in Europe. It was obviously not a pleasing prospect to Fleming. Flem-ing to Clayton, January 18, 1945, with enclosure, *ibid.*

Soviet Russia would greatly strengthen the American economy." In order to avoid a recurrence of economic depression after the war, Nelson maintained, American business would have to export far more than ever before, and war-torn " 'Russia is one of our largest potential customers.' " " 'We're fifty years ahead' " of Russia industrially, Nelson continued, so that the United States would not have to worry about building up an incipient competitor. " 'The Soviets won't be able to compete with us for world markets for a long time to come, except perhaps in countries right next door to her,' " Nelson added, thereby writing off, as did most Washington officials then and later, any interest in American business penetration of the then shattered and always poor Eastern European market area.[25]

Having developed his ideas at some length with his staff, Nelson went to Roosevelt and Hull, who expressed enthusiasm and promptly packed him off to Moscow to talk to Stalin. The only note of skepticism was sounded by the new Ambassador to Russia, W. Averell Harriman, who reminded his colleagues while in London that the lend-lease program had shown the Russians to be "not exactly easy to get on with even in wartime." In Moscow, however, Stalin professed deep interest in Nelson's outline of postwar aid, generally in the form of heavy capital equipment and largely through private business channels. Nelson returned to Washington elated. Harriman, ever the skeptic, demanded that whatever direct postwar aid of the kind agreed to by Stalin and Nelson should be channelled through the American government, and specifically the State Department, and not through private channels.[26] His view prevailed, and upon his arrival in Moscow on the eve of the Tehran conference, Harriman initiated talks with foreign trade commissar Mikoyan to discuss postwar American aid for Russian reconstruction. The Russians continued to respond with intense interest, and finally in early January of 1945, after further discussions at Tehran and elsewhere, Molotov handed Harriman a very detailed *aide-mémoire* which represented "the first formal Russian re-

---

[25] Quoted in Albert Z. Carr, *Truman, Stalin and Peace* (New York: Doubleday & Company, Inc., 1950), pp. 13–15.
[26] *Ibid.*, pp. 18–21.

quest for a postwar loan." Harriman promptly cabled the State Department "that the Soviet Union placed 'high importance on a large postwar credit as a basis for the development of Soviet-American relations.' "[27]

However, criticism of the Soviet Union and its practices, especially in Eastern Europe, increased steadily if slowly in the United States between 1943 and the spring of 1945. Thousands, possibly millions, of Americans remained quite certain that the Soviet government and the Russian people had not changed from Marxian doctrinaires to midwestern earthmovers. They insisted that Stalin was a brutal dictator and not a rough-hewn, pipe-smoking Jacksonian democrat. Eugene Lyons, who spoke with the authority of years lived in Russia, deplored the liberal tendency in the United States to ignore the facts that the "world's largest concentration camps" were in Russia, that "extreme measures of suppression" were still employed there, and that "the last vestiges of economic democracy in the factories" had long since been "obliterated." "A thousand other things which Americans deserve to know if they are to deal realistically and not sentimentally with the problems posed by Russia" were either being withheld or grossly distorted by American liberals, Lyons charged. "The Kremlin rulers are neither impressed nor placated," he said, by our "romantic performance."[28]

Lyons and other social critics, who had observed the Soviet system first hand, were not alone in their condemnation of the wartime cult of Russia. Although somewhat subdued, the Catholic Church reemphasized its traditional opposition to the existence and policies of any Communist state at an early date. By mid-1945 it was reported that such official opposition was threatening to split the Catholic vote in the eastern cities to the enormous detriment of the Democratic Party.[29]

[27] Quoted in Thomas G. Paterson, "The Abortive American Loan to Russia and the Origins of the Cold War," *Journal of American History*, LVI (June 1969), 70–75.

[28] Eugene Lyons, "The Progress of Stalin Worship," *American Mercury*, LVI (June 1943), 695–697. Cf. also Lyons' "Letter to American Liberals," *American Mercury*, LVII (May 1944), 569–575.

[29] "True Dangers of the Great Popular Movement to Acclaim the Soviet," *Catholic World*, CLIV (January 1942), 488–490; Press Research Inc. Release, June 4, 1945,

Polish-Americans formed by far the largest active bloc of anti-Soviet feeling in the United States during the Second World War. Roosevelt's fear of the political power of this group, which he had communicated to Stalin at Tehran, was not exaggerated. By early 1945 Polish nationalist propaganda was flooding the country from two sources. One was the Polish American Congress, Inc., whose outlets were the Polish language newspapers in New York—*Nowy Swiat*—and Detroit—*Dziennik Polski*. A source close to the Democratic National Committee stridently claimed that the Congress was controlled and manipulated by "fascists" and "subversives" from the prewar Pilsudski government in Poland.[30] The other source was the Polish Government Information Center in New York, officially established and run until July 1945 by the London Polish Government in Exile. The Information Center appears to have spawned and controlled a number of spin-off groups, such as the American Friends of Polish Democracy and the Polish Labor Group, who jointly sponsored a weekly news magazine, *Poland Fights*, and the National Committee of Americans of Polish Descent, who in 1944 published a long essay on the Katyn Forest massacre, which clearly implicated the Russians without making an outright charge.[31] The Information Center itself produced a number of pamphlets as well as the weekly *Polish Review*, which after Yalta, of course, became increasingly harsh in its denunciations of the Soviet and Lublinite control of the homeland.[32]

It is impossible to assess the extent of the shift in the public attitude toward Russia by the spring of 1945 as a result of the mounting tempo of anti-Soviet propaganda and the post-Yalta decline in relations between the Soviets and the West. It is probably fair to say that the forces working for a sympathetic view of Russia still predominated, and that the majority of Americans still hoped for a peaceful resolution of differences and a continuation of the Grand

op. cit.: "U.S.–U.S.S.R. Relations, Part I; Propaganda Against Soviet Threatens to Disrupt International Relations," p. 1.

[30] Press Research, Inc. Release, "The Polish Lobby," pp. 1–2, 27.

[31] Numerous copies of *Poland Fights* for 1943 and 1944 are in the author's possession, as is the pamphlet, "Death at Katyn" (New York: National Committee of Americans of Polish Descent, 1944).

[32] Cf., for example, *The Polish Review*, V (March 15 and March 22, 1945).

Alliance into the postwar world to guarantee the peace.[33] But opinion was clearly divided and emotions were high. Truman's early policies, as we shall see, tended to reflect the uncertain mood of his fellow citizens.

Public and popular attitudes toward the Chinese in the latter stages of the war reflected a growing bewilderment that was the product of hope gradually turning to disillusionment. From the turn of the century on, traditional American policy toward China had revolved about the concept of the "open door"—a marvelously imprecise term which has usually elicited from scholars sinister images of banking consortiums and flinty-eyed Boston businessmen seeking to exploit ruthlessly a prostrate Chinese government and an ignorant Chinese peasantry for the sake of capitalistic profit. Certainly the impression is reinforced by the provisions of the Nine Power Treaty on China of 1922. In it the contracting parties stressed adherence to "the principle of equal opportunity for the commerce and industry of all nations throughout the territory of China. . . ." And the Open Door was explicitly defined as "equality of opportunity in China for the trade and industry of all nations. . . ." Furthermore, in October of 1938 the State Department demanded of Japan an end to all discriminatory or impedimental practices which hindered the free flow of international trade in those portions of China under Japanese control.[34]

In practice, however, American activities in China under the umbrella of Open Door policy were from the beginning far less commercially oriented than religiously and morally oriented. Heartbreaking impediments to trade, including wretched transportation

[33] After surveying "scores of polls," Thomas A. Bailey has concluded that "The high point in American good will toward Russia came in April 1945, on the eve of the San Francisco Conference, at which time about half of those polled favored a military alliance with Moscow." Thomas A. Bailey, *A Diplomatic History of the American People*, 4th ed. (New York: Appleton-Century-Crofts, Inc., 1950), p. 856*n*. The following month the Public Opinion Research Poll, conducted from Princeton, concluded that seventy-two percent of the American people favored continued cooperation with the Russians after the war. This figure represented only an eight percent drop from November of 1942. H. Schuyler Foster to Assistant Secretary of State Archibald MacLeish, May 24, 1945, Records of the Department of State, decimal file 711.61/5-2445, National Archives.

[34] Quoted in "Our Far Eastern Record; A Reference Digest on American Policy" (New York: American Council Institute of Pacific Relations, 1940), pp. 5–6, 21–23 (copy in author's possession).

facilities to the interior, inability and disinclination of the poor Chinese peasant, or even broad sections of the urban middle class on the coast, to purchase American goods, the rapid development of an unfavorable trade balance, and finally and most important, an "inveterate Chinese hostility toward the foreigner," all served to place severe handicaps upon American commerce. Possibly a vigorous government policy in support of American business in China might have overcome these enormous handicaps. Certainly "a fiercely competitive struggle for sales and contracts" raged in China between Germany, Great Britain, France, Russia, and Japan during the final decade of the nineteenth century and the first fourteen years of the twentieth. But then all of these nations were far more dependent upon foreign trade than was the United States. The willingness of Washington to lend assistance to American business in China prior to 1914 "was usually little more than an expression of good will." Insofar as the United States was concerned, the "China market" between 1890 and 1914 was a "myth."[35]

Nor did the situation improve during the interwar decades of the twenties and thirties. As late as 1935 an influential American exponent of increased foreign trade admitted "that 92% of our trade is domestic and only 8% foreign."[36] Given the centuries-old predominance of American trading routes with Britain and the European continent over those with Asia, State Department defense of the Open Door in commercial terms as late as 1938 seemed ritualistic at best and wholly irrelevant at worst.

Nor had the situation changed much by 1945. The same strong advocate of foreign trade of a decade before—Will Clayton—now was in a strong position to shape world commercial revival and policy. Yet, Clayton explicitly stated that the revival of trade and commerce in Western Europe must take top priority, and he expressed profound skepticism over the future commercial development and importance of Asia in general. China as a particular case was never mentioned.

[35] Paul A. Varg, "The Myth of the China Market, 1890–1914," *American Historical Review*, LXXIII (February 1968), 742–758 *passim*.

[36] William L. Clayton, "Cotton and Foreign Trade," *The Acco Press*; *A Monthly Magazine for the Cotton Farmer* [Houston, Texas], XIII (June 1935), 1–4, copy in Clayton Papers, Box 42.

The peculiar attraction of China for the American public was not so much commercial as moral. Loss of a "China market" does not adequately explain the widespread anguish in this country in 1949 when Chiang Kai-shek was forced off the mainland by the Communists. False romanticism about the Chinese character and situation does.

Throughout the first three and one-half decades of this century the missionary impulse to moral uplift always exceeded by a wide margin the capitalistic impulse to profit in the American mind. China was perceived as an exotic but backward land, badly in need of being taken in hand by good American Protestant reformers who would educate the quaint heathen in the ways of Christ and democracy. Especially for those disenchanted with the moral crusades in the United States, "The image of China as a *tabula rasa* for American reform" became irresistible.[37]

As the religious reform impulse waned under the impact of early twentieth-century violence and disillusion, the political reform impulse waxed stronger. With American entry into World War II, it reached a climax of emotional idealism. In March of 1943, after conversations with Roosevelt, Cordell Hull, and Sumner Welles on the United Nations Organization, Anthony Eden cabled Churchill of his "strong impression that it is through their feeling for China that the President is seeking to lead his people to accept international responsibilities." After the Cairo conference the following November, Eden despairingly noted that "our American allies were impressed almost to the point of obsession with the merits of General and Mme. Chiang Kai-shek and their Government."[38]

That same month a student of Sino-American relations, Nathaniel Peffer, wrote of the tragedy inherent in the orgy of mutual idealization that had occurred in both China and the United States during the months immediately after Pearl Harbor. Looking first at the United States, he spoke of the rapid emergence of a "China

[37] Cf. Paul A. Varg, *Missionaries, Chinese, and Diplomats* (Princeton: Princeton University Press, 1952); Jerry Israel, "For God, for China and for Yale—The Open Door in Action," *American Historical Review*, LXXV (February 1970), 796–807 *passim*.

[38] Eden, *The Reckoning*, pp. 437, 493.

myth," compounded of shame at not having gone to Chiang Kai-shek's aid earlier, and an earnest hope that China would emerge from the war as a strong democratic state which could stabilize Asian politics in a way pleasing to American idealism. "Suddenly we became China conscious," he wrote.

> Many among us learned about China for the first time. Many went to China for the first time in the prevailing emotional glow and saw only what they wanted to see. Many who had lived in China began to disseminate pictures of China retouched in the same glow. It is an unfortunate fact that a considerable number of Americans who have lived in China are inclined to be incontinently sentimental about the Chinese. . . . Those Americans who like to describe themselves as "friends of China" can sometimes be extremely silly.
>
> China became a country endowed with more than human qualities. It was a democracy pure and Jeffersonian, its leaders selfless, statesman-like beings consecrated to the spread of liberty, every peasant guerrilla a boy on the burning deck. And when Chinese and Japanese met in battle, the Japanese forthwith dissolved.

Peffer added that Americans "rather made fools" of themselves over the first visit of Madame Chiang. "Great as are that lady's charms and attainments, she is hardly the latter day composite of Plato and Joan of Arc that she was hailed as being." By the time Peffer wrote, of course, the pendulum in some circles had already begun to swing in the opposite direction. Now it was "being whispered in Washington" that "China is a fascist dictatorship, China is vilely corrupt."[39] Peffer pled for a realistic and balanced public understanding of Kuomintang China that would shun both extremes.

But his efforts were in vain. If the popular press is in any sense a faithful barometer, opinion in the United States polarized sharply over the China question in 1944–1945. In July of the former year Y. C. James Yen answered in the affirmative the question, which was also the title of his extended essay in *Life* magazine: "Will Postwar China Be Democratic?" Democracy "is rooted deep in China's past," Mr. Yen argued, "and lives in the words of her

---

[39] Nathaniel Peffer, "Our Distorted View of China," *New York Times Magazine*, November 7, 1943, pp. 7 ff.

sages and the deeds of her heroes." True, at present there were disturbing political trends in the country; dictatorship was the current reality. But, Yen claimed in the authentic voice of the American missionary, "mass education" in the postwar period would serve to revive, promote, and ultimately assure the triumph of the presently dormant but potentially vibrant strain of democracy that had run through China's past. "The only way to make the world safe for democracy is by spreading democracy" through mass education. This could and would be done. Yen closed by reminding his readers that what even so bitter a China critic as Theodore H. White had recently called "the great revolution of Asia" was working itself up in China. It could not be stopped.[40] The tragedy of the missionary vision as conveyed by Yen, of course, was that it could conceive of no *successful* Asian revolution working itself out upon any other lines than those established in 1776. The seeds of yet another terrible disillusionment were already deeply embedded in many American minds.

The near collapse of Nationalist China at the end of 1944 and the growing presence of the Chinese Communists forced upon the American public mind the depth of the Chinese torment.[41] But popular opinion remained divided, while government policy remained obdurate in its support of Chiang and the Kuomintang.

In contrast to Russia and China, public opinion toward Japan during World War II was always united. From Pearl Harbor to the final months of the war nearly all Americans agreed upon a policy of total, crushing victory in the Pacific. A pulsating abhorrence of the Japanese swiftly became a fixture of American wartime thinking. According to one scholar the conviction that "the Japs are not human . . . in part accounts for the peculiarly bloodthirsty character of the Pacific fighting," in which enemy prisoners were few not only because of their own fanaticism, but also because of American unwillingness to take them. Wartime films conveyed this ferocious sentiment to the public at home with equal fervor. The Japanese enemy was depicted as "an ape," as "subhu-

---

[40] Y. C. James Yen, "Will Postwar China Be Democratic?" *Life*, XVII (July 10, 1944), 67 ff.

[41] Cf., for example, Mark Gayn, "The Cause of China's Tragedy," *Colliers*, CXV (January 13, 1945), 18–19 ff.

man evil." He never spoke but only killed remorselessly. No attempts were apparently ever made to portray the Japanese in human terms.[42]

As early as March of 1942 a senior American general, on his way to command in the Far East, strikingly echoed the emerging mood of his countrymen toward the Japanese. "When I think of how those bowlegged cockroaches have ruined our calm lives," Joseph Stilwell remarked, "it makes me want to wrap Jap guts around every lamppost in Asia."[43] By January of 1945 a war correspondent home on brief leave from the Pacific gave stunning testimony to the terrible depths which American attitudes toward Japan had reached after three years of unremitting battle.

> Never before has the nation fought a war in which our troops so hate the enemy and want to kill him. This intense hatred was first aroused by the sneak attack on Pearl Harbor. From then on it was fed by countless small incidents of dirtiness and treachery. I remember men who, when they came out to the Pacific, had no particular hatred of or desire to kill Japanese. Then they saw their buddies machine gunned while parachuting from a plane or killed by a hand grenade some wounded Jap held under his armpit and detonated when an American bent down to help him. When treachery like that affects you, or somebody you know, you grow to hate violently.

Two months later the recapture of Manila gave American correspondents on the scene an opportunity to recount lurid and revolting examples of enemy atrocities against the Filipinos. They did not allow the chance to slip by.[44]

The wealthy, powerful, and educated were not immune from this hyper-emotionalism. Behind the careful words and the often judicious and detached argument, anger and fear of the Japanese was as strong as among the common people. In the midst of an unusually balanced essay, *Japan and the Japanese*, the editors of *Fortune* argued in late 1944 that "frustration is the essence of Japan's na-

[42] McNeill, *America, Britain, and Russia*, pp. 4–5n.; Toland, *Rising Sun*, pp. 345–737 *passim*; Richard R. Lingeman, *Don't You Know There's a War On; The American Home Front, 1941–1945* (New York: G. P. Putnam's Sons, 1970), p. 201; Deming, *Running Away from Myself*, p. 10.
[43] White, ed., *The Stilwell Papers*, p. 49.
[44] *Newsweek*, XXV (January 1, 1945), 28; (February 26, 1945), 32.

tional life," and this frustration created a volatile character, one in which "placid acceptance of oppression" could change in a moment to "raging excesses." "Japan's history drips with the blood of lords slaughtered by men whom they raised up, men who in turn were cut down by underlings. . . . the people have many times risen up blindly and madly and assaulted their officials."[45]

So stirred were American passions against Japan—and Germany —during the final year of the war that senior American officials felt compelled to reflect them. On the day of his departure for the San Francisco United Nations Conference Tom Connally, Chairman of the Senate Foreign Relations Committee, characterized the Asian and European foes to his colleagues as "two savage and brutal enemies" and spoke of "the duty we owe to civilization to crush and chain these monsters."[46] On V-E Day President Truman spoke of the Far East as "still in bondage to the treacherous tyranny of the Japanese," while applauding "the abject surrender of the Nazi barbarians."[47]

In such an atmosphere talk of a negotiated settlement short of the unconditional surrender doctrine propounded at Casablanca two years before was deemed unthinkable. Then Assistant Secretary of State Joseph C. Grew, who had been repatriated from Japan in 1942 in an exchange of diplomatic personnel, had himself fallen for a time under intense public criticism for supposedly advocating peace in the Pacific short of unconditional Japanese surrender. By October of 1944 he was obviously eager to demonstrate his own intense will to victory, and in a Navy Day speech he warned his audience "that we must not, under any circumstances, accept a compromise peace with Japan, no matter how alluring such a peace may be or how desirous we may become of ending this terrible conflict." "An enticing peace offer from Japan may come at any time,"

[45] The Editors of *Fortune, Japan and the Japanese: A Military Power We Must Defeat, A Pacific Problem We Must Solve* (Washington: The Infantry Journal, December, 1944), pp. 5–6. This book was a collection of articles that had appeared in the magazine in preceding months.

[46] Quoted in Tom Connally with Albert Steinberg, *My Name Is Tom Connally* (New York: Thomas Y. Crowell, 1954), p. 275.

[47] Harry S. Truman Press Conference, May 8, 1945, in *Public Papers of the Presidents; Harry S. Truman, April 12 to December 31, 1945* (Washington: U. S. Government Printing Office, 1961), pp. 45, 47, hereinafter cited as *Truman, Public Papers, 1945.*

Grew added, but American policy must continue to be, as he had stated over a year before, the "smashing" of "totalitarian aggression . . . first, and then its stump must be uprooted and burned."[48] Some months later the editors of *Fortune* reemphasized these same themes and urged Americans to steel themselves to the necessity of a direct invasion of Japan to end the war.

> The Japanese military know that we have only to wage war on them to defeat them; they are staking their chances on the hope that we shall not want to. . . .
>
> In 1942 the danger for the Allies was that they might be overwhelmed. In 1943 the danger was that the Allies would not be able to fight enough to prevent the Japanese from digesting their empire and growing vastly in strength. . . . From 1944 on, the danger is not that we cannot defeat Japan, but that we shall not want to pay the price of crushing her entire military machine.[49]

The danger of American war weariness seemed remote in the early spring of 1945, however. The columnist Ernest K. Lindley, who had long enjoyed close contact with Roosevelt, wrote in mid-March that "our strategists will not regard as acceptable any peace terms which do not provide for the military occupation and demilitarization of Japan."[50] There were no alarmed letters to the editor in response to the column. Official Washington said nothing. The apparently unshakable Japanese determination to resist was thus matched by an implacable American will to conquer.

Despite underlying divisions and unease, the mood of wartime America toward the Russian and Chinese allies and the Japanese enemy was thus reasonably clear and consistent. But when Americans turned their attention to Britain, her Empire, and the related problems of postwar economic rehabilitation, deep resentments and anxieties came bubbling to the surface. These emotions disturbed and distorted the wartime sense of national purpose and served to confuse and even to paralyze for a time the making of intelligent foreign policy.

[48] Joseph C. Grew, *Turbulent Era; A Diplomatic Record of Forty Years, 1904–1945*, 2 vols. (Boston: Houghton Mifflin Co., 1952), II: 1395, 1403; Zacharias, *Secret Missions*, p. 333.

[49] Editors of *Fortune, Japan and the Japanese*, pp. 140–141.

[50] *Newsweek*, XXV (March 19, 1945), 44.

By 1944 and 1945 most Americans, including, for example, Cordell Hull and John Foster Dulles, could "think in terms of a continuing understanding between the United Kingdom, the U.S., Russia and China" and "hope to see the world covered eventually by a peace system based on a new league assembly, a world court, and a system of commonly accepted international law," presumably based upon the principles of the Atlantic Charter.[51] Economically and socially the planet must be opened to free trade and the free movement of peoples, goods, and ideas. In pursuit of this dream as many barriers to freedom of movement and exchange must be removed as it would be possible to do, and to millions of Americans in 1944–1945 the chief such barrier was not Communism but the British Empire. Roosevelt himself encouraged this attitude by his frequent anti-imperialist pronouncements, leading one scholar to argue with considerable force and conviction "that throughout most of the war President Roosevelt and his advisers worried less about the possibility of conflict with Russia than about the continued existence of Western, particularly British, imperialism. The President believed that a refusal by the imperial powers to grant independence to colonial peoples was far more likely to produce a third world war than anything that Russia might do."[52]

Roosevelt's outlook on this, as on so many other matters, clearly reflected a large measure of public thinking. "Roosevelt's most devoted liberal supporters and his bitterest enemies among the isolationists were united in their distrust of British imperialism; and one of the President's constant fears was that he might be maneuvered into using, or seeming to use, American power to prop up the British colonial Empire."[53] It had not been so very long before that the America First crusaders had begged that this country not go to

[51] The quote referring to the similarity in outlook between Hull and Dulles is from Richard Rovere, *Affairs of State; The Eisenhower Years* (New York: Farrar, Straus and Cudahy, 1956), pp. 58–59.

[52] Gaddis Smith, *American Diplomacy during the Second World War* (New York: John Wiley and Sons, 1965), p. 81. Such thinking even suffused American strategic planning in 1942 and 1943. After the Casablanca Conference in January, 1943, the Joint Chiefs were convinced that the English were determined to tie American military power down to the Mediterranean theater of operations in order to secure British interests in that area. Cf. Kent Roberts Greenfield, *American Strategy in World War II; A Reconsideration* (Baltimore: The Johns Hopkins University Press, 1970), pp. 30–34.

[53] McNeill, *America, Britain, and Russia*, p. 40.

war to rescue Britain and her imperial system, which was fully equated with all of the manifest evils of Nazism. By 1944 self-styled anti-imperialists in this country began to express alarm that the war would not only save Britain but would serve as well to strengthen, not weaken, her Empire. "Less than four years ago, the British Empire was counted down and almost out, not only by its enemies but also by its sorrowing friends," Demaree Bess "wired" from London to readers of *The Saturday Evening Post* late that summer. "Today British imperialists are taking no back talk from anybody, not from Russians, Americans, or their own anti-imperialists." This ostensibly cocky mood was due to the "overwhelming evidence" that "the British Empire is more powerful now than it has been for generations." The imperial ideal had once again taken "firm" hold upon not only the people at home in the British Isles but upon colonials "overseas in the dominions" as well. The Dominion Conference of May 1944 was presented as *ipso facto* proof of the Empire's rejuvenation. The conference had been called, Bess maintained, "to draw up plans for the British Empire's role in the postwar world," and all had apparently been sweetness and light. Thus "London is already the center for continuous conferences designed to adjust and to fortify the British position in every part of the world. . . ."[54]

Only a stunning capacity for credulity can explain this kind of ignorance. Yet most Americans, including some in the highest echelons of government, failed to appreciate the dynamics of imperial decline during, and indeed long after, the war. Britain's vast sterling resources, for example, obscured for most Americans her desperate need of dollars in order to trade and buy in the American market, which would be the world's strongest and richest after victory.[55] Britain's vast oil holdings in the Middle East and her expressed wish to expand her program of regional planning in the area through the agency of the Middle East Supply Center seemed to justify an "anti-imperialist" United States policy including support of "young nationalist rulers such as the Sultan of Morocco and

[54] Demaree Bess, "The British Empire Feels Its Oats," *The Saturday Evening Post,* CCXVII (August 10, 1944), 20 ff.
[55] Cf. Warren F. Kimball, *The Most Unsordid Act; Lend-Lease, 1939–1941* (Baltimore: The Johns Hopkins University Press, 1969), pp. 9–10, 19.

Shah Muhammed Riza of Persia," who asked "that their countries should be freed from 'imperial' treaties or concessions and developed after the war with the aid of United States finance and technique."[56] If the British Empire was gaining the preponderant global strength that critics such as Demaree Bess claimed, then why should American dollars be poured into British coffers and why should the American government supinely acquiesce in further imperial ventures by London in the Middle East and elsewhere? Certainly not all American citizens or officials held such views; many suspected how dreadfully weak Britain had become and how feeble was her hold over imperial affections by the closing months of the war. But for those who could not or would not realistically assess Britain's decline, "anti-imperialism" remained powerfully attractive. "From early in the war there were officials in Washington as well as politicians who were ready to use the pressure of British needs to obtain political and economic concessions on longstanding controversial questions."[57]

Was the American government then bent upon a course of world-wide capitalistic expansion at the expense not only of the British Empire but also of the Soviets and their hopes for a *cordon sanitaire* in Eastern Europe and Asia? It has been seriously argued so. During the latter stages of the war, Gabriel Kolko has asserted, Washington officialdom sought to employ national economic and even military power to crumble the British Empire in the Mid- and Far East as well as to contest Soviet control over Eastern Europe. The purpose of such a policy, he has maintained, was to provide American capitalism with the new markets it so desperately needed. At the same time Washington sought to coerce the Russians to behave "responsibly," *i.e.*, as Washington desired and ordered by the threatened withdrawal of postwar aid.[58] This set of arguments has a certain credibility if study is restricted to Soviet-American affairs. As relations between Washington and Moscow became

[56] George Kirk, *The Middle East in the War* (London: Oxford University Press, 1952, 1953), pp. 24–25.

[57] E. F. Penrose, *Economic Planning for the Peace* (Princeton: Princeton University Press, 1953), p. 208.

[58] Cf. Paterson, "The Abortive American Loan to Russia," *passim*; Gabriel Kolko, *The Politics of War, 1943–1945* (New York: Alfred A. Knopf, 1968), *passim*.

strained in the spring of 1945 a number of American officials, most notably Averell Harriman and Assistant Secretary of State for Economic Affairs William L. Clayton, did strongly urge the withholding of postwar credits from the Soviet Union until the Kremlin improved its conduct. The Russian loan remained in limbo as late as the war's end.[59]

It is also true that throughout the war various agencies in Washington waged total economic warfare with a kind of grim joy and in a spirit of "those who are not for us are against us." Finally, a combination of sincere anti-imperialism and felt military necessity did induce American policy-makers in 1945 to work to whittle down British power in East Asia. But the assertion that wartime economic policy represented a grand and sinister design to create a worldwide American capitalistic empire is dubious in the extreme. For the overriding fact remains that American capitalism at home was at best in an uncertain state of health and American capitalists and their public supporters knew it. They were filled with a sense of foreboding and preoccupation as a result.[60] Indeed, when inquiry

[59] Paterson, *loc. cit.* The matter of the Russian loan, however, is rather more complicated than recent scholarship has suggested. Throughout the war American lend-lease policy toward Russia was, in the words of War Mobilization Director James Byrnes, "to provide everything USSR asks for that can be produced and is lend-leasable and is possible to ship." Looking beyond this generous policy in January of 1945, the American government sought to induce the Russians to agree after the end of the war "to accept at a fair price, machinery, tools, equipment and raw materials being currently supplied" under lend-lease "which have a post war use" and "that will be on hand in the U.S. or under contract." The United States, Washington further proposed, would be reimbursed by the Soviet government over a thirty-year period at the low rate of 2 3/8 percent. The Russians resisted this plan, however, and countered with their application for a $6 billion credit under terms which would guarantee them the same unique trade and credit privileges which they were enjoying under lend-lease during the war. Byrnes and others were exasperated for several reasons. First, "No authority now exists for such a loan," and legislation amending the charter of the Export-Import Bank would have to be secured to cover such a large transaction. And, second, Byrnes and his colleague knew what few inside or outside the government then realized and what few recent historians have been willing to acknowledge, namely that the Russians possessed the means for a rapid, self-generating postwar economic revival in their large and steadily growing gold supply, coupled with the utter lack of an internal debt plus current and future reparations payments from Axis countries. According to OSS figures, for example, the Soviet government in January of 1945 possessed $2½ billion in gold reserves and was mining $250 to $300 million more each year. Cf. James F. Byrnes, "Memorandum for the President, January 18, 1945," Folder 632, The James F. Byrnes Papers of the Robert Muldrow Cooper Library, Clemson University, Clemson, South Carolina; Harriman to Secretary of State, January 6, 1945; Memo from Elbridge Durbrow to Will Clayton, January 11, 1945, Records of the Department of State, decimal files 861.24/1-645 and 861.24/1-1145, National Archives.

[60] Cf., for example, the address by Senator Kenneth S. Wherry of Nebraska,

is broadened to include all the forces influencing diplomatic decision-making, including public opinion and Congressional power of the purse, the thesis of a grand capitalistic design animating American foreign policy during World War II loses most of its force. What is most striking about American international economic policy during and just after the war is not its aggressiveness but its timidity, not its primacy as a tool of American diplomacy but its relegation to a secondary role. There were several compelling reasons which accounted for this situation.

First and foremost was simple general ignorance of the world. In the memorable words of Wendell Willkie, wartime America with its enormous array of censorships "is like a beleaguered city that lives within high walls through which there passes only an occasional courier to tell us what is happening outside."[61] Such ignorance, which permeated all strata of wartime American private and public life, led to "gross" underestimations of the destruction suffered by the European and British industrial economies,[62] and partially explains the tragic miscalculations of the "anti-imperialist" elements in Washington and across the country.

Intimately linked to this wartime ignorance of the true state of the world was the widespread fear in America of a resumption at home of the Great Depression of the thirties. As long as this threat existed, American aid to the postwar world must be limited; American ventures in foreign trade must be limited; American needs must come first. In early April of 1945, as privation and distress lay over most of the Eurasian land mass, the newly converted internationalist Senator Arthur Vandenberg declared "that all American

"What about Our American Economy," delivered before the Sixtieth Annual Dinner of the American Tariff League, New York City, January 18, 1945, and the entire folder entitled "Reciprocal Trade Agreements Act, June, 1945," in Kenneth S. Wherry Papers, Box 3, Nebraska State Historical Society, Lincoln. An arch-conservative and unreflective defender of primitive capitalism, Wherry was minority whip in the upper chamber at this time.

61 Willkie, *One World*, p. i.

62 Dean Acheson, *Present at the Creation; My Years in the State Department* (New York: W. W. Norton and Company, 1969), p. 230; Acheson oral history interview with Ellen Clayton Garwood, November 2, 1958, "Marshall Plan" Folder, p. 1, Ellen Clayton Garwood Papers, Box 1, Harry S. Truman Library, Independence, Mo. In late February of 1945 then Acting Secretary of State Joseph C. Grew, in the midst of a cable on reciprocal trade agreements, spoke casually of the "unsettled" condition of the "French market brought about by the war and four years of enemy occupation." Grew to Ambassador in France (Caffery), February 21, 1945, *Foreign Relations, 1945; Diplomatic Papers*, IV: 758–759.

expenditures for relief and rehabilitation must be from a budget 'wholly separate' from lend-lease and thus subject to the pruning and close scrutiny of Congress itself." The Senator

> stressed that he suggested "no intimation that we shall not do our full part in helping the United Nations to reconstruct a healthy, happy world. But I do suggest . . . that we are neither big enough nor rich enough to become permanent almoner to the whole world. . . . I am only asserting . . . that we, too, have desperately difficult American post-war problems of our own to which our resources must be primarily dedicated, that there are limits to the external post-war burdens which our people can carry."[63]

How narrow those limits were had already become obvious. Two weeks earlier *Time* magazine's Congressional correspondent astutely concluded that at that moment the proposal for an international monetary fund would be killed in the House Banking Committee, that the Reciprocal Trade Agreements bill would be drastically watered down as to length of duration and Presidential bargaining discretion on tariff schedules, and finally, that "Congress would not authorize large loan commitments. There is little enthusiasm for big postwar loans to other governments."[64] Congress, in fact, had consistently declined throughout 1943 and 1944 to spend large sums of money for what had appeared to many to be gratuitous American efforts to revive the world—and especially Great Britain—singlehandedly. Speaking of UNRRA appropriations, one scholar-bureaucrat has written that so with postwar "relief, so with reconstruction; the political atmosphere in Washington set limits on what could be done."[65] Roosevelt was always aware that the atmosphere in Washington inhibited bold American economic action. At Yalta, for instance, he told Stalin and Churchill in the midst of discussions over German reparations that the American people would not directly or indirectly underwrite any such payments as they had after World War I, in large measure because "the United States would emerge from the war in poor financial

[63] Quoted in *New York Times*, April 10, 1945, p. 1:1.
[64] Frank McNaughton Report, March 30, 1945, McNaughton Papers, Box 6.
[65] Penrose, *Economic Planning*, p. 169.

condition and that we would have no money to send into Germany for food, clothing or housing."[66]

The strong American aversion to any massive commitment to postwar rehabilitation was matched by a corresponding apathy to postwar foreign trade questions in many sectors of Congress and the business community. As late as July of 1944 Will Clayton had little luck in converting even such liberal-minded corporate executives as Paul Hoffman and such liberally oriented organizations as the Committee for Economic Development to an enthusiasm for foreign trade problems. Along with their fellow citizens Hoffman and his colleagues on the C.E.D. were preoccupied with postwar domestic problems. Hoffman would only promise Clayton vaguely that "As C.E.D. goes along, I am quite sure we may find ways to be of real assistance in promoting an understanding of the importance of international trade." Clayton, a zealot on the subject, was clearly disturbed by Hoffman's attitude.[67] And well he might be, for in coming months even the comparatively innocuous Reciprocal Trade Program ran into deep trouble in Congress, and it found few vocal supporters among the members of the C.E.D. The program itself was essentially conservative and backward-looking, embodying as it did "the principle that trade treaties should be negotiated between pairs of countries in separate negotiations." In terms of the restoration of world trade, such bilateral arrangements could only mildly ameliorate, not solve, the enormous problems to be overcome. Yet Reciprocal Trade was persistently attacked by parochial Congressmen and lobbyists for vested domestic interests, and such attacks imbued the State and Treasury Departments with a strong sense of caution when formulating broader and bolder programs for international economic recovery.[68]

The combination of ignorance and anxiety expressed by so many American citizens and officials in the realm of domestic and foreign economic matters strongly influenced the policies of those within the United States government who were vitally interested in post-

---

[66] Quoted in Byrnes, *Speaking Frankly*, p. 28.

[67] Paul Hoffman to Robert Patchin, July 10, 1944, Will Clayton to Hoffman, July 12, 1944, Hoffman to Clayton, July 18, 1944, Clayton Papers, Box 17.

[68] Penrose, *Economic Planning*, pp. 88, 90–91.

war global reconstruction. Always properly concerned with what they could get through Congress, the internationalist-minded economic planners in Washington were frequently forced to make stronger demands for the protection of American interests than either they wished or than was proper given the specific problem. This was true from the time of lend-lease through Bretton Woods to the beginnings of the bilateral postwar loan program in early 1945.

It was through Article VII, written into each of the numerous lend-lease protocols, that American economic planners, led by Treasury Secretary Morgenthau, first sought to induce the wartime allied nations, including Britain and Russia, to abandon their previous policies of economic exclusivism embodied in imperial preference systems or monopolistic state trading corporations. An open postwar world of free and unfettered international trade was the American objective. In accepting lend-lease aid, the recipient nations in turn pledged themselves to

> the betterment of worldwide economic relations . . . directed to the expansion [of trade and commerce], by appropriate international and domestic measures of production, employment, and the exchange and consumption of goods . . . to the elimination of all forms of discriminatory treatment in international commerce, and to the reduction of tariffs and other trade barriers; and in general to the attainment of all the economic objectives set forth in the Joint Declaration made on August 14, 1941, by the President of the United States of America and the Prime Minister of Great Britain.

This last reference pertained, of course, to the Atlantic Charter.[69]

This was not an ignoble conception of the ideal postwar economic order. The fundamental goal sought was an international co-

[69] The most authoritative statement of liberal American postwar international trade objectives is found in "Postwar Economic Policy and Planning; Sixth Report of the House Special Committee on Postwar Economic Policy and Planning, . . . May 8, 1945," a copy of which is in the Clayton Papers, Box 28. The chairman of this committee was Representative Colmer of Mississippi. Cf. also Penrose, *Economic Planning*, pp. 14–30; McNeill, *America, Britain, and Russia*, pp. 448–449. Article VII of the lend-lease agreements may be found, along with a contemporary partisan discussion of the entire program, in Edward R. Stettinius, Jr., *Lend-Lease; Weapon for Victory* (New York: The Macmillan Co., 1944), esp. pp. 342–343.

operative effort "to bring about an expanding [world] economy" in terms "of production, employment and the exchange and consumption of goods." In the beginning responsible American authorities wished to exclude nothing—not even imperial preference—that might advance this goal.[70] In view of the ruthless practices of economic nationalism that defined the gloomy international history of the nineteen-thirties, epitomized by the efforts of Dr. Schacht and Nazi Germany, Washington's policy objectives can only be termed common-sensical and broad-minded. But they were consistently hobbled and compromised by the domestic and anti-imperialist concerns of the American public and Congress. The practical result, seen at the Bretton Woods Conference, which sought to implement and expand the ideals of Article VII of the lend-lease accords, was an emergent American policy of enlightened and generous economic nationalism. The conference climaxed months of conversations and planning for a postwar international monetary fund and international bank for reconstruction and rehabilitation (popularly known as the World Bank). The United States pledged a significant share of its resources to these enterprises. But its representatives were forced to demand much in return. Generous and enlightened as American international policy was to become, it nonetheless remained essentially nationalistic at heart. The American people would have it no other way.[71]

Morgenthau, whose department led in the drive to establish the international fiscal institutions to aid postwar reconstruction and stability, clarified the American approach beyond doubt in his closing remarks at Bretton Woods. "The American delegation," he said, "has been, at all times, conscious of its primary obligation—the protection of American interests." After adding that the Americans presumed that each of the other delegations had behaved in the same fashion, he concluded that "none of us has found any in-

[70] Acheson, *Present at the Creation*, pp. 32–33.
[71] A brilliantly argued and impressively researched counter-opinion stressing America's generous and even revolutionary approach to postwar economic planning is Alfred E. Eckes, Jr., "Open Door Expansionism Reconsidered; The World War II Experience," *Journal of American History*, LIX (March 1973), 909–924. In my opinion Professor Eckes fails to take into account traditional American prejudices against the British empire and the lingering influence of isolationism.

compatibility between devotion to our own country and joint action."[72] This was surely a debatable point.

Bretton Woods represented the triumph of American will and planning over that of the British, led by John Maynard Keynes, and the implications were enormous. As early as 1942 Keynes had handed Washington a comprehensive plan for what amounted to a postwar international central bank—designated the International Clearing Union—designed to aid debtor nations, such as Great Britain surely would be in the immediate postwar period, through temporary periods of balance of payments deficits. Keynes focused upon the creation of new and flexible international bank money to supplement gold—called *bancor*—which would be based upon the existing trade volume and financial balances of each member country.

> Countries which ran favorable international balances would pile up credit balances of bancor units with the International Clearing Union. On the other side, countries incurring deficits in their international account would run debit bancor balances. In effect the Union would extend short-term loans to the debtor countries, financed from the surpluses accumulated by those countries whose balance of payments was favorable.[73]

Naturally there were to be sharp limits placed upon the ability of the debtor nations—such as Britain or France or Italy—to call upon the resources of the creditor nations—such as the United States—within the Union. Repeated and excessive borrowing, strictly defined, would lead to a declaration of default and the possibility of a suspended account. But the plan in essence was designed to help debtor nations in world commerce by drawing upon the excessive resources of the creditors.

Keynes' supple mind did not stop there. He also proposed to give the Union specific short-term functions, particularly the underwriting of a certain amount of relief and reconstruction activity. By making the resources of the International Clearing Union avail-

---

[72] Blum, *Morgenthau Diaries*, III: 276.
[73] Robert Lekachman, *The Age of Keynes* (New York: Random House, 1966), p. 181.

able to such agencies as the United Nations Relief and Rehabilitation Agency (UNRRA), the burden of postwar reconstruction would not fall so heavily and all at once on a few particular nations, notably the United States.[74] Indeed, Keynes' plan was keyed to the short-term problems of immediate postwar reconstruction, both of international currency and trade and/or relief and rehabilitation work.

Britain and other European nations would obviously emerge from the war as dollar-poor creditors to the United States, and this dollar gap would become far more acute before it eased, for shattered Europe needed far more imports than it could balance with exports. Possibly the Empire could have eased Britain past the ordeal had there been sufficient dollar stocks within its various trading areas, but both British and American planners had early come to the sensible conclusion that trade barriers, imperial preferences, exclusions, and the like had during the thirties contributed materially to the economic world war that preceded and helped to generate the military conflict. The British, in fact, had, as Keynes' plan indicated, gone much farther toward an acceptance of a truly open and interdependent world trade than the Americans at this time were willing to go. Essentially the British were asking that the United States, through the medium of the International Clearing Union, accept an arrangement whereby the debtor countries, led by England, would be initially favored in terms of short-term borrowing of international money—*bancor*—at the expense of the creditor nations, such as America, until the prostrate debtor nations could revive their war-devastated exporting industries to the point of balancing their international payments.

The explicit orientation of Keynes' plan toward the postwar debtor—as opposed to creditor—nations was fully revealed in his provisions for voting and borrowing powers within the Clearing Union. Such powers were to be based not upon existing national wealth of the respective countries, but upon their foreign trade volume.[75] Thus Keynes' plan was designed to hasten the rapid revival and then to stabilize international postwar trade through the swift

[74] *Ibid.*, pp. 181–182; Penrose, *Economic Planning*, pp. 42–43.
[75] Lekachman, *Age of Keynes*, p. 183.

recovery of the shattered economies of the industrial nations. In order to revive trade and rebuild economies, however, the few creditor countries remaining after years of world war, such as the United States, would have to be willing to have their monetary and credit surpluses drawn upon rather extensively through the agency of the International Credit Union for an indeterminate period until debtor nations could achieve a favorable balance of trade and payments.

American officials, at once reflecting and comprehending public opinion, were unwilling to do this. "Even though no nation would be free to accumulate debits beyond its [debt] quota, the quotas themselves were sufficiently generous" under Keynes' plan "to cause American apprehension that the United States would incur a vast liability to finance the deficits of most of the rest of the world."[76] Behind this opposition, of course, rested the deep-seated suspicions of the British Empire held by many Americans in and out of Congress.

Mindful of these problems and prejudices, American planners countered Keynes' scheme with one of their own, establishing a far more conventional and rigid international monetary fund to help meet problems of postwar international trade and finance. The American plan, drawn up by Harry Dexter White in the Treasury Department, "resembled the Keynes Plan in many of its aims but differed in its methods." The International Monetary Fund would provide advances to tide over temporary balance of payments difficulties, but the money would come not from a new and flexible international currency reflecting prevailing trade patterns, but from a fixed fund of gold initially voted by participating governments. Moreover there were crucially important political motives in the American plan. According to it the United States would subscribe roughly five times the sum to the fund as any other contributor, and votes within the organization were to be proportional to contributions. But this was not all, for White's plan "measured borrowing privileges according to the criteria of initial gold contribution and size of national income," whereas Keynes' proposal, as we have

[76] *Ibid.,* p. 182.

seen, placed voting and borrowing powers within the Fund on the basis of foreign trade volume. "By no special accident," White's "criteria as substantially favored the American position" within the Fund as "Keynes' standards would have strengthened the Brittish situation." The American plan would have created "an aristocracy of wealth. . . . the Keynes Plan . . . would have set up an aristocracy of commerce."[77]

Beyond the immediate political question as to whether Britain or the United States would control the Fund lay the fact that White's plan by its very rigidity and narrowness of conception ignored the short-term problem of rejuvenating prostrate world trade through a flexible international monetary structure that would allow debtor nations generous long-term borrowing privileges to revive their postwar economies.

> [The] Fund was suited to deal with short-period fluctuations affecting international balances of payments, but not with long-continued and deep-seated economic maladjustments resulting from drastic wartime changes in the economic positions of countries, nor with the disruption of the network of multilateral world trade. The Fund was adapted to help a country to tide over a temporary shortage of foreign exchange without disrupting its own monetary system. . . . But the shortage had to be temporary and the advances repayable within a few years.

The American International Monetary Fund plan was ably suited to deal with the kind of breakdown in international trade and finance that would accompany a great international depression such as that of 1929–1939. It had little relation to the materially shattered world of 1944. The Fund was not designed to deal adequately with the coming postwar dollar gap between debtor and creditor nations; it had no authority to use its resources for relief or reconstruction; it made no provision for large and/or *sustained* outflows of capital suffered by one or a group of member nations. Temporary assistance in financing balance of payments deficits was the object of the IMF, not the regeneration and stabilization of international trade. Yet Washington, not London, held the economic and political resources to prevail. And Washington—always con-

---

[77] *Ibid.*, p. 183; Penrose, *Economic Planning*, pp. 45–52.

cerned with what could be got through an often parochial and suspicious Congress—surrendered to ignorance, to traditional conceptions, and to prejudice against the British, which took the form of insisting upon an aristocracy of wealth that would favor the United States in any area of fiscal cooperation jointly chosen. And so, "circumscribed by the perverse politics of Washington, the representatives at Bretton Woods . . . prepared to deal with a recurrence of the last great depression. Their work might bear fruit in a more distant future; for the early postwar period it was of little value."[78]

The depth of ignorance, prejudice, reaction, and selfishness which often existed in post-depression, wartime America is reflected in the suspicious and often hostile reception accorded the International Monetary Fund plan by American business on the eve of Bretton Woods. Randolph Burgess of the New York Federal Reserve Bank, acting as spokesman for the American Bankers Association, told Morgenthau in mid-June 1944 of his "severe objections." Despite the fact that the IMF obviously favored American capitalism, "Few New York bankers, Burgess said, understood the proposal, and most of them were suspicious of it. 'They are distrustful of any program . . . for giving away American gold; they are distrustful of all spending programs, especially when sponsored by Lord Keynes [who, of course, had not sponsored the IMF, though he and his British colleagues would accept it as the best they could get].' " The United States, Burgess continued, "should not commit itself 'to put up money until other countries are prepared to make some commitment as to how they will use it and how they will pay it back. . . . making a big pot of money available . . . would accentuate . . . inflationary tendencies.' " Moreover, American subscription of some sixty to sixty-five percent of all resources in the Fund angered Burgess "and he interpreted Keynes's views as expressing 'the philosophy of deficit spending over again —the use of credit as a cure-all.' "[79] Burgess' use of the term *deficit spending* was of course meant as an epithet, for in those days such a policy was generally considered in conservative circles to be al-

[78] Penrose, *Economic Planning*, p. 60; McNeill, *America, Britain, and Russia*, pp. 451–452.
[79] Quoted in Blum, *Morgenthau Diaries*, III: 253.

most as great a sin as sexual perversion. That Burgess' jaundiced
view found widespread support may be seen by recalling the fact
that ten months later the House Banking Committee was still sitting
on the IMF bill and threatening to kill it.[80]

The revival of the advanced industrial nations thus remained a
critical issue, since both the International Monetary Fund and the
International Bank for Reconstruction and Development, which accompanied it into being at Bretton Woods, did not directly or sufficiently deal with the problem of immediate postwar rejuvenation. By early 1945, with Morgenthau preoccupied with his plan
for Germany, the center of economic decision-making shifted to
the State Department. There officials were already thinking in
terms of a series of individual postwar loans, should Congress refuse to convert lend-lease aid from wartime uses to projects related
to peacetime reconstruction in the industrial nations. Prospects for
the latter course of action dimmed swiftly in April. At that time the
third wartime lend-lease bill had come up for a vote in the Senate.
Vandenberg, as has been noted, was asserting that no lend-lease
aid would go to postwar economic revival. Following the lead of
his Republican colleague, Robert A. Taft promptly tacked on an
amendment prohibiting "the President from contracting for the use
of the Lend-Lease program for postwar relief, rehabilitation, or reconstruction. . . ." The result was a tie vote, thirty-nine to thirty-
nine, which one observer correctly labeled a "significant straw in the
wind," inasmuch as the British, under prior arrangements, were in
fact being permitted to use lend-lease aid indirectly for postwar
reconstruction.[81] Any attempts to blatantly convert lend-lease to a

---

[80] As late as March 1945 the ostensibly "liberal" Committee for Economic Development publicly expressed grave reservations about the entire structure established
by the Bretton Woods agreements. The C.E.D. applauded the International Bank as
an agency to ensure world stabilization of national currencies, but it expressed grave
reservations about the place and purpose of the monetary fund and in the midst of
global economic prostration loftily warned that "Uneconomic international debt
should not be created for the purposes of relief or to bring about an internal expansion which might be better produced by and within the borrowing country itself."
"A Statement on National Policy by the Research Committee of the Committee for
Economic Development on the Bretton Woods Proposals" (n.d.), copy in Tom Connally Papers, Box 103 (received by Connally's office, March 22, 1945).

[81] Harry S. Truman, *Memoirs*, 2 vols. (New York: Signet Books, 1965), Vol.
I: *Year of Decisions, 1945*, p. 116. Truman as Vice President cast the deciding
vote, defeating the amendment. Cf. also Drury, *Senate Journal*, p. 409; Ehrman,
Grand Strategy, p. 241.

program of postwar reconstruction would clearly run into deep trouble in Congress, which was already mulling over the American-
initiated International Monetary Fund plan with vocal mistrust.
Moreover, a peacetime lend-lease program would run into deep
trouble from at least one key figure in both the Roosevelt and later
Truman administrations. Admiral Leahy never obscured his opposition to use of lend-lease funds for international rehabilitation.[82]

So bilateral loans it must be if the United States should decide
to redeem its oft-stated commitment to direct, immediate, and meaningful postwar aid to the industrial nations of the world devastated
by war. The inherent perils in such a policy of economic bilateral-
ism were many and profound. Those not favored by American lar-
gesse were sure to become sullen and spiteful. Those who were were
just as surely liable to become embittered at the cost of their reciprocal responsibilities.

At this point Will Clayton, "a big tall, well-built Texan in his
60's,"[83] stepped forward as a leading policy-maker. He would not
relinquish that role until the ideas which underlay the Marshall
Plan of 1947 were far advanced. Clayton's plan was to use an ever-
expanding postwar international trade to correct weaknesses within the American domestic economy. "What he basically wanted in
the post war period," a close colleague later recalled,

> was to move the world into a place or sphere where trade would be
> free to reach the heights, and where because of the picture's getting
> bigger the uneconomic policies and occurrences in the U.S. would be
> amenable to correction or better whittled down to size until they fi-
> nally disappeared . . . you couldn't get trade going right in the U.S. un-
> less you made the world trade picture harmonize and get going.
>
> Clayton believed that it was necessary to start with the reconstruction
> of Western Europe because it was the place where you could make
> progress quickest, for the people, the skills, and the materials were
> there. With money and time, Europe could do the job itself. He doubted
> how far you could move and how fast in the underdeveloped countries
> —in Asia, and Africa, and the Far East; also there was trouble recon-
> ciling the U.S. views with the Latinos [South Americans] because of
> their protectionist views.[84]

[82] Leahy, *I Was There*, pp. 376–377.
[83] Drury, *Senate Journal*, p. 247.
[84] Emilio G. Collado oral history interview with Ellen Clayton Garwood, November 6, 1958, pp. 6–7, "Marshall Plan" folder, Garwood Papers, Box 1.

Herein lay all of the strengths and weaknesses of the most advanced American economic thinking of the time. Clayton's vision is appealing, and it was surely sound, because it presupposed the ultimate creation—or re-creation—of a world economy dominated by no single power. Indeed, it is clear that Clayton was willing to run the risk that after helping to revive the economies of Western Europe, America might for a time suffer from the consequences of "uneconomic policies and occurrences" at home until the sheer volume of international exchange became so great as to obliterate them. The realism in this vision had distinct limits, however. Although the idea of a large postwar loan to Russia had surfaced and been enthusiastically endorsed in certain quarters, Clayton clearly either did not favor it or did not feel that such a loan could be comfortably incorporated into his scheme of things. Apparently in his thinking the Soviets were banished to the nether land of backward economic societies such as those in Asia and Africa. Obviously, too, Eastern Europe did not fit into his plans, though at Potsdam he would speak sympathetically to the Poles about postwar aid.

In overall conception and implementation, in fact, American economic planning and practice during the latter stages of the Second World War and the first months of the peace that followed proved to be quite traditional, quite narrow, and plagued by the possibility that a frequently recalcitrant and parochial Congress would not provide the resources necessary to carry out any single plan or cluster of plans. It was surely not aggressive. The argument that American planners were consciously seeking to build an "American Empire" in 1945–1946 simply does not make sense. Throughout the history of the world, imperial systems had been strongest when rival empires existed to challenge and be challenged—and incidentally to trade with openly or clandestinely. The world was prostrate in 1945; no single nation could long dominate the ruined world economy without itself collapsing. Even if the ultimate goal of American planners was to expand the national capitalistic system in the postwar years, it was incumbent upon them to revive certain portions of the industrial and agricultural world so as to have someone for American capitalists to trade with. Clayton's thinking clearly reflected these ideas. But Congress and key figures in the Roosevelt and early Truman administrations constantly opposed any such sweeping plans or policies.

American economic initiatives during the war often *gave the appearance* of aggressiveness because of the prevailing public mood of anxiety within the country concerning the postwar domestic economy. Fears of postwar depression, finding expression in the dour and mistrustful Yankee trader mentality within Congress, often forced American officials to formulate partially self-defeating plans so that the United States could invariably realize some immediate and tangible benefits. This was particularly true of the International Monetary Fund, which was clearly inferior to Keynes' International Clearing Union. It was true, for that matter, of Clayton's thinking, which obviously rested not upon a multipronged approach to the rapid revival of world commerce but upon a slow trickledown process in which American aid would be limited to Western Europe, which then, in partnership with the United States, might begin the economic uplift of the other devastated areas of the globe. But Clayton, after years of government service as Director of Surplus Property Disposal and then Assistant Secretary of State for Economic Affairs, knew his often petulant Congress, and what he could get through it and from it.[85] So did his fellow planners in the State and Treasury Departments, and they drew up their ideas and governed their conduct in and beyond Washington accordingly. Thus the paradox in American wartime economic planning: a series of essentially conservative and backward-looking plans wholly unsuited to the realities of a prostrate world could be interpreted as reflections of an aggressive design.

One final example of the restraints of public opinion upon wartime planning occurred between 1943 and 1945 over the issue of Mideast oil. Petroleum, of course, lay at the very heart of wartime American needs and figured centrally in Washington's felt necessity to maintain a measure of postwar military strength to guard the peace. Several scholars, however, have scented a deeper motive

---

[85] Allen Drury, who covered the Senate in the later war years, claimed that Clayton possessed "the smoothest manner imaginable when it comes to handling recalcitrant committees." *Senate Journal*, p. 247.

behind American interest in the far shores of the Mediterranean at this time. The strong anti-imperialist sentiment in the United States, it is claimed, provided the perfect shelter within which greedy oil interests could and did pressure Roosevelt and his advisers to replace British political and financial influence with American power. "While the United States government had not yet felt the need to evolve a coherent policy for the Middle East, her business men were at this time turning their eager eyes upon undeveloped economic resources in the region so that the President's 'anti-imperialist' interest" regarding Britain "may not at bottom have been as altruistic as he imagined it to be."[86] Certainly American influence in Iran had grown steadily since 1942, despite several *contretemps* on the part of overzealous civil and military officials stationed in or passing through Tehran. American "tutelage" of the Iranian government had replaced that of the British. And as late as Potsdam, when the American troops initially sent to protect and expand the Mideast supply corridor to Russia were leaving in droves, the War Department determined to maintain two military advisory groups in the country. This was at the express wish of Tehran's officialdom in order to provide some counterweight to the Soviet and British presence.[87]

But American interest in the Mideast was at best sporadic prior to the outbreak of the Cold War in 1946. The argument that United States penetration into the area during World War II was encouraged or manipulated by American oil interests simply does not stand the test of objective fact. The history of the "Great Oil Scare" of 1943 and its aftermath, among other incidents, amply supports this contention.

During that mid-war year "sudden startling reports" began to circulate "about the drain upon our underground supplies" of crude oil. It swiftly appeared "that the United States was consuming known domestic reserves faster than these were being replaced by new discoveries." The alarmed Petroleum Administrator for War,

---

[86] Kirk, *The Middle East in the War*, pp. 24–25.

[87] T. H. Vail Motter, *The Persian Corridor and Aid to Russia* (Washington: Department of the Army, 1952), *passim*, esp. pp. 163–168, 454–460, 476–478; Acting Secretary of State (Grew) to Secretary of State (Byrnes), July 17, 1944, in *Foreign Relations, 1945*; *Conference of Berlin*, II: 1389–1390.

Harold Ickes, anxiously queried whether America could " 'oil another war,' " while "other countries," obviously referring to Russia and Britain, "grasped the remaining undeveloped sources of supply."[88]

Attention immediately turned to the Middle East, where already American oil companies held a small concession in the sheikdom of Kuwait and a very large concession in Saudi-Arabia. It quickly developed that the oil companies, especially the Arabian-American Oil Company in Saudi-Arabia, "felt that their operations were at the mercy of British diplomacy." They feared that the British, who had vast holdings throughout the entire area, might in the future try to drive them out or greatly restrict their operations through pressure upon Ibn-Saud. Moreover, should the now friendly sovereign die, his nation might not survive the struggle for succession. And finally "there were the unpredictable currents of war. Who knew where the armies of Britain or Russia might end up?" The State Department and its economic adviser, Herbert Feis, discounted the idea of Russian pressures to dislodge American interests in the region since the American holdings were so far down the Persian Gulf.[89]

The British seemed more of an immediate problem. A swirl of controversy swiftly enveloped the relevant departments of the American government, with the Navy joining the Arabian-American Oil Company in its quest for semi-official status for its concessions. The company argument was countered with the assertion that mere official government protection for the concessions could not save them from enemy seizure in the event of another war, since the Middle East was not—and apparently would not be—an area of predominant American military interest in the postwar world. Yet something had to be done, for by early 1944 it was clear that "a great new refinery" would be needed on the Persian Gulf to supply our forces in the Pacific.[90]

The problem was finally referred to FDR, who never showed much interest in such matters, during July of 1944. With brisk

[88] Kirk, *loc. cit.*; Herbert Feis, "The Government Gives Attention to the Oil of the Middle East," in *Three International Episodes; Seen from E.A.* (New York: W. W. Norton & Company, Inc., 1966), pp. 95, 99, 101.

[89] *Ibid.*, pp. 104–109, 111.

[90] *Ibid.*, p. 131.

jocularity he decided that the American government should simply buy out the company. The company, which had approached the government for protection, now found the government proposing extinction as the only solution! This was too much; the company balked. The force of its intransigence was reinforced by the knowledge in administration circles "that any deal would have to survive the scrutiny of some members of Congress who would oppose any terms that gave the private owners a profit, and other members whose constituents were engaged in domestic oil operations."[91]

At last, in August of 1944, the government did what it should have done months earlier; it proposed talks with the British to determine their attitude. Agreement on joint cooperation in worldwide oil was reached with gratifying rapidity. In essence the Anglo-American oil agreement of 1944 proposed mutual sale of oil on a non-discriminatory basis, equality of opportunity in the acquisition of concessions, and mutual respect for existing concessions. Finally, an Anglo-American International Petroleum Commission was to be created " 'to analyze . . . short-term problems of joint interest' " across the entire spectrum of oil operations from initial discovery to final sale.[92]

It was at this point that public opinion in the United States came to play a decisive role. Domestic oil operators, particularly those in Oklahoma and Texas, raised a storm of protest, most of which was directed at senior Texas Senator Tom Connally, who also happened to be Chairman of the Senate Foreign Relations Committee. "We do not relish having our oil or any other thing under control of European governments," Connally was told by one editor, who stressed "the outspoken disfavor" which the agreement "has received here in Texas." A small oil operator in Oklahoma charged that under the agreement "the destiny of the oil business in this country" would be placed "in the hands of a small group." A number of correspondents invoked the traditional states-rights argument with respect to oil regulation. Another writer expressed dismay "as a Texan and an American" over "the impending ruin of our greatest industry, the Oil Business."[93] And so it went, on and

[91] *Ibid.*, p. 128.
[92] Quoted in *ibid.*, pp. 158–161.
[93] J. E. Dickey to Tom Connally, November 15, 1944, Lt. Commander Hobart Key, Jr., to Connally, November 16, 1944, Fennell Dibrell to Connally, November

on. Connally preserved literally hundreds of such letters in his files.

Connally quickly crumbled under this unremitting pressure. He prevailed upon the administration to submit the oil agreement to the Senate Foreign Relations Committee as a treaty. At the same time he assured his oil constituents that in his opinion the agreement "will . . . never be ratified by the Committee. . . . it is unfair to the American oil industry and is not necessary for the general welfare." True to his word, Connally in December of 1944 had the treaty killed. Not until the autumn of 1945, when emerging difficulties with the Soviets were beginning to create an entirely new international atmosphere, were negotiations undertaken looking toward a new and more specific agreement.[94] Once again domestic interests, formally expressed through Congressional opinion and action, had impinged upon, and in this case clearly triumphed over, foreign economic policy planning. The irony lay, of course, in the fact that in this instance American domestic interests served to strengthen, not to weaken, ostensible British imperial power abroad.

American interest in postwar economic reconstruction thus ran the gamut from timidity to disinterest to mistrust and revealed along the way a powerful, if inconsistent, anti-imperialist impulse directed at Great Britain. Indeed the whole American mood throughout World War II was divisive and irrational, burdened as it was by ignorance and emotional prejudices. A volatile yet ill-informed public, preoccupied by the overpowering drama of mass participation in an unprecedented world war and overwhelmed by propaganda from private and public agencies, was in a poor position to comprehend logically the magnitude of the forces battering the planet.

The prejudices generated by the war were inevitably complex and contradictory. They were certainly not invariably pejorative. Japan was deeply hated by all, and Britain and her Empire were widely disliked. Despite a frequently expressed hope that in the

17, 1944, Segrun and Guadalupe County Chamber of Commerce to Connally, November 23, 1944, F. H. Dunn to Connally, November 27, 1944, Connally Papers, Box 99.

[94] Tom Connally to J. E. Dickey, December 11, 1944, *ibid.*; Feis, "Government Attention to the Oil of the Middle East," pp. 167–171.

postwar world everyone would "sit down at the same table" with "equal shares for all," there was demonstrable public hostility in the United States throughout the war to a comprehensive program of postwar reconstruction that might in any way retard the quest for affluence and economic security at home. Americans quite literally wanted to have their pumpkin pie—and eat it too. But there remained as late as the early spring of 1945 a widespread, though far from universal, hope that in the postwar world we could "get along with the Russians" in keeping the peace. And the aspirations for a democratic, friendly, and ultimately powerful China, which could help the United States maintain stability in East Asia, were far from dormant. At the heart of all of these prejudices, of course, lay the tremendous passions generated by total war. Japan and, to a somewhat lesser extent, Germany were not only "the enemy"; they represented barbaric evil incarnate. Russia was widely perceived not only as a wartime ally and potential co-partner in keeping the postwar peace, but also as a nation of stout-hearted comrades whose democratic impulses were throbbing mightily despite an outworn political system. At its worst, American wartime romanticism portrayed Stalin as "good old Uncle Joe."

To describe such prejudices and ignorance so baldly is not, of course, to describe their effects. All societies at any given moment exist on myths and cults which have their origin in prejudice and ignorance of a greater or lesser extent. What made the American condition so ominous at this particular point in history was that the United States already possessed the power—and soon would possess immeasurably greater power—to carry out its emotions as international policy of the most influential nature.

What held these prejudices in fairly firm balance and order was the relative coherence of Franklin D. Roosevelt's policies and the enormous force of his personality. The quality of those policies and of that personality are surely matters for debate. But the fact of coherence was of crucial importance at a time of rapid change and flux in the world's and America's history.

And then the man was suddenly gone. Would his successor follow a policy of continuity or change? No one knew. Coherence threatened to crumble. Confusion and uncertainty threatened to rule affairs.

3

"A Farmer Boy from Jackson County"

The appalling news reached wartime Washington near the close of a dank, rainy spring afternoon. It was April 12, 1945, and Franklin Roosevelt was suddenly dead in Georgia—victim of a massive stroke. The warm voice, the vibrant personality, the buoyant man who in twelve years of Presidential leadership had ultimately guided the nation out of its most extensive and demoralizing depression and then through the storms of history's most devastating war was abruptly no more. His unsuspecting successor, summoned to the White House to receive the dreadful message, haltingly asked the widow what he could do to help. Putting her arm around Harry Truman's shoulder, Eleanor Roosevelt replied with infinite compassion and perfect candor: "Is there anything *we* can do for *you*? For you are the one in trouble now."[1] A shocked and grieved Allied world could only concur with those terrible words.

To a young *New York Times* reporter the thought of Roosevelt's passing "was like the pillars of the temple coming down." The successor "was a cardboard figure, a brash midwestern politician

[1] Acheson, *Present at the Creation*, p. 103; Truman, *Year of Decisions*, pp. 14–15.

whom FDR had picked almost capriciously as Vice President, as the least aggravating compromise between Jimmy Byrnes and Henry Wallace." To David Lilienthal out in Tennessee reaction was "Complete unbelief. That was first. Then a sick, hapless feeling. The consternation at the thought of the Throttlebottom Truman. 'The country and the world doesn't deserve to be left that way, with Truman at the head of the country at such a time.' " Across the Atlantic Harold Nicolson forlornly wrote: "It is really a disaster. I feel deeply for Winston [Churchill], and this afternoon, from his manner, I could see that it was a real body blow. . . . He [Truman] may, as Coolidge did, turn out to be a person of character." Only hours later did the full impact of "the death of the man who, like the rivers, had seemed ageless, begin to impress itself fully on the national mind." "The gravest question-mark in every American heart," Senator Vandenberg said that evening, "is about Truman. Can he swing the job?" The object of such anxious solicitude, having taken the oath of office and held a hurried Cabinet meeting in order to pledge continuity, quietly returned to his Connecticut Avenue apartment for a quick bite of the neighbor's supper and then tumbled into bed before facing his first full day in office.[2]

Shortly after his surprise nomination for the Vice Presidency in July of 1944, Harry Truman had assured his neighbors in Independence, Missouri, that his new status had not changed a thing about him. "I'm just a farmer boy from Jackson County," he said. Few could fault this personal analysis of an apparently simple, plain, and unassuming character. The brief journalistic portrait which contained the above quote labelled the sixty-year-old Senator and Vice President-to-be as a "farmer, soldier, storekeeper and small town politician," and that seemed to about sum him up.[3] He was the product of village and rural western Missouri, a land of wooded rolling hills sloping gently down to the river which gave

[2] Cabell Phillips, *The Truman Presidency; The History of a Triumphant Succession* (New York: The Macmillan Co., 1966), p. 2; *Lilienthal Journals*, p. 690; Nigel Nicolson, ed., *Diaries and Letters of Harold Nicolson*, 3 vols. (New York: Atheneum Press, 1966–1968), Vol. II: *The War Years, 1939–1945*, p. 447; *Newsweek*, XXV (April 23, 1945), 26; "Later Diary Entry, April 12, 1945," in Arthur H. Vandenberg and Joe Alex Morris, eds., *The Private Papers of Senator Vandenberg* (Boston: Houghton Mifflin Co., 1952), p. 165; Truman, *Year of Decisions*, p. 23.

[3] "Truman of Missouri," *Life*, XVII (August 21, 1944), 75 ff.

the state its name. Some ten miles to the west lay downtown Kansas City, but in Truman's youth and early manhood it seems to have influenced him but little, though he worked and lived there for several years in his mid-twenties. He was a farmer during much of his young adulthood. When he was not, the mores and habits of his time and place—which Independence fully exemplified, with its courthouse square, the quiet tree-lined streets, the habits of sobriety and discipline through hard work, and the comparatively leisurely pace of living—suited him perfectly. After doing his share in the AEF to keep the world safe for democracy in 1917 and 1918, Truman returned home at age thirty-five to open a haberdashery store in Kansas City, but the venture was quickly swept away in the short but sharp depression of 1921. The Pendergast machine picked the young man up in apparently absolutely honest fashion. According to Truman, he had served with several members of the machine, including Jim Pendergast, when he was in France with Battery D during the "Great War." These men frequently dropped into the haberdashery for gossip and chat. It was natural, if not inevitable, that Truman should drift into Pendergast and Jackson County politics once the haberdashery folded. After serving a two-year term as district judge in the early twenties, Truman in 1926 was elected, with Pendergast backing, as presiding judge of the county court. The "court" system in Missouri at that time was administrative, not judicial. Among other responsibilities, it levied taxes, made expenditures for roads, schools, homes for the aged. It was a perfect position from which to extract graft, and many men under the Pendergast wing did just that. Truman did not. He ran his court with honesty, efficiency, and fair economy. He became a shining symbol of Pendergast integrity at a time when the image of the machine as a whole was steadily darkening under revelations of gross corruption. By 1934 Truman was eager for a broader stage. The national House beckoned, but he claimed that "two fine gentlemen" already held the available seats, and so he turned to the Senate. His connections in Kansas City and across western Missouri served him well, and on January 3, 1935, he entered the Senate chamber in Washington for the first time.[4]

[4] The above biographical material is taken from Truman, *Year of Decisions*, pp. 131–214; Cabell Phillips, *The Truman Presidency*, pp. 3–37.

There was little to distinguish Harry Truman's Senate service in the years prior to Pearl Harbor. Tom Connally of Texas later recalled that the future President only spoke once in the upper chamber during those seven years and that "he had played no significant role" in the revolutionary legislation of the middle and later New Deal era. Truman's eagerness to "go along" was revealed in 1938 when he ducked out of a critical vote on an anti-lynching bill, not wishing to antagonize northern liberals or southern conservatives within his party or his own evenly-divided constituents.[5] Vice Presidents have been fashioned from lesser material. Truman loved the Senate, loved the circumstance, if not pomp, that has long accrued to the upper chamber, loved the comradeship of the Club.[6] For one with no college education and no formal training in the law, possession of a United States Senate seat in one's fifties was a notable achievement. Truman seemed content with it. Except when truly divisive issues such as race came to the fore, he was a good, consistent New Dealer, possibly too good, for he almost lost his seat in 1940. If he did little that was strikingly positive, he did little that was glaringly negative in relation to his President, his party, or his Senate. He was always a happy and likeable man in those years and indeed remained so down to the end of his Senate service.[7] In return, he was warmly regarded by his colleagues, who in their initial skepticism had labelled him "the Senator from Pendergast."[8] If his friendliness occasionally seemed almost spaniel-like, the Senate press corps soon came to realize that it masked

[5] Connally, *My Name is Tom Connally*, p. 274; Samuel Lubell, *The Future of American Politics*, 3d ed. (New York: Colophon Books, 1965), p. 26.

[6] " 'It's wonderful, this Senate,' " he told correspondent Allen Drury in early April 1945. " 'It's the greatest place on earth. . . . The grandest bunch of fellows you could ever find anywhere.' " Someone then remarked that it was a good place for public service. " 'It's the best place there is,' " Truman replied soberly. " 'If you really want to do public service, this is the place for it.' " Quoted in Drury, *Senate Journal*, p. 410.

[7] *Ibid.*, pp. 221, 283–284; Connally, *My Name is Tom Connally*, p. 274.

[8] Truman's personal loyalty to the Pendergasts was consistent and legendary. Senator Burton K. Wheeler recalled that " 'When Tom Pendergast was indicted Harry Truman came up to me. "Should I resign?" I said, "Why should you resign?" He said, "They've indicted the old man. He made me everything I am, and I've got to stand by him." And he did to the day of his [Pendergast's] death.' " Quoted in Studs Terkel, *Hard Times; An Oral History of the Great Depression* (New York: Pantheon Books, 1970), p. 270. Cf. also Maurice M. Milligan, *Missouri Waltz* (New York: Charles Scribner's Sons, 1948), pp. 219 ff. for a scathing indictment of Truman's relations with the Pendergast machine. Milligan had successfully prosecuted Tom Pendergast in 1936 while United States District Attorney for western Missouri.

a very shrewd judge of people.[9] After Pearl Harbor his chairman-ship of the celebrated Truman Committee to investigate honesty and fairness in the awarding of wartime contracts was just and ef-ficient. It gave him a sudden national prominence he had never before enjoyed and possibly did not relish.[10] And so when Truman took the oath of office that gloomy evening in April 1945, he was affectionately characterized by one observer as "farm boy, soldier, failure, child of Pendergast, Senator, Vice-President, one of the most honest people in creation."[11] And certainly one of the most tragically unprepared.[12]

Truman, like the people he led, was assuming at least partial custodianship of a world he never made and scarcely understood. All of his experience and interests had lain in domestic affairs. Now he was suddenly to become a world leader. The sense of bur-den must have been almost unbearable.

It was compounded, of course, by the nature of his predeces-sor's leadership. Throughout the war years Franklin Roosevelt had most emphatically been his own foreign secretary, save when he chose to delegate certain problems and negotiations to his intimate adviser, Harry Hopkins. The increasingly embittered State Depart-ment was often in the dark regarding Roosevelt's—and therefore America's—foreign policy. In July of 1943 Morgenthau recorded in his diary Cordell Hull's plaintive query concerning negotiations over the International Monetary Fund: " 'What is it we can do to improve the situation? . . . The President runs foreign affairs. I don't know what's going on.' " Characteristically, at Yalta not even Secretary of State Stettinius was included in the Roosevelt-Stalin discussions that led to the Far Eastern agreements. Roosevelt en-joyed at all times a fairly intimate knowledge of major internation-

---

[9] Drury, *Senate Journal*, p. 327.
[10] " 'I was getting along fine until I stuck my neck out too far and got too famous —and then they made me V.P. and now I can't do anything. No, sir, I can't do any-thing,' " Truman told a group of reporters on the afternoon before Roosevelt's death. Quoted in *ibid.*, p. 410.
[11] *Ibid.*, p. 412.
[12] Truman only saw Roosevelt a total of eight times during the entire year before the latter's death. And "when they met Roosevelt was not taking time to instruct his Vice-President in all the problems that were crowding in upon his weariness." Jonathan Daniels, *The Man of Independence* (Philadelphia: J. B. Lippincott Com-pany, 1950), p. 259.

al issues plus the enormous power of decision-making accrued during an unprecedented dozen years in the Presidency.[13] His aides and counselors thus pressed their own policy proposals upon a man fully as knowledgeable, if not more so, than themselves.

Truman's abrupt accession created at least a temporary vacuum and fluidity in American policy-making. Others were now more knowledgeable—or claimed to be—than the President. The result was an almost immediate scramble among Presidential counselors —official and unofficial—to get Truman's ear in order to shape or help shape his major policy decisions. Truman was therefore exposed to a much wider range of foreign policy arguments and options during the critical early months of his administration in the spring and summer of 1945 than his predecessor had ever been since Pearl Harbor.

From the beginning, however, Truman appeared firmly resolved to meet the incredible challenges of the Presidency with strength and purpose. He seemed to Tom Connally to be "nervous and ill at ease" when he returned briefly to the Senate during the first full day of his administration. But to his White House staff he presented a figure of confidence. He told Admiral Leahy that "I want you to tell me if you think I am making a mistake. Of course, I will make the decisions, and after a decision is made, I will expect you to be loyal." Some days later he imparted to David Lilienthal that air of brisk decisiveness that was rather quickly to become the hallmark of his public personality.[14]

The transformation of Harry Truman from the homespun, simple, friendly President of the Senate to the apparently purposeful President of the United States and world leader may have been ascribed by the more pious of the time to a benevolent act of God, but in fact it was the shadow of Jimmy Byrnes and not the altruism of the Almighty that forced Truman to pick up the reins so swiftly and resolutely. For there were many in and out of Washington on April 13, 1945, who felt that the one man in the nation qualified to succeed Roosevelt had been denied his, and his country's, opportunity

---

[13] Blum, *Morgenthau Diaries*, III: 241–242; Churchill, *Triumph and Tragedy*, pp. 333–334; Leahy, *I Was There*, p. 348.

[14] Connally, *My Name is Tom Connally*, p. 275; Leahy, *I Was There*, pp. 347–348; *Lilienthal Journals*, pp. 698–699.

by the connivance of cheap politicians a year before. "All over the Hill on Friday there was one fervent prayer," a Congressional reporter noted. " 'God grant that Harry Truman will call in Jimmy Byrnes.' " The *New York Times* instantly speculated that Byrnes, who had resigned as Mobilization Director a dozen days before, might "take an important post in the Cabinet." So, evidently, did a number of Cabinet officials, for Navy Secretary Forrestal had immediately dispatched a plane to South Carolina to bring Byrnes back to Washington, and Byrnes and Truman met for an hour that first day of Truman's Presidency. At that time Truman first told the South Carolinian that he was "considering" him for Secretary of State. Several days later the consideration became a wish, though it would not be carried out until the close of the San Francisco Conference to preserve continuity. To the press, however, the first Truman-Byrnes meeting confirmed all hopes. "After an hour's conference," the *Times* reported, "it was understood that Mr. Byrnes would, in effect, replace Harry Hopkins as Presidential confidant, and it was asserted [by whom it was never made clear], would receive more authority than a President has yet yielded to any man."[15] The inference could readily be drawn from such eager assumptions that Truman was for all practical purposes about to turn the Presidency over to Byrnes. Behind these speculations lay a questionable but oft-stated premise, namely that Truman and Byrnes were friends and that each admired the other. Time and events were to prove the idea groundless. And the confused and ultimately embittered Truman-Byrnes relationship would play a profound role in the shaping of American policy in the coming months.

But for the moment Secretary of State Stettinius had to be allowed to play out his role as host and co-organizer of the San Francisco Conference while a new and ill-informed President coped with foreign policy questions on his own. The most ominous of these were emerging across the ruined landscape of Eastern Europe.

[15] Frank McNaughton Report, April 14, 1945, Box 7, McNaughton Papers; *New York Times*, April 13, 1945, p. 1:4; Truman, *Year of Decisions*, pp. 34–35; Byrnes, *Speaking Frankly*, pp. 48–49.

4

The April Crisis over Eastern Europe

By mid-April 1945, only eight weeks after Yalta, the Grand Alliance was crippled by dissension. The Crimean accords on Europe had obviously broken down. This was an inevitable development, given the conflicting objectives of their authors. But breakdown was no less frightening for all of that.

In Rumania, only two weeks after the close of the Yalta Conference, the Russians, with the internal aid and support of their followers, who had kept the country in turmoil for some time, pressed a Communist government upon King Michael, in flagrant violation of the Anglo-American interpretations of the Declaration on Liberated Europe. Andrei Vyshinski, who had flown to Bucharest to talk with the King, claimed that conditions of unrest in the country were grave enough to warrant the demand for governmental reorganization. Vyshinski further stated that he had given Michael sufficient opportunity to find some non-Communist to form a strong government before directly intervening to announce Petru Groza as the Soviet choice. And in a conversation with the American representative on the Rumanian control commission, Vyshinski protested that the Soviets were acting in accordance with democratic principles, since the Communists comprised one of the largest political factions in the country. American officials and public opinion were shocked by the consistently unilateral and heavy-handed Russian behavior. The Soviet initiative was viewed as all the more grim by the fact that under the terms of both the Rumanian Armistice Agreement and the Declaration on Liberated Europe, Britain and the United States were jointly responsible—legally and morally—along with the Russians, for the change in King Michael's government.[1]

To the dismay of American officials in Moscow, however, the Roosevelt administration refused to risk a rupture with the Kremlin over events in the remote regions east of the Elbe. The United States merely chose to "assail" the Russians with notes "in which expressions of plaintive surprise were mingled with empty pleadings to the Soviet authorities to do otherwise than they were doing."[2]

In mid-March Soviet-American relations were further strained. The United States seemed unwilling to allow Russian military observers to sit in on exploratory talks in Switzerland between Western representatives and German officers seeking to surrender the Nazi army in Italy. The Russian response represented the ultimate in righteous anger, in view of the oft-repeated agreement among Stalin, Churchill, and Roosevelt that the bedrock of Big Three partnership lay in the mutual pledge not to make a separate peace with the enemy or any of his forces. On March 22 and 23 Molotov sent identical notes to both the British and American ambassadors which said in part that " 'the Soviet Government sees not a misunderstanding but something worse' " in the exclusive Anglo-American negotiations with the Germans. " 'In Berne for two weeks behind the backs of the Soviet Union, which is bearing the brunt of the war against Germany, negotiations have been going on' " be-

---

[1] Events in Bucharest in late February and early March may be traced in the almost daily reports of the American Control Commission Representative, Burton Y. Berry, to the State Department, esp. that of March 1, in *Foreign Relations, 1945; Diplomatic Papers,* V: 465–499. Reaction in both Britain and America may be found in Byrnes, *Speaking Frankly,* pp. 50–53; Eden, *The Reckoning,* pp. 604–605; Grew, *Turbulent Era,* II: 1443; *Newsweek,* XXV (March 26, 1945), 62.

[2] Kennan, *Memoirs,* pp. 253–254.

tween German and Western representatives. " 'Soviet Government,' " Molotov concluded, " 'consider [*sic*] this completely impermissible. . . .' "[3] The United States response, in turn, was one of injured innocence, since Washington had readily agreed with the British to keep the Russians fully informed of the course of early conversations and had arranged that Russian officers would be in attendance once full and serious negotiations with the Germans commenced. Referring to an earlier and less vigorous Soviet protest on the subject, Ambassador Harriman cabled from Moscow on March 17 that the Soviet attitude "confirms the growing impression that General Deane and I have received, particularly since the Crimea Conference, that the Soviet leaders have come to believe that they can force their will on us on any issue."[4]

The issue did not die quietly. As late as April 1 Roosevelt felt constrained to inform Stalin that no hard and fast negotiations had taken place between Anglo-American representatives and emissaries of the German forces in Italy. Two days later Stalin replied with a note which indicated at once how deeply the euphoric spirit of Yalta had eroded and with what great fears and certainty the Russians regarded the conclusion of a separate peace between Nazi Germany and the Western democracies. Charging that Roosevelt was receiving fragmentary and, by implication, erroneous information, Stalin asserted that according to his sources secret negotiations between Western representatives and German military officials had indeed taken place in Switzerland, and that according to the sweeping agreements reached "the German Commander on the Western Front, Marshal Kesselring, is to open the front to the Anglo-American troops and let them move east, while the British and Americans have promised, in exchange, to ease the armistice terms for the Germans." The Soviet Premier concluded: "And so what we have at the moment is that the Germans on the Western Front have in fact ceased the war against Britain and America. At the same time they continue the war against Russia, the Ally of Britain and the U.S.A." "With astonishment," and "bitter resentment toward your

---

[3] Quoted in Ehrman, *Grand Strategy*, pp. 123–128.
[4] Leahy, *I Was There*, p. 332; *Foreign Relations, 1945; Diplomatic Papers*, III: 732.

informers," Roosevelt on April 5 denied any such duplicity in the strongest cable that he sent Stalin between Yalta and his death. There the matter rested as Truman took office.[5]

The chief source of deteriorating relations between Russia and the West in the spring of 1945, however, was Poland. In conformity with the Yalta Polish agreements, a commission composed of Soviet Foreign Minister Molotov and the British and American ambassadors in Moscow was established to guide negotiations between the Lublin Poles and the "democratic leaders" from within Poland itself and from the exiled government in London. The Western representatives and their governments were acting on the assumption that the Lublin government would be completely reorganized along democratic lines. The Russians and their Lublin allies quickly revealed that their interpretation of the Yalta Polish accords provided only for inclusion of a few non-Lublin elements in a Lublin-controlled provisional government. Deadlock ensued almost at once. According to Harriman, Molotov deferred from the beginning to the wishes of the Lublin Poles, who in effect demanded a veto over the names of anyone proposed by the Western ambassadors for inclusion in the reorganization negotiations. The Lublinites were particularly incensed by the vehement reaction of the London Poles to the territorial as well as political settlement of the Polish issue at Yalta.[6] Negotiations soon broke down, and Harriman assumed an ostentatious posture of pessimism. He, General Deane, and the other officials at the American Embassy in Spaso House had had their suspicions of Russian aims and practices sharpened by several years of near-daily contact with Soviet officials. Negotiations had often been tedious and frustrating and always ex-

---

[5] The cables are found in *Stalin's Correspondence with Roosevelt and Truman, 1941–1945* (New York: Capricorn Books, 1965), pp. 204–208. Cf. also Leahy, *I Was There*, pp. 330–334. Soviet fears of a separate German-Western peace were raised once again in an interview between Assistant Secretary of State James Dunn and Soviet Ambassador Gromyko on April 4, in which Gromyko excitedly claimed that the British were trying to modify the unconditional surrender doctrine in the European Advisory Council. Dunn assured Gromyko that the United States would not countenance such a modification. *Foreign Relations, 1945; Diplomatic Papers*, III: 217–219.

[6] Cf. cables to Secretary of State (Stettinius) from Harriman and from Chargé to Polish Government in Exile (Schoenfeld), February 24–March 1, 1945, Acting Secretary of State (Grew) to Schoenfeld, March 9, 1945, Harriman to Secretary of State, April 3, 1945, in *ibid.*, V: 123–197 *passim*.

hausting. The embassy staff had been particularly shaken and depressed by Stalin's brutal decision in August of 1944 to halt the Red Army before Warsaw so as to allow the Nazi garrison to wipe out the Polish uprising in the city. Now, after some hesitation due to Harriman's belief that "the Russians cannot afford to let the Crimea decisions break down," disenchantment deepened. "Boredom and disgust" filled Spaso House.[7]

On April 6 Harriman in effect demanded a sharp revision of American policy toward the Soviet Union. He urged that the United States "should maintain positions that would be hard for the Soviet authorities if they maintained positions hard for us; and that we should hurt them if they hurt us." The ambassador's motive in urging such a reversal of traditional policy was not to precipitate a cold war, but to prevent one. He repeatedly hammered home the idea that Moscow consistently mistook America's generous impulses for weakness or for sinister design. "I hope I will not be misunderstood when I say that our relations with the Soviet Government will be on firmer ground as soon as we have adopted a policy which includes on the one hand at all times a full place for cooperation with the Soviet Union but on the other a readiness to go along without them if we can't obtain their cooperation." On April 11 Harriman in another cable urged that the possible postwar Russian loan should be placed before the Soviets in such a way " 'at all times' " as to " 'make it plain that our cooperation is dependent upon a reciprocal cooperative attitude of the Soviet Government on other matters.' " Harriman's position was supported within the administration at this time by Forrestal and Will Clayton and possibly others.[8]

On April 7 Stalin sent his Western colleagues a cable that was at once a challenge and a proposal. The Premier began by charg-

---

[7] Deane, *Strange Alliance*, pp. 31–140 *passim*; Kennan, *Memoirs*, p. 222; Harriman to Secretary of State, March 2, 1945, *Foreign Relations, 1945*; *Diplomatic Papers*, V: 136.

[8] The April 6 telegram is paraphrased in Herbert Feis, *Churchill, Roosevelt, Stalin; The War They Waged and the Peace They Sought* (Princeton: Princeton University Press, 1957), pp. 597–598, and may be found in Records of the Department of State, 1945, decimal file 711.61/4-645, National Archives. Harriman's cable on the Russian loan is quoted in Paterson, "The Abortive American Loan to Russia," pp. 79–80. Cf. also Walter Millis, ed., *The Forrestal Diaries* (New York: The Viking Press, 1951), pp. 40–41.

ing the American and British ambassadors in Moscow with trying to ignore the Lublin Poles and the provisions of the Yalta Polish agreement. He reiterated his demand that the only non-Lublin Poles to be invited to the negotiations should be those who publicly embraced the Yalta accords. Finally, he advanced a new and tougher proposal, namely, that the formula previously used to reorganize the Yugoslav government be applied to Poland. This would have given the Lublin Poles four of every five ministries in the reorganized provisional government.[9]

A totally exasperated Winston Churchill at once proposed to Roosevelt that a joint and public Anglo-American statement be prepared on the Polish impasse. Roosevelt and his current Secretary of State, Edward R. Stettinius, however, continued to cling to the policy that had been pursued throughout the war. Even as Harriman cabled Washington on April 6, asking for a tougher line, Stettinius publicly stated once again his unshaken belief "that the Crimea Agreement on Poland will be carried out." Five days later, in the last message he ever sent the Prime Minister, Roosevelt rejected the strategy of an immediate showdown with Stalin over Poland and urged Churchill to "minimize the general Soviet problem as much as possible because these problems, in one form or another, seem to arise every day and most of them straighten out. . . ."[10]

Time was to show that Roosevelt's assessment was not the dithering of a tired and dying man, but was fairly close to the mark. The Polish situation at the time of his death was bad, and it would get worse. But the elements of an ultimate resolution, inevitably favorable to the Russians, were there all the time. In the first place, both the British and the Americans had become disenchanted with the bellicose pretensions of the London Poles, particularly after Mikolajczyk's resignation at the end of 1944 had thrown control of the government into the hands of the anti-Russian intransigents. In fact, Eden bluntly told Mikolajczyk as early as

---

[9] The cable is in *Stalin's Correspondence with Roosevelt and Truman*, pp. 211–213.

[10] Truman, *Year of Decisions*, p. 37; "Council on Foreign Relations Proceedings at the Opening of the Harold Pratt House, . . . New York, April 6, 1945," in Clayton Papers, Box 30; Roosevelt to Churchill, April 11, 1945, *Foreign Relations, 1945; Diplomatic Papers*, V: 210.

mid-January 1945 that "obviously in some not too distant future we will have to recognize the Lublin Provisional Government, and therefore withdraw recognition from the Polish Government in London." Several days later Hopkins in London declined to comment on whether the Americans favored either the Curzon or Oder lines as the postwar boundaries of Poland.[11]

The skids were obviously being greased for the intransigent London Poles. But not for Mikolajczyk. He was the prize for each side, a figure who enjoyed great popularity in Poland and a man of demonstrated political flexibility. Indeed, he had lost his leadership of the London Poles because of that flexibility in advocating acquiescence in the Curzon Line. After Yalta his former colleagues among the London Poles had prevailed upon him to denounce the Crimean Polish accords, which obviously surprised and angered Stalin. Yet Mikolajczyk would be a good man to have back inside Poland and enveloped within the provisional government if he could just be made to say the right things. Churchill and Roosevelt were eager to have him there as a strong pro-Western representative. Thus it was that on the same day that Stalin cabled FDR, he also sent Churchill a lengthy note in which Mikolajczyk was first denounced as wholly unacceptable to the Lublin Poles. But then Stalin added: " 'However, if you think it necessary, I should be ready to use my influence with the [Lublin] Provisional Polish Government to make them withdraw their objections to inviting Mikolajczyk, if the latter would make a public statement accepting the decisions of the Crimea Conference on the Polish question. . . .' " Churchill immediately commenced "painful discussions" with Mikolajczyk and the other London Poles to obtain their acquiescence.[12] There the matter rested at Roosevelt's death.

Flexibility of mind was not an attribute possessed solely by Stanislaw Mikolajczyk. Harriman's own attitude and behavior need to be studied as best we can at this juncture. Superficially, of course, he appeared to be the most rigid of hard-liners, first advocating use of a postwar loan to compel Russia to behave as the United States saw fit, then demanding that America draw a line for Russia in the

[11] Rozek, *Allied Wartime Diplomacy*, pp. 332, 334.
[12] Quoted in Churchill, *Triumph and Tragedy*, p. 377.

diplomatic dust which, should she step over it, would summon forth an equally tough response from Washington. But was Harriman pressing a carefully thought-out and fixed policy line on his superiors? Or was he simply taking the most extreme of positions from time to time in order to insure that all possible options would be studied by his superiors? Years later one who worked closely with him remarked:

> Harriman would cogitate out loud, debate vigorously with anyone present, and sometimes seem to stick stubbornly to a wrongheaded position. Then, he might suddenly switch, for Harriman had an unusual objectivity and generosity toward others and their views—he was a man who could and frequently did change his mind under the weight of argument. . . . Harriman always asked two questions: first, "What course do we want events to take?" and then, "Do we have the power to bring it about?"[13]

In the spring and summer of 1945 the United States clearly did not have the power—or did not feel that it had the power, either militarily or economically—to affect events beyond the Elbe. Harriman's comments on the Russian loan, given the suspicious and parsimonious mood of Congress, simply made eminently good sense at the time. There would be no way of getting a massive postwar credit to Russia through Congress if the Soviets were to use naked coercion and force to dominate Eastern Europe, and the Russians should be told this. As for the composition of the Polish government, even *before* the events of early May led to total breakdown of the Polish talks, Harriman—along with Stettinius—told Anthony Eden that all the non-Lublin elements, *i.e.*, both from within Poland and from the London exiles, could hope at most for about forty percent of the posts in any reorganized government.[14]

The ingredients for a settlement of the Polish issue were thus present at Roosevelt's death as that doomed man mildly pointed

[13] Roger Hilsman, *To Move a Nation; The Politics of Foreign Policy in the Administration of John F. Kennedy* (New York: Doubleday & Company, Inc., 1967), p. 57.

[14] E. L. Woodward, *British Foreign Policy in the Second World War* (London: Her Majesty's Stationery Office, 1962), pp. 511–512; Feis, *Churchill, Roosevelt, Stalin*, p. 572. The Feis account also would seem to indicate that Harriman believed "that the Yalta agreement contemplated that the Warsaw [Lublin] group would have the leading part both in the consultations and in the reformed government" **even** *before* Roosevelt's death.

out. It would not be a "good" nor an advantageous settlement, but it would be the best that the West could get, and that fact would soon be fully appreciated. Truman's abrupt accession, his need to familiarize himself with foreign policy problems and to sift through as much advice as he could get, allowed the issue to drift rather dangerously until the Hopkins mission laid to rest the political if not the territorial issue of postwar Poland. But in his first exchange with Churchill on April 13 Truman clearly indicated that compromise and not showdown was in his mind. He first rejected the idea of publicizing the apparent Soviet-Western impasse over Poland. Then, turning to Stalin's telegram of April 7, the President, while admitting that the Soviet Premier "does not leave much ground for optimism," nonetheless added: "I feel very strongly that we should have another go at him." Churchill grudgingly submitted, and two days later another Anglo-American negotiation formula, which nonetheless adhered fairly strictly to the standard Western demands, was dispatched to Moscow. It was coupled with a sharp denial of Stalin's charge that the Western governments were seeking to undermine the Lublin faction and an equally sharp rejection of the Yugoslav precedent as a solution for the Polish crisis. As Truman later wrote, "I felt that military and political collaboration with Russia was still so important that the time was not ripe for a public statement on this difficult and still unsettled Polish situation." At the same time Churchill began the break of the Polish logjam by successfully working on Mikolajczyk in order to soften his stand on the Yalta accords.[15]

Within a few days an opportunity arose to continue the Soviet-Western dialogue over Poland. Stalin, apparently sincerely touched by Roosevelt's death, reversed an earlier disquieting decision and dispatched Molotov to the San Francisco United Nations Conference. The Soviet Premier suggested to his Western colleagues that Molotov might stop over in Washington for several days of talks before proceeding on to the coast.[16] Harriman and one of his offi-

[15] Truman to Churchill, April 13, 1945, *Foreign Relations, 1945; Diplomatic Papers*, V: 211–212; Truman and Churchill to Stalin, received April 18, 1945, *Stalin's Correspondence with Roosevelt and Truman*, pp. 215–217; Churchill, *Triumph and Tragedy*, pp. 416–418; Truman, *Year of Decisions*, pp. 36–38.

[16] Stalin to Roosevelt, March 27, 1945, *Stalin's Correspondence with Roosevelt and Truman*, pp. 199–200; Harriman to Secretary of State, April 16, 1945, *Foreign Relations, 1945; Diplomatic Papers*, V: 223–224.

cers, Charles Bohlen, returned to Washington several days before
Molotov's arrival to meet the new President and receive whatever
new instructions he might have. On April 20 Harriman spoke personally to the President for the first time. In the presence of the Secretary and Undersecretary of State he told Truman bluntly that "in
effect what we were faced with was a 'barbarian invasion of Euo-
rope,' that Soviet control over any foreign country did not mean
merely influence on their foreign relations but the extension of the
Soviet system with secret police, extinction of freedom of speech,
etc., and that we had to decide what should be our attitude in the
face of these unpleasant facts." Harriman emphasized to the President that he spoke from an attitude of realism, not pessimism.
Stalin and his advisers thought they could pursue two simultaneous
policies, the ambassador said. One looked to a continuation of
cooperation with the West; the other, toward Soviet expansion
over Eastern Europe. Only by taking a firm stance on its own interpretation of the Yalta agreements could the United States force the
Russians to realize that their two policies were in fundamental con-
tradiction. Truman responded moderately; he intended to be "firm
but fair" with the Russians.[17]

For the President knew that the United States in the spring of
1945 still needed the Soviet Union fully as much as Russia needed
America. This fact clearly emerged at the end of the interview.
The Soviets were pressing for inclusion of the existing Lublin Polish government in the San Francisco Conference. Truman "definitely" stated that the Senate would not accept a United Nations
Charter signed by the Lublin faction as representative of the Polish
government, but then went on to admit that if the Russians chose
to withdraw from the San Francisco Conference over the Polish issue, the future outlook of the world organization would be grim.
"The President said that the truth of the matter was that without
Russia, there would not be much of a world organization."[18] Having but recently left the Senate, the President was well aware that
American acceptance of United Nations membership was a reflec-

[17] "Memorandum of Conversation Between the President, Secretary of State, Undersecretary of State Grew, Ambassador Harriman, and Mr. Bohlen, by Bohlen,
April 20, 1945," *ibid.*, V: 231–234.
[18] *Ibid.*

tion and the ultimate triumph of internationalism in the United States. At that moment American public interest in the coming world organization was reaching unprecedented heights. The State Department alone was receiving from five to seven thousand letters per day on the subject.[19] To jeopardize the entire future of the United Nations over the immediate reorganization of the Polish government would have constituted the gravest political risk. It was one that Truman, in office only a week, was not prepared to assume.

The necessity for continued American reliance upon Soviet aid was most profoundly stressed, however, in a conference which Truman held with his advisers on April 23, just before the President was to receive Molotov for a second time. The Soviet Foreign Minister had arrived in Washington the day before and had immediately plunged into long conversations at the State Department with Stettinius and Eden over reorganization and recognition of the Polish government. Continued stalemate was the result, as Molotov now demanded not only the Yugoslav precedent as the basis of a new Polish government, but also the inclusion of such a government in the United Nations Charter Conference at San Francisco. These escalated demands put Russia and the West much further apart than ever before and mocked the earlier compromises which both Harriman and Mikolajczyk ultimately had been willing to make.[20]

Now, on the afternoon of the twenty-third, Stettinius reported the discouraging result of the talks to a gathering in the Oval Office of the White House. "A complete deadlock had been reached" on the Polish question, the Secretary of State said. According to Bohlen's notes, Truman reacted angrily. He "said that he had told Mr. Molotov last night that he intended fully to carry out all of the agreements reached by President Roosevelt at the Crimea. He added that he felt our agreements with the Soviet Union so far had been a one-way street and that he could not continue; it was now or never. He intended to go on with the plans for

---

[19] Divine, *Second Chance, passim*; U.S. State Department *Bulletin*, XII (April 29, 1945), 806; (June 24, 1945), 1163–1164.

[20] *Foreign Relations, 1945; Diplomatic Papers*, V: 237–239, 241–251; Arthur Bliss Lane, *I Saw Poland Betrayed* (Indianapolis: Bobbs-Merrill Co., 1948), pp. 102–103.

San Francisco and if the Russians did not wish to join us they could go to hell."[21]

Truman's comments have been interpreted as marking the beginning of a major American policy change toward Russia—from Rooseveltian generosity and cooperation to a Trumanite hardness and determination to crack Russian control over Eastern Europe, using the atomic bomb as a major diplomatic lever.[22] Such an interpretation rests partly upon the suspension of any further examination of what was said at this meeting, especially by Truman. The President, in fact, found his opening remarks fully supported by only one man—Secretary of the Navy James Forrestal. A self-driven, sensitive, frequently suspicious, and ultimately tortured soul, Forrestal had long entertained apprehensions about postwar Soviet desires in both Europe and Asia. He had also developed, much to the discomfort of the White House, a fixation upon the inevitability of a third global holocaust even as the second was reaching a climax of violence. Following Truman's opening outburst, Forrestal argued that the Polish crisis was not an isolated incident but all of a piece. "He said that he felt for some time the Russians had considered that we would not object if they took . . . all of Eastern Europe into their power. He said that it was his profound conviction that if the Russians were to be rigid in their attitudes we had better have a showdown with them now than later."[23]

Admiral Leahy noted that Forrestal's view reflected a consensus and "that no particular harm could be done to our war prospects if Russia should slow down or even stop its war effort in Europe and Asia. The Joint Chiefs were about to change our military policy anyway on the basis of studies made in Moscow by General Deane."[24] However, the further record of the meeting, as well as

[21] *Foreign Relations, 1945; Diplomatic Papers,* V: 251; Millis, ed., *Forrestal Diaries,* p. 50; Truman, *Year of Decisions,* p. 93.

[22] Gar Alperovitz, *Atomic Diplomacy; Hiroshima and Potsdam; The Use of the Atomic Bomb and the Confrontation with Soviet Power* (New York: Vintage Books, 1967), pp. 13–14, 19, 25.

[23] Arnold A. Rogow, *James Forrestal; A Study of Personality, Politics and Policy* (New York: The Macmillan Co., 1963), pp. 123–125; Forrestal to Capt. James K. Vardaman, May 26, 1945, with enclosure, Vardaman to Forrestal, May 31, 1945, Rosenman Papers, 1945, Box 4. This exchange was not declassified until 1962. *Foreign Relations, 1945; Diplomatic Papers,* V: 253; *Forrestal Diaries,* p. 49.

[24] Leahy, *I Was There,* p. 351.

the subsequent pattern of strategic decisions on the course of the war in the Pacific, refute the admiral's contention.

Stimson, who spoke next, stressed the fact that the Russians had so far kept their word "in the big military matters. In fact, he said that they had often been better than their promise." Turning to the Polish question, which he admitted he knew little about, Stimson "remarked that years ago virtually all of Poland had been Russian" and later added "that he would like to know how far the Russian reaction to a strong [American] position on Poland would go. He said that he thought that the Russians perhaps were being more realistic than we were in regard to their own security." Expanding his comments later in his diary, Stimson added that he knew "very well from my experience with other nations that there are no nations in the world (except the U.S. and the U.K.) which have a real idea of what an independent free ballot is." Stimson in fact was angered far less by the Russians than by the State Department, which "has got itself into a mess. Contrary to what I thought was the wise course they have not settled the problems that lie between the United States and Russia and Great Britain and France, the main powers, by wise negotiations before the public meeting in San Francisco. . . . Why to me it seems that they might make trouble between us and Russia in comparison with which the whole possibilities of the San Francisco meeting amount to nothing." And Stimson added that he had been surprised that afternoon that Forrestal had "for once" become "a yes man."[25]

Harriman and Leahy followed Stimson in trying to calm troubled waters, and although their remarks were quiet and brief they obviously served to bring the meeting back to a more traditional perspective. Harriman "said obviously we were faced with a possibility of a real break with the Russians but he felt that if properly handled it might be avoided." Leahy then remarked that he had left Yalta with the definite impression "that the Soviet Government had no intention of permitting a free government to operate in Poland and that he would have been surprised had the Soviet Government behaved any differently than it did." And he added

[25] *Foreign Relations, 1945; Diplomatic Papers*, V: 253–254; Stimson Diary, April 23, 1945.

that he felt that it was "a serious matter to break with the Russians."[26]

It was Generals Marshall and Deane, however, who finally brought up the major consideration lurking behind the arguments against an immediate showdown with the Soviets over the Yalta Polish accords. Marshall stated "that from a military point of view the situation was secure" but that the army "hoped for Soviet participation in the war against Japan at a time when it would be useful to us. The Russians had it within their power to delay their entry into the Far Eastern war until we had done all the dirty work. He said that difficulties with the Russians . . . usually straightened out." Deane then flatly stated that Russia could not be kept out of the Pacific war in any case. She would enter the conflict, he said, as soon as she was able, no matter what happened in other fields. "He felt that the Russians had to do this because they could not afford too long a period of letdown for their people who were tired." Deane added that his experiences in Moscow had convinced him "that if we were afraid of the Russians we would get nowhere, and he felt that we should be firm when we were right." Essentially what both Deane and Marshall were saying was that since Soviet entry into the Pacific war was inevitable, the task of American policy-makers was to manipulate that entry in such a fashion as to maximize American interests, aims, and planning. That could only be accomplished in an atmosphere of at least minimal cordiality and harmony. In conclusion, Stimson reiterated his opinion "that the Russians would not yield on the Polish question," nor should the United States expect them to. Faced with this barrage of skepticism concerning the possibility of a major American policy change, Truman rapidly retreated. In response to Harriman's comments, the President "said that he had no intention of delivering an ultimatum to Mr. Molotov but merely to make clear the position of this government."[27]

Thus the first real debate among American officials concerning future policy toward the Soviet Union after Roosevelt's death

[26] *Foreign Relations, 1945; Diplomatic Papers*, V: 254.
[27] *Ibid.*, pp. 252–254; Truman, *Year of Decisions*, p. 96; Pogue, *Marshall*, pp. 580–581.

ended on a note of decided caution. The Russians, through Molotov, were subsequently admonished in plain and unvarnished language to keep their Yalta Polish commitments, a stand that was "more than pleasing" to Admiral Leahy. But as Leahy added: "I did not believe that the dominating Soviet influence could be excluded from Poland, but I did think it was possible to give to the reorganized Polish Government an external appearance of independence."[28] In other words American policy-makers in the weeks just after Roosevelt's death followed the deceased President's policy with fair consistency despite some ostentatious tough talking. Eastern Europe in general and Poland in particular continued to be considered as a sphere of preponderant Soviet influence. What particularly disturbed the United States was the constant Russian insistence that the San Francisco Conference accept the Lublin faction as the *de facto* government of Poland and thus a charter member of the organization. On this point Truman, as Roosevelt before him, made the American position firm. But, as shall become clear, once the United Nations was established without the participation of the Lublin Poles, the United States quickly capitulated to Soviet pressure to have Poland dominated by the Lublinites. Behind this American policy lay the overriding desire to secure continued formal Soviet friendship and assistance in the triumphant prosecution of the war against Japan.

In the days and weeks following the April 23 White House meeting, however, American policy toward Russia was put to further strain by developments in Eastern Europe, which seemed flagrantly to violate the Western interpretation of the Yalta accords. Stalin signed a twenty-year mutual assistance pact with the Lublin faction in direct violation of the Crimean agreements. In so acting, the Russian leader again emphasized his insistence that this group must constitute the legitimate core of any future Polish government.[29] At the same time reports began to circulate widely that in early March leading members of the surviving Polish underground

---

[28] Leahy, *I Was There*, p. 352. The official transcript of the Truman-Molotov interview of April 24, in which the President "talked tough" to the Russians, is in *Foreign Relations, 1945; Diplomatic Papers*, V: 256–257; Truman's own account is in *Year of Decisions*, pp. 97–99.

[29] Lane, *I Saw Poland Betrayed*, p. 101.

had been lured to a meeting with Russian political police by promises of participation in the Moscow reorganization talks, only to be arrested and incarcerated. On May 4 Molotov finally admitted that the men were being held in Russia awaiting trial on charges of " 'diversionary tactics in the rear of the Red Army.' " The following day Moscow added that the men had maintained illegal radio stations.[30]

During the first few days of May Truman received disquieting information from other quarters of Eastern Europe. In early March, only three weeks after Yalta, the State Department had warned the Russians through the American representative in Bulgaria that the United States expected the Crimea Declaration on Liberated Europe fully implemented in the former Axis nations lying in the Danube Valley.[31] Now, two months later, Acting Secretary of State Grew, in summarizing weeks of gloomy reports from Bulgaria and Rumania, told Truman of the increasing "difficulty of maintaining the position of this Government in an area where the Soviet Government considers its interests paramount." And Grew added: "Since Bulgaria and Rumania surrendered to the Allies last autumn they have been under strict Russian control though nominally subject to Anglo-American-Soviet Control Commissions. The American representatives on the Control Commissions have hardly more than the status of observers, although in the case of Bulgaria, the armistice terms provide for their participation in the work of the Commission." The point that so perturbed Grew and the State Department was that the presence of these American representatives in Bulgaria and Rumania "associates this Government with measures taken in the name of the Commission by the Soviet authorities on which we are not consulted and with which we are often in disagreement." And the Acting Secretary reminded the new President that only two weeks after Yalta "the Soviet Government . . . intervened directly" in Rumanian political affairs "to bring about the installation of a minority government dominated by the

[30] Quoted in Churchill, *Triumph and Tragedy*, p. 426. Cf. also Eden, *The Reckoning*, p. 619; Lane, *I Saw Poland Betrayed*, p. 104.
[31] Acting Secretary of State (Grew) to U.S. Representative in Bulgaria (Barnes), March 3, 1945, *Foreign Relations, 1945; Diplomatic Papers*, IV: 169.

Communists." In Bulgaria, Grew continued, the Russians "have exerted pressure directly and indirectly on behalf of the Communist party." Grew enclosed a long supplementary memorandum from the American representatives in Bulgaria to buttress his depressing tale. Two days later the Chief Military Representative in Rumania, General Van Schuyler, submitted a similar statement directly to Truman.[32]

These developments in Poland and Moscow, Rumania and Bulgaria, formed a somber background to Stalin's adamant refusal to consider or negotiate the Anglo-American interpretation of the Yalta agreements on the reorganization of the Polish government. Despite Truman's tongue-lashing, Molotov in a further conversation with Stettinius and Eden late on April 23 refused to consider further discussion of the Polish issue until Stalin had replied to the joint Truman-Churchill message of April 15.[33] The following day the Premier's cable reached Washington. He denounced what he called the stubborn Anglo-American determination to view the currently functioning Lublin Polish government as "a group on a par with any other group of Poles" and not as "the core of a future Polish Government of National Unity." Stalin added that the Western rejection of the Yugoslav precedent was further proof of the desire of both Truman and Churchill to strip the existing Lublin government of its legitimate pre-eminence. Stalin then reminded his Western colleagues of the uncomfortable fact that in October of 1944, in order to save Greece from the possibility of falling into the Communist orbit, Churchill had gone to Moscow and had agreed to establish *de facto* spheres of influence in Eastern Europe. The Prime Minister had obtained assurances from the Premier of future British pre-eminence in Greece in exchange for future Soviet dominance over Bulgaria and Rumania. Stalin had steadfastly kept his part of the bargain, while Churchill and Roosevelt—and later Truman—worked on the assumption that the Yalta Declaration on Liberated Europe superseded the October 1944 ac-

---

[32] Memo from Acting Secretary of State (Grew) to President Truman, May 1, 1945, *ibid.*, pp. 201–203, 205–207, V: 540–544.
[33] "Minutes of Third Meeting Regarding Polish Question, Held at State Department," April 23, 1945, *ibid.*, V: 260–262.

cords in the two Danubian countries. Now Stalin sought to use his good faith regarding Greece as a bargaining counter for Poland. Poland was to the security of Russia what Belgium and Greece were to the security of Britain, he said.

> I do not know whether a genuinely representative Government has been established in Greece, or whether the Belgian Government is a genuinely democratic one. The Soviet Union was not consulted when those Governments were being formed, nor did it claim the right to interfere in those matters, because it realises how important Belgium and Greece are to the security of Great Britain. . . . I am ready to . . . do all in my power to reach an agreed settlement. But you are asking too much. To put it plainly, you want me to renounce the interests of the security of the Soviet Union. . . .

He then closed by reiterating his demand that the Polish question be settled by the Yugoslav formula.[34]

It is difficult to suppress some sympathy for Stalin at this point. He thought he had reached a spheres of influence agreement with Churchill respecting Europe the previous October—and indeed it had been the Prime Minister who had initiated the suggestion. The Yalta accords seemed so vaguely drawn as to constitute merely a cynical sop to the principles of the Atlantic Charter by realistic statesmen, who understood that the existing balance of power in the world precluded an open and fluid political system across Europe. Now, suddenly, Stalin was made to realize that many in the West, led by Churchill and even certain elements in the American government, did mean to enforce the Yalta accords with respect both to Poland and other parts of "liberated Europe." The Generalissimo's frank letter to Truman may well have represented an attempt to wrench the new, untried, and uncertain President back to the generous Roosevelt policy respecting Russian interests in Eastern Europe. If so, it ultimately succeeded brilliantly.

For the moment, however, Churchill's hold on Truman was stronger than that of Stalin. On April 29 the Prime Minister wrote his Soviet colleague to remind him once again that "it was on ac-

---

[34] Stalin to Truman, April 24, 1945, *Stalin's Correspondence with Roosevelt and Truman*, pp. 219–220; Churchill, *Triumph and Tragedy*, pp. 421–422.

count of Poland that the British went to war with Germany in 1939." Churchill concluded unhappily: "There is not much comfort in looking into a future where you and the countries you dominate, plus the Communist Parties in many other States, are all drawn up on one side, and those who rally to the English-speaking nations and their associates or Dominions are on the other. It is quite obvious that their quarrel would tear the world to pieces. . . ."[35] The following day the Prime Minister phoned Truman and adroitly obtained the President's renewed acquiescence to the British interpretation of the Polish crisis. Stettinius had just reported from San Francisco that further talks with Molotov had gotten nowhere: The Soviets continued to demand the resolution of the Polish issue along the lines of the Yugoslav formula. Four days later, with definite news of the Russian arrest of the sixteen members of the Polish underground, the Moscow negotiations on Poland were suspended by the Western powers.[36]

By the first week of May relations between Russia and the West had deteriorated to their lowest post-Yalta level and probably their lowest level of World War II.[37] To the dismay of a number of State Department officials, who deplored the current drift in East-West relations, talk of a future war with the Soviet Union began to seep into portions of the American press and became a common topic of gossip at Washington cocktail and dinner parties, even among officials with the highest civil service ratings. From Rome Ambassador Kirk begged the State Department not to permit a precipitate withdrawal of American troops from Europe at war's end. Grew quickly passed the message on to Truman and to Stim-

---

[35] Churchill, *Triumph and Tragedy*, pp. 423, 425.

[36] "Transcript of Trans-Atlantic Telephone Conversation between President Truman and British Prime Minister Churchill," April 30, 1945, *Foreign Relations, 1945; Diplomatic Papers*, III: 767; Truman, *Year of Decisions*, p. 128; Lane, *I Saw Poland Betrayed*, p. 104.

[37] It was at this time that French Communist leader Jacques Duclos launched his series of attacks against what Arthur Schlesinger, Jr. has called "American universalism," while Stalin stood before a visiting Yugoslav delegation in the midst of a late night drinking party in the Kremlin and cried out: "The war is nearly over. We will recover in fifteen or twenty years and then we'll have another go at it." (Schlesinger, "Origins of the Cold War," *Foreign Affairs*, XLVI [October, 1967], 43; Milovan Djilas, *Conversations with Stalin* [New York: Harcourt, Brace & World, Inc., 1962], pp. 114–115.) Whether these incidents marked a fateful and irreversible departure in Soviet policy is left to the reader to judge in light of subsequent events discussed in the following pages.

son.[38] But a cluster of powerful and often unrelated countervailing influences were at work in Europe, America, and Asia to arrest the trend. Within a surprisingly short time a substantial rapprochement occurred in Soviet-American if not in Anglo-Soviet affairs. The personal outlook of the American President, concurrent events elsewhere in Europe, and above all, the overriding priorities generated by the Pacific war, all played important roles in rescuing Washington's relations with Moscow from the brink of disaster.

[38] Memorandum of Conversation between Charles Bohlen, Archibald MacLeish, and Raymond Gram Swing, May 22, 1945; MacLeish to Acting Secretary of State Grew, May 26, 1945; Memorandum from Acting Secretary of State Grew for the President, May 26, 1945; Memorandum from Acting Secretary of State Grew to the Secretary of War, June 4, 1945, Records of the Department of State, decimal file 711.61/5-2245, 711.61/5-2645, and 740.00119E.W./5-2545, National Archives.

5

Countervailing Influences in Washington and Europe--April, May, and June

Harry Truman had not wanted to be President of the United States. Having succeeded to that office, he wasted no time in demonstrating how little he relished the role of world leader. His initial remarks at the White House meeting of April 23, and even his later "dressing down" of Molotov for having ostensibly broken the Yalta accords, reflected a character that was not only uneasy, but exasperated as well by having to take the time to carry out duties that were essentially of secondary interest. Like the people whom he now led, Harry Truman longed to turn the bulk of his attention and energies inward upon the American scene as World War II in Europe reached its close. The Rooseveltian zest for the high adventure of helping to remake a shattered globe in a nobler image was gone from the White House now. In its stead remained a dogged determination to see the war through to a victorious conclusion and to see the United Nations become a living reality with the least possible strain and drama. In the realm of foreign policy, vision and enthusiasm apparently ceased beyond these immediate goals. In the realm of domestic policy, however, the challenges of reorganization, reconversion, and reform quickly fastened upon the man from Missouri. Truman indicated the drift of his thinking to David Lilienthal several weeks after his accession. "I want to win two wars. I want to insure getting a peace organization. And I want to carry forward the policies of Franklin Roosevelt just as he did, if I can. That goes for TVA, I want to see some other Valley authorities established. . . ."[1]

Between April 13 and June 30 Truman sought to reshape and reorganize the entire bureaucratic structure of the Executive Department. He moved to make the Cabinet into the chief administrative arm of the Presidency, while simultaneously staffing it with his own people, from whom he demanded immediate organizational reforms within their individual departments. Concurrently the President publicly fought for the expansion of certain New Deal political reforms, notably in the areas of regional development, unemployment compensation, and social security. During the first weeks he also met frequently with Director Harold Smith on the approaching 1946 budget, the contours of which were difficult to assess or shape because of the probability of an end to at least some wartime controls and restrictions.[2]

At the same time the President found his sleeve frequently plucked by harried and anxious liberals within the bureaucracy, especially in the war agencies and particularly in O.P.A. These New Dealers feared that with "the boss" now gone their position and powers might be undercut by a conservative reaction.[3]

All of these commitments took time and attention, but Truman begrudged neither. Where he clearly felt that Presidential time was being questionably consumed was in foreign policy. On the eve of

[1] *Lilienthal Journals*, p. 699.

[2] "Notes after Cabinet Meeting, April 20, 1945," Stimson Papers, Box 420; "Statement by W. R. Ronald . . . before the Eisenhower Reorganization Committee, Department of Agriculture, August 1, 1945," Clinton P. Anderson Papers, Box 11, Harry S. Truman Library, Independence, Mo.; Lewis Schwellenbach to Alvanley Anderson, to William Green, June 22, 1945, Schwellenbach Papers, Box 1 (correspondence); Frank McNaughton Report, June 1, 1945, McNaughton Papers; Harold D. Smith Diary, April 18, 26, May 3, 4, June 19, 1945, Harold D. Smith Papers, Franklin D. Roosevelt Library, Hyde Park, N.Y.; Truman, *Public Papers, 1945*, pp. 32–35, 36–38, 40–41, 62–64 ff., 77, 82; *New York Times*, May 25, 1945, p. 1:2, 3; Truman, *Year of Decisions*, pp. 72–74, 113–117.

[3] Chester Bowles to Harry Truman, April 18, May 28, July 4, 1945, Fred Vinson to Truman, April 25, 1945, Truman Papers, Office File 28.

Truman's departure for Potsdam Harold Smith obtained the distinct impression that the President "seemed concerned that he was having to spend so much time on international matters."[4]

Such concern was a clear reflection of Truman's basically moderate approach to the Soviet problem throughout the ten weeks between Roosevelt's death and Potsdam. Preoccupation with domestic affairs only partially explains this mood. Disturbing events elsewhere in Europe and in the Middle East at this time, while not on a commensurate scale of importance with those involving Stalin, did tend to deprive Soviet conduct in Eastern Europe of any degree of uniqueness. Influential and experienced American policy-makers thus could and did argue that the Russian crisis fell within the framework of a general behavioral pattern created by immediate postwar breakdown and that it could be managed and mastered through the traditional arts of diplomacy. Certainly Stalin was difficult to deal with in the late spring of 1945, but so were deGaulle and Tito, each of whom attracted at one time or another as much Presidential attention as did the Soviet Premier.

The wartime history of Anglo-American relations with Gaullist France had been unhappy at best. Before Pearl Harbor and again during the North African campaign, principle had been sacrificed to expediency in American dealings with the German puppet Vichy government and its officials. Understandably, a profound and not wholly misplaced distrust of Anglo-American intentions had grown up among the Gaullist "Free French" forces. Most of them came to feel that they were perpetually on the point of being sold out by their American allies, who preferred to deal with Petain, Laval, and Darlan when it came to questions involving the French government. Roosevelt had always disliked deGaulle, largely for personal reasons, and one of the President's last major acts was to keep the Free French leader away from the Yalta Conference. Having successfully used deGaulle throughout the war, Churchill was not uncharacteristically ready to dispense with him at its close. The Prime Minister told Truman in early July of 1945 that " 'after five long years of experience, I am convinced' " deGaulle " 'is the

---

[4] Harold D. Smith Diary, July 6, 1945, Harold D. Smith Papers.

worst enemy of France in her troubles.' " He said that he considered deGaulle " 'one of the greatest dangers to European peace.' "[5]

Deeply embittered by the arrogant treatment he had suffered at the hands of the Anglo-Americans, deGaulle in the spring of 1945 had become convinced that French influence could only be revived by French mischief. As he told his Foreign Minister, Georges Bidault, "Since we have been reduced to our present situation our most successful moves have been those that have raised the most violent storms."[6] With a new untried hand at the American helm of state, the General wasted little time in raising violent storms to test the President's instinct for navigation. In late April, with the war against Nazi Germany not yet finally concluded, deGaulle instructed General de Tassigny to disregard Eisenhower's instructions to the French to evacuate Stuttgart. Eisenhower's request was based on the fact that the city was included in the operational zone of the American Seventh Army. DeGaulle, however, had been brooding about his exclusion from the Yalta Conference, where the Big Three rather desultorily had agreed to give France a zone of German occupation to be carved out of the Anglo-American zones. Obviously offended that he had been grudgingly given this gift without being handed any opportunity to demand it as a right, deGaulle was now determined to hold Stuttgart and all adjacent areas occupied by the French army until France's occupation zone had been clearly defined.[7] Eisenhower properly passed the problem on to Truman. On May 2 the President in a sharp note informed deGaulle that he was fully prepared to undertake a "complete reorganization" of the Allied Military Command. This threat implied

[5] William L. Langer, *Our Vichy Gamble* (New York: Alfred A. Knopf, 1947), *passim*; McNeill, *America, Britain, and Russia*, pp. 44–46; Eden, *The Reckoning*, pp. 519–520, 526, 531, 574; Grew, *Turbulent Era*, II: 1503. Churchill was never fond of deGaulle. An apocryphal wartime story goes that having endured one of the general's interminable harangues on the glories of France, the Prime Minister turned to his Cabinet upon deGaulle's departure and intoned, "We have found our Joan of Arc; now we must find the archbishops to burn her."

[6] General Charles deGaulle, *War Memoirs*, 6 vols. (New York: Simon & Schuster, 1960), Vol. VI: *Salvation, 1944–1946, Documents*, pp. 236–237.

[7] Eisenhower to deGaulle, April 28, 1945, quoted in deGaulle, *Salvation, Documents*, pp. 220–221; and in Alfred D. Chandler *et al.*, eds., *The Papers of Dwight David Eisenhower; The War Years*, 5 vols. (Baltimore: The Johns Hopkins University Press, 1970), IV: 2657–2659. Cf. also Churchill, *Triumph and Tragedy*, p. 303; Snell, *Meaning of Yalta*, pp. 48–49, 67–69.

future French expulsion from combined operations against Germany and the end of essential American supplies to the French army if deGaulle did not immediately comply with Eisenhower's directive. DeGaulle backed down only after reiterating his long-standing complaint that "no large French unit has been fully equipped by the United States since the beginning of operations in Western Europe."[8]

The brute fact that the French army moved on an American-built stomach dictated the extent of deGaulle's probes and the nature of Truman's responses. As early as the end of March disturbing news had reached Washington that deGaulle might seek to annex the Val d'Aosta area in northwest Italy, adjacent to the French border.[9] As in the Stuttgart area, French troops had moved in toward the end of the war and refused to move out when ordered to do so by the Supreme Allied Commander. DeGaulle followed a wavering course throughout as befitted his weak position. He at first vigorously disclaimed any designs upon Val d'Aosta, then in early May told Ambassador Caffery that he did hope "at a later date to take up amicably and through regular channels with the Italian Government the question of very minor adjustments of the tracing of the frontier in that region." Two weeks later Bidault told Undersecretary of State Grew in Washington that "He agreed completely with General deGaulle that France should have no annexationist claims to the area. . . ." However, further orders from Eisenhower to the French to move out of the region during this time proved unavailing, and American army intelligence reported that the French were infiltrating troops and civilian agents "under military cover who change to civilian clothes and parade as Italians favoring French annexation." Soon Truman learned that American troops advancing into the area were "being impeded by passive French resistance, including road blocks."[10]

---

[8] DeGaulle to Eisenhower, May 1, 1945, Truman to deGaulle, May 2, 1945, deGaulle to Truman, May 4, 1945, deGaulle, *Salvation, Documents,* pp. 223–226; Truman, *Year of Decisions,* p. 266; Dwight D. Eisenhower, *Crusade in Europe* (Garden City, N.Y.: Permabooks Edition, 1952), p. 455.

[9] Secretary of State (Stettinius) to Ambassador in France (Caffery), March 31, 1945, *Foreign Relations, 1945; Diplomatic Papers,* IV: 726.

[10] Caffery to Secretary of State, April 7, May 6, May 17, 1945, Alexander C.

Throughout this period Truman and his counselors were deeply immersed in the concurrent crisis with Tito and the Yugoslavs over territorial conflicts on the other side of the Italian peninsula and could give the Val d'Aosta problem only limited attention. However, in an interview with Bidault on May 21 Truman politely put his "cards face up on the table" and told the Foreign Minister that in stirring up territorial issues at that time, the French, like the Yugoslavs, were "prejudicing the ultimate settlement of these matters at the eventual peace conference" and were giving "ammunition to those in our country who may be trying to stir up trouble between the United States and France. . . ." Bidault promised to impart Truman's sentiments to deGaulle and then skillfully deflected the conversation to various French demands on Germany. There the matter rested for some weeks.[11]

By early June Field Marshal Sir Harold Alexander, the Supreme Allied Commander in the Mediterranean, became impatient with the stubborn refusal of the French forces to leave Val d'Aosta. He began sending cables to both Churchill and Truman asking for permission to establish an Allied government in the region, by force if necessary. First learning of the incident at a weekly meeting of the Secretaries of State, War, and Navy, Henry L. Stimson became deeply concerned. It appeared to him that both the British and American governments and their respective military staffs were about to accede to Alexander's wishes, thus raising the threat of open war between France and the Anglo-Americans. Stimson went to Truman and begged him not to grant Alexander discretionary power and not to issue a joint Anglo-American press release condemning deGaulle. Stimson reasoned that public opinion in the three countries had been sufficiently inflamed by the recent crisis in Syria. Further Anglo-American pressure on France might well drive that sensitive and unhappy nation to the point of an open diplomatic rupture with England and the United States. The

Kirk, political Adviser to S.A.C. Mediterranean, to Secretary of State, May 17, 1945, *ibid.*, 696–697, 726–729; Truman, *Year of Decisions*; p. 267.

[11] "Memorandum of Conversation by Acting Secretary of State Grew," May 21, 1945, *Foreign Relations, 1945; Diplomatic Papers*, IV: 698–699; Grew, *Turbulent Era*, II: 1513–1514.

Secretary of War urged the President instead to write a very strong private letter to deGaulle. Truman agreed and asked Stimson to do the job for him.[12]

At the same time the President again determined to use economic sanctions to bring deGaulle into line. After having taken the situation up with the Joint Chiefs and the State Department on June 5, "I ordered that further issues of munitions and equipment to the French troops be stopped." According to Leahy, who was present at the meeting, Truman's response to the crisis was swift: " 'The French are using our guns, are they not? . . . All right, we will at once stop shipping guns, ammunition, and equipment to deGaulle. . . .' " Having employed the economic stick, Truman reverted to the diplomatic carrot. Stimson's letter was sent over Truman's signature on June 7. It had been drafted at Stimson's request by General Marshall and Assistant Secretary of War John J. McCloy. It was a strong note, although lend-lease cut-off was not mentioned. Truman condemned as "an extremely churlish declaration" the recently announced French decision to remain in Val d'Aosta and denounced the "almost incredible threat that French soldiers, equipped with American arms, were prepared to fight American Allied soldiers whose efforts and sacrifices have contributed so recently and so effectively, to the liberation of France herself." The President concluded by requesting deGaulle to reconsider the question and to withdraw his troops from the region, implying a general territorial settlement at the postwar peace conference.[13]

DeGaulle now came under incessant pressure to withdraw his forces from northwest Italy. His commander in Val d'Aosta, General Juin, who expressed skepticism of deGaulle's sanity on several occasions, first indicated on June 9 a break in the French position. The following day, an hour after Ambassador Caffery had taken Bidault "to task . . . on the subject of northwestern Italy,"

---

[12] Stimson Diary, June 5, 6, 1945.

[13] Leahy, *I Was There*, p. 373; Truman, *Year of Decisions*, pp. 267–269; Truman to deGaulle, June 7, 1945, deGaulle, *Salvation, Documents*, pp. 269–271; *Foreign Relations, 1945; Diplomatic Papers*, IV: 735–737.

the French formally capitulated and agreed to withdraw their forces.[14]

The Middle Eastern crisis of May and June seemed the most serious of all the problems existing between Washington and General deGaulle. It erupted suddenly in late May and revolved around French attempts to retain special rights in the former mandates of Syria and Lebanon, whose independence had been previously recognized by the French as well as the United States, Russia, and Britain. When French demands for retention of certain privileges appeared exorbitant and when the French proceeded to reinforce their existing garrisons in the two countries in the midst of the talks, the Arabs broke off negotiations, and street demonstrations in support of the Syrian and Lebanese governments broke out. The French claimed that as the result of an agreement signed between deGaulle and the British in June of 1941 "it was clearly specified that France would continue to exercise all her [mandated] rights in Syria and the Lebanon." In the spring of 1945 deGaulle specifically sought to maintain French control of the Syrian and Lebanese military forces, and it was over this issue, as well as the ostentatious reinforcement of French garrisons during talks between France, Syria, and Lebanon, that the negotiations broke down. The crisis was primarily an Anglo-French affair. When initial street demonstrations led to rioting and rioting to open warfare between Syrians, Lebanese, and the French garrisons, Churchill determined to impose peace on the Levantine area by force. On May 31 he informed deGaulle that units of the British army were moving in from Egypt to restore order, and he asked that French troops be confined to their barracks until order was restored. "Once firing has ceased and order has been restored we shall be prepared to begin tripartite discussions in London."[15] The French were in no position to argue, although deGaulle's fury was reflected in the cables he sent to his commander in Beirut just prior to the arrival of the British. The appearance of the British troops restored or-

[14] Alexander C. Kirk to Secretary of State, June 9, 1945, Caffery to Secretary of State, June 10, 1945, pp. 737–740; Grew, *Turbulent Era*, II: 1517.

[15] *New York Times*, May 22, 1945, p. 1:7; deGaulle press conference, June 2, 1945, Churchill to deGaulle, May 31, 1945, in deGaulle, *Salvation, Documents*, 249, 253–259; Churchill, *Triumph and Tragedy*, p. 482.

der,[16] and the issue of French rights in their former mandated areas was ultimately referred to the United Nations.

American anxiety grew as the crisis developed and deepened. When Bidault was in Washington during the third week in May, before Franco-Levantine negotiations had broken down, Acting Secretary of State Grew told him that the United States government was "considerably disturbed" over the mounting tension and animosity in Syria and Lebanon. Grew noted that among other considerations the area would soon be "a highly important avenue" for redeployment of Allied troops from Europe to the Far Eastern theater of operations. He laid major stress, however, on the point that even an act of minor provocation by a great power against a small nation at this juncture would surely jeopardize the future of the United Nations Organization, then in a state of such laborious creation at San Francisco. As usual, Bidault was evasive in the face of American pressure, simply replying that the French had the responsibility to keep order in the region.[17]

When violence broke out a week later the State Department promptly issued a statement urging that the French, "in a most friendly spirit, carefully review" their Mideast policy so as to make clear to everyone French intentions to respect Syrian and Lebanese sovereignty. The note politely condemned the French for seeking "a special position in those countries" and pointed out that both nations were members of the fledgling world organization. Several days later Truman reiterated this careful condemnation in a private letter to deGaulle.[18]

American reaction to the Near Eastern crisis ultimately passed beyond simple remonstrance. When Churchill decided to move he immediately notified Truman, who called a round of Cabinet meetings on the problem on May 30 and June 1. The decision to approve Churchill's action was quickly taken, and a subsequent request that several American warships aid in the British show of force

---

[16] DeGaulle to General Beynet, June 1, 1945, 3 a.m., 3:30 p.m., in deGaulle, *Salvation, Documents*, pp. 250–252; Churchill, *Triumph and Tragedy*, p. 483.
    [17] Grew, *Turbulent Era*, II: 1508–1509; *Foreign Relations, 1945*; *Diplomatic Papers*, IV: 692–693.
    [18] U.S. Department of State *Bulletin*, XII (June 3, 1945), 1013–1014; Truman to deGaulle, June 1, 1945, deGaulle, *Salvation, Documents*, pp. 249–250.

was enthusiastically supported by Leahy, who carried the day. On June 1 Grew reported that British firmness had swiftly restored calm, if not good feeling, to the area.[19]

The Anglo-American crisis with Marshal Tito over Venezia Giulia was fraught with more imponderables and deeper peril than the concurrent difficulties with deGaulle, for it seemed nearly certain that up to a point Moscow was behind and in support of Yugoslav actions. Yet the Venezia Giulia crisis also gave Truman and his military advisers the opportunity to demonstrate that their essentially moderate views toward the Soviet Union—and their determined policy *not* to retain American troops in Europe or to use such forces for diplomatic purposes while they were still on the Continent—might prove to be the best means of calming things down and of bringing final peace to that shattered and devastated corner of the earth.

The Venezia Giulia or Istrian region, lying on the northeast corner of the Adriatic and including the strategic port of Trieste, had long been in dispute between Yugoslavia and Italy. In the early spring of 1945 it was garrisoned by confused and demoralized units of the German army. On March 20 Yugoslav partisans launched an offensive into the region. They were well-supplied, as they had been for months, by arms and ammunition provided from British and American depots. By April 30 Marshal Tito announced that his troops had reached the suburbs of Trieste. British fears for the future of the area were immediately stimulated. The British particularly feared that Yugoslav occupation of Trieste would jeopardize the eventual settlement of the province's fate at the postwar peace conference and meanwhile might affect the supply of the proposed English occupation zone in Austria. The previous February Field Marshal Alexander had apparently secured Tito's agreement that Alexander should be placed in charge of all operations and forces in Venezia Giulia.[20] In early April, however, Tito had gone to Moscow, and in an interview published in *Red Star* he declared the " 'population of Istria and Trieste de-

---

[19] Leahy, *I Was There*, p. 373; Grew, *Turbulent Era*, II: 1515–1516, 1519*n*.
[20] Ehrman, *Grand Strategy*, pp. 128–130; U.S. Department of State *Bulletin*, XII (May 13, 1945), 902.

sire to be part of Yugoslavia and we are assured that their wishes will be realized.' "[21] The only possible source of such assurance was, of course, Russian officialdom. Now, at the end of the month, with Yugoslav forces entering Trieste, Tito announced that " 'our troops continued their glorious offensive drive for the liberation of our brothers in the towns of Trieste, Istria and Gorica,' " adding that " 'the liberation of our brothers pining under a foreign yoke' " was the chief goal of the Yugoslav offensive.[22] Did the " 'foreign yoke' " refer to Germany or Italy? No one could be sure.

Alarmed by these developments, Alexander as early as April 26 requested permission to move his own units into Venezia Giulia in force. Truman and Churchill swiftly concurred, and on the 28th the Supreme Commander was ordered to establish Allied military government over the province, including that portion already occupied by Tito's forces. On April 30 a New Zealand division penetrated the province, and by May 2 some of its troops entered Trieste, formally received the German surrender, and took control of the docks. Two days later the Yugoslavs warned that the New Zealanders had come to Trieste " 'without permission' " and that such action might result in " 'undesirable consequences.' "[23] Once again a potentially explosive situation had suddenly arisen to strain the Grand Alliance.

The State Department, spearheaded by Acting Secretary Grew, once again pressed for strong action. In an interview on April 30 Grew alerted the President for the first time that American troops within Alexander's command might have to be used to compel Tito's forces to withdraw. The President promptly said that he did not intend to have American forces used to fight Yugoslav forces nor did he wish to become involved in Balkan political questions. Truman then drafted a cable to Churchill in which this point was driven home.[24]

That same day Stimson entered the picture, informing Grew that the Joint Chiefs "think we are taking chances in following Alex-

21 Quoted in A.P. dispatch from Moscow, April 15, 1945, *San Francisco Chronicle*, April 16, 1945, 1:4.
22 Quoted in Grew, *Turbulent Era*, II: 1474.
23 Quoted in *ibid*. Cf. also Ehrman, *Grand Strategy*, p. 130.
24 Grew, *Turbulent Era*, II: 1475–1476.

ander in what he is to do and are inclined to stay off completely."[25] Three days later, as Alexander's New Zealand troops and Tito's partisans uneasily and suspiciously joined forces in Trieste, Stimson again contacted Grew on the developing crisis. The Secretary of War had discovered that the State Department was proposing to go beyond the British position of basic cooperation with Tito in return for Tito's acquiescence in Alexander's overall rule and wished for Tito's total removal from Venezia Giulia. "The whole plan of the State Department was apparently based on a direction [*sic*] of Mr. Roosevelt before he died," Stimson recorded. "This very strongly affected the position which I had misunderstandingly taken the other day in advising Marshall to back up our State Department. I thought that the State Department was backed by the British instead of opposed by it."[26] Stimson told Grew "that I thought the whole matter ought to be carefully reexamined with a view not to entangling our troops in that matter at all." Grew responded that Truman felt the same way, and later, while both men waited in the Presidential anteroom, Grew showed Stimson "correspondence which recently passed between Churchill and Truman. This was very illuminating, giving Churchill's objections to the State Department plan much as I felt them myself."[27] According to Stimson both Churchill and Truman at this point rejected any heavy-handedness on Alexander's part in Venezia Giulia, although they had authorized him to move into the province.

On May 5, however, Alexander cabled Churchill that " 'Tito . . . now finds himself in a much stronger military position than he foresaw when I was in Belgrade [the previous February] and wants to cash in on it. Then he hoped to step into Trieste when finally I stepped out. Now he wants to be installed there and only allow me user's rights. We must bear in mind that since our meeting he has been to Moscow.' " Churchill's response, that " *'The destiny of this part of the world is reserved for the peace table, and you should certainly make him aware of this,'* "[28] clearly reflected a sudden

---

[25] *Ibid.*, pp. 1477–1478.
[26] Stimson Diary, May 2, 1945.
[27] *Ibid.*
[28] Quoted in Churchill, *Triumph and Tragedy*, p. 473; italics his.

toughening in the British mood and a total commitment to a hard line stance by Alexander.

The new tenor of British reaction to Tito's obstinacy in holding on to Trieste and Venezia Giulia swiftly transmitted itself to the State Department. Stimson noted gloomily on May 7 that "The State Department have been trying to put over a direction [*sic*] to Field Marshal Alexander to undertake things which everybody else thinks are very hazardous and will provoke an open clash of arms with Tito. . . . Marshall came to me with the papers this afternoon and . . . I called up Grew and told him that my advice was very strongly against [that of] the State Department's. . . ."[29]

May 10 represented the high tide of State Department influence on Truman. At his daily conference with the President, Grew asserted that the situation in Venezia Giulia "was growing more serious hourly" as the Yugoslavs not only refused to leave but "had raised their own flags and had changed the names of the streets from Italian to Yugoslav." The Acting Secretary argued "that Russia was undoubtedly behind Tito's move with a view to utilizing Trieste as a Russian port in the future, that the Socialists and Communists —in Italy—argued that the United States and Great Britain are no longer able to oppose the Soviet Union in Europe. . . ." Truman momentarily caved in. "The President replied that he had been giving the most serious consideration to this matter and had finally come to the conclusion that the only solution was to clear Trieste" of the Yugoslavs. "He realized that this was a reversal of his former position but that developments were such that it left no alternative." Leahy, who saw Truman later in the day, noted that the President "seriously contemplated taking a strong stand even if it should result in hostilities between the Anglo-American and Yugoslav troops. We were determined to preserve the neutrality of the area." Stimson saw Grew at roughly the same time and gloomily found that both he and the President were beginning to 'get their wind up' over the incident. Two days later a surprised and pleased Winston Churchill received a long message from Truman, in which

[29] Stimson Diary, May 7, 1945.

the President concluded that the Anglo-Americans "should be prepared to consider any necessary steps to effect Tito's withdrawal."[30]

Thereafter, however, Truman swiftly backed away from any suggestion of an armed clash between American and Yugoslav units. Military counsels and military considerations resumed preponderant influence over the President's thinking. Late on May 10, when the cable to Churchill may have already left the White House, Leahy and Grew discovered that General Marshall continued to believe "that every effort should be made to avoid a military clash," and, therefore, "It was decided to try, through diplomatic channels, to induce Tito to withdraw" from Venezia Giulia. At the same time Stimson went directly to Truman and in a long talk told the President politely to steady down. These excitements happened after the end of most wars, the experienced Secretary informed his new President, and the best policy was to try to ride things through and not to take any action in this case without consulting General Marshall.[31] Truman assured Stimson that he would follow his advice, and on May 14 a disappointed Churchill heard from the President of a new American policy. Truman "declared that we should await reports about our messages to Belgrade before deciding what forces to use if our troops were attacked. Unless Tito did attack it was impossible to involve the United States in another war." Two days later Truman flatly told the Prime Minister that "he was unable and unwilling to involve his country in a war with the Yugoslavs unless they attacked us."[32]

At this point American policy shifted somewhat, for after conferences with Grew and the Joint Chiefs on May 19 and 20 Truman decided to send a number of American divisions to the Brenner Pass north of Trieste while the navy was requested to make a show of force in the Adriatic. The air force was also alerted for possible action.[33] Simultaneously, however, the major American emphasis

---

[30] Grew, *Turbulent Era*, II: 1479; Leahy, *I Was There*, p. 368; Stimson Diary, May 10, 1945; Churchill, *Triumph and Tragedy*, p. 474; Bryant, *Triumph in the West*, p. 356.

[31] Leahy, *I Was There*, p. 368; Stimson Diary, May 10, 1945.

[32] Churchill, *Triumph and Tragedy*, p. 476; Bryant, *Triumph in the West*, pp. 356–357.

[33] Truman, *Year of Decisions*, p. 278.

fixed upon diplomatic solution. This despite the fact that the State Department had noted the existence of some "thirty or more territorial questions in Europe which require careful study before satisfactory decisions can be reached" and despite also a personal warning from Anthony Eden on May 15 that a firm attitude had to be taken toward Tito, "otherwise problems by the hundreds would arise in the future." Stalin's aid was sought in crumbling Tito's obdurate attitude, and progress was gratifyingly rapid.[34] For while Stalin defended Yugoslavian claims to the entire province, he seems to have pressed Tito into assuming a more open mind toward settlement, given the obvious British and American determination to have their way in the region. As late as May 19 the Yugoslav chief rejected British and American demands that an Allied Military Government be established in Venezia Giulia, and he called together a "General Assembly of the City of Trieste." This assembly, composed of "delegates from local factories and Workmen's Circles," was wholly Yugoslav in composition, and the propaganda it produced simply assumed that Trieste was a Yugoslav city.[35] The flamboyant Yugoslav next asserted that " 'the honor of our army and the honor of our country demand the presence of the Yugoslav army in Istria, Trieste and the Slovene coastline.' " Grew quietly and publicly responded "that Marshal Tito's reply had not been satisfactory." The Marshal swiftly deflated his claims. His commanders first moved their main headquarters out of Trieste, and on May 22 Tito accepted " 'in principle' " Allied proposals which, when made public on June 9, provided for the retention of token Yugoslav civil and military units in the province under Alexander's control and supervision.[36]

In the Trieste affair Truman came as close to authorizing use of United States military forces for postwar territorial and political purposes in Europe as he ever did during the first year of his admin-

---

[34] U.S. Department of State *Bulletin*, XII (May 13, 1945), p. 902; Grew, *Turbulent Era*, II: 1481–1482; Herbert Feis, *Between War and Peace; The Potsdam Conference* (Princeton: Princeton University Press, 1960), p. 50; Truman, *Year of Decisions*, pp. 278–280; Truman to Stalin, May 21, 1945, Stalin to Truman, May 22, 1945, *Stalin's Correspondence with Roosevelt and Truman*, pp. 235–237.

[35] *New York Times*, May 19, 1945, p. 1:6.

[36] Quoted in Grew, *Turbulent Era*, II: 1484–1485n. Cf. also U.S. Department of State *Bulletin*, XII (June 10, 1945), 1050.

istration. He was pressed in this direction by a State Department whose suspicions of Russia and suggestions for a possible Anglo-American confrontation with Soviet power almost perfectly matched those of Churchill and the British. Yet Truman rejected these pressures. He chose rather to employ the American military machine solely for the defeat of the Axis powers and the occupation of their homelands and for nothing else. In pursuing this policy the new President was vigorously supported by his chief military advisers, Stimson and Marshall. He was no doubt steadied as well by the realization that the American public would not at this time countenance the policies advanced by the State Department. Despite real and serious differences with Russia over Eastern Europe, military victory, not diplomatic advantage or showdown, dominated Truman's thinking and that of his most influential aides throughout the late spring and early summer of 1945.[37] This simple policy underwent its severest test amidst the complexities and confusions surrounding East Asian diplomacy and strategic planning to end the war in the Pacific. It survived intact, but only after the most searching debate.

[37] Writing years later of his thinking in mid-May, Truman stated: "The thought now uppermost in my mind was how soon we could wind up the war in the Pacific. . . ." *Year of Decisions*, p. 262. All of his remarks and actions at the time fully support his assertion.

6

The Riddle of the Far East--April and May

Three major considerations shaped American policy toward the Pacific war in the final months of that conflict. First was the near collapse of Kuomintang China in 1944–1945 and the simultaneous, dramatic emergence of the Chinese Communists. Second were the many implications, particularly for China, of the coming Russian entry into the Asian conflict. And third was the assumed ability and certain determination of the Japanese militarists to wage and maintain the war even after an invasion of the home islands. Conjecture, doubt, and ceaseless argument surrounded these problems. Policies were shaped and implemented in an atmosphere of sensed ambiguity and frequent skepticism.

Washington's response to the Chinese agony was distressingly —perhaps inevitably—unimaginative. Coalition governments composed of Communist and non-Communist elements had become the pattern of ideal political solution in the smaller states of Europe, such as Yugoslavia, Poland, and elsewhere. Why not in China also? The attractiveness of this policy was heightened in China's case by the fact that a significant number of American military and State

Department personnel there had come by late 1944 to express not
only open contempt for Chiang, but a corresponding admiration
for the Chinese Communists as well. They argued that while "the
Chinese Communists have a background of subservience to the
U.S.S.R., . . . new influences—principally nationalism—have come
into play which are modifying their outlook." Since "Russian intentions with respect to the Far East, including China, are aggressive," and since the Kuomintang National Government was "dis-
integrating," there were only two ways to keep the Russians out of
China. The first was to impose reforms and "revitalization" upon
the Kuomintang government "so that it may survive as a significant
force in a coalition government." The second, to be undertaken
if Chiang remained obdurate, was to "limit our involvement with
the Kuomintang and . . . commence some cooperation with the
Communists, the force destined to control China." Ambassador
Gauss tended to share this view, as did General Stilwell, whose
hatred for Chiang and his regime was literally bottomless by the
time he was relieved of command in the autumn of 1944. Stilwell
wrote in July of that year that if the current condition in China
persisted, the country "will have civil war immediately after Japan
is out. If Russia enters the [Pacific] war before a united [Kuomin-
tang-Communist] front is formed in China, the Reds, being immediately accessible, will naturally gravitate to Russia's influence
and control."[1]

In retrospect, abandonment—or threatened abandonment—
of Chiang late in 1944 might have been the wisest course for the
United States to follow in China. Chiang certainly was not receptive to the idea of a true coalition government. Rather than coalition, he preached absorption. The Communists should "agree to
support the [Kuomintang] Government," he told Vice President
Wallace that summer, "and accept a peaceful and political role in
the administration of the country." In short, Mao and his cohorts
should agree to be swallowed up and smothered within the Kuomintang bureaucracy.[2] Washington certainly would not have had to

[1] *China White Paper*, I: 64–65; II: 564–576; White, ed., *Stilwell Papers*, pp.
132–133, 209–211, 215, 262, 315–316, 317, 322.
[2] *China White Paper*, I: 56.

throw itself into the arms of the Chinese Communists in reaction. But the possibility that Mao and his followers could have been split off from Russia at this time and nurtured as an independent Communist force, as John Service and John Davies were suggesting, was certainly not a fanciful scheme in light not only of subsequent history but also of the contemporary comments of Stalin and Molotov regarding the Yenan forces. In any event, such a policy was never seriously considered. Formation of a coalition government in which the pre-eminent interests of the Kuomintang were to be protected became the official American strategy to avert civil war in China.

In August of 1944 Major General Patrick J. Hurley, a noisy and aggressive Oklahoman who had been Herbert Hoover's Secretary of War and a diplomatic troubleshooter and troublemaker for Roosevelt throughout the war, was dispatched to Chungking primarily to try and keep a Chinese army in the war and to unify Chinese efforts against Japan. The formation of a joint Kuomintang-Communist Chinese government was an almost inevitable precondition to the successful completion of the assignment.[3] On his way to China Hurley stopped off at the Kremlin to sound out Soviet attitudes toward the Chinese Communists. At this point Hurley shared Stilwell's concern about the influence of a Russian entry into the Japanese war upon events in China. Molotov, however, seemed to be gratifyingly disdainful of the Yenan forces, attributing to them an ideological moderation which disqualified them from serious consideration as Marxist-Leninist comrades in arms. Molotov heatedly denied Chiang Kai-shek's repeated charge that Russia was covertly supporting the Chinese Communists, thereby contributing to China's weakness and division.[4] At Yalta, of course, the Russians imparted a sense of sincere friendliness toward the Nationalist Chinese. Stalin's commitment to the making of a formal treaty of alliance and friendship with Chiang constituted the firmest kind of Soviet recognition of the Kuomintang government. Yet some top

[3] Acheson, *Present at the Creation*, pp. 133–134; *China White Paper*, I: 59, 71; Feis, *China Tangle*, p. 178.

[4] Feis, *China Tangle*, pp. 178–181; *China White Paper*, I: 71–72, 93; Hurley to Secretary of State, February 4, 1945, Records of the Department of State, Record Group 84, Foreign Service Post File (Chungking), 710 Series, National Archives.

American officials—Harriman and Stettinius among them—left the Crimea skeptical of the very number and extent of the commitments Stalin had bound himself to keep. Even if Stalin were sincere, might not the politburo rebel?[5] And might not this possible Soviet reaction against the Yalta accords redound to the great detriment of China and of American policy there?

Eight weeks after Yalta and two weeks after Roosevelt's death Hurley was back in Moscow to probe Soviet intentions once more. He had enjoyed only some tentative success in his repeated attempts since the end of 1944 to heal the Nationalist-Communist rift, and he evidently felt that the Yalta accords had been a hindrance rather than a help in his endeavors. While in Washington at the end of March he told the dying Roosevelt with uncharacteristic tact and quietude that the Far Eastern concessions to Stalin "affected" the "territorial integrity and political independence of China." According to one authoritative account, Roosevelt initially denied Hurley's charge, but once the Ambassador "reinforced his arguments by citations of the text of the agreement," the President gave in and "agreed that something should be done, in Hurley's later phrase, to 'ameliorate' the Yalta accord."[6] Hence the Ambassador returned to Chungking via the Kremlin. According to his telegram to the State Department after talking to the Generalissimo, Hurley told Stalin that the United States had once again reaffirmed its decision "to support the National Government of China under the leadership of Chiang Kai-shek." Stalin in reply

> stated frankly that the Soviet Government would support the policy. He added that he would be glad to cooperate with the United States and Britain in achieving unification of the military forces in China. He spoke favorably of Chiang Kai-shek and said that while there had been corruption among certain officials of the National Government of China, he knew that Chiang Kai-shek was "selfless," "a patriot" and that the Soviet in times past had befriended him.

Hurley was elated. So, initially, was Stettinius. In a memorandum of April 18, covering dispatch of the Hurley telegrams to the White

[5] Stettinius, *Roosevelt and the Russians*, pp. 309–311; *Military Situation in the Far East, August 1951, Part 5*, pp. 3341–3342.

[6] Romanus and Sunderland, *Time Runs Out in CBI*, pp. 249–254, 338–339; Feis, *China Tangle*, pp. 214–225.

House, the Secretary of State pointedly compared Churchill's and Eden's lukewarm support of Washington's China policy—"the great American illusion," the Prime Minister had called it — with Stalin's and Molotov's generous comments on Russian hopes for "closer and more harmonious relations" with a strife-free and dominant Nationalist China. The way seemed open to continued efforts in China to bring Communists and Nationalists together without fear of adverse Soviet intervention either of an overt or covert nature. By the time he reached Chungking, Hurley's mood of general benevolence was positively expansive. He said that the Chinese Communists "are not in fact Communists, they are striving for democratic principles." As late as June he described himself as " 'the best friend the Communists had in Chungking.' "[7] China was truly filled to bursting with democrats in the spring of 1945. They simply failed to see eye to eye on most of the fundamental social, economic, and political questions facing mankind in the middle of the fifth decade of the twentieth century.

The invariably dubious Kennan, meanwhile, came away from the Hurley-Stalin talks with a different impression of Stalin's remarks. Stressing that "to the Russians words mean different things than they do to us," Kennan informed the State Department that in his opinion, "future Soviet policy respecting China will continue what it has been in the recent past: a fluid resilient policy directed at the achievement of maximum power with minimum responsibility on portions of the Asiatic continent lying beyond the Soviet border." To achieve this objective the Kremlin preferred in China as elsewhere "to work through others and to veil the means by which her real power is exerted." If this could be achieved by working on and through the Kuomintang, then Stalin would certainly move in this direction. Implied but not stated in Kennan's assessment was the thought that if Chiang proved obdurate, Stalin would then seek to work through the Chinese Communists. Specificially, Kennan argued that the Russians would seek to recapture "all the diplomatic and territorial assets" previously enjoyed in Asia

[7] *China White Paper*, I: 94–96; Richard H. Rovere and Arthur Schlesinger, Jr., *The MacArthur Controversy and American Foreign Policy* (New York: Farrar, Straus and Giroux, 1965), p. 210; *Foreign Relations, 1945; Diplomatic Papers*, VII: 329–332, 338–340.

by the czars. Obviously unaware of the secret Yalta agreements which provided for this very contingency, the charge concluded that Stalin would seek "Domination of the provinces of China in Central Asia contiguous to the Soviet frontier" and would also attempt to acquire sufficient control in all areas of North China now dominated by the Japanese to prevent other foreign powers from repeating the Japanese incursion.[8]

Despite frequent lamentations throughout his *Memoirs* that his scholarly advice was never taken and seldom even noted in Washington at this time, Kennan's message went directly to the President from the State Department with the added interpretive comment " 'that it would be tragic if our anxiety for Russian support in the Far East were to lead us into an undue reliance on Russian aid.' "[9] This State Department comment, which reflected a rapid change of mind on the part of the mercurial Stettinius, doubtless derived not only from Kennan's message but also from Harriman's reaction to the Hurley cable. Reading it in Washington on April 19, the Ambassador to Russia immediately informed E. F. Stanton of the Far East desk that Hurley had formed a "too optimistic impression of Marshal Stalin's reactions" and that upon entry into the Pacific war the Russians would probably break immediately with Chiang and support the Chinese Communists "even to the extent of setting up a puppet government in Manchuria and possibly in North China. . . ." Harriman later passed these views on to Admiral Leahy, as well, and Leahy concurred in their essential soundness. Stettinius meanwhile cabled Hurley: "I attach great importance to Marshal Stalin's endorsement at the present time of our program for promoting Chinese military and political unity under Chiang Kai-shek. At the same time I feel, as I am sure you do also, the necessity of facing the probability that Stalin's offer is given in direct relation to existing circumstances that may not continue for long." While the Secretary of State did not share Harriman's fears that Stalin would break with Chiang immediately upon a Soviet en-

<hr/>

[8] *China White Paper*, I: 96–97; Kennan, *Memoirs*, pp. 250–251; *Foreign Relations, 1945; Diplomatic Papers*, VII: 342–344. There are slight linguistic differences in the three sources cited, but they in no way compromise the thrust of Kennan's meaning.
[9] Quoted in Truman, *Year of Decisions*, pp. 100–101.

try into the Pacific war, he did ask Hurley to "impress (repeat impress)" upon Chiang the fact that if China were not unified at the time of Russian entry into the Asian conflict, Stalin would have legitimate option of siding with Yenan rather than Chungking.[10]

Truman received Kennan's report and the State Department comment on April 24, the day after his first long conference with key advisers on the worsening state of Soviet-American relations regarding Eastern Europe. Here was yet another warning that the Russians could not be trusted and that the game of luring the Soviets into the Pacific war was not worth the candle of Kuomintang-American interests. The President seemed momentarily impressed.[11]

At this moment the issue of Russian participation in the Pacific war was being reconsidered by the American military itself. Would Soviet contributions to victory over Japan be commensurate with the American diplomatic and matériel aid it entailed? And finally, on that same day, April 24, Secretary of War Stimson asked Truman for an early appointment to discuss thoroughly a new weapon which might indeed make the need for Soviet intervention in Asia superfluous. The temptation, then, to harden suddenly and sharply the American policy line toward Russia at this point in time, less than two weeks after Truman assumed office, must have been almost overwhelming. Never again before the end of the war would adverse diplomatic developments so perfectly meld with newly favorable policy options. Yet the State Department hard line was not assumed. After some hesitation, military necessity, including the attractiveness of a Soviet entry into the Pacific war, once again won out in official thinking.

At Yalta the Stalin-Roosevelt agreements in the Far East had extended much further than the simple provision for a Soviet entry into the Pacific war. In order to intensify the American bombing offensive against Japan, Stalin readily agreed to the rapid establishment of United States air bases in the Komsomolsk-Nikolaevsk region along the Amur River in southern Siberia. Reconnaissance

---

[10] *China White Paper*, I: 97–98; *Military Situation in the Far East, August 1951, Part 5*, pp. 3336–3337; Leahy, *I Was There*, p. 369; Secretary of State Stettinius to Ambassador Hurley, April 24, 1945, Records of the Department of State, Record Group 84, Foreign Service Post File (Chungking), 710 Series, National Archives.
[11] Leahy, *I Was There*, p. 369.

and survey teams were to enter the area immediately. Actual construction of the bases was to be a Russian task. Stalin also agreed to open additional weather stations "if the details will be presented to the Russian authorities." In turn the Russians asked for the opening of a Pacific sea and air supply route to the Siberian Maritime Provinces, "particularly for the delivery of foodstuffs and petroleum products."[12]

Joint Soviet-American planning for the final assault against Japan thus seemed about to be realized. Yet in subsequent discussions Stalin carefully hedged making any strategic commitments on the scope and scale undertaken by the British and American high commands in Europe. He simply promised that "from our side we shall fulfill your desires to carry on the planning vigorously"—vigorously but separately. In similar fashion Stalin did not commit himself to a promise that American personnel would man the new Siberian weather stations.[13]

Stalin thus kept a great deal of planning initiative in his own hands. Promises concerning air bases had been made; this did not necessarily imply fulfillment. Presumably separate planning would be finally coordinated by the three heads of state at some future date. The Russian attitude at Yalta seemed to bear out General Deane's earlier conclusion that "the Russians believed that we should simply agree on the tasks each nation should perform and then proceed to carry them out independent of each other."[14] It was indeed a strange alliance and one that might hinder as well as help long-range American interests in China and throughout East Asia.

The post-Yalta decline in East-West relations swiftly and adversely affected Soviet-American cooperation in the Pacific. In mid-March, after first informing Harriman and Deane in Moscow that the American survey party should proceed to Alaska in anticipation of an early passage to Siberia, the Russians abruptly refused clear-

---

[12] U.S. Department of Defense, *The Entry of the Soviet Union into the War Against Japan; Military Plans, 1941–1945* (Washington: 1955), p. 48 (typescript copy in Harry S. Truman Library, Independence, Mo.).

[13] *Ibid.*, p. 49.

[14] Deane, *Strange Alliance*, p. 255.

ance for the unit to proceed. By April 6, after repeated but fruitless attempts to break the impasse, Deane had had enough. He
cabled Washington that "I thought it was undignified to have our
party sitting in Fairbanks awaiting Soviet pleasure and recommended that it be returned to the United States. My recommendation was approved, and the prospect of B-29s being based in the
Amur River district receded still further." Deane's anger and that
of his colleagues at Spaso House had steadily grown during March
and April over Russian violation or failure to carry out the Crimean
agreements respecting Soviet-American collaboration in the Pacific theater, especially in light of the fact that the United States "continued to exert unusual efforts to deliver supplies for [Russia's] Siberian reserve." Only two meetings were held between members of
the American military mission and Red Army officials, and "they
consisted for the most part in the Soviet delegation making notes
of American proposals and questions and promising that the matters would be studied and the answers forthcoming. There was no
discussion or joint examination of any of the problems involved."
The American planning team in Moscow "was wasting its time,"
the impatient Deane concluded, so he decided to set it working on
more interesting tasks, chief among which would be to examine
whether Soviet aid in the Pacific war was in fact at all vital to victory.[15]

The conclusions of his study group became available to Deane
around April 1, and they were startling. Both the Amur River B-29
bases and the Pacific supply route to Siberia would simply not yield
benefits commensurate with the effort. The Amur River site in Siberia was roughly as far from Japan as the already operative air
bases in the Marianas, and the capture of Iwo Jima and particularly
the upcoming seizure of Okinawa would provide air bases far closer
to the Japanese homeland than any in Siberia. The conclusion on
the need to maintain the supply route was more balanced. It was
concluded that the route "would not be vital to the success of the
Soviet offensive" in Manchuria, "but that it would provide assur-

[15] *Ibid.*, pp. 254, 261–262; *Entry of the Soviet Union into the War Against
Japan*, p. 52.

ance against initial reverses and an unexpectedly long duration of the war."[16]

In mid-April Deane returned to Washington with Harriman and promptly began pressing for a partial reversal of existing Pacific strategy. In conversation with his superiors, he "noted that military collaboration with the Soviet Union was no longer vital to the United States, and he recommended limiting future collaboration to projects that would be of primary importance to the United States in the prosecution of the war." In a separate paper Deane recommended "that the [Siberian] air base project be cancelled and that the United States await Soviet initiative before pursuing the supply route project" further.[17] The general did *not* state, nor did he imply, that Soviet *aid* in the war against Japan was not still a vital element in victory. All he said was that attempts to forge a *collaborative coalition* with the Russians to prosecute the final phases of the Pacific war, as was accomplished between the Anglo-American military staffs in Europe, was "no longer vital to the United States." Deane accepted, and he wished his superiors to accept, the idea that there would now be two separate battles within one war.

Nonetheless, the general's conclusions disturbed the Joint Chiefs. In the weeks immediately following Yalta MacArthur had been queried about his views concerning Soviet entry into the Pacific war, even as he was told of the Yalta agreements. MacArthur's reaction was surprisingly close to that of Marshall, Stimson, and others.

MacArthur told Brigadier General George A. Lincoln on February 25 that he considered "it essential that maximum number of Jap divisions be engaged and pinned down on Asiatic mainland, before United States forces strike Japan proper." As for Russia, MacArthur told Lincoln that

politically they want a warm water port which would be Port Arthur. He considered that it would be impracticable to deny them such a port because of their great military power. Therefore, it was only right they should share the cost in blood in defeating Japan. From the military standpoint we should make every effort to get Russia into the

[16] Deane, *Strange Alliance*, pp. 263–265.
[17] *Entry of the Soviet Union into the War Against Japan*, pp. 60–61.

Japanese war before we go into Japan, otherwise we will take the impact of the Jap divisions and reap the losses, while the Russians in due time advance into an area free of major resistance.

And MacArthur "considered the President should start putting pressure on the Russians now."[18] Three days later Secretary of the Navy Forrestal, stopping off in Manila on a tour of the Pacific front, also heard MacArthur's views. The general

> expressed the view that the help of the Chinese would be negligible. He felt that we should secure the commitment of the Russians to active and vigorous prosecution of a campaign against the Japanese in Manchukuo [Manchuria] of such proportions as to pin down a very large part of the Japanese army; that once this campaign was engaged we should then launch an attack on the home islands, giving, as he expressed it, the *coup de main* from the rear while substantial portions of the military power of Japan were engaged on the mainland of Asia.

Forrestal further noted that MacArthur's conversation "indicated a fear that the Russian plan would be to try to persuade us into a campaign on the mainland of China which would be more costly than on the home islands, and at the end of which Stalin could increase his prestige in Asia by pointing out that he had to come in and assure the victory."[19]

MacArthur's eagerness to force Soviet entry into the Pacific war at an early date reflected a prevailing concern with the possible imminence of a great Asian campaign among army planners. The Japanese units in Manchuria and North China could not be expected to reinforce the garrison in the home islands, because the United States naval and air blockade of Japan had, by the late spring of 1945, largely cut off communications between Japan and the Asian continent. But the army feared that "large-scale landings and operations on the mainland of Asia . . . may be necessary anyway, for neither strategic bombing nor actual invasion may force the Japanese [in Asia] to accept unconditional surrender. A substantial element of the American general staff believes that the

[18] *Ibid.*, pp. 50–51.
[19] Millis, ed., *Forrestal Diaries*, p. 31.

Japanese Army can resist for a long time in the Asiatic mainland, even if the Japanese in the metropolitan islands surrender."[20]

The Joint Chiefs were clearly perplexed by these and other conflicting views of Soviet participation in the Pacific war. Their concern was given urgency on April 6, when Russia suddenly announced that she would not renew her Neutrality Pact with Japan. There was much ambiguity in the action since the pact still had a year to run, and it could be argued that the Soviets might honor the remaining twelve months of the agreement. Also, the only official Soviet explanation of the action taken was the longstanding Japanese aid to the Third Reich. "For the moment the statement should be read for exactly what it is and no more," the *New York Times* stated, and their opinion seems to have reflected Washington's thinking.[21] On April 12, the day of Roosevelt's death, Marshall asked MacArthur for a further exposition of his views on future Pacific strategy, since " 'there is an honest difference of opinion on this problem.' " According to Marshall, two distinct schools of thought existed. One group, composed largely of navy and air force people, led by Admiral Nimitz, argued that much more preparation was needed for a successful invasion of Japan " 'than is possible with [current] target dates of 1 December [1945] and 1 March [1946] for the main operations.' " The admirals and generals therefore urged " 'a campaign of air-sea blockade and bombardment' " of Japan, ultimately involving secondary American invasions of Korea or the Chinese Shantung peninsula to establish needed close-in air bases and supply depots for the final invasion. " 'Movement to the China coast,' " Nimitz stated on April 20, " 'will have the additional effect of assuring Russia's entry into the war.' " Opposed to this view of slow and inexorable strangulation were those who believed " 'in driving straight into Japan proper as soon as forces can be mounted from the Philippines and land based air established in the Ryukyus [Okinawa].' "[22]

In a long reply, also sent on April 20, MacArthur unequivocally sided with the second "school." " 'I am of the opinion,' " he wrote,

---

[20] *Newsweek*, XXV (May 28, 1945), 38.
[21] *New York Times*, April 6, 1945, p. 1:8; U.S. Department of State *Bulletin*, XII (April 29, 1945), 811.
[22] Quoted in *Entry of the Soviet Union into the War Against Japan*, pp. 54–58.

" 'that the ground, naval, air and logistical resources in the Pacific are adequate' " to carry out an invasion of Kyushu. And he concluded: " 'From the standpoint of weather it appears that November would be the best month to initiate operations.' " To buttress his argument, MacArthur added that the " 'Japanese fleet has been reduced to practical impotency. The Japanese Air Force has been reduced to a line of action which involves uncoordinated suicidal attacks against our forces, employing all types of planes including trainers. Its attrition is heavy and its power for sustained action is diminishing rapidly. These conditions will be accentuated after the establishment of our air forces in the Ryukyus.' "[23]

The Marshall-MacArthur-Nimitz exchange in the first week of Truman's Presidency laid bare the dilemma of American strategists as they contemplated the best ways and means of concluding World War II in the Pacific. MacArthur's rather airy dismissal of the very substantial kamikaze threat,[24] for example, revealed a strain of special pleading that had been a hallmark of his leadership since the Bataan and Corregidor campaigns. How strong was Japan? How long and tenaciously could she resist an invasion? Might she be induced to surrender short of a massive assault upon her home islands? These questions remained unanswered in mid-April, yet they held the key to the potential necessity for a massive Russian intervention with all that it implied for the future stability of Asia and especially of Nationalist China.

For the moment the Joint Chiefs decided to accept Deane's recommendation, which, after all, in no way implied any foolish American attempt to bar Russian entry into the Asian war. On April 19, the same day that Harriman was warning the State Department that Stalin would probably support the Chinese Communists, and the day before the Ambassador told Truman that, in light of Russian advances into Germany, "we are facing a barbarian invasion of Europe," the Joint Chiefs "asked the United States Mili-

---

[23] Quoted in *ibid.*, p. 57.

[24] Morison notes that between April 6 and June 22 the Japanese sent a total of 1,465 suicide planes against the American fleet off Okinawa, killing 4,900 men, wounding an additional 4,824. Sherrod's statistics show a total of thirty-three American ships sunk and two hundred thirty-three damaged as a result of these attacks. Morison, *Victory in the Pacific*, pp. 233, 282; Sherrod, *On to Westward*, pp. 324–333.

tary Mission in Moscow to abandon all efforts to introduce additional personnel into the Soviet Union except on matters essential to the prosecution of the war." On April 24, the day that Kennan's gloomy memo on the Stalin-Hurley conversations reached Truman's desk, the Joint Chiefs "cancelled the Siberian air based project" and held an overall review of Pacific strategy. They decided first "that the early invasion of the Japanese home islands represented the most suitable strategy to accomplish unconditional surrender," and, second, "Soviet entry into the war was no longer considered necessary to make the invasion feasible." On May 10 the Joint Chiefs officially made this report the basis for future planning, and two weeks later, on May 25, "the directive for the Kyushu operation was issued . . . setting the target date at 1 November 1945, as recommended by the field commanders."[25] When informed by Deane in Moscow that the Amur River B-29 base project had been abandoned, Antonov, the Soviet commander-in-chief, "made no comment whatsoever."[26]

These decisions immediately raise a number of intriguing questions, which one leading revisionist historian has seized upon.[27] First, did the April–May conclusion to suspend attempts at close cooperation with Russia in military planning and to ignore Russia as a prime factor in any successful invasion of Japan reflect a new sense of hostility toward the Soviet Union on the part of Truman and his military and civil advisers—a hostility generated by current Russian behavior in Europe as much as by the Soviet stubborn unwillingness to collaborate in planning an end to the Pacific war? Second, did the imminent emergence of the atomic bomb play a significant role in the apparent decision to downgrade the Soviet role in forthcoming Pacific operations and the possible decision to take a much harsher stand against Russian expansion in Asia? Third, did the bomb give American policy-makers such an entirely new sense of power and confidence as to cause them to consider the possibility of concluding the Pacific war *before* Russia entered the conflict, thus offering the possibility of nullifying the Yalta Far

[25] *Entry of the Soviet Union into the War Against Japan*, pp. 61–62, 68.
[26] Deane, *Strange Alliance*, p. 266.
[27] Alperovitz, *Atomic Diplomacy*, pp. 30–33.

Eastern accords, restricting Soviet expansion in Northeast Asia, and saving Chiang Kai-shek and the Nationalist government from an overt military as well as political Soviet-Chinese Communist alliance?

An affirmative answer to these questions—which would clearly imply the existence of an East-West cold war by May of 1945 and its recognition and acceptance by top American officials—must rest upon three assumptions, all of which are susceptible to the test of fact. But first and foremost one crucial fact must be kept in mind when examining subsequent official thinking upon the desirability of a Soviet entry into the Pacific war. The May 10 declaration of the Joint Chiefs was meant to be construed very narrowly. For what they said was that Soviet aid was not vital to the success of a direct invasion of the home islands. Yet this had not been considered the prime benefit of a Soviet intervention at any time! As has been noted, the chief gain for the Americans of a Soviet military thrust in Asia was on the mainland, not in the home islands. Russian invasion of Manchuria would obliterate the haunting possibility of the need for American military operations against the fanatical Kwantung Army in Northeast Asia *after* the home islands had been conquered. By their silence the Joint Chiefs clearly did not mean to imply that a Soviet entry was not wanted at all. They simply said it was not vital to the successful invasion of Japan proper. And, in fact, it had never been so considered.

With respect to the three assumptions upon which rests the thesis that the United States no longer wanted Russia in the Pacific war, the first is that American officials might have decided upon an open or subtle policy of stiffening Nationalist China's resistance to the Yalta accords. Second, they might well have developed a serious and sustained diplomatic offensive to induce Japan to surrender swiftly and suddenly, not only prior to American invasion, but also and especially prior to Soviet attack upon Manchuria. If Stalin's statement at Yalta was anywhere close to the truth, then the United States had three months after the Nazi collapse to maneuver Japan out of the war. Or third, and finally, American officials privy to the atomic secret might well have disclosed in private correspondence their determination to practice an overt or covert form of atomic diplomacy against the Russians, utilizing a "strategy of delay" on all substantive issues between East and West until the bomb was perfected and delivered. Such a policy would not necessarily preclude working to induce a Japanese surrender before the Russians could attack Manchuria, but obviously a "battlefield" demonstration of the bomb's power would prove far more effective in showing American military superiority, thus opening the possibility of restraining further Soviet expansion in both Europe and Asia. Do the actions and assertions, private and public, of top American officials between April and July of 1945 support a thesis of emergent, mutually cognizant East-West cold war and the practice of atomic diplomacy by the United States between Roosevelt's death and the Hiroshima raid?

These questions all hinge upon the attitude of American policy-makers and military strategists toward the Pacific war. If Truman and his advisers believed that Japan was finished and the need for an invasion unnecessary and unlikely, then the use of the atomic bomb, along with the need for Soviet aid, obviously took on a far different significance than if the need to defeat Japan was felt to be the major policy priority in the spring and summer of 1945. And the dominant, indisputable fact of these months was the very real dread of an apparently necessary assault upon Japan in order to bring World War II to a close.

The April 19 decision of the Joint Chiefs to suspend all moves toward close tactical cooperation with the Russians in no way reflected either a subsidence of this dread or of the assumption that the Russians would come in. The day before the Joint Chiefs made this decision Eden, stopping off in Washington on his way to the opening of the San Francisco Conference, was briefed on coming operations in the Pacific by Marshall. "Marshall's stern report forecast a prolonged struggle in the Far East, if conventional weapons only were used. The sober reserve with which he recited his appraisal made it all the more disturbing. He was, I knew, no alarmist."

Later that day Eden cabled Churchill some specifics.

The Japanese are doing all that they can to build up their strength on their mainland. They have, it seems, brought one or two divisions back from Korea [this was just before the Americans were able to close the Korean straits through air and submarine blockade], and also one from Manchuria. . . . Marshall was inclined to think that the Russians underestimated the extent of the challenge they would have to meet if they engaged the Japanese on a large scale by land. He thought that they would have very heavy losses. He emphasized the difference between a landing on [Pacific] islands where the Japanese garrison was limited and a major engagement with a large Japanese field army.[28]

Marshall's remarks reflected two major assumptions: first, that the Russians would indeed enter the Pacific conflict despite the prospect of heavy losses and, second, that an invasion of Japan would also be very costly to the Anglo-Americans. A profound implication also lurked behind the comment "if conventional weapons only were used." Here Marshall was alluding, as Eden knew he was, to the atomic bomb.

How did American policy-makers view the bomb in the context of the Pacific war and our relations with Russia in these crucial transitional months? First and foremost it must be stressed and stressed again that as early as 1944 American officials privy to the atomic secret had agreed without question or comment that the bomb would be used *and used against Japan*. There was never any serious debate on this point prior to May–June 1945.[29] A second and equally crucial decision was reached at Hyde Park between Churchill and Roosevelt in September of 1944: The atomic secret would remain an Anglo-American monopoly. There would be no immediate postwar sharing of the secret with Russia or anyone else.[30] These decisions were never reversed. Truman and his advisers, determined to carry on the work of Franklin Roosevelt, did just that. The bomb was used against Japan. Russia was not really informed of its existence beforehand. The fascinating debates and arguments among top American officials in the spring of 1945 and the frantic efforts of some atomic scientists to prevent the bomb's

---

[28] Eden, *The Reckoning*, pp. 612–613.
[29] Richard G. Hewlett and Oscar E. Anderson, Jr., *A History of the United States Atomic Energy Commission*, 2 vols. (University Park, Pa.: The Pennsylvania State University Press, 1962, 1970), Vol. I: *The New World, 1939–1946*, pp. 253, 334; Arthur Holly Compton, *Atomic Quest; A Personal Narrative* (New York: Oxford University Press, 1956), p. 233; Stimson and Bundy, *On Active Service*, pp. 613, 633.
[30] Hewlett and Anderson, *The New World*, pp. 326–327.

use and force a policy of international control upon their government, which are discussed below, occurred within this atmosphere of expected use and monopoly. As General Leslie Groves later was to write, the ultimate decision to drop the bomb "was one of non-interference . . . basically a decision not to upset existing plans."[31]

The course of the atomic question, the point at which the atomic decision was made, and the effect of the coming atomic monopoly upon American views of Soviet Russia in the spring and early summer of 1945 are most readily traceable in the diary entries of Henry L. Stimson, since the elderly Secretary of War had been deeply immersed in the research and development of the atomic bomb from the beginning.

It had been on April 2, ten days before Roosevelt's death, a little more than two weeks after Stimson had held a final, ambiguous session with the President on the developing bomb and the possibility of its subsequent international control, that Stimson "had a very important conference with Stettinius and Forrestal" concerning the recent deterioration of American relations with the Soviets. "A good many of these incidents have passed through my hands and I knew about them—at least certain phases of them," Stimson recorded. He then went on to enumerate "the unwillingness of the Russians to let us send planes and officers behind their lines in Poland and eastern Germany in order to help collect and send home the American prisoners of war who are being uncovered by the Russian advance through Germany," the difficulties with the Russians over the Nazi surrender to Anglo-American officials in northern Italy, and other outstanding issues. Poland seemed the major issue of the moment. Yet Stimson concluded: "we simply cannot allow a rift to come between the two nations without endangerous [*sic*] the entire peace of the world." So disturbed was Stimson by this trend that he spoke to Marshall about it as soon as Stettinius and Forrestal had departed. "Marshall told me that he had anticipated these troubles and thought they would be pretty bad and irritating but thought that we must put up with them." Phoning Stettinius later, Stimson remarked "that in retrospect Russia had been very good to us on the large issues. She had kept her word and carried out her

---

[31] Groves, *Now It Can Be Told*, pp. 265–266.

engagements. We must remember that she has not learned the amenities of diplomatic intercourse and we must expect bad language from her."[32]

Two weeks later, on April 16, Stimson attended a stag dinner at the British Embassy given in honor of Eden. The English present pronounced a series of jeremiads against Russia and against Soviet behavior, "and when I came away I felt that the only thing I could hang on to with any hopefulness was the fact that Russia and the United States had always gotten along for a hundred and fifty years history with Russia friendly and helpful." But then another source of hope obviously occurred to the old man, for he added: "Our respective orbits do not clash geographically and I think that on the whole we can probably keep out of clashes in the future."[33] Stimson was here alluding to spheres of influence. The subsequent Soviet-American *quid pro quo* on trusteeships and regional pacts worked out at San Francisco and incorporated in the United Nations Charter could only have confirmed the Secretary's basic outlook of hopefulness.

Stimson's April 24 letter to Truman "suggesting a talk on S-1 [code name for the atomic bomb]" was sent during a day filled with reading and analysis of the whole atomic project "and the problems which it presents to the country." In conjunction with Harvey Bundy, Stimson finally "wrote a memorandum giving an analytical picture of what the prospects of S-1 are, . . ." and the following day he took it with him when he went to the White House to see Truman.[34]

The discussion appears to have been exploratory rather than conclusive. General Groves was present, having been slipped quietly past the invariable ring of White House reporters, and the President read both the Stimson-Bundy memo and one prepared by Groves concerning the progress of the Manhattan Project. According to Groves' report,

A gun-type bomb [used at Hiroshima] would be ready about August 1 (no test was necessary). A second should be on hand before the end

---

[32] Stimson Diary, April 2, 1945.
[33] *Ibid.*, April 16, 1945.
[34] *Ibid.*, April 24, 1945.

of the year. Early in July, Los Alamos should be able to test an implosion weapon. If necessary, it could hold another trial by the first of August. Less than a month after that, it could have a Fat Man [implosion type] ready for combat. Unfortunately, this model would require more material and yield less explosive effect than had been hoped. *Japan had always been the target.* A special Twentieth Air Force group was about to leave for its overseas base.[35]

Truman listened to Groves' report without comment. His quiet posture had momentous consequences. For in failing to question Groves' report in any way, *Truman at this point acquiesced in the actual use of the bomb against Japan.* Only a flat declaration, and probably a written order, could have reversed the enormous momentum of preparation that was building for the bomb's use. Such a declaration, such an order, was never given. By the time of Potsdam such a reversal of policy would have been shattering and viewed as nearly unthinkable by every American official privy to the secret. *Harry Truman made the decision to drop the bomb on Japan as early as April 25, 1945,* and he did so not positively, but negatively, by deciding, to use Groves' words—"not to upset existing plans."[36]

Having read Groves' report, Truman next turned to Stimson's memorandum. It was a curious essay, balanced between hope, fear, and caution, its brief paragraphs suffused with the urgency of conveying to the reader the fact that the atomic bomb, when completed, would be " 'the most terrible weapon ever known in human history, one bomb of which could destroy a whole city.' " The monopoly of this dreadful force, moreover, probably could not long be maintained by the United States and Great Britain, Truman was told. The spectre of such a weapon " 'constructed in secret and used suddenly and effectively with devastating power by a willful nation or group against an unsuspecting nation or group of much greater size and material power' " was a certain nightmare of the future unless some sort of control could be established. Yet Stim-

---

[35] Hewlett and Anderson, *The New World*, p. 343. Italics added.

[36] A closely parallel argument, but one that seems to ignore the importance of the April 25 meeting and assigns Truman's negative decision to a later point, sometime in May, can be found in Len Giovannitti and Fred Freed, *The Decision to Drop the Bomb* (New York: Coward-McCann, 1965), pp. 240–246.

son's respect for the United Nations Organization coming into being at San Francisco was low.

"To approach any world peace organization of any pattern now likely to be considered, without an appreciation by the leaders of our country of the power of this new weapon, would seem to be unrealistic. . . . the control of this weapon will undoubtedly be a matter of the greatest difficulty and would involve such thorough-going rights of inspection and internal controls as we have never heretofore contemplated.

Furthermore, in the light of our present position with reference to this weapon, the question of sharing it with other nations and, if so shared, becomes a primary question of our foreign relations. . . .

On the other hand, if the problem of the proper use of this weapon can be solved, we would have the opportunity to bring the world into a pattern in which the peace of the world and our civilization can be saved. . . ."[37]

With these curious sentences, each carefully counterbalancing the other, Stimson left the entire question of future international control of atomic weaponry, and particularly the tangled question as to whether to share the secret with the Russians, completely up to the new President. Very possibly, since the three men read the report together,[38] Stimson was more precise in stating his preference —maintaining the atomic secret beyond the immediate use of the bomb or opting for a full exploration of the possibilities for meaningful international control. The record is not clear. We do know that the Secretary urged Truman to appoint a committee "to study and advise [the President] of the implications of this new force,"[39] which would seem to have been a sufficiently ambiguous suggestion as to satisfy Stimson that he had pushed the case for international control far enough to calm the fears of the concerned atomic scientists, led by Vannevar Bush and James Conant, while not personally committing himself to such a course. In any case, Stimson felt that "a great deal had been accomplished" by the interview, and his aides, Harvey Bundy and George Harrison, concurred.[40]

[37] Quoted in Stimson and Bundy, *On Active Service*, pp. 635–636.
[38] Hewlett and Anderson, *The New World*, p. 343.
[39] Truman, *Year of Decisions*, pp. 104–105.
[40] Stimson Diary, April 25, 1945.

In fact, little had been accomplished beyond the momentous if implicit reaffirmation of the decision to use the bomb, when ready, against Japan.[41] Should the Soviets be told about the bomb, and if so, when? Or should the bomb be kept a secret from them, a silent but powerful diplomatic counter to be revealed at such a time as to shake the Russians into a reasonable attitude?

Concerned atomic scientists, led by Niels Bohr, working through Vannevar Bush and Harvey Bundy in Stimson's office, urged in the last week of April, as they had a number of times in the past, that comprehensive plans be made for an American-sponsored program of international control. The San Francisco Conference seemed the perfect time and place for such a program to be discussed, Bohr suggested; and he, as others before him, raised the awesome possibility of a future Russian-American nuclear arms race if something were not swiftly done.[42]

Bundy and Harrison successfully worked on Stimson. Bohr had failed to appreciate the American desire for absolute secrecy concerning the Manhattan Project before it was brought to fruition, secrecy that utterly precluded any discussion at San Francisco. But on May 1, after reading Harrison's "very good paper" on the need to at last consider postwar atomic problems in comprehensive fashion, Stimson agreed to the formation of an "Interim Committee." By May 3 the committee was complete.[43] Five days later Nazi Germany surrendered, and the attention of American officials and planners gravitated inevitably toward the Pacific.

Four days after the German surrender Joseph Grew, who was Acting Secretary of State while Stettinius was in San Francisco, raised an entirely new question, one that was, implicitly at least, closely tied to the rapidly developing atomic bomb: Did America want Soviet Russia in the Pacific war *at all?* Not even General Deane had gone this far.

The genesis of this question seems to have been the weekly meeting between the Secretaries of State, War, and Navy on May 1.

---

[41] On April 23 and again on April 30 British officials on the Combined Policy Committee on Atomic Affairs in Washington informed London that " 'the Americans propose to drop a bomb sometime in August.' " Quoted in Ehrman, *Grand Strategy*, pp. 275–276.

[42] Hewlett and Anderson, *The New World*, p. 344.

[43] Stimson Diary, May 2, 3, 1945; Millis, ed., *Forrestal Diaries*, p. 54.

The official who first raised the question was not Grew, but James Forrestal, whose deep and early suspicions of Soviet Russia have already been noted. Forrestal asked Stimson and Grew "whether or not it was time to make a thorough study of our political objectives in the Far East. . . ." Specifically, Forrestal inquired, "How far and how thoroughly do we want to beat Japan?" Should the islands be "Morgenthaued"? "What is our policy on Russian influence in the Far East?" Forrestal continued. "Do we desire a counterweight to that influence? And should it be China or should it be Japan?" Grew's response was limited to proposing deferral of "the decision on the question of the Japanese Emperor until we had effected a military occupation," thereby implying his continued belief at this time in the necessity for demanding unconditional surrender and achieving it through direct invasion of the Japanese home islands.[44]

The interrelated issues of Japanese surrender and Soviet entry into the Pacific war were not to be settled so swiftly, however. Germany's defeat brought the question of Japan's surrender squarely to the forefront of official American thinking. By mid-May reports were circulating publicly that the American First Army under General Hodge—"First Across the Rhine"—in Europe, was now on its way to the Pacific with a brief leave scheduled in the United States. Units of the Eighth and Fifteenth Air Forces were also heading toward the far Pacific. Plans called for some 280,000 men per month to be transferred from the ETO westward. Soon thereafter—on June 7—Truman issued a public statement on domestic transportation in which he said that "The plan of battle now requires that our armies be transferred to the Far Pacific in the very short time of 10 months," thereby insuring participation in the March 1, 1946, assault on the Tokyo Plain by the forces seasoned in European combat.[45] The great buildup for the invasion of Japan had begun. In sheer size, weight, and momentum—as Truman himself implied—it had never before been matched in human history. Only a courageous, last-minute decision or the employment of a massive new force, such as the atomic bomb, could deflect this vast military thrust.

---

[44] *Ibid.*, pp. 52–53.
[45] *New York Times*, May 22, 1945, p. 1:6, May 23, 1945, p. 38:2, 3, 4; *Newsweek*, XXV (May 21, 1945), 35; Truman, *Public Papers, 1945*, p. 114.

Nonetheless, American officials continued to explore the fateful questions raised by the need to subdue Japan. On May 11 Forrestal met in his office with Harriman and key members of the naval establishment. The Ambassador came right to the point. "Harriman said he thought it was time to come to a conclusion about the necessity for the early entrance of Russia into the Japanese war. He said he was satisfied they were determined to come in it because of their requirements in the Far East (he described the territorial concessions made at Yalta)." Harriman went on to state his belief that the Russians

> much more greatly feared a separate peace by ourselves with Japan than any fear of ourselves about their concluding such an arrangement. He said he thought it was important that we determine our policy as to a strong or weak China, that if China continued weak Russian influence would move in quickly and toward ultimate domination. He said that there could be no illusion about anything such as a "free China" once the Russians got in, that the two or three hundred millions in that country would march when the Kremlin ordered.

The admirals present were divided in their reaction. Vice Admiral Cooke "thought the necessity for Russia's early participation was very much lessened as a result of recent events." Cooke added, however, the significant reservation that "the Army he didn't think shared that view." Admiral Edwards just hoped "the Japanese would agree to a basis of unconditional surrender which still left them in their own minds some face and honor."[46] Edwards' comment reflected the developing feeling among some military strategists, notably in the navy and air force, that an air and sea blockade with an implied modification of unconditional surrender, might bring Japan to her knees without the necessity of invasion.

Discussions of the problem at the Cabinet and sub-Cabinet levels continued into the following days. On May 12 Harriman bluntly asked for "a clear outline of American policy" and submitted a long questionnaire concerning the whole range and structure of future Far Eastern policy. Should the Yalta Far Eastern agreements be "reexamined in the light of the fact that Russia has not observed

[46] Millis, ed., *Forrestal Diaries*, p. 55.

its part of that contract"? How "urgent is the necessity for quick Russian participation in the war against Japan?" Should the Soviets participate in the postwar occupation of Japan? What of Korea? Could it be saved from a Bolshevized government or not with the planned Russian drive into the area against Japanese troops? What of our relations with the British over Hong Kong, with the French over Indochina? These questions were to be "formulated" more clearly " 'for discussion with the President.' "[47] But Grew deemed them of such immediate and overriding importance that a Presidential decision should be sought at once. His sense of urgency had been quickened in recent days, not only by what he clearly regarded as ominous Soviet behavior in Europe, but also by the emergence of unofficial Japanese peace seekers in Europe who had been querying and prodding the American government ever since January.

The Acting Secretary had become deeply alarmed at Soviet actions in the months since Yalta. He was convinced that the American people, and perhaps a significant portion of the American leadership as well, either did not understand or refused to recognize the developing Soviet menace. In a long private memorandum summarizing his thinking, which he did not write until May 19 and then, significantly, showed only to Harriman and Bohlen, Grew labeled Communist Russia " 'the one certain future enemy.' " The United Nations would be ineffective in the postwar world because, thanks to the various Yalta agreements, there could be no effective restraints upon Soviet power. From her rapidly consolidating power base in Eastern Europe, Grew gloomily predicted, " 'Russia's power will steadily increase and she will in the not distant future be in a favorable position to expand her control, step by step, through Europe. The Near East and the Far East will in due course be brought into the same pattern.' "[48]

As early as the middle of 1943 a number of high-ranking officials in Tokyo had concluded that the tide of battle across Oceania must inexorably turn against Japan if a negotiated peace was not secured soon with Britain and the United States.[49] The mounting

---

[47] *Ibid.*, p. 56.
[48] Quoted in Grew, *Turbulent Era*, II: 1445–1446.
[49] Butow, *Japan's Decision to Surrender*, pp. 17–18.

series of catastrophes which brought the American enemy perilously close to Nippon's doorstep by the time of Yalta galvanized a growing number of Japanese in semi-official and unofficial positions to quietly seek ways out of the war short of unconditional surrender.

From January of 1945 on a steady stream of reports began trickling into Washington from OSS units and embassies all over Western Europe of anxious queries from minor Japanese officials concerning ultimate American intentions in the Pacific. In January such reports came from the Vatican, in April from Stockholm, by early May from Lisbon, Stockholm, and Switzerland.[50] The pattern was invariably the same. Minor Japanese civil or military officials were seeking to explore the limits, if any, of unconditional surrender. Would this policy preclude retention of the Emperor? Would it mean the inevitable termination of Japan's traditional *Tennō* system or "national polity" which the imperial throne defined and symbolized? As late as May 12 the American government officially clung stubbornly to the argument that there was nothing to discuss or that unconditional surrender was self-explanatory.[51]

The Japanese government itself said nothing. It was publicly committed to a fight to the finish—in the home islands if necessary. This official policy never changed. Not until August 10, 1945, four days after Hiroshima and twenty-four hours after Nagasaki, did the Japanese government approach Washington concerning surrender and peace.[52] Prior to August 10 the military for all practical purposes ruled Japan. "In terms of physical accomplishment, the Japanese military had already lost the war," Professor Butow has remarked, "but *spiritually* they were still indestructible. For want of a better solution they now insisted that, if given the chance to concentrate their forces against the invader when he came, they

---

[50] "Memorandum by the Director of the Office of Far Eastern Affairs to the Undersecretary of State," Washington, January 30, 1945; Minister in Sweden to Secretary of State, April 6, 7, 19, May 11, 1945; Ambassador in Portugal to the Secretary of State, May 7, 1945; "Memorandum of the Director of the Office of Strategic Services to the Secretary of State," Washington, May 12, 1945, in *Foreign Relations, 1945; Diplomatic Papers*, VI: 475–481.

[51] Acting Secretary of State (Grew) to Minister in Sweden, May 12, 1945, *ibid.*, pp. 480–481.

[52] Representative Bertrand W. Gearhart to Acting Secretary of State Acheson, December 9, 1945, Acheson to Gearhart, December 18, 1945, *ibid.*, pp. 495–497.

could win a decision on the battlefield of the homeland that would permit Japan to end the war on favorable terms." To the peace seekers within the government who appear to have individually and fitfully been behind *some* of the queries sent out in Europe, such a course represented pure madness.[53] "Hundred Million Die Together," the slogan of the fanatics, was an invitation to national suicide. But the army was in control; they were not. Their only hope was to enlist the aid of the Emperor, to whose ultimate will all bowed, and to develop such powerful arguments in favor of peace that not only the Emperor and the army, but also the Americans, would listen.

It was with precisely these twin aims in mind that Prince Konoye approached the Emperor with a carefully written memorial on February 14, 1945, even as Churchill, Roosevelt, and Stalin were meeting at Yalta. "I think that there is no longer any doubt about our defeat," Konoye's memorial began. Yet a defeat, while serious, could be kept from being catastrophic *if* the national polity could be maintained intact. The main threat to the *Tennō* system, however, lay not with the United States but with Russia. "What we have to fear . . . is not so much a defeat as a Communist revolution which might take place in the event of a defeat." The recent "notable ascendancy of Soviet Russia in world affairs" had inevitably focused popular attention in Japan as elsewhere upon the Kremlin. Inside Japan the "rapid deterioration of the people's living conditions, increase in the voice of the laboring class, rise of pro-Soviet feelings as enmity against America and Britain increases," all were dangerous signs of a potential for Red revolution should the present regime and political system of Japan be crushed in war. But all this was merely by way of preliminary. For the Communist enemy was already deeply embedded in Japan. Already there were powerful "and disguised" signs of the "activities of the Communists behind both the military and bureaucrats within the Japanese Government itself." Indeed, the greatest threat to the national polity came from "an extremist group in the military" which sought "to achieve radical changes in internal politics." It was the army,

[53] Butow, *Japan's Decision to Surrender*, p. 50.

or at least a portion of it, that very institution pledged to protect the *Tennō* system, which was really seeking to undermine it in order to introduce social radicalism into Japan. Therefore, the longer the army fought, the longer the national polity suffered under the physical blows of the enemy, the longer the country was unbearably strained by war, the more certain would be a radical revolution. "In the last few months," Konoye continued, "the slogan 'Hundred Million Die Together' has become increasingly louder, seemingly among the right wing people, but has its real basis in the activities of the Communists."

What was the solution to this fearful appearance of internal subversion? Konoye at first proposed to "stop the war as soon as possible," since "the longer we continue the war, the greater will be the danger of revolution." But in the next paragraph the Prince completely changed his mind. "If we try to stop the war abruptly," he told the Emperor, "these military extremists together with both the right and left wings, might attempt anything—even a bloody internal revolt, and thereby nullify our efforts" to retain the existing national polity. "The prerequisite to the conclusion of the war, therefore, is to wipe out the influence of these dangerous people and reform the Army and Navy." The war, therefore, *must* be ended, but *not* before the army and navy were "reformed."[54]

It was, taken measure for measure, a most remarkable document. For what Konoye did was to deflect the attention of the Emperor and the peace party away from the overriding problems involved in ending the war immediately and toward a quixotic crusade to "reform" the supposed Communist elements within the Japanese armed services before the war could be "abruptly" terminated. The cause of Japanese military fanaticism, of "Hundred Million Die Together," could not have been better served. The war must be continued until the Communists were rooted out of the military. Yet the longer the war went on the stronger was the proof that the Communists were more deeply embedded in the armed services than

---

[54] The Konoye memorial has been reprinted in several places. I have used the translation in United States Strategic Bombing Survey, *Japan's Struggle to End the War* (Washington: 1946), pp. 21–22. Cf. also Butow, *Japan's Decision to Surrender*, pp. 47–50, which is substantially the same.

anyone had yet imagined! Caught in a vicious circle of self-fulfilling prophecies, Japanese officials who truly wished to end the war truly could not. Only the Americans could end it for them in the mountains and rice fields of Kyushu and on the Tokyo Plain. Terrified of the armed services for their "Communist" leanings, their police power, and their custodianship of the Japanese spirit, fearful that the Americans meant just what they said about unconditional surrender, yet fearful too of the ideological attractiveness as well as military power of the Soviets, Konoye and his "peace" colleagues in the Japanese government acted in a manner in the spring and summer of 1945 which can only be defined—if we may use an American colloquialism to cover the complexities of oriental politics—as dithering.

There *was* one point, however, at which Konoye's goals might possibly have touched existing realities. If the Americans could be convinced that it was in their interest to spare Japan and to cooperate with her existing leadership to construct an anti-Communist bulwark in East Asia, then the Konoye memorial might become the basis of a revitalized national polity. Should the United States agree to call off the war, to permit Japan to retain her territorial integrity and her imperial system, then the peace reformers within the government in Tokyo would be given the time necessary to carry out their program.

On May 7, just before the whole subject of American aims in Asia was brought up by Harriman in Washington, the Counselor of the Japanese legation in Lisbon, Masutaro Inouye, approached an OSS agent and made the following statements to him: " 'There can be no "unconditional surrender" as the Emperor would never do that.' " However, with Germany gone and with the realization that " 'Japan will be hopelessly smashed by United States bombers,' " perhaps the time had come for America and Japan to sound each other out. Inouye had no concrete proposals to make, save " 'to give up all the conquests in their war,' " which were rapidly slipping from Japan's grasp in any case. But he did have reminders to be whispered in American ears. Did the United States really want " 'Russia . . . to drive them out of the Far East' "? Did the United States truly want to " 'lose the great Chinese market[?] The way Molotov acts at San Francisco shows plainly that Stalin has reverted to Imperialism or to Isolationism,' " Inouye confusingly stated. " 'There can be no other solution for the western powers than to get up a united front against Stalin.' " And why not with Japan? " 'We hold the richest parts of the Chinese sub-continent and we have an important Chinese following. We have the argument of "Asia for the Asiatics." So instead of waging a very long war against Japan in China and finally losing the Far East markets to Russia the western powers should come to some sort of an arrangement, however bad it might be for us. We do not think that after the Polish experience the USA will grant a six billion dollar credit to Stalin and we think that the Russians will drift even farther apart from the western powers. We hope,' " Inouye concluded, " 'that the United States will see this in the same light.' "[55]

It cannot be presumed that Joseph Grew knew of the Konoye memorial at this time. But did he see Inouye's remarks, which may well have come originally from Konoye or one of his circle? If so, Grew may well have divined Konoye's thoughts, for he knew most of the Japanese officials well. The Acting Secretary need not have subscribed to all of the aims Konoye hoped to achieve. Every piece of available evidence points to the fact that Grew was steadfast in his determination to see the Pacific war through to a decisive United States victory which would destroy the power of the Japanese military class. But, of course, this aim did not conflict in any way with Konoye's hopes. Grew's and Konoye's thinking could easily converge in an agreement to retain the Emperor as the symbol of Japan's ongoing national polity while both men would agree also on the need to destroy utterly the military group whose actions in one way or another now threatened ruin to that polity. By retaining the Emperor the way might be opened for a diminution of Russian Communist influence in the Far East, and the foundations for a firmly anti-Bolshevist Japan could be laid. Should Grew decide, as he quickly did, to push for an amelioration of the unconditional surrender formula to the degree that the Japanese people would be permitted to retain the imperial institution, a substantial basis for negotiation would suddenly exist.

[55] Quoted in Ambassador in Portugal to Secretary of State, May 7, 1945, *Foreign Relations, 1945; Diplomatic Papers*, VI: 478–479.

Possibly influenced, then, by current Japanese attitudes toward Russia as well as by the deep pessimism he shared with Harriman concerning Soviet intentions, Grew swiftly packaged the Ambassador's questions of May 12 into a formal note and dispatched it to Forrestal and Stimson that same day. " 'Is the entry of the Soviet Union into the Pacific War at the earliest possible moment of such vital interest to the United States as to preclude any attempt by the United States Government to obtain Soviet agreement to certain desirable political objectives in the Far East prior to such entry?' " Grew inquired. He asked specifically if the Yalta agreement should not be revised and if Soviet requests for a share in the Japanese occupation should not be rebuffed unless and until the Russians firmly agreed to help bring about the unification of China under Chiang Kai-shek, agreed to return Manchuria to Chinese sovereignty, agreed to discuss the future of Korea looking toward the creation of a United Nations trusteeship there, and at least agreed to consider the possibility of American emergency landing rights in the Kuriles.[56]

Stimson and Forrestal submitted their formal reply on May 21, but either just before or just after they did so Truman entered the debate with apparently decisive results. This was probably on May 19, the day that he gave Harry Hopkins his instructions for the meeting with Stalin. "Before Hopkins left for Moscow," Truman later wrote, "I had impressed upon him the need for getting as early a date as possible on Russia's entry into the war against Japan."[57] As we shall see Hopkins took these instructions very much to heart, and their successful fulfillment formed the basis of official American optimism over the the results of the Hopkins mission.

The Stimson and Forrestal replies of May 21 were thus undoubtedly written with the sure knowledge of Truman's position. But Stimson's own thinking did not diverge widely from that of his President. Harriman's concern over Soviet policies, which he so frequently expressed in the weeks just after Roosevelt's death, had stirred Stimson into further reflection upon the coming impact of the atomic bomb upon East-West relations. In assessing Stimson's

[56] Quoted in Grew, *Turbulent Era*, II: 1455–1457; and *Entry of the Soviet Union into the War Against Japan*, pp. 69–70. Cf. also Stimson Diary, May 13, 1945.
[57] Truman, *Year of Decisions*, p. 293.

comments, it must be borne in mind that they were made in an atmosphere which assumed the necessity for a costly invasion of Japan to end World War II. Indeed, Stimson's remarks concerning a round of meetings with Harriman and Marshall on May 10 convey this point very explicitly. Stimson wanted to get Harriman's "views on the situation in Russia and the chance of getting a Russia that we could work with." "It was a rather gloomy report that he gave us," Stimson recorded that night. "He didn't think that there was any chance of getting the seeds of liberalism into Russia. . . . Yet he thought that Russia would be afraid to throw down the Dumbarton Oaks plan or the associations with us altogether. He thinks that Russia is really afraid of our power, or at least respects it and, although she is going to try to ride roughshod over her neighbors in Europe, he thought that she was really afraid of us. I talked over very confidentially our problem connected with S-1 in this matter."[58]

Stimson's remarks in the above connection would suggest that the seeds of a future policy of "atomic diplomacy" were germinating in his mind. Later that day, however, the Secretary "had a short talk with Marshall on rather deep matters—the coming program of strategy for the operations in the Pacific where I wanted to find out whether or not we couldn't hold matters off from very heavy involvement in casualties until after we had tried out S-1. I found out that probably we could get the trial before the locking of arms came and much bloodshed." In other words, Stimson's first and foremost thought was to use the bomb *before*, if possible, the invasion of Japan, "the locking of arms . . . and much bloodshed." That the bomb would become a major factor in international diplomacy after its use, if effective, was only to state an obvious point. Thus, upon receipt of Grew's long May 12 memo concerning Russia and the Japanese war, Stimson commented, "These are very vital questions and I am very glad that the State Department has brought them up and given us a chance to be heard on them. The questions cut very deep and in my opinion are powerfully connected with the success of S-1."[59]

---

[58] Stimson Diary, May 10, 1945.
[59] *Ibid.*, May 13, 1945.

The following day Stimson called in his close adviser, John J. McCloy, and asked his opinion of Grew's queries. "I told him that my own opinion was that the time now and the method now to deal with Russia was to keep our mouths shut and let our actions speak for words. The Russians will understand them better than anything else. It is a case where we have got to regain the lead and perhaps do it in a pretty rough and realistic way." Stimson claimed that the Soviets had seized the initiative "because we have talked too much and have been too lavish with our beneficences to them." But now, with the coming of the atomic bomb, "this was a place where we really held all the cards. I called it a royal straight flush and we mustn't be a fool about the way we play it. They can't get along without our help and industries and we have a weapon coming into action which will be unique. Now the thing is not to get into unnecessary quarrels by talking too much and not to indicate any weakness by talking too much."[60] Whether Stimson ever passed these rough sentiments on to the President in such forthright fashion is unclear.

What is clear is that the following day at the weekly State-War-Navy meeting attended by Averell Harriman, among others, Stimson made explicit his concept of a strategy of delay. After a night's sleep, he felt Grew's and Harriman's questions were "premature."

> The trouble is that the President has now promised apparently to meet Stalin and Churchill on the first of July and at that time these questions will become burning and it may be necessary to have it out with Russia on her relations to Manchuria and Port Arthur and various other parts of North China, and also the relations of China to us. Over any such tangled wave of problems the S-1 secret would be dominant and yet we will not know until after that time probably, until after that meeting, whether this is a weapon in our hands or not. We think it will be shortly afterwards, but it seems a terrible thing to gamble with such big stakes in diplomacy without having your master card in your hand.

This very strong suggestion of a coming "atomic diplomacy" was again diluted, however, by further references in Stimson's diary that day to the overriding problem facing American officials at the

[60] *Ibid.*, May 14, 1945.

time, which was the defeat of Japan and *not* the confrontation with
Soviet power. T. V. Soong, the Chinese Foreign Minister, in Washington for talks, tried "to persuade the President that the easiest
way for America to win the war over Japan is to fight it out in
China on the mainland of Asia—the very thing that I am resolved
that we shall not do unless it is over my dead body. . . ." And Stimson added that "Marshall has got the straightforward view," which,
of course, involved an American invasion of Japan, a Soviet invasion of Manchuria and North China, "and he feels that we must
go ahead. Fortunately the actual invasion will not take place *until
my secret is out* [*i.e.*, until the atomic bomb was used]. The Japanese campaign involves therefore two great uncertainties; first,
whether Russia will come in, *though we think that will be all right*;
and second, when and how S-1 will resolve itself."[61]

One fact seems plain. In Stimson's mind as in Marshall's, the military defeat of Japan through direct assault upon the home islands
with accompanying Russian aid in Northeast Asia was the prime
strategic and tactical consideration facing the United States in the
late spring and early summer of 1945. Beyond this point all becomes murky, and conjecture assumes command. Despite its horrendous power, Stimson and Marshall apparently were not at all certain at this time that the atomic bomb in and of itself could bring
about the defeat of Japan. The bomb, Stimson's secret, *was* envisioned as having a tremendous potential shock value upon the Japanese *once used, as it surely would be*. But whether the bomb
would make an assault upon Japan unnecessary was at best unclear.
It was obvious that America's possession and justifiable use of such
a weapon was certain to have an impact upon Soviet-American relations. But the depth of that impact was as difficult to surmise as
was the ultimate force of the completed bomb. There is little doubt
that at times during the late spring of 1945 Stimson seriously pondered a future policy, however vague, of atomic diplomacy. But
the fact remains that he was as unsure of the bomb's ultimate efficiency and power as was everyone else. Moreover, he had not and
for many months would not despair for the future of Soviet-Ameri-

[61] *Ibid.*, May 15, 1945. Italics added.

can relations. That these relations were felt by Stimson—and obviously Truman as well in light of his dispatch of Hopkins to Moscow and especially Davies to London—to be of crucial importance to world peace, is indisputable. At the conclusion of a report to Truman on May 16 urging the President *not* to dispatch large military forces to the Asian mainland to help China as Soong had requested, Stimson stated once again: "We must find some way of persuading Russia to play ball."[62] The "pretty rough and realistic" way of the atomic bomb could be considered legitimate *so long as* the major focus of atomic deployment was against active Japanese militarism and not Soviet diplomatic and political expansionism. This was obviously the way Stimson's mind was operating.

Thus it was that in his long, May 21 reply to Grew's earlier note Stimson stressed the fact that Soviet entry into the Pacific war was inevitable and would " 'be decided by the Russians on their own military and political basis with little regard to any political action taken by the United States.' " Moreover, " '*Russian entry will have a profound military effect in that almost certainly it will materially shorten the war and thus save American lives.*' " Franklin Roosevelt could not have put the case for a Soviet entry more eloquently or precisely. Stimson went on to add that " 'the concessions to Russia on Far Eastern matters which were made at Yalta are generally matters which are within the military power of Russia to obtain regardless of U.S. military action short of war.' " Presumably such " 'military action' " included by this late date of analysis the forthcoming atomic strike against Japan. Stimson's lesson was clear and forceful. Even in late May of 1945 the United States seemed still to need Russia far more than the Soviets needed the United States. That same day Forrestal informed Grew that he, too, shared Stimson's views fully and completely.[63]

The great debate over whether or not to seek some modification of the Yalta Far Eastern accords and/or to try to end the Pacific war without Soviet entry thus came to at least a temporary close.

---

[62] *Ibid.*, May 16, 1945.

[63] Stimson's reply may be found in Grew, *Turbulent Era*, II: 1457–1459, italics added. The replies of both Stimson and Forrestal are in *Entry of the Soviet Union into the War Against Japan*, pp. 70–71.

Plans for the invasion of Japan and for perfection and use of the atomic bomb went forward.[64] Grew, isolated in his concern and skepticism after Harriman's return to Moscow, now prepared a new approach to the problem of minimizing, if not eliminating, Soviet entry into the Asian conflict and the resultant rise of Russian influence in Asia. On May 28 he sounded Truman out on the possibility of inducing a Japanese surrender short of invasion, use of the bomb, or Soviet entry into the war. The carrot to be used was an "indication" by the American government to the Japanese people that "once thoroughly defeated and rendered impotent to wage war," they would "be permitted to determine their own future political structure." Grew tried to induce Truman to include these phrases in his May 31 address on the Japanese war. But Truman sent his Acting Secretary to his chief military advisers, Stimson, Marshall, and Forrestal. At a meeting on May 29 they all vetoed the idea. "The question of timing was the nub of the whole matter, . . ." with the military chieftains apparently not wishing to indicate any sense of American war weariness as the battle for Okinawa reached its climax. Grew's initiative was thus too late. Truman, now keyed to the advice and mood of his military advisers, most notably Marshall, deferred to them once again at this time, and the matter was dropped.[65] The President had told Lilienthal that his first priority was to "win two wars." The invasion of Japan, therefore, would proceed. The shock and power of Russian intervention should be utilized to the fullest since the Soviets could not be kept out of Northeast Asia in any case. To compress the scope and scale of that intervention to the diplomatic and geographic framework of the Yalta accords, friction with Stalin must be minimized, his good will cultivated. There is no available record that Truman and his advisers reasoned thus. None is necessary.

[64] The *formal* ratification by Truman's Interim Advisory Committee of the earlier April 25 decision to use the bomb was made after long discussions on May 31 and June 1, 1945. The committee decided that the bomb could and should be used and that only a sudden, unannounced demonstration would achieve maximum military and psychological results. Several accounts of these Interim Committee meetings have been published. The most authoritative is in Hewlett and Anderson, *The New World*, pp. 356–360.

[65] Accounts of the May 28 and 29 meetings may be found in Grew, *Turbulent Era*, II: 1423–1424; Millis, ed., *Forrestal Diaries*, p. 66; Stimson Diary, May 29, 1945; and *Foreign Relations, 1945; Diplomatic Papers*, VI: 545–549.

For while all seemed confusion at the time, with events piling upon events in a random and aimless fashion, a distinct pattern of international Big Three relations was beginning to reemerge during the confused weeks of May and early June. Amidst the foggy springtime hills of San Francisco, as well as across the shattered landscape of central Europe, agreements were reached and decisions made or reconfirmed that went far to establish the promise of a stable postwar world order based upon mutually recognized spheres of influence maintained by Soviet and Western military power of roughly proportionate force and balance. That this emerging reality was far from displeasing to Truman and his influential advisers may be confidently inferred from the actions of the American government in these weeks, if not from any particular official statements.

7

Toward a Rapprochement--San Francisco and Central Europe, May and June

During the final weeks of April and the first week in May 1945, the vast Anglo-American armies moved inexorably toward victory in central Europe while the Russians concentrated upon the rape of Berlin. As Nazism finally collapsed Churchill for the last time tried to lure the Americans into using their powerful military presence on the Continent as a political and diplomatic counter to Soviet expansion. One of the agreements reached at Yalta after months of haggling between British and United States officials in and out of the European Advisory Commission provided for the division of Germany and Austria into zones of occupation.[1] By mid-April units of the American Third Army were driving down the Danube Valley toward Linz, the Seventh Army was already deep inside Austria, while other battle groups from both the First and Ninth Armies had reached the Elbe along a broad front. By the end of April the irrepressible General George Patton commenced a deep thrust into what had been agreed at the Crimea would be the Soviet zones of occupation. By the first days in May

[1] Mosely, "Occupation of Germany," pp. 155–182.

164

his army had penetrated into Czechoslovakia almost as far as Pilsen and Karlsbad to protect his flank along the Danube and to harry the fleeing and disorganized Wehrmacht.[2]

To the Prime Minister the final and finest moment to influence Soviet behavior in Europe had arrived. No "stop" order had been given by either British or American authorities. No political or military agreement restraining the forward movement of the Western armies existed. As early as April 11 Eisenhower, with Marshall's concurrence, had advised Moscow direct that he considered that both the Soviet and Western forces should advance until contact was imminent. Three days later, following a flurry of cables between London and Washington, the combined Chiefs of Staff ratified Eisenhower's free advance proposal.[3] Under the influence of this idea, the British Chiefs of Staff asserted on April 9 that withdrawal into zones of occupation was a matter to be considered by the three heads of government.[4]

On April 13 Sir Alexander Cadogan, at Eden's behest, wrote American Ambassador Winant "pointing out how important and valuable it would be if the American forces could press forward into Czechoslovakia and liberate Prague, supposing that military considerations allowed." Continued American silence redoubled British urgency. Soon thereafter Churchill was told of the Eden proposal and the "conviction" of his foreign minister "that such an action by the Americans, were it possible, might make the whole difference to the postwar situation in Czechoslovakia and might influence that in nearby countries." On April 26, with Prague still a prize for either the Americans or the Soviets, Churchill cabled Eden to take the matter up with Stettinius. The Foreign Secretary found his American counterpart surprisingly receptive. Stettinius told Eden "that he entirely shared our views and had sent word accordingly to the President and Admiral Leahy."[5] In the meantime Chur-

---

[2] Eisenhower, *Crusade in Europe*, pp. 464–465; Churchill, *Triumph and Tragedy*, p. 433; Omar N. Bradley, *A Soldier's Story* (New York: Henry Holt and Company, 1951), pp. 548, 551.

[3] Quoted in Chester Wilmot, *The Struggle for Europe* (London: Fontana Books, 1959), p. 792. Cf. also Ehrman, *Grand Strategy*, pp. 151–153; Chandler, ed., *Eisenhower Papers*; *War Years*, IV: 2591n.

[4] Ehrman, *Grand Strategy*, p. 152.

[5] Eden, *The Reckoning*, p. 615.

chill applied direct pressure on Truman. In an April 18 cable the Prime Minister pressed the case for two zones. One would be a tactical zone " 'in which our troops must stand on the line they have reached unless there is agreement for a better tactical deployment against the continuing resistance of the enemy.' " The other would constitute the already-drawn and agreed-to occupational zones to which the Western Allies should not retire until some deliberately obscure date, certainly after V-E Day and possibly not until the conclusion of another Big Three meeting. " 'I do not wish our Allied troops or your American troops to be hustled back at any point by some crude assertion of a local Russian general,' " the Prime Minister concluded. A dozen days later, with Prague still in German hands, the Prime Minister cabled Truman again, repeating Eden's earlier argument almost verbatim: " 'There can be little doubt that the liberation of Prague and as much as possible of the territory of Western Czechoslovakia by your forces might make the whole difference to the post-war situation in Czechoslovakia, and might well influence that in near-by countries,' " Churchill asserted. " 'On the other hand, if the Western Allies play no significant part in Czechoslovakian liberation that country will go the way of Yugoslavia.' "[6]

Here was Churchill's final cast of the dice. In 1943 and 1944, with British and American military power at a rough parity in Europe, the Prime Minister had begged Roosevelt to concentrate the secondary Western thrust in Europe at the Balkans rather than at southern France. The Americans had refused. In the autumn of 1944 the British, already looking toward the occupation of as much of Central and Eastern Europe as possible for diplomatic bargaining purposes against the Russians, pleaded for a single powerful and rapid Western drive toward the Ruhr and Berlin. The Americans, however, supported Eisenhower's strategy of slow, massive assault along a broad front in order to obliterate the Wehrmacht and achieve total victory over Germany. Six months later, in March of 1945, with the seizure of Berlin still beckoning but with American military power unquestionably preponderant, the British were

[6] Quoted in Churchill, *Triumph and Tragedy*, pp. 433, 439–440. Cf. also Truman, *Year of Decisions*, pp. 239, 243.

forced to wring their hands once again. Eisenhower cabled Stalin direct to assure him that the American "broad front" strategy was not keyed to Berlin but rather focused primarily upon capture of what became the mythical Nazi "redoubt" in Bavaria and secondarily upon Leipzig, the Elbe, and portions of the Danube Valley.[7] A fortnight later, on the eve of the Soviet offensive against the Nazi capital, Eisenhower made it plain to all that unless expressly ordered to do so he intended to "clean up my flanks" on the Elbe while to the north Montgomery concentrated upon the capture of Denmark and the western Baltic ports. Berlin was the Russians' problem. The drive of American armies down the Danube Valley and into Czechoslovakia and parts of northern Yugoslavia was a sideshow.[8]

The final decision as to serious Western penetration into the outskirts of Eastern Europe thus belonged to the Americans, who had never in the past seriously given in to Churchill's political and military preoccupations. Eisenhower would not do so now. Immediate strategic considerations and steady pursuance of the broad front concept dominated his thinking to the last, even though German resistance in these last days was largely confined to "ambushes and desperate stands, . . . pockets of fanatic resistance in wood and ruined town," and occasional desultory road blocks.[9] If a change in policy should come, it would have to come from Truman, and the new President began to receive steady pressure along this line from the State Department, particularly from Stettinius and Grew, who asked that the Joint Chiefs of Staff "consider the idea seriously."[10]

The President, however, resisted the pleadings of both the British and the State Department. On April 23 he responded to Chur-

[7] Wilmot, *Struggle for Europe*, pp. 510–543, 788–792; Ambrose, *Eisenhower and Berlin, passim*; Bryant, *Triumph in the West*, p. 338. Much controversy has been generated over the failures of Eisenhower's intelligence section to properly evaluate the "National Redoubt" fiction. There can be no question, however, that at the time SHAEF's G-2 believed that it existed and was about to function. The Wagnerian scenario dreamed up at Ike's headquarters was faithfully passed on to the American public by the highly respected Drew Middleton. Cf. "Nazi Die-Hards Man Their National Redoubt," *New York Times*, April 8, 1945, p. E3:3; Eisenhower to Combined Chiefs of Staff, April 14, 1945, in Chandler, ed., *Eisenhower Papers*; *War Years*, IV: 2604–2606.

[8] Bryant, *Triumph in the West*, p. 342; Truman, *Year of Decisions*, p. 238.

[9] Wilmot, *Struggle for Europe*, p. 792; Bryant, *Triumph in the West*, p. 342.

[10] Truman, *Year of Decisions*, p. 243.

chill's suggestion that Western forces seize and hold great chunks of eastern Austria and western Czechoslovakia. After thorough study and with full realization of "the intentions of the Russians to act on their own, without our co-operation, in all the countries they had liberated, . . ." Truman nonetheless concluded that "Our commitment on the occupation zones was . . . an established fact, and our government had been proceeding on that basis ever since Yalta." "I could see no valid reason," he subsequently wrote in justification, "for questioning an agreement on which we were so clearly committed, nor could I see any useful purpose in interfering with successful military operations. The only practical thing to do was to stick carefully to our agreement and to try our best to make the Russians carry out their agreements."[11] The major source of Truman's thinking is not difficult to trace. Five days later George C. Marshall, upon whom the President had already come to rely, cabled Eisenhower: " 'Personally and aside from all logistic, tactical or strategical implications I would be loath to hazard American lives for purely political purposes.' "[12]

Churchill's message of April 30 provoked further consideration of the issue among American policy-makers. Following Marshall's lead, Eisenhower on April 23 had registered dismay over Churchill's determination "to intermingle political and military considerations in attempting to establish a procedure for the conduct of our own and Russian troops when a meeting takes place." Eisenhower subsequently informed Marshall on April 29 that he would move into Czechoslovakia as far as Pilsen and Karlsbad only after clearing his flanks and only if conditions were propitious. "I shall *not* attempt any move which I deem militarily unwise," Eisenhower emphasized, "merely to gain a political prize unless I receive specific orders from the Combined Chiefs of Staff." The Chiefs of Staff concurred, for both they and the President were haunted by knowledge "that after the defeat of Germany there still remained Japan. To bring Japan to her knees would require the transfer of many troops from Europe to the Pacific." While agreeing with Churchill "that it would be desirable to hold the great cities of

[11] *Ibid.*, pp. 240–241.
[12] Quoted in Ambrose, *Eisenhower and Berlin*, p. 84.

Berlin, Prague, and Vienna," the Americans knew "the fact was that, like the countries of Eastern Europe, these cities were under Russian control or about to fall under her control. The Russians were in a strong position, and they knew it." The Americans, eager to get out of Europe and into the Pacific, were not. On May 1 Truman cabled Churchill of the American decision to support Eisenhower's severely limited advance.[13]

So Prague fell to the Soviets. But Churchill was not yet done. Quick convening of a Three Power conference on Europe might yet discomfit the Soviets if American troops had not yet completed their withdrawals back to the western zones of Germany and Austria. And so the Prime Minister launched the initiative that led to the Potsdam Conference two months later. On May 6, with the final Nazi surrender only hours away, Churchill again urged that the American armies stand firm in Czechoslovakia and Yugoslavia, pending another meeting of the Big Three.[14]

But with victory Truman's interest in European affairs began to ebb. He responded on May 9 that a Big Three meeting was desirable, but that "in regard to timing, it will be extremely difficult for me to absent myself from Washington before the end of the fiscal year (30 June)," an obvious reference to the domestic problems which crowded around him. In the meantime, the President continued, "it is my present intention to adhere to our interpretation of the Yalta agreements, and to stand firmly on our present announced attitude toward all the questions at issue."[15] With this cable Truman committed himself to the total withdrawal of all American forces from the fringes of Eastern Europe.

Administrative delays and frictions in establishing four-power control over Berlin and the confusions attending the mass surrender of Nazi military units all over Central Europe delayed this withdrawal until mid-June and permitted Churchill one final plea for delay until the forthcoming Big Three meeting. Truman bluntly turned him down. For although Soviet friction with the Western

---

[13] Chandler, ed., *Eisenhower Papers*; *War Years*, IV: 2640, 2662. Cf. also Eisenhower to John Russell Deane, May 4, 1945, *ibid.*, p. 2679; Truman, *Year of Decisions*, pp. 241–244.
[14] *Foreign Relations, 1945*; *Conference of Berlin*, I: 3.
[15] *Ibid.*, p. 4.

powers developed over the issue of access routes to Berlin and de-layed the arrival of British and United States occupation forces in the city,[16] one overriding fear continued to bind Russians, Ameri-cans, and British closely together in Germany during the month of June. A Nazi revival of power amidst the ruins of Big Three discord over Germany was too terrible for anyone to seriously con-template.[17] The crude attempts by Admiral Doenitz in mid-May to create a rift between Anglo-Americans and Russians from his po-sition as final head of the Nazi government frightened the Western Allies, led to the Admiral's swift removal from all access to pow-er and influence, and tended to discourage any subsequent initia-tives by Western leaders to coerce Soviet behavior in Germany and elsewhere in Europe during the early summer of 1945.[18]

Truman's sense of restraint and his accommodation to the real-ities of Russian power in Europe were carried over into the United Nations Conference, where further agreements were concluded

[16] Feis, *Between War and Peace*, p. 143.

[17] "There's . . . *got* to be agreement" among the Big Four Allies, Marshal Zhukov told reporters at Berlin in mid-May, "if we don't want to play into the hands of the Germans." The Soviet de-Nazification campaign in Berlin during the nearly two months of sole Russian occupation seems to have been sincere and as thorough as time and chaos permitted. Werth, *Russia at War*, pp. 890, 894, 899; Erich Kuby, *The Russians and Berlin, 1945* (New York: Ballantine Books, 1969), pp. 302–303.

[18] Robert Murphy, *Diplomat among Warriors* (New York: Pyramid Books, 1965), pp. 272–273. The strenuous efforts of revisionist historians Gar Alperovitz and Gabriel Kolko to prove an intense and aggressive American interest in Eastern Europe throughout the spring and summer of 1945 are simply not supported by the published and unpublished records of the time. It is quite true that American repre-sentatives on the control commissions in Rumania and Bulgaria energetically con-tested Soviet efforts to promote Communist rule, to subvert non-Communist opposi-tion, and to impose a news "blackout." It is equally true that Harry Truman dreamed for a time of linking the "breadbasket" nations of Eastern Europe with the Western capitalistic heartland through internationalization of continental waterways. But at no time did the decision-makers in Washington allow idealistic hopes to conflict with Soviet power. When in August Maynard Barnes in Bulgaria went so far as to seek postponement of elections which would have been flagrantly rigged in direct vi-olation of the Declaration on Liberated Europe, he was sternly rebuked by Secretary of State James Byrnes, who refused to risk a direct confrontation with Soviet inter-ests and chose instead to maintain the fiction that the Bulgarian people were still sufficiently free—with the Red Army patrolling their streets—to shape their own po-litical destiny. As for Truman's aspiration for internationalization of *all* the world's waterways—including, it should not be forgotten, the Suez and Panama Canals—there is little evidence that this was ever a well-defined and coordinated or dog-gedly pursued policy within the American bureaucracy. Nor does evidence exist that the Truman administration ever seriously considered pursuing such a plan once Sta-lin contemptuously dismissed it at Potsdam. (Alperovitz, *Atomic Diplomacy*, pp. 137–233; Kolko, *Politics of War*, pp. 389–427; *Foreign Relations, 1945*; *Diplomatic Papers*, IV: 163–419, V: 474–666.)

concerning the respective spheres of postwar influence and interest of the Soviet and American governments. By the time of the San Francisco Conference the major substantive issues of structure and power distribution within the new international organization had already been largely resolved. At Dumbarton Oaks and at Yalta the outlines of the new league had been sketched. To many of the smaller states the result had seemed "a caricature of democracy in international relations," since it clearly "gave the Big Powers complete control in the . . . security organization."[19] Though drawn to San Francisco, many of the smaller nations hoped to modify, though they knew they could not change, certain aspects of the charter.

The two most important problems facing the American and Russian delegations, beyond the Polish question, revolved about the regional bloc and trusteeship issues, both of which drew the smaller powers in as interested participants. The salient achievement of the conference lay in the ultimate ability of the Big Three, still divided until near the very end over Poland, to fashion mutually acceptable compromises on these two potentially disruptive issues while maintaining a generally united front against the pretensions of the smaller nations for a more equitable balance of power in the organization.

The most stubborn East-West problem, save for Poland and for the final flareup over the veto question in early June, revolved around the place of regional pacts within the organization. Early in the conference the Russians became aware of what they considered "the enormous influence exercised by the Latin American Republics even including the very small ones." Molotov claimed that these states "seemed . . . to have a voice out of all proportion to their power and resources." The Soviets had been particularly incensed by the determination of the smaller Western Hemisphere nations to push the membership of Fascist Argentina while denying a like consideration to the Lublin Poles. The question was ultimately resolved on a *quid pro quo* basis—the Latins voting to seat the two Soviet Republics, Byelorussia and the Ukraine, promised

[19] Ciechanowski, *Defeat in Victory*, p. 349.

representation by the Yalta agreements, in exchange for the inclusion of Argentina.[20] Russian anger with the Latins was thus already high when the regional pact issue emerged, and it quickly built to new heights of indignation.

Basically the Soviets claimed to distrust any weakening of the international organization, which was, after all, rather firmly under the control of the Great Powers through the Security Council. The State Department, on the other hand, had committed itself at the recently concluded Chapultepec Conference to push for revisions of the Dumbarton Oaks outline, looking to the inclusion of largely autonomous regional pacts free from control by the Security Council. The response of the smaller nations, led by the Latin Americans, to this evidence of United States willingness to compromise had been enthusiastic. To the smaller nations the American proposal necessarily lessened the influence of the Great Power-dominated world organization over purely regional affairs and promised a degree of local autonomy in international relations which might even lead eventually to a reduction of American dominance over the Western Hemisphere.[21] The fact cannot be overemphasized that at San Francisco the initiative to make the Western Hemisphere a *de facto* American sphere of influence insofar as great power politics was concerned came as much from the Latin American delegates as from the State Department. Indeed, the American delegation itself soon split over the issue, with some members echoing the Soviet argument that regional blocs would drastically weaken the entire concept, fatally hindering the operation of the world organization. Others countered with the argument that, in line with the traditional Monroe Doctrine, the United States had committed itself to a regional pact arrangement through the elaboration of hemispheric defense policies and other collaborative efforts throughout the course of the war.[22]

20 *Foreign Relations, 1945; Diplomatic Papers,* I: 386–389, 482–501, 510.
21 *Ibid.,* pp. 591–597, 695.
22 *Ibid.,* pp. 662–698 *passim*; Arthur M. Vandenberg to Edward R. Stettinius, May 5, 1945, Correspondence, April–December 1945, Vandenberg Papers, William L. Clements Library, Ann Arbor, Michigan. America's role in generating hemispheric defense during World War II may be traced in William L. Langer and S. Everett Gleason, *The Undeclared War, 1940–1941* (New York: Harper & Brothers, 1953), pp. 147–168, 593–624. It is also briefly sketched in Dexter Perkins, *A History of the*

After several weeks of heated debate, Assistant Secretary of War John J. McCloy, who was his department's representative on the American delegation, phoned Henry Stimson and in a disjointed conversation revealed the depth of confusion and division within the United States contingent. McCloy stressed America's "very strong interest in being able to intervene promptly in Europe where . . . twice now within a generation we've been forced to send over our sons over some . . . relatively minor Balkan incident." Yet McCloy was also firmly attached to the regional pact idea, and so, he told Stimson, "I've been taking the position that we ought to have our cake and eat it too; that we ought to be free to operate under this regional arrangement in South America, at the same time intervene promptly in Europe, that we oughtn't to give away either." Stimson's response was a series of grunted affirmatives. Whether the Americans could "have our cake and eat it too" was ultimately up to the Latins on the one hand and the Russians on the other. As time passed the Latins grew increasingly shrill in their demands "for greater freedom for the existing inter-American system to act in matters of hemispheric concern." On May 15 Truman took a direct hand in events by promising the Latin Americans that he would conclude a postwar treaty "under which all the American Republics would assist each other against any aggressor, American or non-American." The Latins responded with effusive thanks.[23]

Truman's initiative might be interpreted as an aggressive act in which he threw down the gauntlet to the Russians and revealed in the process an insatiable American appetite to meddle and intervene anywhere and everywhere. But the act was far more apparent than real. In the first place, the President was acting in response to small power demands that great power influences be reduced in

Monroe Doctrine (Boston: Little, Brown and Company, 1955), pp. 353–364. David Green's brilliant essay, "The Cold War Comes to Latin America," appeared too late to be fully incorporated in the text. However, Green's emphasis upon Latin American desires in 1945 juridically to bind overweaning American political and economic power in the hemisphere through regional pact arrangements must be stressed in assessing South American behavior at the San Francisco Conference. See esp. pp. 157–158.

[23] "Telephone Conversation between the Secretary of War and Mr. McCloy in San Francisco," May 8, 1945, Stimson Papers, Box 420; Stettinius to Grew, May 6, 1945, *Foreign Relations, 1945*; *Diplomatic Papers*, I: 614, 731, 734–735; *New York Times*, May 16, 1945, p. 1:2–3.

local affairs. The Latins would find it much easier to restrain American power at the regional level than in the Security Council of the United Nations. Secondly, the Soviets, despite their virulent opposition to Latin American proposals, proved to be as interested as any other nation in provisions for autonomous regional security within the United Nations structure. How else could their determined quest for security against Germany through control of Eastern Europe be formally legitimatized in international law?[24] Indeed, as early as December 10, 1944, Stalin had begun to build his diplomatic wall around all sides of Germany by concluding a treaty with France aimed at preventing the rise of a Fourth Reich. For this treaty—and the policy it initiated—to have United Nations sanction and true international legitimacy the Soviets would be forced to acknowledge United States and Latin American demands for largely autonomous regional pacts. The Soviets clearly had as much to gain from such arrangements as did the United States and her Latin American neighbors. Thus when, on May 12, Eden proposed a draft article on regional pacts which sought to legitimatize their existence and function, while stressing the supremacy of the United Nations Organization, both Stettinius and Gromyko (who had replaced Molotov by this time) expressed great interest, and with Truman's promise to the Latin Americans three days later, the way was paved for a formal settlement between May 20 and 23.[25] From that settlement ultimately emerged not only the Organization of American States and NATO, but also the Warsaw Pact and COMECON.

The regional pact settlement greatly heartened the American delegates. Senator Vandenberg, whose suspicion of the Russians was exceeded only by his dislike of Franklin Roosevelt's policy toward them, confessed that:

> I am deeply impressed by what has happened. . . . At the outset many of the Nations were far, very far, apart. Our own delegation was not wholly united. The subject itself was difficult—how to *save* legitimate regionalism . . . and yet not destroy the essential over-all authority of

[24] *Foreign Relations*, 1945; *Diplomatic Papers*, I: 591–592.
[25] *Ibid.*, pp. 706–707, 819, 825–826.

the International Organization. By hammering it out . . . we have found an answer which satisfies practically everybody. In my view, that is the great hope for the League itself. If we do nothing more than create a constant forum where nations *must* face each other and *debate* their differences and strive for common ground, we shall have done infinitely much.[26]

The struggle over the trusteeship question was quieter but in some ways more intense. American officials had long been deeply remorseful over the disastrous results of national unpreparedness in the Pacific during the months following Pearl Harbor. By April of 1945 they were determined to claim the entire ocean rim from the Philippines, Okinawa, and Japan on around to the edge of the continental United States as a *de facto* postwar sphere of military influence. Roosevelt had conceived of the forthcoming United Nations trusteeships as the ideal means of fulfilling this policy. He envisaged the capture of as many trusteeships as were necessary to secure firm military and naval predominance over the entire ocean. Stimson and Forrestal were both skeptical of this line of approach, involving as it did the acquiescence of the other member nations. The two Secretaries wished to avoid any discussion of trusteeship at San Francisco, desiring instead a simple unilateral American declaration that this country would retain in peace those islands won by blood in war.[27] Addressing the United States delegation on the eve of the conference, Stimson told "how in this war" America "rescued Australia and the Philippines and was now engaged in rescuing the Dutch East Indies and China. Under these circumstances the character of the bases we were seeking did not at all represent exploitation or selfish conquest; they were policies of defense for the entire ocean and all its neighbors." America had never been an exploiting nation, Stimson loftily continued, and this was particularly true of the current war. The United States had for three and one-half years been selflessly "fighting a battle of freedom and justice." In conclusion, the Secretary of War recalled "that when he went to the Philippines in 1928 it had been his duty as

[26] Vandenberg and Morris, eds., *Private Papers of Senator Vandenberg*, pp. 197–198.

[27] Millis, ed., *Forrestal Diaries*, pp. 33, 44.

Governor-General to know the defense lines. Everyone knew then that Corregidor and the Philippines were defenseless" with the then current military power of the United States. It had been his unhappy fate, Stimson added, "that what he predicted would happen did happen [after Pearl Harbor]. . . . We tried to get arms to them but could not sail the seas or fly our planes because we were cut off by Jap held bases. We had to see those doomed men, the garrison at Corregidor, and the Commonwealth trampled under by unspeakable methods of warfare. . . ." Forrestal followed Stimson and fully supported his argument, concluding that "Power must remain with the people who hate power."[28]

When it became clear that neither the trusteeship nor regional pact questions could be ignored at San Francisco, Stimson and McCloy began to examine the possibility of balancing American desires for *de facto* spheres of influence in Latin America and the Pacific with similar Russian interests in Eastern Europe. Discussing the problem with McCloy the day after the conference opened, Stimson calmly observed that "our position in the western hemisphere and Russia's in the eastern hemisphere could be adjusted without too much friction."[29] It is not fanciful to presume that the Secretary had conveyed these thoughts to Truman the day before when the two first met to explore the atomic problem in depth.

At San Francisco the Americans did not try to hide the fact that they were tying the issue of trusteeship to national security and a Pacific sphere of influence. The Soviets in turn sought to modify the trusteeship concept in practice and limit it in time. However, the issue was not laced with the same rancor that had occasionally marked the debates over regional pacts. And ultimately the Russians allowed the United States to have its trusteeships pretty much as it had planned.[30]

The Americans, and particularly the Senate, War, and Navy Department representatives on the delegation, wanted United Nations trusteeships divided into "strategic" and "non-strategic" categories with the generous concern for training native populations in self-

[28] Stimson Diary, April 17, 1945; *Foreign Relations, 1945; Diplomatic Papers,* I: 311–318.
[29] Stimson Diary, April 26, 1945.
[30] *Foreign Relations, 1945; Diplomatic Papers,* I: 597, 612–615.

rule obviously subordinated to military considerations in those areas falling in the former category. On May 4 the Russians, French, and Chinese "indicated that they would in general go along with it."[31]

Two weeks later the Russians and Chinese changed their minds and suddenly disclosed that they jointly "wished to introduce the word 'independence' as an objective of the trusteeship system." The Americans, lining up with those imperial powers, Britain and France, whose colonial policies were supposedly anathema to democratic sensibilities, continued to press for use of the phrase first employed in the United States draft: " 'progressive development toward self-government.' " According to Commander Harold Stassen, who headed the American delegation to the Trusteeship Committee, "there was no limit to self-government. It might lead to independence. The word 'independence,' however, suggested full national independence and was a provocative word. Our position . . . was based on the feeling that we should not go beyond the area of agreement that was [initially] possible among the [five major] powers."[32]

By introducing the term *independence* into the trusteeship article the Soviets were obviously seeking to place some sort of time limit upon a development—American control of the Pacific and possibly elsewhere through trusteeship—which they were momentarily unable to combat. Stassen's weak defense of the weasel-worded phrase *progressive self-government* in turn revealed the extent of American determination to subvert possible aspirations for self-determination among the peoples of the Pacific to immediate, deeply felt national security needs.

In the following days, however, the Russians generally chose to exercise restraint in projecting both their proposal and the potential propaganda line—Soviet patronage of self-determination for all peoples—which lay behind it. State Department officials actively feared such a Soviet propaganda offensive,[33] but in the event the Russians did not make much of it. The Americans and British, in

[31] *Ibid.*, p. 598.
[32] *Ibid.*, p. 792.
[33] Cf. Grew to Stettinius, May 8, 1945, *ibid.*, p. 652.

turn, quickly perceived the folly of contesting the vibrant influence of independence. Within the week of May 18 a compromise agreement was worked out conceding that independence should be "a possible objective for 'trusteeship' territories" but that mere " 'self-government' should remain the objective for other territories such as the British Colonies."[34]

The Soviets, again joined initially by the Chinese, next sought to lock the other Great Powers into a specific series of steps and processes leading to the independence of the various trusteeships, and more fatiguing diplomacy ensued. These Russian probes, however, never materially threatened the American trusteeship position in the Pacific, although they did try American patience for a time. Insistent Soviet pressure, however, did lead to a major blunder on Stettinius' part that would have major repercussions upon the international diplomacy of the coming autumn. For when at last, at Stalin's direction, the Russians formally agreed to support the trusteeship compromise worked out during the week of May 18, Gromyko broached the subject of possible Russian participation in the trusteeship program. This was during the final days of the conference, and the euphoric Secretary of State, filled with joy at the coming end of a conference whose undoubted success was due in great measure to Russian compromise, eagerly responded. On June 23 he placed his government on public record as supporting the Soviet request.[35] Nothing good was to come of this generous impulse.

But conflict seemed far off in those happy final hours at San Francisco during the last week of June. A significant measure of cooperation and a significant degree of compromise had marked the deliberations and set the tone of Soviet-American relations. Indeed, both delegations found much in common in their frequent opposition to the aspirations of the smaller nations for a greater share of power within the international organization. As has been noted, the Soviets were completely exasperated for a time with the clamorous demands of the Latin Americans for inclusion of Argentina and United Nations recognition of regional pact arrangements. The Latins, in turn, were alienated by what they considered

---

[34] *New York Times*, May 25, 1945, p. 1:4.
[35] *Foreign Relations, 1945; Diplomatic Papers*, I: 1111–1117, 1428–1429.

arrogant Soviet obstructionism.[36] The Americans' frequent *bête noire* turned out to be the strident Australian, Dr. Evatt, who particularly angered Arthur Vandenberg. According to the Republican Senator, "the Australians were the ones that were throwing monkey-wrenches into the works" whenever discussion came around to questions involving relative power parity between the Big Five permanent members of the Security Council and the smaller nations.[37]

Countless frictions as well as major conflicts divided Soviet and United States delegates at San Francisco. The lack of independent decision-making powers within the Russian delegation constantly irritated the excitable Americans. On at least two occasions, once with respect to the trusteeship question and later in regard to the veto issue, Russian officials made tentative agreements which were soon repudiated by Moscow, thus necessitating long, and to the Americans, nerve-wracking, delays before the affairs were smoothed out to everyone's satisfaction.[38]

Nonetheless, at the end of May, despite—or very probably because of—the deliberate pace of the conference, knowledgeable American observers concluded that the meetings had ended their first four weeks "with more accomplishments than failures and with excellent prospects of attaining the goal which its sponsors established at Dumbarton Oaks nine months ago." Only the rumbling discontent of the small nations with the Yalta veto power agreement signalled the possibility of yet another crisis.[39] Of chief importance was the developing atmosphere of mutual esteem within which the Soviet and American delegates worked. Vandenberg, for example, remarked of Molotov that "He is an earnest, able man for whom I have come to have the profoundest respect—despite our disagreements."[40]

[36] On April 30 Vandenberg wrote that Molotov "has done more in four days to solidify Pan-America against Russia than anything that ever happened." Vandenberg and Morris, eds., *Private Papers of Senator Vandenberg,* p. 182.

[37] *Foreign Relations, 1945; Diplomatic Papers,* I: 843.

[38] Vandenberg and Morris, eds., *Private Papers of Senator Vandenberg,* pp. 199–203.

[39] *New York Times,* May 25, 1945, p. 1:4; *Foreign Relations, 1945; Diplomatic Papers,* I: 778–779.

[40] Vandenberg and Morris, eds., *Private Papers of Senator Vandenberg,* p. 184.

Thus the San Francisco Conference, while not fully reviving the elusive "spirit of Yalta," did serve to appreciably lessen recent Soviet-American, if not East-West, tensions. At only one point in the conference, during the first week in June, did despair of a successful outcome descend upon the American delegates, and it was quickly dissipated by the exertions of Harry Hopkins in Moscow. For the most part, despite constant irritations and frictions, American delegates at San Francisco felt that they could work with the Soviets, although the most suspicious among them, such as Vandenberg, believed that only firmness would bring results.

Doubtless the major substantive achievement of the San Francisco Conference, beyond the establishment of the United Nations itself, was the implicit acceptance by both Russians and Americans of the reality of postwar spheres of influence. While the Western powers *en bloc* still refused officially to recognize Eastern Europe as a current and future Soviet sphere of influence, Truman's refusal to maintain any troops there and his demonstrable determination to pull them back into their formal occupation zones in Germany and Austria so as to get on with the war against Japan could only have meant one thing to Stalin. Had the Generalissimo, as he now styled himself, been able to hear Stimson's remarks to McCloy concerning the respective Soviet and American hemispheric interests, he could have been even more certain of his intuition. As it was the Russians for their part did not at San Francisco significantly or at length obstruct proposals designed to make the Western Hemisphere and vast stretches of the Pacific an American sphere of influence. For this a growing number of American officials, including many in the State Department, led by the mercurial Secretary Stettinius, were increasingly appreciative.[41]

The new—or renewed—pattern of Big Three relations was clearly emerging by the third week of May. Truman had told Churchill in unmistakable terms that American troops would be withdrawn from advanced positions in Europe. Agreements on regional pacts and a tentative accord favorable to the United States

---

[41] Cf. "Address by Assistant Secretary of State Archibald MacLeish over the National Broadcasting System, May 26, 1945," U.S. Department of State *Bulletin*, XII (May 27, 1945), 950–952.

position on trusteeships were in the making at San Francisco. It was at this point that Truman dispatched Harry Hopkins to Moscow. The timing, purpose, and significance of the Hopkins mission have been matters of some dispute, particularly since Hopkins apparently received only verbal, not written, instructions from his President. Available evidence, the tenor of the conversations, and the agreements reached, when viewed in the context of the time, all suggest, however, that Hopkins' mission was principally aimed at burying the Polish issue once and for all[42] and at making clear to Stalin once again that America was not interested in expanding her influence east of the Elbe nor of contesting *de facto* Soviet predominance there. With these objectives achieved, the Hopkins-Stalin talks then proceeded to the most pressing problem facing the United States government at the moment—joint Russian and American action to end the Pacific war as rapidly and as cheaply as possible. The Hopkins mission was thus designed implicitly to clarify and ratify the new power relationships that World War II had created between Russia and the United States—power relationships that gave the Soviets a sphere of influence in Eastern Europe while the Americans dominated their own hemisphere and wide areas of the Pacific. On this foundation of *Realpolitik* rested the Soviet-American rapprochement of mid-1945.

[42] James F. Byrnes later asserted bluntly that the "principal cause of Hopkins' trip" was "the situation in Poland." *Speaking Frankly*, p. 63.

8

Healing the Breach--The Hopkins Mission

The origin of the Hopkins mission is not clearly traceable. But it is clear that by the second week in May events in Eastern Europe, the fears of Harriman, Kennan, and others concerning future Soviet intentions in China, and even the menacing movements of Tito in Venezia Giulia had obviously created a crisis mentality in the State Department. Showdown or negotiation seemed the only alternatives. Harriman, Bohlen, Grew, and the rest of the department opted for negotiation. The man who led them in this direction and decisively imposed his will upon Soviet-American relations at this critical juncture was Harry Truman. As early as April 30 Truman determined to dispatch to Moscow Roosevelt's most effective and influential contact with the Kremlin. This was only seventeen days after the torch was passed in Washington and but a week after the first full discussions between the new President and his advisers on the Polish issue. There is some evidence, though inconclusive, to indicate that Truman might have first broached the subject to James Byrnes and others on the train returning from Hyde Park on April 15.[1] Certainly he had firmed

[1] Byrnes, *Speaking Frankly*, p. 49.

up his decision by the end of the month; for on the thirtieth he sent for Joseph E. Davies, the former Ambassador to Moscow and notorious Russophile, and told him that he needed "personal, on-the-spot reports from men with judgment and experience" concerning the current attitudes of both the Prime Minister and the Generalissimo on the entire range of issues facing the Big Three. Truman then proposed to send Davies to Churchill! "Hopkins, I added, was to see Stalin in Moscow, and I considered both assignments to be of primary importance because it was imperative for me to know whether the death of Roosevelt had brought any important changes in the attitudes of Stalin and Churchill."[2]

Not until May 4, however, two days before Churchill's first strong plea for an early meeting of the Big Three, did the President call in the perennially ill Hopkins and successfully urge upon him the trip to Moscow despite his clearly failing health. According to Truman, both Byrnes, the presumptive heir apparent to the Secretaryship of State, and the State Department itself opposed the Hopkins mission. Cordell Hull supported the initiative, however, and Truman pressed on with it,[3] once again overriding his cautious and suspicious diplomats in favor of a policy of accommodation with the Russians.

Yet it was not until May 19 that Hopkins went to the White House to receive his final instructions. Why the delay? There are a number of possible explanations. The most obvious centers around Hopkins' health. He apparently spent most of early May in bed, where Averell Harriman and Charles Bohlen found him when they returned from California on May 12. But Hopkins was not in materially better health on the day of his departure, which was the twenty-third.[4] The anxieties and actions of Harriman and Bohlen suggest a second reason for Hopkins' delay, namely, that Truman, in the face of State Department opposition, sought to rouse more support for the Hopkins endeavor before allowing it to proceed. Harriman and Bohlen played right into the President's hand.

The Ambassador to Russia and his aide had passed the previous three weeks in San Francisco, where Harriman's continued preoc-

---

[2] Truman, *Year of Decisions*, p. 129.
[3] *Ibid.*, p. 287.
[4] Sherwood, *Roosevelt and Hopkins*, II: 536; Leahy, *I Was There*, p. 369.

cupation with promoting American influence in Eastern Europe had caused him mounting agony as he perceived the American delegation at many points giving way to Soviet designs. He tried to warn his colleagues, reminding them "of the Russian attempt to chisel, by bluff, pressure, and other unscrupulous methods to get what they wish." Yet what in fact could be done to reverse this trend with regard to Eastern Europe? Harriman had no answer. "While we cannot go to war with Russia," he said, "we must do everything we can to maintain our position as strongly as possible in Eastern Europe."[5] But how? That was the problem which continued to torment the Ambassador, which caused "despair in the heart" as he and Bohlen gloomily discussed what they fancied to be the progressive deterioration in Soviet-American relations during the long plane trip across springtime America back to Washington. With considerable trepidation Bohlen "suggested the possibility that President Truman might send Hopkins to Moscow to talk things out directly with Stalin and Molotov." Bohlen's hesitancy was due to the belief that Harriman might resent Hopkins' intrusion upon his ambassadorial domain. But Harriman had apparently worked himself up to such an emotional state that he agreed with the suggestion at once and enthusiastically. Arriving in Washington, Harriman and Bohlen immediately rushed to Hopkins' bedside in Georgetown and proposed the trip. According to his biographer, Hopkins' response was at first sanguine at the thought of the possibilities of such a mission, then despondent at the realization that his intimate identification with Roosevelt might well alienate the Presidential successor, who was busy building his own administration. The only explanations that satisfactorily account for Hopkins' strange response at this point, eight days after Truman had already talked to him, are either that his illness had caused him to forget his earlier interview with the President—which is unlikely—or that he was playing the President's game, building support for his mission. The latter explanation seems far more likely. Whatever the facts, Harriman was not put off and drove on to the White House to obtain Truman's approval.[6]

[5] *Foreign Relations, 1945; Diplomatic Papers*, I: 389–390.
[6] Sherwood, *Roosevelt and Hopkins*, II: 535–536.

Truman's outward response was cool, though inwardly he must have been delighted. He simply told Harriman that "he was much interested in the idea but would need some time to think it over."[7] Two days later, however, the fire, which the President had apparently kindled himself, roared higher as Admiral Leahy "broached to the President the desirability of a three-power meeting," and the following morning, May 15, in a conference with State Department officials, Truman was further pressed by Harriman, Bohlen, and Grew to assent to a meeting with Churchill and Stalin before July. Here was a perfect opportunity for the President to justify the Hopkins and Davies missions to himself and his colleagues as necessary preliminaries to a summit conference. For Truman was simply unwilling to leave the country before the end of June. The domestic problems which interested him most were crowding about. In response to the urgings of his three State Department advisers the President said "that he agreed . . . but that his difficulty was that he had a number of pressing domestic questions particularly the preparation of a budget message before the end of the fiscal year which made it difficult for him to leave before then."[8] Four days later Hopkins received his instructions from Truman, and four days after that he departed for Moscow, while Davies proceeded to London.

So much for the timing of the mission. What of its motivation? Was it a deliberate attempt to delay a diplomatic showdown with the Russians in both Europe and the Far East until the atomic bomb came into existence as the "master card" of American power? Much has been made in this connection of the alleged "secrecy" of the Hopkins trip—apparently none of those in the State Department who should have been notified were told of the mission until the very eve of Hopkins' departure. However true this may have been, there is nothing sinister about it. Gar Alperovitz's horror over the fact that the Secretary of State and others were not informed is a bit contrived.[9] A number of explanations for Truman's

[7] *Ibid.*, p. 536.

[8] Leahy, *I Was There*, p. 369; Grew, *Turbulent Era*, II: 1462–1464; *Foreign Relations, 1945; Conference of Berlin*, I: 12–14.

[9] Alperovitz, *Atomic Diplomacy*, pp. 68–71, 270–275. The integrity of Alperovitz's scholarship has recently been attacked by Robert James Maddox: "*Atomic Di-*

reticence come to mind, each of which plausibly fits into the pattern of continuing Presidential determination to pursue a generous policy toward the Russians. In the first place, the Secretary of State was fully occupied in San Francisco with the multitudinous problems involved in bringing the United Nations Organization into being. Secondly, Truman was simply following a Rooseveltian precedent in launching a diplomatic initiative without prior and full consultation with the State Department, Admiral Leahy, or anyone else. Third, Truman did speak at length with Grew, Leahy, Harriman, and Bohlen about the early resumption of personal, high-level, Soviet-American negotiations before Hopkins was officially sent on his way, and the Hopkins mission was fully in accordance with the consensus reached by the President and his advisers. Fourth, because of Hopkins' health, his departure or even his ability to undertake the trip may have been a questionable factor until that last moment when both Stalin and the Presidential advisers were simultaneously informed of the trip. Fifth, Truman may have been waiting day-by-day until a markedly favorable trend in Soviet-American relations should manifest itself (the agreements at San Francisco between May 18 and May 20 on regional pacts and trusteeships may well have been the sign Truman was waiting for). And, finally, Truman's desire for "secrecy"—if such it was—*vis-à-vis* the State Department fits in perfectly with the thesis that, far from trying to deceive the Russians as to American intentions, he really did mean to placate them in the sincere spirit of wartime comradeship that had marked his predecessor's efforts to work with the Kremlin. For it had been the State Department, after all, that had so frequently joined Churchill in the first month of Truman's Presidency to demand a much tougher line toward the Russians. Since the Hopkins mission was designed instead to accelerate the slowly emerging trend toward the healing of relations between Washington and Moscow, the President had very good reasons for keeping the news of Hopkins' departure and his instructions from the men at State. In this connection it should be noted that Truman at this time exhibited a carefully stated but unmis-

plomacy: A Study in Creative Writing," *Journal of American History*, LIX (March 1973), 925–934.

takable impatience with State Department jeremiads against the Russians. This applied particularly to Harriman, who was politely but obviously told by the President at the May 15 meeting to stop running about the United States making anti-Soviet speeches and to get back to Moscow where he belonged.[10]

The most persuasive explanation for the Hopkins mission is also the most obvious. On April 30, when Truman first decided to send personal envoys to both Churchill and Stalin, and again on May 4, when he called Hopkins in, the White House—as well as the entire United States—was caught up in the excitement of the war's end in Europe. During the last few days of April and into early May, "Every day brought important developments or sensational rumors."[11] In this atmosphere it was inevitable that the new President's sense of satisfaction should be strongly diluted by an awesome realization of what still seemed to lie ahead in the Pacific. Only half the battle had been won. Another, greater and more costly, invasion must be mounted, and another long and desperate and bloody battle remained to be fought in the Far East before the Second World War could be brought to an end. Inevitably, the official attention which had become increasingly fixed upon the military situation in Asia would now become riveted there. Was continued East-West conflict over Poland worth the chance of a Russian reversal of the Crimean Far Eastern accords? And what of the bomb at this time? Surely it would be used when available. But it would not be available for at least another two months. And would it be available at all? The influential Admiral Leahy, who constantly paraded his expertise in high explosives, thought the atomic quest " 'the biggest fool thing we have ever done.' " " 'The bomb will never go off,' " he told Truman at about this time, " 'and I speak as an expert in explosives.' "[12] And even if available, how much *more* destructive would one or even three or four atomic bombs be than the hideous mass fire bomb raids currently being mounted as a matter of routine against Japanese cities? As late as 1949 Presidential scientific advisers were still debating that ques-

[10] *Foreign Relations, 1945; Conference of Berlin,* I: 14.
[11] Leahy, *I Was There,* p. 356.
[12] Quoted in Truman, *Year of Decisions,* p. 21.

tion, though the Russians never did.[13] Despite Stimson's eloquent preachments on its enormous destructive force, the atomic bomb was simply too slender a reed for any responsible diplomatist to rely upon in May and June of 1945, no matter what his feelings were toward Soviet Russia. And Truman's sentiments toward the Kremlin were far from hostile at this time. Indeed, the President's motives in sending Davies to London as well as Hopkins to Moscow reflected a determination to maintain the Soviet attachment even at the risk of weakening the British alliance. It is against this background that the President's controversial curtailment of lend-lease must be viewed.

The abrupt curtailment of lend-lease after V-E Day did not represent a conscious effort to restrain Soviet behavior in Eastern Europe, as some have charged.[14] It stemmed from a variety of conflicting decisions which neatly dovetailed to create an unhappy result. According to Truman himself, Joseph Grew and Foreign Economic Administrator Leo Crowley came in on May 8 with an unsigned order, supposedly prepared at Roosevelt's direction, authorizing the Foreign Economic Administration and the State Department to cut back severely lend-lease supplies to the Allies upon Germany's surrender. Feeling that the order made "good sense," the President, according to his account, "reached for my pen and, without reading the document, . . . signed it." Almost immediately a storm of anger and recrimination broke forth from the Allies as Crowley used the order in draconian fashion, "even to the extent of having some of the ships" already at sea "turned around and brought back to American ports for unloading." Faced with the sharp Allied reaction, led by the Russians, Truman rescinded the order and subsequently sought to clarify American lend-lease policy in terms of further extension—but only if such aid should be directly

---

[13] "The fire raids upon Japan were much more terrible, ... It was indeed the bizarre nature of the bomb, and the uncanny sort of future it suggested, rather than its actual results in the war, that impressed people." Vannevar Bush, *Modern Arms and Free Men* (New York: Simon and Schuster, 1949), p. 91.

[14] See, for example, Alperovitz, *Atomic Diplomacy*, pp. 35–39; Barton J. Bernstein, "American Foreign Policy and the Origins of the Cold War," in Barton J. Bernstein, ed., *Politics and Policies of the Truman Administration* (Chicago: Quadrangle Books, 1970), pp. 27–28.

employed in the war against Japan.[15] In fact, the story was more complex than the President has suggested, and the chief victim of his action was not Russia, but Britain.

At the Second Quebec Conference in September of 1944 Churchill had at last managed to persuade Roosevelt of the desperate straits of the British economy. As a consequence the two had agreed that during the period between the end of the war in Europe and victory in the Pacific the United States would continue to supply England with sufficient "food, shipping and goods," as well as ammunition, so as to "free" at least a part of "British labour for essential civilian tasks. The supplies, as before, would be in the form of lend-lease." In other words, Roosevelt agreed to use lend-lease aid as a *de facto* wartime loan to Britain. However, during the first months of 1945 the British became aware of strong pressures within the American government to reverse this policy. In April the British Ambassador warned his government to expect " 'something like a crisis' " within the next several months over lend-lease.[16]

The crisis was not long in appearing. On April 26 Budget Director Harold Smith spoke to Truman about the forthcoming lend-lease appropriations to be submitted to Congress. Smith had already established a strong influence over Truman, evidenced by the President's constant allusion to his need to stay home to work on fiscal matters. Now the President, perhaps aware—perhaps not—of the Roosevelt-Churchill lend-lease agreement of the previous September, told Smith that he knew that there was "a good deal of isolationist propaganda under various guises at the present time" on Capitol Hill, "and the isolationist spirit might break out into the open." Truman added that "he did know what was bothering the Senate. He was very clear that if we use lend-lease for rehabilitation purposes we will open ourselves to a lot of trouble." This would be particularly the case, the President went on, should lend-lease be employed in such a way as to constitute a unilateral loan to Britain. Not only would Congress be up in arms, but so would the Russians. Smith replied that "while I did not pretend to be an

---

[15] Truman, *Year of Decisions*, pp. 254–259.
[16] Ehrman, *Grand Strategy*, pp. 241–243.

expert in these matters, it would seem to me that such arrangements would only serve to give Russia an excuse, if she needed one, for similar unilateral arrangements," *i.e.*, in Eastern Europe. "The President said, 'I think you have something there.' "[17]

On May 11, after the initial curtailment order had been released and while Crowley was enthusiastically at work implementing it, Stimson approached Truman "to give my views of the necessity of a more realistic policy in regard to the Russians and the use of Lend Lease towards them." Stimson argued that with the war in Europe at an end, the Soviets should cease to enjoy the special privileges granted them under the lend-lease protocol. Truman's response was "enthusiastic," but not for the reasons which Stimson may have anticipated. Truman "said it was right down his alley. He was trying to pull in the extravagance. . . ." In other words, he was responding to growing Congressional pressures for a cutback in wartime spending. The ever-pugnacious State Department, which does seem to have been thinking of using lend-lease aid as an economic club against the Soviets, happily seized the initiative, sending Stimson, among others, "a proposed aide-memoire to the Russians telling them that we could no longer give them everything they wanted and they must apply and justify their needs in the same way others did." Truman's desire to appease Congress with lend-lease curtailment thus served the needs of the State Department hard-liners quite well, and according to Stimson, Grew "seemed very much pleased" by the decision to cut lend-lease shipments across the board.[18]

[17] Harold D. Smith Diary, April 26, 1945.

[18] Stimson Diary, May 11, 1945. It would be erroneous to assume that *everyone* in the State Department looked upon lend-lease as strictly a weapon to mold Soviet conduct in Eastern Europe. In a mildly written memo to his chief, Will Clayton, in mid-April, Emilio Collado recalled that "It is the announced policy of the American Government to use lend-lease only for war purposes." Collado then discussed the current status of lend-lease aid to each of the Allied nations. Coming to the Soviet Union, Collado admitted, "There is no provision in the Lend-Lease Act or in the Master Agreement with Russia, that would require the discontinuance of lend-lease aid on V-E Day if Russia is not in the Pacific war at that time." Nonetheless, "If Russia does not enter the Pacific war lend-lease shipments should stop as of V-E Day, unless overriding political and military considerations make such a step unwise." And, if possible, Collado continued, "arrangements should be made, in accordance with the terms of the Master Agreement, for the recapture of any lend-lease supplies now in the possession of Russia that are needed in the Pacific war, or would otherwise be useful to the United States." It is clear from these remarks

The new American lend-lease policy was summed up in a statement issued by Stettinius at San Francisco on May 15:

> The central principle which has been applied in the administration of lend-lease in the past and will continue to be applied now that the war is over in Europe is the same for all countries.
>
> Lend-lease *has been* and *will be* supplied to our Allies—be it the Soviet Union, United Kingdom, France, the Netherlands or other countries—on the scale which is necessary to achieve final victory as speedily and effectively as possible. . . .
>
> In the practical application of this fundamental principle, the type and quantity of supplies furnished any country has always been and will continue to be reviewed and adjusted in the light of changing circumstances of the war.

In one respect this statement represented a clear victory for the State Department. By asserting that lend-lease aid would be dispensed in the same way to all countries, it promised an end to the special immunity from justification of requests which the Russians had enjoyed throughout the war. Indeed, Grew himself specifically stipulated on May 14 that from then on "lend lease shipments to the Soviet Union be reviewed and continued where they are justified on the basis of adequate information regarding the essential nature of Soviet military supply requirements and in the light of competing demands."[19]

Stalin reacted unhappily to the new policy. He complained to Hopkins in Moscow several weeks later that the "scornful and abrupt manner" in which lend-lease aid had been cut off and then resumed under new and stricter provisions symbolized a rapid cooling in Soviet-American relations following the German surrender. Hopkins, however, was able to "satisfy fully" the Soviets, to use Stalin's term, that lend-lease aid was never intended to influence

that if Collado entertained any hope of "coercing the Russians through lend-lease," it lay in the direction of trying to force the Russians into an early entry into the Pacific war by a dramatic American demonstration that lend-lease was strictly a wartime measure to be enjoyed only by those engaged in battle. Memo from Emilio Collado to Will Clayton, "Lend-Lease Policy at the End of the European War," April 18, 1945, Records of the Department of State, decimal file 840.24/4-1845, National Archives.

[19] U.S. Department of State *Bulletin*, XII (May 20, 1945), 940; McNeill, *America, Britain, and Russia*, p. 24.

Russian actions, and in July the Russians were granted additional generous lend-lease shipments for their effort against Japan.[20]

It was the British who suffered the major blow. For the new American policy abrogated the earlier Roosevelt-Churchill accord. Despite repeated pleas and urgings from both Churchill and the British Chiefs of Staff before and during the Potsdam Conference, American lend-lease aid to England continued to be dispensed in such a stiff and correct fashion that neither a suspicious American public nor the Soviet diplomatic corps could complain that the United States was seeking to restore the economic health of the British Isles through the program. As late as mid-July "the U.S. War Department informed the Joint Staff Mission that in future no military supplies could be made available" to Britain "under lend-lease except for direct employment against Japan."[21]

Truman's actions in mid-May exemplified a determination not only to avoid special economic relations with Britain, but also to keep American foreign policy regarding Russia free of identification with the Churchill government. The President made his position clear in an exchange of cables with the Prime Minister on the eleventh and twelfth and through the Davies mission. On the eleventh Churchill urged Truman to "come here in the earliest days of July and that we leave together to meet U.J. ["Uncle Joe"—Stalin] at wherever is the best point outside Russian-occupied territory to which he can be induced to come." Truman's response of the following day—dispatched either just before or just after hearing Harriman propose a Hopkins mission to Moscow—was rather chilly. "I would much prefer to have Stalin propose the meeting, . . ." the President said, adding: "When and if such a meeting is arranged, it appears to me that in order to avoid any suspicion of our 'ganging up' it would be advantageous for us to proceed to the meeting place separately."[22]

A fortnight later Davies stunned the British upon his arrival in London with the assertion that the Americans wished to meet *first* with the Russians "and that the representatives of His Ma-

[20] Truman, *Year of Decisions*, p. 256; Sherwood, *Roosevelt and Hopkins*, II: 546, 547; *Entry of the Soviet Union into the War Against Japan*, pp. 74–75.
[21] Ehrman, *Grand Strategy*, pp. 242–243.
[22] Truman, *Year of Decisions*, p. 286.

jesty's Government should be invited to join a few days later."
Churchill "reacted violently against this" proposal, and Truman
later wrote that "I had at no time proposed seeing Stalin alone at
any separate conference."[23]

Whether Davies had either carelessly or willfully misunderstood
his instructions is a fascinating question. Eden, for one, thought
that he had.[24] But Admiral Leahy has flatly stated that "One of
the requests that the President had asked Davies to put to Churchill was that he, Truman, would like to see Stalin alone before
the tripartite conference opened."[25] Certainly the fact that Truman
had seen fit to send to Churchill's side a man whose Russophilia
was notorious, a man certain to make—as indeed he did make—
"an unfavorable impression" upon British officials, who considered
him "a vain amateur" at best and a "born appeaser" at worst, argues
that the President longed to set out upon an independent diplomatic course toward warmer and closer relations with the Russians,
even at the expense of the British.[26]

But the argument that Truman used various pressures from
Churchill, Grew, Harriman, Bohlen, and Leahy for his own purposes—namely, to cultivate the Soviet alliance rather than to risk
its dissolution through showdown—is most thoroughly supported
not only by the words of Davies at London but by the deeds of
Hopkins at Moscow.

In his first conversations with Stalin between May 26 and May
31—conversations from which the British representatives in Moscow were conspicuously excluded[27]—Hopkins conceded every
point concerning the Polish issue to the Russian dictator. Having

---

23 *Ibid.*, p. 289; Churchill, *Triumph and Tragedy*, pp. 492–496; Eden, *The Reck-oning*, p. 623; Leahy, *I Was There*, p. 379.

24 Eden, *The Reckoning*, p. 623. On his way back to Washington Davies stopped at Eisenhower's headquarters and lunched with the general's naval aide, Capt. Harry C. Butcher, who recorded in his diary that evening that Davies had said that "The President had been explicit in his direction that nothing should be done which would give the Russians the idea that the British and Americans were ganging up on them." Very probably Davies decided on his own to blunt British hopes for bilateral Anglo-American talks before Potsdam by raising the possibility of private Soviet-American conversations. Cf. Capt. Harry C. Butcher, *My Three Years with Eisen-hower* (New York: Simon and Schuster, 1946), pp. 855–856.

25 Leahy, *I Was There*, p. 379.

26 Eden, *The Reckoning*, pp. 623–624; Leahy, *I Was There*, pp. 378–380.

27 "Memorandum by Harry Hopkins," Washington, June 13, 1945, *Foreign Re-lations, 1945; Diplomatic Papers*, V: 337–338.

first conveyed to Stalin the President's acceptance of a Big Three meeting in or near Berlin during the middle of July,[28] Hopkins turned immediately to Poland. While he impressed upon the Generalissimo "in unmistakable terms how greatly . . . disturbed" Truman and the American people were "with the action of the Soviet Government in relation to Poland," Hopkins repeatedly emphasized the fact

> that the United States was not only not interested in the establishment of a *cordon sanitaire* around Russia, but on the contrary was aggressively opposed to it; that the United States had no economic interests of substantial importance in Poland and that we believed that the United States, the Soviet Union and England in working together to help create a new Polish state that would be friendly to Russia could have an immense moral and political effect in the task of bringing about genuine Polish-Soviet friendship.

Hopkins later "said he wished to state here and now that the United States did not desire to have involved in the execution of the Crimea Decision any present agents of the London Government, whether in Poland or out."[29]

Here was the American position baldly presented to Stalin. It openly invited the Generalissimo's determined statements that the Polish government must be organized his way. Elections there would ultimately be, but basic freedoms of political action and association could not be permitted, Stalin asserted, before Nazism and Fascism were extirpated within Poland and throughout Europe. While the American principles of democracy "are well known and would find no objection on the part of the Soviet Government," nonetheless "specific freedoms" could only be applied in Poland "in full in peace time and even then with certain limitations." Hopkins' response signalled his capitulation. "Mr. Hopkins said he thoroughly understood the Marshal's opinions."[30]

Capitulation, in turn, paved the way for agreement and unity. Stalin graciously agreed at first that Mikolajczyk and one London Pole should come to Moscow and resume negotiations with mem-

[28] Feis, *Between War and Peace*, pp. 139–140.
[29] *Foreign Relations, 1945; Diplomatic Papers*, V: 300–301, 306.
[30] *Ibid.*, p. 302, 303.

bers of the existing Polish provisional government and with certain others residing in Poland but not then members of that government. Ultimately it was decided that no more than five non-Lublin Poles from within the country would join no more than three, including Mikolajczyk, from the London government-in-exile in negotiating with eight Lublin representatives for permanent reorganization of the existing provisional government.

Hopkins then cabled Truman on May 30 the erroneous interpretation that Stalin "is prepared to return to and implement the Crimea decision and permit a representative group of Poles to come to consult with the Commission." The Poles so mentioned were not representative at all. They first had passed through Stalin's screening process, to which Hopkins completely deferred. Each was individually examined and passed upon by the Generalissimo in conversations with Hopkins between May 28 and May 30, and their cases were reviewed again before final selection in the Hopkins-Stalin talks of May 31. Nearly all—with the possible exception of Mikolajczyk—were thus acceptably pliable to the Soviets and their Lublinite followers in the existing Polish provisional government. After his discussions with Stalin on May 31, Hopkins asked Truman to accept the list he and Stalin had jointly agreed upon. "In recommending this to you," Hopkins cabled, "I believe that this carries out the Yalta agreement in all its essential aspects." Truman happily chose to ignore the fact that the accord did no such thing when he signalled his agreement to Moscow.[31]

The following day the enthusiastic President wired Churchill that "Harry Hopkins has just sent me a most encouraging message about the Polish situation." Then, after outlining the Stalin-Hopkins agreements, the President concluded: "I feel that this represents a very encouraging, positive step in the long drawn out Polish negotiations, and I hope that you will approve the list as agreed to in order that we may get on with this business as soon as possible." Not until June 9 did the dejected Churchill respond. His reply indicated a deep awareness of how thoroughly he and his country had been shouldered aside by the brash and impatient Americans on an

---

[31] *Ibid.*, pp. 307–308; Truman, *Year of Decisions*, p. 293.

issue that had been of central importance to British foreign policy for years. "I agree with you," the Prime Minister wired, that Hopkins "has obtained the best solution we could hope for in the circumstances, . . ." though "he has not obtained substantial satisfaction on any of Mikolajczyk's points."[32] Mikolajczyk himself seemed more resigned to the situation. He quickly agreed to go to Moscow and negotiate his way into the provisional government, obviously under the impression that he could do more to influence future developments in Poland from inside the new government than beyond.[33]

Having finally bargained away any significant American influence in Poland, Hopkins found his attempts to secure the release of the sixteen Polish political prisoners incarcerated in March utterly frustrated. Hopkins' approach to Stalin on the matter was characteristically conciliatory and deferential. On June 3 he cabled Truman that "I specifically exempted from the discussion anyone charged with killing Russians and confined my discussion to those who were charged only with possession of illegal radio transmitters." But despite the American warning that the case had dangerously stirred up public opinion in the United States and that failure to resolve the problem "would stir up endless trouble and probably take most of the time" of the forthcoming Potsdam Conference, Stalin refused to make any commitments. There was no reason for him to do so. One far less astute and determined than the Generalissimo would have perceived by this time that any policy of evasion mingled with deceit and determination concerning Poland would soon wear down the Americans. After further desultory discussion, Hopkins was forced to console himself and his President with the impression that the Russians were taking the issue under advisement.[34]

And so the melancholy affair of Poland wound down to its inevitable end. Stalin had secured a complete victory as the attitudes of Hopkins and Truman guaranteed that he would.

---

[32] *Foreign Relations, 1945; Diplomatic Papers,* V: 314, 334.
[33] "Chargé to Polish Government in Exile (Schoenfeld) to Secretary of State, June 2, 1945," *ibid.,* pp. 316–317.
[34] *Ibid.,* 318–319.

Although no written record of Hopkins' instructions apparently exists, there is absolutely no doubt that his posture at Moscow faithfully reflected the wishes of his President. Truman made his position crystal clear at his press conference on June 13 when formally announcing the final agreements reached at Moscow on Poland. "The all important thing which confronts us," the President told his fellow citizens, "is that the unity, mutual confidence, and respect which resulted in the [European] military victory should be continued to make secure a just and durable peace." He simply dodged questions about the ultimate fate of the sixteen Poles then in Russian hands. "I want to make no statements that will in any way embarrass the Russian government." And he added, "At least, we are in a much better position now than we were before Mr. Hopkins went to Moscow and Mr. Davies went to London."[35]

Others were not so certain. Jan Ciechanowski, the London Polish Ambassador to the United States, called at the State Department the day of the Presidential press conference to state frankly "his feeling that he did not expect a satisfactory solution from the coming talks among Polish leaders in Moscow. His principal complaint was that we had consented to hold the talks before obtaining the release of the sixteen Polish leaders."[36] Ciechanowski's concern was underscored and justified by the sudden trial of the sixteen on June 17, the day after negotiations began among the various Poles in Moscow.[37] Yet the United States government did nothing. When the Poles in Moscow finally did come to an agreement on allocation of offices in late June, the new provisional government immediately came into being. It was quickly recognized by the United States, which peremptorily severed relations with the London Poles, who reacted with great grief and bitterness.[38]

Senator Vandenberg quickly registered his displeasure with the Polish settlement. Possessed of a large Polish-American constituency, the Senator on July 9 wrote Grew to inform him bluntly "that

[35] Truman, *Public Papers, 1945*, pp. 120–122.
[36] *Foreign Relations, 1945; Diplomatic Papers*, V: 338.
[37] Harriman to Secretary of State, June 17, 18, 1945, *ibid.*, pp. 346–349.
[38] Harriman to Secretary of State, June 21, 1945, *ibid.*, pp. 352–353; "Statement of the President, July 5, 1945," in U.S. Department of State *Bulletin*, XIII (July 8, 1945), 47; Ciechanowski, *Defeat in Victory*, pp. 385–386.

the settlement of the Polish question thus far made is inadequate and unconvincing to millions of our citizens among whom I may say that I am numbered." "I wish to inquire," Vandenberg continued, "whether our responsibility under the Yalta agreement is presumed to have been discharged by the creation of this new Provisional Government?" Vandenberg then proceeded to answer his own rhetorical question in the negative. "There still seems to be no clear assurance that the Polish people will themselves have the final opportunity of untrammelled self-determination."[39] Fortunately for American policy-makers, Vandenberg had access only to the bare textual statement of the Soviet-American accords on Poland and not to the full transcript of the Hopkins-Stalin talks.

Stalin had characteristically conceded something to the Americans in exchange for United States acquiescence in the Soviet solution to the Polish crisis. In front of Hopkins on June 6, the Generalissimo overrode Molotov and agreed to accept the interpretation of the United States and all the other member countries concerning voting procedures in the United Nations Security Council. According to Hopkins' account, Stalin claimed that he had misunderstood the nature of the problem, and he gave in swiftly over Molotov's protests.[40] The way was thus cleared for the successful completion of the United Nations Charter. The following day in San Francisco the mercurial Vandenberg, who but a week before had written that the conference was "at its lowest ebb today" and who would soon condemn the means of its rescue, wrote jubilantly, "*America* wins! The 'veto' crisis broke today—and it broke *our* way."[41]

More than the veto crisis or even the Polish issue had been solved by the Hopkins and Davies missions. Truman had successfully asserted his own diplomatic goals and had seen them achieved. There would be no diplomatic showdown with the Russians in Eastern Europe employing existing military force and occupation as the

---

[39] Vandenberg to Grew, July 9, 1945, in U.S. Department of State *Bulletin*, XIII (July 22, 1945), 109.

[40] *Foreign Relations, 1945; Diplomatic Papers*, V: 330–331.

[41] Vandenberg and Morris, eds., *Private Papers of Senator Vandenberg*, p. 208; Unpublished entry, May 31, 1945, Arthur M. Vandenberg Diary, 1945, Vandenberg Papers; U. S. Department of State *Bulletin*, XII (June 10, 1945), 1043.

pawn. There would be no economic coercion of the Soviets through lend-lease or any other medium. Following the lead of his predecessor, *Truman wished to be rid of the burden of Eastern Europe beyond the point where American advisory and consultative rights had been satisfied.* He wished to clear his decks of the complex problems involved in the political reconstruction of the countries east of the Elbe, and Hopkins had done that for him. The price paid was the total sacrifice by Washington of British interests. London, increasingly aware of its impotent and deteriorating position within the Grand Alliance, could only acquiesce. Now planning could proceed in uncluttered fashion for the forthcoming Potsdam Conference. As Truman had said to the press on June 13, "In other words, Mr. Churchill, Mr. Stalin and the President of the United States must be able to meet and talk and trust each other in that we want to believe that each of us wants a just and durable peace. That is one of the reasons for the preliminary visits of Mr. Hopkins and Mr. Davies. . . ."[42]

Even Harriman expressed satisfaction over Hopkins' mission. " 'Hopkins did a first-rate job,' " Harriman admitted to Truman. The Ambassador ruefully admitted " 'that Stalin does not and never will fully understand our interest in a free Poland as a matter of principle. The Russian Premier is a realist in all of his actions, and it is hard for him to appreciate our faith in abstract principles.' "[43]

The President's critics within the State and Navy Departments were forced to acknowledge a major upswing in international affairs by the end of the first week in June with the success of the Hopkins mission and the final subsidence of the Trieste and Val d'Aosta crises. Grew was particularly elated at the "great progress on the international crises that had been active during the past ten days."[44] Europe at long last seemed to be calming down despite Stalin's continuing displeasure over the persistent unwillingness of the American government to grant outright recognition to the Soviet-dominated governments of Hungary, Bulgaria, and Rumania.[45] The success of the San Francisco Conference at long last

[42] Truman, *Public Papers, 1945,* pp. 120–122.
[43] Quoted in Truman, *Year of Decisions,* pp. 292–293.
[44] Grew, *Turbulent Era,* II: 1518; Millis, ed., *Forrestal Diaries,* p. 67.
[45] Stalin to Truman, June 23, 1945, *Foreign Relations, 1945; Conference of Ber-*

was assured. The prospects for significant achievements at Potsdam seemed bright.

But transcending all of these crucial considerations was the Pacific war. Soviet participation in that conflict was obviously deemed essential by both Truman and Hopkins, not only for its undoubted military value, but also as a symbol of continuing Big Three unity. No more fascinating nor more important conversations took place between Stalin and Hopkins at Moscow in late May and early June than those relating to East Asia and the entry of the Soviet Union into the war against Japan.

The Hopkins-Stalin talks on the Far East took only a portion of the third meeting between the two on May 28. Stalin first reaffirmed and clarified his Crimean commitment to enter the Pacific war no more than three months after Germany's defeat. By August 8, three months to the day after the Nazi collapse, " 'the Soviet Army will be properly deployed on the Manchurian positions.' " But Stalin also reemphasized the Crimean reimbursements promised the Soviets for their efforts. China, therefore, must " 'agree to the proposals made at Yalta.' " Then " 'For the first time' " Stalin " 'stated that he was willing to take these proposals up directly with [Chinese Foreign Minister T. V.] Soong when he comes to Moscow.' " And Stalin added that he wished to see Soong no later than July 1.[46]

After categorically reaffirming his commitment to support Chiang—" 'He specifically stated that no Communist leader was strong enough to unify China' "—and after firmly stating " 'that he wanted a unified and stable China and wanted China to control all of Manchuria as part of a United China,' " Stalin " 'went out of his way to indicate that the United States was the only power with the resources to aid China economically after the war. He observed that for many years to come Russia would have all it could do to provide for the internal economy of the Soviet Union.' "[47]

After agreeing with Hopkins that a trusteeship should be established for Korea under the joint supervision of the United States,

---

lin, I: 387. A much milder version of this note, in which Stalin asked only for recognition of the Bulgarian and Rumanian governments, may be found in *Stalin's Correspondence with Roosevelt and Truman*, p. 250.

[46] Quoted in Sherwood, *Roosevelt and Hopkins*, II: 553.

[47] Quoted in *ibid.*, pp. 553–554.

Russia, China, and Britain, Stalin turned the talks toward Japan. Since February various individual Japanese, acting in both unofficial and semi-official capacities, had begun to approach the Russian government, asking that it act as a " 'divine outside force' " to bring about peace between Nippon and the United States.[48] Stalin therefore told Hopkins that Japan was doomed, that she knew it, and that various peace feelers were being sent out " 'by certain elements in Japan.' " All this was by way of background to Stalin's intent. For he told Hopkins that, in the American's words, " 'The Soviet Union prefers to go through with unconditional surrender and destroy once and for all the military might and forces of Japan.' " Were Japan not crushed, her military power totally extinguished, she might rise again to haunt the world with the spectre of further military aggression.[49]

Stalin then added his opinion " 'that if we stick to unconditional surrender the Japs will not give up and we will have to destroy them as we did Germany.' "[50] Was Stalin deliberately trying to drive the Americans into a costly invasion of Japan to make up in some measure for what the Red Army had had to suffer in 1942 and 1943 while the Western Allies supposedly fumbled and hesitated over a direct invasion of Europe? Was his philosophy "let them pay for their victories as we had to"? Perhaps. It has been so suggested by one respected scholar.[51] But in the course of further discussion with Hopkins, the Genereralissimo let it be known that he was not averse to a Japanese capitulation *short of* invasion *if* a subsequent Allied military occupation of the home islands could be assured. Once again the sleepless Soviet self-interest showed itself. " 'Should the Allies depart from the announced policy of unconditional surrender and be prepared to accept a modified surrender,' " Hopkins wired Truman, " 'Stalin visualizes imposing our will through our occupying forces and thereby gaining substantially the same results as' " unconditional surrender. " 'In other words,' " Hopkins continued bluntly and vividly, " 'it seemed to us

48 Quoted in Werth, *Russia at War*, p. 929.
49 Quoted in Sherwood, *Roosevelt and Hopkins*, II: 554.
50 Quoted in *ibid.*
51 "In Europe, his [Stalin's] allies had made the Red Army take the bloodbath; now he could let the Americans and British carry the burden of battle, and he could take his share of the spoils." James MacGregor Burns, "FDR; The Untold Story of His Last Year," *Saturday Review*, LIII (April 11, 1970), 15.

that he proposes . . . to agree to milder peace terms but once we get into Japan to give them the works. The Marshal expects that Russia will share in the actual occupation of Japan and wants an agreement with the British and us as to occupation zones.' "[52]

Stalin's influence upon American strategic thinking with respect to concluding the war against Japan has never been adequately appreciated. And yet it was of crucial importance. For Stalin's attitude inevitably served to stiffen the resolve of those who were determined to pursue the policy of unconditional surrender. He, too, wanted the harshest possible peace, achieved either through bloody battle that would extirpate all existing Japanese military force, or by "milder" means, so long as those means insured an Allied occupation which would *then* give the Japanese "the works." The Generalissimo all but told the Americans outright that the continued price of Soviet trust and cooperation in East Asia hinged upon the determined United States implementation of the *de facto* unconditional surrender of Japan. No half-measures would do. George Marshall's memo to Stimson of June 9—some ten days after Hopkins communicated Stalin's sentiments to Washington—takes on an added significance. " 'We must be careful,' " Marshall wrote, " 'to avoid giving any impression that we are growing soft.' "[53] Impression to whom? The Japanese? Surely—and also to the Russians. Harriman's comment to Forrestal and the Navy chiefs on May 11 that the Russians more greatly feared a separate peace between America and Japan than United States officials feared a similar Soviet-Japanese agreement seemed fully borne out by Stalin's remarks to Hopkins. Once again, the Russians had put the Americans on the spot. If the Grand Alliance were to continue, Japan must in some way be beaten into the dust.

And so by mid-June American thinking focused upon Potsdam and Japan. But the Japanese dilemma assumed the largest proportions. How close were the Japanese to defeat? Could they be induced to surrender short of invasion? Should they be so induced, given Stalin's expectations? How costly would the invasion of Ja-

---

[52] Quoted in Sherwood, *Roosevelt and Hopkins,* II: 554–555.
[53] Quoted in Herbert Feis, *The Atomic Bomb and the End of World War II* (Princeton: Princeton University Press, revised ed., 1966), p. 188.

pan be? How soon could it be mounted? These and related questions preoccupied and perplexed American officials during the latter half of the month and on into early July.

9

The Decision to Invade Japan--June and July

During the first few weeks in June a series of meetings were held in both Tokyo and Washington which apparently insured that the Pacific war would be fought to a bloody, unyielding conclusion.

On June 6 the Japanese army suddenly called a full conference of the Supreme Council for the Direction of the War. The council represented the top military and civil leadership of the Japanese government, and the army's purpose was plain. It asked for speedy ratification of its "final, comprehensive demand" that the nation

engage the enemy on Japan's own shores, for only thus, said the military, could the imperial land be preserved and the national polity maintained. As they saw it, Japan's "one hundred million" people, ever steadfast in their loyalty to their imperial father through all eternity, would arise together from the vantage ground of their sacred land to strike the invaders dead!

The military was not to have its way without "hours of explanations and reports." But as "morning passed into afternoon . . . the final decision became a foregone conclusion." Japan would fight on through an American invasion to the last man and the last ditch.[1] The Japanese Cabinet formally ratified the decision of the council the following day, and twenty-four hours later the Emperor, in Imperial Audience, gave his assent in the traditional manner—through silence.[2]

The decision was, of course, an unmitigated defeat for the peace faction within the government. Yet, as we have seen, that faction had been paralyzed from the beginning, in large measure because of its stress upon the "Communist revolution" issue above and beyond any simple expedient to end the war. Other factors were also at work sapping the will and energy of the peace faction. Those who sought to end the war were fatally restrained, not only by their numerous and justified terrors of the fanatical militarists and what they might do if the peace plots were exposed, but also by what the victorious Americans surely would do if any peace initiatives should succeed. Few members of the peace faction had a record of opposition to the war sufficiently documented to convince the Allies of their sincerity. All of them had served in cabinets which had propagated war as an instrument of national policy. They knew that atrocities had been committed by the army against Allied prisoners of war during the period during which they had held office, that there were war crimes charges facing all Japanese politicians who had served in the Cabinet from 1936 onward.[3]

Thus the conflicting pressures on these men to continue the war —to soften and blur peace overtures, to hope against hope that the armed forces could hold out long enough to exhaust the Americans on the one hand, while creating a climate favorable to internal anti-Communist "reform" on the other—were immense. They readily succumbed to hesitation, timidity, faint-heartedness, and inertia in the weeks and months after Germany's surrender.

Admiral Baron Kantarō Suzuki had come to the premiership in early April. A septuagenarian, the old man proved a riddle to all

---

[1] Butow, *Japan's Decision to Surrender*, pp. 93, 96; Shigenori Togo, *The Cause of Japan* (New York: Simon and Schuster, 1956), pp. 290–293.

[2] Butow, *Japan's Decision to Surrender*, pp. 99–102.

[3] Leonard Moseley, *Hirohito, Emperor of Japan* (New York: Avon Books, 1967), p. 298. Butow is not insensitive to this point. Cf. *Japan's Decision to Surrender*, p. 73.

who came in contact with him. Did he desire peace? No one could be sure. He would later tell American interrogators that the Emperor had called him to leadership in early April in order to end the war. Yet on May 3, anticipating Germany's fall, he issued a statement reaffirming his own government's " 'faith in certain victory.' "[4] Nor could the Emperor's opinion and will, if they existed, be divined. The collapse of Germany propelled one of the more venturesome members of the peace group, Foreign Minister Togo, toward the throne "to try to get agreement to making peace while our military strength was not yet wholly exhausted." Hirohito merely replied that it was his wish that Japan end the war "as early as possible."[5] Just how this was to be accomplished, the Emperor, as tradition dictated, would not say. It would take two atomic bombs and a Soviet declaration of war to destroy the tradition and permit Hirohito to transmit his wishes into policy. After another month of characteristically clandestine dithering, the peace faction finally decided to approach the one great power with potentially sizable interests in Asia which was not yet at war with Japan—Soviet Russia.

The absurd logic of this decision is obvious. Soon after Yalta the Kremlin had announced that it would not renew its non-aggression treaty with Japan. While that treaty had not yet expired, only the most foolish of men could have assumed that the Soviets would not soon come to the active aid of their Anglo-American allies. Moreover, any successful Russian mediation would surely have promoted the popularity and cause of Communism inside Japan. But these were desperate, nay frantic, men whose concern was uneasily balanced between the preservation of the national polity and the protection of their own lives. Russia would have to be lured away from Britain and the United States, they apparently concluded, but not so far into the Japanese orbit that Moscow might acquire the opportunity to intervene actively in Japan's internal affairs. The only way to accomplish this end would be to offer the Kremlin a bigger bribe in northeast Asia than Tokyo would have to assume the Americans had given Stalin at Yalta. Japanese diplo-

---

[4] Quoted in Butow, *Japan's Decision to Surrender*, pp. 71, 79. Cf. also U.S. Strategic Bombing Survey, *Japan's Struggle to End the War*, pp. 6–7.
[5] Togo, *The Cause of Japan*, p. 276.

macy, in short, would have to destroy the Grand Alliance. And this immense task would have to be performed from a position of constantly deteriorating national power. As early as the previous September the then Foreign Minister Shigemitsu had suggested giving the Soviets everything in northeast Asia, Sakhalin, and the Kuriles that the Americans later granted at Yalta, plus Japanese acquiescence in the "peaceful activities" of Russia in China. But now continued military reverses had drastically whittled away what it was in Japanese power to grant the Soviets. Nonetheless, the attempt had to be made and so it was. In early June the peace faction decided to approach the Russians through their Ambassador, Jacob Malik. Former Premier Hirota, "one of our top-ranking Russian experts of the time," was chosen for the task. He botched the job miserably. Instead of stressing Japan's desire for Russian mediation to end the war, Hirota consumed most of the month strenuously trying to bribe Malik with territorial concessions. The Soviet Ambassador exhibited a marked lack of interest. He often yawned and even glanced at newspapers from time to time, while the Japanese day after day tirelessly reiterated his tasteless proposals. At last the Russian agreed to forward Hirota's proposals to Moscow, but they went by routine courier rather than by cable.[6]

The peace faction thus offered little in the way of a resolution of Japan's terrible dilemma. Could the military offer anything better? The decision of June 7–9 to fight on is a sufficient answer. Evidently the majority of the Supreme War Council and the Cabinet, as well as the Emperor, still believed that there were some grounds for hope, if not optimism, that a threatened fight to the death might yield fruitful results. And while the closest student of Japanese politics at this time has castigated the decision of early June as pure madness—a romantic gesture which flew in the face of all reality[7] —it is well to look at just what resources the High Command of the Japanese army was counting upon to back its claims.

Current sober assessments by Japanese military analysts seemed to indicate beyond the shadow of a doubt that whatever Japan's

<hr />

[6] Butow, *Japan's Decision to Surrender*, p. 89; Togo, *The Cause of Japan*, p. 88; Moseley, *Hirohito*, p. 307.

[7] Butow, *Japan's Decision to Surrender*, p. 116.

will to resist might be in mid-summer 1945, her *ability* to resist was
steadily wasting away toward the vanishing point.[8] Yet was this
in fact a correct assessment? Some Japanese writers think not. And
even a cursory study of the Japanese military situation at this time
reveals that despite her desperate condition, Japan was far from
beaten. Her army would have met the Americans on the beaches of
Kyushu and Honshu with something far more than what one
writer has derisively called "bamboo spears."[9]

Japanese preparations to meet an American assault had begun
early in the winter of 1945. In the following months, despite severe
and growing shortages in matériel and food, the army prepared its
defenses and stockpiled its supplies. On April 7, the day after Russia announced that she would not renew her non-aggression pact
with Tokyo, divisional district defense chiefs—veteran generals all
—were appointed to posts throughout the islands. All told, between February 28 and May 23 forty-nine divisions were activated,
while Imperial General Headquarters began laying plans to meet
an actual invasion. Conservation of air strength was stressed to the
point that by June some twelve hundred "regular planes" had been
husbanded, in fair safety, from American air attacks in order to
meet the general assault. This policy partly explains the comparatively light loss ratio of American bombers over Japan in the spring
of 1945. These "regular aircraft" were to do battle with the American bomber forces that were expected to begin "softening up" the
islands during the immediate pre-invasion bombardment period. In
addition another 2,100 suicide planes had been readied to attack the
invasion fleets. By August the Japanese army expected to muster
all told some 2,350,000 men in the home islands to oppose an Allied landing.[10]

The morale of these troops was determinedly high. Despite the
steady American march across the Pacific that had consumed two
years and thousands of Japanese lives, "most officers and men had

[8] U.S. Strategic Bombing Survey, *Japan's Struggle to End the War*, "Appendix
A-2, Survey of [Japanese] National Resources as of 1-10 June 1945," and "Appendix B, Japanese Military Resources near the End of the War," pp. 16–21.
[9] Moseley, *Hirohito*, p. 294.
[10] Saburo Hayashi, *Kogun; The Japanese Army in the Pacific War* (Quantico,
Va.: The Marine Corps Association, 1959), pp. 150–169; U.S. Strategic Bombing
Survey, *Japan's Struggle to End the War*, p. 1.

an easy-going confidence of winning . . . without any sense of *effort*."[11] In part this arrogant confidence stemmed from a long and intensive propaganda campaign by the High Command. But it stemmed in part also from some shrewdly analyzed factors on the part of the Japanese military. Defense of the homeland, with all its favorable factors such as security of internal lines of communication and intimate knowledge of the terrain, could be expected to be far more successful even than the bloody battles out in the Pacific islands that had cost the Americans such heavy casualties.

> In appraising the characteristics of operations to defend Japan proper, the Army High Command judged that the odds were not impossible for a number of reasons: . . . there would be no fear that Japanese shipping would be sunk (unlike the situation during the previous island campaigns) . . . it had become possible to preserve planes from severe bombing by U.S. forces prior to landings. The main strength of the army remained almost intact and, since the battles would be fought ashore, it could operate very well without the Navy. American landing operations against the Japanese homeland would require more than three times the number of transports used in the war against Germany [*i.e.*, during the Normandy invasion]; hence there would be more chances to attack the U.S. supply lines, which extended across great distances.

Finally, and most important, "Taking advantage of the actual American landings, the Japanese Army would be able to inflict heavy casualties by employing strong points prepared beforehand."[12] Those Americans who had lived through the hell of Tarawa, Iwo Jima, and other islands could attest to the Japanese genius in constructing multi-layered and incredibly obstinate "strong points" that could be reduced only by the most savage and costly means.

Pure fanaticism, too, remained as a prime factor in Japanese morale. As late as the first week in August Japanese planners had concocted a scheme involving two hundred bombers and two thousand troops. This force was to be dispatched on a one-way suicide mission to the Marianas to knock out the B-29 bases. The plan

[11] Hayashi, *Kogun*, p. 179.
[12] *Ibid.*, pp. 177–178.

was wrecked by a raid upon the Japanese air field in northern Honshu by Allied carrier aircraft.[13]

One other factor played a crucial role in Japanese strategic thinking. There was no expectation that the Americans could or would launch any but conventional blows at the homeland. "Full credence was lent [by the Japanese High Command] . . . to the contention of the nuclear physicists . . . that 'during World War II no nation in the world would be able to perfect atomic bombs.' " Even after Alamogordo "there were . . . reports that the United States had been conducting experiments in New Mexico with a new weapon of high explosive power, but nobody imagined that it was actually an atomic bomb."[14]

Viewed from the perspective of fanaticism, then, there was cause for profound concern but not total despair within Japan's ruling military circles in June of 1945. In contrast to the always clandestine, always fearful, and—the term is not too strong—always anxiety-ridden peace faction within the Japanese government, the army projected a consistent image of bellicose confidence which, by the dynamics of the situation, paradoxically waxed ever stronger as disaster followed disaster.

The fall of Okinawa on June 22 did signal something of a break in the official wall of fanaticism which the Japanese government had erected around itself. Marquis Kido approached the throne the day before the loss of that island, armed with all the gloomy reports he could muster and also carrying with him the agreement of his Cabinet colleagues, including even War Minister Anami, that Japan's only hope now for "peace with honor" was to agree to surrender all conquests and possessions now held. Might it be possible, he asked Hirohito, to commence peace initiatives based upon these considerations? The Emperor agreed and went even further the next day. Hastily summoning an Imperial Conference, Hirohito, in "carefully chosen phrases," admonished his ministers to seek actively the path to peace.[15] The enemy had now appeared in front of the gates. Time was of the essence. Yet it must be stressed

---

[13] Morison, *Victory in the Pacific*, p. 332.
[14] Hayashi, *Kogun*, p. 162.
[15] Butow, *Japan's Decision to Surrender*, pp. 114–121.

that Hirohito did *not* demand that means be immediately found to end the war on any terms up to and including an Allied occupation and subversion or extermination of the imperial institution. All the Emperor really did was to legitimatize the fumbling and formerly clandestine efforts of the peace faction. He went no further. And for its part, the peace faction promptly and unimaginatively returned to its fruitless efforts to induce the Russians to break the Grand Alliance and work with Japan either as a mediator in ending the war with the imperial government intact or as a collaborator in ruling over all of East Asia. Konoye, Kido, and the others had obviously reached bankruptcy, both morally and intellectually. The army continued its preparations to defend the homeland to the death.

Peering through the smoke of battle in the far Pacific, then, American policy-makers were justified in concluding that the Japanese will to resist remained unshakable in June of 1945. The question now was whether the Americans retained their implacable determination to conquer. The military and naval operations of June and July left no room for doubt. The battle fleet—"the greatest mass of sea power ever assembled"—was finally released from its duties around Okinawa on June 10. It had been continuously at sea for ninety-two days. Aboard the great carriers and battleships and on the small destroyers fear and exhaustion seeped down bulkheads, flowed through passageways, and spread across the decks wherever men congregated. Yet after only a fortnight for rest and replenishment at Leyte, the admirals ruthlessly pushed their ships and sailors northward again, back to the Japanese coast, where the entire month of July was spent in hurling blow after blow—including several "thousand plane raids" by fleet carrier aircraft—directly at the islands. Between July 10 and August 6 Halsey's fleet destroyed or damaged 2,804 enemy planes and sank or damaged 148 Japanese combat ships and 1,598 merchant ships.[16]

---

[16] E. B. Potter and Fleet Admiral Chester W. Nimitz, *Triumph in the Pacific* (Englewood Cliffs, N.J.: Prentice-Hall, 1963), p. 179; Fleet Admiral Ernest J. King with Walter Muir Whitehill, *Fleet Admiral King; A Naval Record* (New York: W. W. Norton & Company, Inc., 1952), pp. 619–620; Morison, *Victory in the Pacific*, pp. 312–314, 330–332; Lewis L. Strauss, *Men and Decisions* (New York: Popular Library, 1963), p. 197; Millis, ed., *Forrestal Diaries*, p. 76.

The Army Air Force was, if possible, even more active. In early May General LeMay diverted some of his B-29s to the task of sowing mines in Japanese waters. By the middle of that month, however, fighter planes were beginning to operate from Okinawa bases directly against southern Japan, and they took over tactical operations, while LeMay's B-29s returned to their primary task of strategic bombing. Throughout the month of June the bombers continued their nightly incendiary attacks against Japan's cities and mixed them increasingly with high-level, daylight, "precision" bombing. "The result was both flexibility and devastating power." The toll of Japanese dead, civilian as well as military, continued to rise appallingly. Amidst scenes of unimaginable mass horror Japan's urban areas settled into ruins and ashes. When the Seventh Air Force moved into Okinawa in July, Japan was subjected to round-the-clock bombing and strafing assaults. "The Japanese Air Force at first aggressively contested the daylight bombing raids . . . but soon it was practically eliminated. Night-fighting P-47's and the more effective P-61's harassed the enemy . . . targets included railroads, bridges, shipping, and even civilians in the field. Everything was considered fair game in the effort to shorten the war and avert the need for invasion." General Arnold, visiting the Marianas at the end of June, publicly warned the Japanese that if they did not surrender, their homeland "would be a target for 2,000,000 tons of bombs in the year beginning July 1, 1945."[17] Within days after Arnold's grim promise the islands were facing yet a third terrible threat. This came from the American submarine force. Employing new technological devices and tactics which neutralized enemy minefields, the navy's submarines worked all around the Japanese shores during the final six weeks of the war, sinking nearly every supply vessel which ventured in or out of port, clamping an ever-tightening and efficient blockade around the islands.[18] Above and beyond these vast operations lay the enormous buildup for the invasion. Already by June, according to a civilian member of Eisenhower's staff, "Four hundred thousand soldiers

---

[17] Buchanan, *United States and World War II*, II: 579–580; Vern Haugland, *The AAF Against Japan* (New York: Harper & Brothers, 1948), pp. 459–467.
[18] Buchanan, *United States and World War II*, II: 580–581.

were being transported monthly from Eisenhower's command to the other side of the earth, together with incredible amounts of war matériel."[19]

Japan was thus isolated in every way by mid-July 1945. A month after the fall of Okinawa her military situation had so deteriorated from what it had been as late as the June 7 decision to fight to the end that even the prospect of a bloody standoff in the home islands which might induce the Americans to cease their efforts was no longer seriously conceivable. Resistance to an invasion could only be suicidal. For with the last approaches to the home islands actively in enemy use, crushing power could not only be fully exerted against Japan for the first time, it could be and was exerted continually. "The construction of airfields on Okinawa is the main activity," Stimson noted on July 4, "and the United States is building a very large and threatening series of jumping off places for the increase of our air attack on Japan." Planning assumed that by October at the latest the United States Army Air Force would be in the Ryukyus *en masse*, ready to support an invasion of Kyushu. But under such circumstances was invasion necessary at all? The air force and navy did not think so. The terrible unrelenting aerial blows against the islands, coupled with the submarine and surface blockade, were reducing the Japanese to starvation. Why risk the lives of three quarters of a million men in the invasion of Kyushu alone when Nippon could be defeated by air and sea power?[20] This idea, long held in certain quarters in both the air force and navy, began to spread more widely in the early summer of 1945 as Japan's supine aerial and naval posture became ever clearer. The postwar conclusion of the United States Strategic Bombing Survey, which supported the air force and navy view, seems incontestable in the light of facts generally available both in July of 1945 and now: "certainly prior to 31 December 1945, and in all probability prior to 1 November 1945, Japan would have surrendered, even if the

---

[19] Murphy, *Diplomat among Warriors*, p. 283. Cf. also Eisenhower to Marshall, April 18, 26, 27, 1945, in Chandler, ed., *Eisenhower Papers; War Years*, IV: 2621–2622, 2647–2648, 2651–2652.
[20] Stimson Diary, July 4, 1945; Haugland, *AAF Against Japan*, p. 474; Buchanan, *United States and World War II*, II: 578, 581; King and Whitehill, *Fleet Admiral King*, p. 598; Leahy, *I Was There*, pp. 384–385.

atomic bombs had not been dropped, even if Russia had not entered the war, and even if no invasion had been planned or contemplated."[21]

Yet an invasion was not only planned, it was confidently expected that it would have to be carried out. Kyushu would be invaded on November 1, 1945, and the Tokyo Plain would be assaulted the following March. The war against Japan would be total. Attack from the clean blue sky and sea must be supplemented by massive battle in the mud and dust ashore. This was the army's plan. And it carried the day within the American government over both Grew's efforts to modify unconditional surrender and over the hopes of the air force and navy that Japan could be starved, bombed, and shelled into surrender. The determination to employ maximum military force to compel Japan's capitulation dictated that Truman's earlier assent to the use of the atomic bomb would in no way be reversed. For if there was to be an invasion all available power must be employed in its behalf. Top level discussions in Washington between June 6 and July 3 thus reconfirmed already existing policies. The atomic bomb would be used when ready; the invasion of Japan would proceed. There was no sentiment within the Truman administration strong enough to reverse the long-standing policies for the final prosecution of the Pacific war.

On June 6, the day that the Japanese government in Tokyo decided to fight on to the end, Henry Stimson met with Truman to brief him fully on the results of the deliberations of the Interim Committee, which the President had established the previous month to review atomic policy from every conceivable perspective. The primary motives for the creation of the committee seem to have been the desire to appease those concerned atomic scientists who hoped against hope that their invention would never be used at all. But the debates which took place on May 31 and June 1, both within the committee and between the committee and advisory panels of scientists and businessmen, seemed to preclude all options save use of the weapon without any prior warning and as soon as it was ready "against a Japanese war plant surrounded by work-

[21] U.S. Strategic Bombing Survey, *Japan's Struggle to End the War*, p. 13.

ers' homes." The man who put this consensus into words was special Presidential delegate James Byrnes.[22]

Having relayed the committee's recommendation, which Truman received without comment, Stimson immediately turned to the problem of Russia. The committee had agreed, in Stimson's words, "that there should be no revelation to Russia or anyone else of our work in S-1 until the first bomb had been laid on Japan." But what would happen in the interim at Potsdam? Stimson brought the question up, and Truman, for the first and only time, indicated that he postponed the Potsdam meeting "until the 15th of July on purpose to give us more time" to develop the bomb.[23] Why? Were the President's earlier statements—notably those of May 14—that he could not leave the country until after July 1 at the earliest because of budgetary and domestic problems simply a screen to mask his real motive? Dr. Alperovitz wishes us to believe that Truman deliberately delayed the three-power summit until such time as the atomic bomb was ready for testing in order to have the weapon on his hip when he met Stalin. The President went to Germany, Alperovitz argues, armed with an almost certain assumption of the bomb's workability and therefore determined to pursue a tough, non-concession diplomacy toward the Soviets.[24] All the known facts, however, argue against such a conclusion and lead inexorably toward another. Truman had clung steadfastly to his predecessor's policy of securing Soviet aid in the Pacific war and of abandoning any conceivable American interests in Eastern Europe while granting Moscow a severely limited sphere of influence in Northeast Asia as the inevitable price of such a policy. The whole tenor of the Hopkins mission and of its positive results was in line with this policy. By June 6 Truman had clearly in mind not only that Russia would enter the Pacific war but also precisely when. Existing evidence indicates that knowing this, the President logically concluded that now was the time to put all the cards on the table. Should American possession of the bomb become known to Stalin during the Berlin Conference, and should other major decisions by the American

---

[22] Hewlett and Anderson, *The New World*, pp. 358, 360.
[23] Stimson Diary, June 6, 1945.
[24] Alperovitz, *Atomic Diplomacy*, pp. 62–126 *passim*.

government affecting the shape of the postwar world be finalized just before or during the meeting, then the relative power and interests of the Soviet and American governments would be fully known to each other. The way would presumably be open for the kind of tough, honest, friendly, face-to-face negotiation and adjustment of conflicting postwar interests that would maintain the Grand Alliance intact into the coming months and years of peace. It is significant that just prior to his departure for Potsdam Truman told Senate Majority Leader Alben Barkley that " 'it would strengthen my hand very much in the Big Three Conference if the Bretton Woods legislation were to be enacted before the Conference was concluded.' "[25] Of even greater importance in this connection was the report of *Time*'s Congressional correspondent on June 22: "Within 40 days," Frank McNaughton wrote, Truman

> will be sitting down with Churchill and Joe Stalin to do some international horse trading. He wants, as a poker player, to have a pat hand. This week the House and Senate presented him with a three year extension of the reciprocal trade program. . . . He is confident the Bretton Woods monetary plan will be approved by the Senate in practically the same form it passed the House.
>
> He would like to have as his final trump card either when he arrives for the Big 3 meeting in Berlin or before leaving, the ratification of the San Francisco instrument. Then he can lay it on the dotted line with Stalin and Churchill, say "I've done my part, the U.S. has done its part, now let's see you do your share." This was the tenor of his thoughts.[26]

How much stronger would Truman's bargaining position be at Potsdam if he could throw a successful atomic bomb test into the pot, if he could tempt Stalin with the possibility of sharing the nuclear secret in exchange for modifications in Soviet designs? Indeed, Truman hints that this was precisely what he had in mind when he notes in his memoirs that the atomic test was being rushed to completion.[27]

[25] Quoted in J. Joseph Huthmacher, *Senator Robert Wagner and the Rise of Urban Liberalism* (New York: Atheneum Press, 1968), p. 305. The legislation passed Congress on August 2.
[26] Frank McNaughton Report, June 21, 1945, "Security Treaty," McNaughton Papers, Box 7.
[27] Truman, *Year of Decisions*, pp. 458, 460.

But would the bomb really work? Could it be delivered by the target date of August 1? Even at this late moment, six weeks before Alamogordo, no one was sure. "I pointed out that there might still be delay" in developing the weapon, Stimson wrote of his conversation with Truman. Leahy remained unconvinced of the feasibility of the entire project. Eden later recalled that in talking with Stimson and others about the bomb in mid-May, there was agreement that "At this stage there was still no certainty as to what this fearful, but untried, weapon could do, and some skepticism even among the initiated."[28]

And supposing the Soviets had gotten wind of the project and asked for an immediate share in its development, or in the fruits of that development, without recognizing that the bomb had to be the subject of negotiations. What then? Stimson and others in the know had become convinced as early as December 1944 that the Russians were spying on S-1. Now the Secretary of War raised just this question with Truman and promptly answered it in firm and certain terms. "I thought that our attitude was to do just what the Russians had done to us, namely to make the simple statement that as yet we were not quite ready to do it."[29]

Here Stimson was quite clearly playing a kind of atomic diplomacy. But Truman quickly indicated that he, personally, was not yet ready to follow his Secretary's lead. Elation with the success of the Hopkins mission to that point, and especially Stalin's heartening remarks on Soviet entry into the Japanese war and the limited nature of Soviet aims in Northeast Asia, obviously dominated Presidential thinking. As Stimson rose to leave, Truman

asked me if I had heard of the accomplishment which Harry Hopkins had made in Moscow and when I said I had not he told me there was a promise in writing by Stalin that Manchuria should remain fully Chinese except for a ninety-nine year lease of Port Arthur and the settlement of Dairen which we had hold of. I warned him that with the fifty-fifty control of the railways running across Manchuria, Russia would still be likely to outweigh the Chinese in actual power in that country. He said he realized that but the promise was perfectly clear and distinct.[30]

[28] Stimson Diary, June 6, 1945; Eden, *The Reckoning*, p. 620.
[29] Hewlett and Anderson, *The New World*, p. 335; Stimson Diary, June 6, 1945.
[30] Stimson Diary, June 6, 1945.

The June 6 meeting between Stimson and Truman brought to light several crucial points. Above all else, the President was still thinking in positive terms about the Russians and the probability of continued cooperation in the postwar world. Stimson was increasingly preoccupied with the atomic bomb both in terms of its military power and its diplomatic implications. He was approaching the firm conviction—and in this subsequent events proved him indubitably correct—that American possession of the bomb threatened to undo irretrievably the existing delicate balance of interests and power across the earth which bound Moscow and Washington in uneasy concert. Only the most careful assessment of existing realities incorporated within the most delicate diplomacy could sustain the *status quo*.

Yet there was obviously no hesitation in Stimson's mind—or anyone else's—regarding use of the bomb against Japan. All of the speculation regarding Russia and the bomb in which the Secretary indulged during his June 6 conference with Truman came after Stimson faithfully passed on the Interim Committee's conclusion that an atomic strike must be "laid on" Japan without warning at the earliest possible date. The momentum of a total military solution to the Japanese question remained uppermost in American thinking, and a week later Truman asked that his top military advisers gather to complete their plans for the invasion of Japan.

The Joint Chiefs first met on June 14 and 15 to draw up the outline which was to govern their presentation to the President. At this time it was decided "that invading and seizing objectives in the Japanese home islands would be the main effort and that no other operations would be considered that did not contribute toward this objective. . . . While preparing for the invasion, sea and air blockades of Japan were to be maintained, the air bombardment pressed, and the destruction of enemy air and naval forces continued with all possible vigor." The Joint Chiefs "also agreed to encourage Russian entry into the Japanese war in accordance with the contingent conditions accepted by Roosevelt at Yalta."[31]

These recommendations were submitted to Truman at a long White House meeting three days later, where, among other things,

[31] Leahy, *I Was There*, p. 383.

the divisive strategic split between the army on the one hand and the navy and air force on the other was finally bridged, with Marshall once again carrying the day for the ground forces. "The Army seemed determined to occupy and govern Japan by military government as was being done in Germany," Leahy grumbled. "I was unable to see any justification, from a national-defense point of view, for an invasion of an already thoroughly defeated Japan."[32] Nonetheless the invasion of Kyushu was authorized.

What justification did indeed exist for such a costly operation at this late date? Marshall seems not to have explained his motives for demanding an invasion and armed governance thoroughly at this time or at any other, and it is the measure of his influence over Truman that he was able to carry the day in spite of the impenetrability of his thinking.[33] In the absence of documented explanation, conjecture becomes irresistible. There were several considerations which could well have prompted Marshall and the army to continue their firm demands for an invasion, even in light of the palpable erosion of Japan's military fortunes since Yalta and the German collapse.

A two-and-a-half-million-man army, never defeated nor even tested in battle as a unit, remained intact in the cities and villages, plains and mountains of Japan. Should some sort of armistice spare this military force from combat and destruction, the consequences could be ominous for the future peace and stability of the Pacific. Japan could claim that she had never been completely subdued. The Allies had before them the lessons of 1918 when, to Pershing's dismay, the German army was allowed to disband essentially undefeated and with the sense that it had been "betrayed" and "stabbed in the back" by the civil authorities at home. "It was a subject the General of the Armies never tired of discussing . . . ceaseless in his resolve to found many schools to develop the multiple techniques of the next inevitable war with Germany. . . . 'They never knew

---

[32] *Ibid.*, pp. 384–385.

[33] "It was natural for me to turn to General Marshall and Secretary of War Stimson" when seeking to bring the Pacific fighting to a speedy conclusion, Truman said later. Significantly, he excluded Navy Secretary Forrestal and Admirals King and Leahy from his mind, although the Pacific theater had always been considered primarily a "Navy show." Was this due to the influence of Captain Truman of Battery D upon President Truman? Or due solely to the force of Marshall's personality? Truman, *Year of Decisions*, p. 262.

they were beaten in Berlin,' he said. 'It will have to be done all over again.' " Pershing had been right, and another generation of Americans had had to finish a job his doughboys had not been allowed to complete.[34]

A second consideration flowed easily from the first. The American military tradition from Grant to Eisenhower had been based upon the unrelenting application of crushing superiority on a broad front to destroy the opposing military force. During the latter stages of the Civil War Grant ruthlessly pursued Lee and brought the dwindling Confederate forces to battle at every opportunity until, in the words of one authority, "the South simply ran out of manpower—rather as Hitler's Germany did in 1945."[35] The suggestion of a connection between Grant's strategic thinking and that of Eisenhower eighty years later was not casual. Eisenhower's overriding aim, the idea which suffused his "broad front" strategy in Europe, was to destroy the German army in a series of killing matches so as to break German morale as well as Nazi power. The death of enemy personnel, not simply the conquest of enemy territory, was Eisenhower's aim from the moment that his troops jumped off from the area west of the Rhine in their last great offensive in the spring of 1945. In " 'the destruction and dismemberment of the German armed forces' " lay the key to victory.[36] There was no reason to assume that the Japanese problem was substantially different. Only by killing thousands of Japanese soldiers in

[34] Captain B. H. Liddell Hart, *The Real War, 1914–1918* (Boston: Little, Brown & Co., 1964), pp. 383–384; Laurence Stallings, *The Doughboys; The Story of the A.E.F., 1917–1918* (New York: Harper & Row, 1963), p. 374.

[35] Walter Millis, *Arms and Men; A Study of American Military History* (New York: Mentor ed., 1956), p. 116. Cf. also Bruce Catton, *U.S. Grant and the American Military Tradition* (New York: Universal Library, 1945), esp. p. 120; and Bruce Catton, *A Stillness at Appomattox* (New York: Pocket Books, 1958), esp. pp. 105–106.

[36] Stephen E. Ambrose argues this point most persuasively in *Eisenhower and Berlin, 1945*, pp. 56, 60–61, 64–65. Cf. also Wilmot, *Struggle for Europe*, p. 791. The quote is from Eisenhower's own press conference of March 28, 1945, reprinted in Butcher, *My Three Years with Eisenhower*, pp. 780, 783–784, 786. Bradley has written unequivocally on this point: "Our primary objective, after all, lay not in Berlin nor in any other terrain feature; rather we were primarily intent on destruction of the German army." Bradley, *A Soldier's Story*, p. 502. This philosophy carried forward into the Korean conflict, of course. It formed the rationale for pursuit of the North Korean army above the thirty-eighth parallel in October of 1950 and led to great grief when China felt sufficiently provoked to intervene. Cf. Truman, *Years of Trial and Hope*, p. 411; David Rees, *Korea; The Limited War* (Baltimore: Pelican Books, 1970), pp. 98–99.

their homeland could American might be ultimately expressed and American will ultimately imposed. Only with these objectives achieved and American military government established would Japanese militarism be finally eradicated.

There was yet a third factor that must have deeply influenced Marshall's thinking at this time. The magnificent sweep of the Anglo-American armies across France and up through the low countries the previous summer, following the breakout from the Normandy beachhead at St. Lô, had bred an atmosphere of supreme optimism in both Washington and London. Germany seemed on the verge of defeat in 1944 at comparatively little cost to the Allies. Marshall had permitted himself to surrender to the general euphoria, and indeed had communicated it to the skeptical Eisenhower and Bradley on a trip to Europe that autumn. The subsequent Allied slowdown caused by insuperable logistical problems, followed by the shocking German counteroffensive in the Ardennes in December, had thrown both the Pentagon and Whitehall into dismay and depression. The lesson seemed clear beyond doubt: Victory could not be counted upon until it was achieved.[37]

Then, too, there was the growing influence of Stalin upon American strategic planning. Truman had earlier admonished an astounded Molotov to "keep your commitments." If the Grand Alliance were to survive, the Americans could do no less than keep their own promises, which Stalin had clearly indicated to Hopkins he expected them to do. There was also the massive thrust of public opinion, demanding righteous retribution for Pearl Harbor, Bataan, and Corregidor, and all the grief and shame that those events and memories evoked.

And finally there were the intelligence reports. Presumably Marshall kept himself fully briefed on estimates of Japan's capacity to resist. Just precisely what those estimates were in mid-June is unknown at present, but they could only have been sobering, for there is available a report written three weeks later, on July 8, which seemed to indicate that mass invasion was the only way to defeat the enemy. According to this report, the Japanese navy had been

[37] Bradley, *A Soldier's Story*, pp. 428–429; John S. D. Eisenhower, *The Bitter Woods* (New York: Ace Books, 1970), pp. 102–103.

reduced to the size of a small and unbalanced task force, and the Japanese air force was strictly limited to suicide tactics. However, the Japanese army remained substantially in force. By the end of 1945 it was estimated that Tokyo could put about thirty-five effective divisions totalling two million men in the field in Kyushu and Honshu. To be sure, this formidable force retained little, if any, strategic mobility in an island countryside devastated from one end to the other by incessant and savage pounding from the air. Also it was exposed to increasing shortages of supplies. For these reasons, the report stated, Japan "In general . . . will use all political means for avoiding complete defeat or unconditional surrender." This meant that Japan would "make desperate efforts to persuade the U.S.S.R. to continue her neutrality, . . ." despite the belief of American intelligence officers "that a considerable portion of the Japanese population now consider absolute military defeat to be probable." The Japanese people were not running the war, however; the military was, and "The Japanese ruling groups still find unconditional surrender unacceptable." The report's conclusion, therefore, was stark and grim: "The Japanese believe . . . that unconditional surrender would be the equivalent of national extinction. There are as yet no indications that the Japanese are ready to accept such terms."[38] Unless unconditional surrender were to be modified in some way, invasion seemed the only answer.

Or so Marshall stipulated to his military colleagues and his President on June 18. Before Truman, Stimson, Forrestal, McCloy, and the Joint Chiefs, Marshall summed up current army thinking. An invasion of the China coast near Amoy, long favored by the navy as a means of intensifying the blockade of Japan, was no longer necessary since "the movement of Jap shipping south of Korea" had already been "greatly reduced" and should "in the next few months" be cut to a trickle. "General MacArthur and Admiral Nimitz are in agreement with the Chiefs of Staff," Marshall continued, "in selecting 1 November [or 'X Day'] as the target date to go into Kyushu." The Kyushu operation, code-named OLYMPIC, would be the essential prelude "to forcing capitulation by inva-

---

[38] Quoted in *Entry of the Soviet Union into the War Against Japan*, pp. 85–88.

sion of the Tokyo Plain." That operation, code-named CORONET, was tentatively scheduled for March 1, 1946, as soon as winter weather conditions in Japan subsided.

Marshall then turned to the knotty problem of subduing Japanese forces in Northeast Asia. "With reference to clean-up of the Asiatic mainland, our objective should be to get the Russians to deal with the Japs in Manchuria (and Korea if necessary) and to vitalize the Chinese. . . ." Somewhat later Marshall added: "An important point about Russian participation in the war is that the impact of Russian entry on the already hopeless Japanese may well be the decisive action levering them into capitulation at that time or shortly thereafter if we land in Japan."[39] In other words, a sufficient *show* of force by both Russia and the United States might be enough to cow the Japanese into surrender without its use. This was clearly a conjectural point in Marshall's mind.

As to the actual Kyushu invasion force itself, total combat and ground support strength would ultimately number 766,700 men, comprising the Sixth Army, organized into thirty-eight divisions. The initial assault wave of nine army and marine divisions would be met on or beyond the landing beaches at Miyazaki, Ariake Wan, and west of Kagoshima, on Kyushu's eastern and southern coasts respectively, by an estimated eight Japanese divisions totalling about 350,000 troops. The navy would muster a staggering total of three thousand war and support ships for the operation. The air force would provide eight thousand aircraft of all types. Here was a stupendous undertaking which easily dwarfed in size the Normandy landings of the year before. As Marshall told his colleagues, "We are bringing to bear against the Japanese every weapon and all the force we can employ."[40]

But unease underlay his remarks. How much more war could the American armed forces stand? In its August 1945 issue, which was apparently sent to press at the end of June, the authoritative magazine, *Infantry Journal*, warned its predominantly military

---

[39] *Ibid.*, pp. 77–79; Haugland, *AAF Against Japan*, p. 475; *Foreign Relations, 1945; Conference of Berlin*, I: 904–905.

[40] *Entry of the Soviet Union into the War Against Japan*, pp. 78, 82; *Foreign Relations, 1945; Conference of Berlin*, I: 904; Haugland, *AAF Against Japan*, p. 475; *New York Times*, October 10, 1945, pp. 13:1ff.

readership that the task of defeating Japan would be "vastly more
widespread" and "much bigger" than that entailed in the destruction of Nazi Germany. The magazine then launched into a typical
propaganda tirade.

> We must not get to expect an easy finish in the Pacific. . . . the Jap
> soldier fights an inhuman, dirty war. . . .
>
> All Americans—those in combat and those at home—must still re-
> member how the Jap soldier has mistreated and killed Americans—sol-
> diers and civilians—men, women and children—how he has marched
> honorably surrendered American troops in the hot sun until they died.
>
> How he has kept American prisoners on starvation rations—treated
> them in ways so completely uncivilized that thousands died before our
> troops could save them.
>
> These things are still happening. The fighting men of the Pacific
> know it well and they fight their battles accordingly, never giving the
> treacherous Jap the chance to put the full measure of his treachery into
> effect.
>
> Most Americans—all fighting men and most of those at home—are
> still remembering what the Japanese have done and what they stand
> for—how the Jap thinks he's the best man living—how he despises
> us and all our Allies, and everybody who stands for what we think is
> decent. . . .
>
> . . . the Japanese ideas have not changed at all. They are still ideas
> that must be wiped out of this world.[41]

Marshall thus sought to justify the army's position on June 18,
while further stiffening the resolve of all who were to be engaged
in the enterprise. He told the meeting "that it was his personal
view that the operation against Kyushu was the only course to pursue. He felt that air power alone was not sufficient to put the Japanese out of the war." After all, it had failed in and of itself to
knock Germany out, as both Generals Eisenhower and Eaker had
readily admitted. And "against the Japanese, scattered through
mountainous country, the problem would be much more difficult
than it had been in Germany." Therefore, "he felt that this plan
offered the only way the Japanese could be forced into a feeling
of utter helplessness. The operation would be difficult but not more
so than the assault in Normandy. He was convinced that every

individual moving to the Pacific should be indoctrinated with a firm determination to see it through."[42]

Confusion and contention surrounded the delicate subject of American casualties in the Kyushu operation. Marshall estimated that in the first thirty days of fighting the loss ratio could be kept to about the level sustained in the Luzon campaign, which was thirty-one thousand total. Leahy, however, invoked the much grimmer Okinawa figure of thirty-five percent of the invading force and arrived at a total of sixty-three thousand.[43]

In the face of this impressive presentation the navy and air force capitulated. King "said that the more he studied the matter, the more he was impressed with the strategic location of Kyushu, which he considered the key to the success of any seige operations" directed at the main island of Honshu. Air Force General Ira C. Eaker, speaking for himself and Arnold "said that those who advocated the use against Japan of air power alone overlooked the very impressive fact that air casualties are always much heavier when the air [force] faces the enemy alone and that these casualties never fail to drop as soon as the ground forces come in."

At this point in the conversation Truman turned to Stimson, who raised some fresh and disturbing considerations. The Secretary first "agreed with the Chiefs of Staff that there was no other choice." But "he felt that he was personally responsible to the President more for political than for military considerations." And in that area Stimson felt that there was "a large submerged class in Japan who do not favor the present war" but who would "fight and fight tenaciously if attacked on their own ground." Something should be done to "arouse" them, Stimson added, "and to develop any possible influences they might have before it became necessary to come to grips with them." In response, Truman revealed a surprising sensitivity. Obviously alluding to Grew's earlier efforts, of which Stimson was, of course, fully aware, yet without specifying precisely how or at what pace peace initiatives were being developed, the

---

[42] *Entry of the Soviet Union into the War Against Japan*, p. 80; *Foreign Relations, 1945; Conference of Berlin*, I: 906.

[43] Leahy, *I Was There*, p. 384; *Foreign Relations, 1945; Conference of Berlin*, I: 905, 907.

President "stated that this possibility was being worked on all the time." Then he asked "if the invasion of Japan by white men would not have the effect of more closely uniting the Japanese." Stimson "thought there was every prospect of this." Forrestal quickly swung the conversation back to more hawkish channels. Even if the United States wished to carry through a plan to beseige Japan for eighteen months, "the capture of Kyushu would be essential." McCloy in swift rebuttal "said he felt that the time was propitious now to study closely all possible means of bringing out the influence of the submerged group" mentioned by Stimson.[44]

After further discussion, in which Leahy stubbornly reasserted that "he could not agree with those who said to him that unless we obtain the unconditional surrender of the Japanese that we will have lost the war," Truman gave the go-ahead for the Kyushu operation. "He had hoped," he said, "that there was a possibility of preventing an Okinawa from one end of Japan to the other," but he seemed convinced that that hope was chimerical. Indeed, it is quite obvious that he had prepared himself days before to accept the responsibility of ordering OLYMPIC carried out. In his Special Message to Congress of June 1, on the winning of the war, the President had not only rejected Grew's effort to include a passage suggesting modification of unconditional surrender, but had taken an uncompromisingly firm position. "All of our experiences," he had said then, "indicate that no matter how hard we hit the enemy from the air or the sea, the foot soldier will still have to advance against strongly entrenched and fanatical troops, through sheer grit and fighting skill, backed up by all the mechanical superiority in flamethrowers, tanks and artillery we can put at his disposal. There is," the President grimly concluded, "no easy way to win." And then Truman had summoned his countrymen to steel their sinews and summon up the blood for one final effort: "We are faced with a powerful Japanese military machine. These are the same Japanese who perpetrated the infamous attack on Pearl Harbor three and one-half years ago; they are the same Japanese who ordered the

---

[44] *Entry of the Soviet Union into the War Against Japan*, pp. 81–83; *Foreign Relations, 1945; Conference of Berlin*, I: 906, 908–909.

death march from Bataan; they are the same Japanese who carried out the barbarous massacres in Manila."[45]

Now, on June 18, he told his military strategists that "he was clear on the situation now and was quite sure that the Joint Chiefs of Staff should proceed with the Kyushu operation." This being the case, the President "stated that one of his objectives in connection with the coming [Potsdam] conference would be to get from Russia all the assistance in the war that was possible." King's subsequent observation that Soviet assistance was not necessary was passed by in silence.[46] Then, in closing, the President suddenly hedged his decision. Planning and preparation for OLYMPIC should proceed. But he wished to be consulted once again before its execution in November. And he reserved judgment on the necessity and feasibility of CORONET, the climactic invasion of the Tokyo Plain. His inner thoughts were an enigma to even his closest advisers at this time. "Truman was always a good listener," Leahy later recalled, "and I could not gauge exactly what his own feeling was." He had made it clear "that he was completely favorable toward defeating our Far Eastern enemy with the smallest possible loss of American lives. It wasn't a matter of dollars. It might require more time—and more dollars—if we did not invade Japan. But it would cost *fewer lives*."[47] Torn by conflicting advice and loyalties, the President obviously continued to place the probability of an invasion in the front of his mind. But he seemed determined to keep his options open as long as possible. The excitable comments of John J. McCloy at the close of the meeting could have only hardened this inclination.

As the generals, admirals, and secretaries prepared to depart, a fidgety McCloy was approached by Truman, who said that no one was going to leave the room without expressing himself. What the Assistant Secretary of War then said is not exactly clear. Accord-

[45] *Foreign Relations, 1945; Conference of Berlin,* I: 909; Truman, *Public Papers, 1945,* pp. 95–96, 98.

[46] *Entry of the Soviet Union into the War Against Japan,* p. 84; *Foreign Relations, 1945; Conference of Berlin,* I: 909.

[47] *Entry of the Soviet Union into the War Against Japan,* p. 84; *Foreign Relations, 1945; Conference of Berlin,* I: 909; Millis, ed., *Forrestal Diaries,* p. 70; Leahy, *I Was There,* p. 385.

ing to one account McCloy burst out that invasion was a "fantastic" proposal. "Why not use the atomic bomb?" McCloy later claimed to recall "the chills that ran up and down the spines assembled there, but the President replied that this was a good possibility." McCloy then told the assembly that "the United States with its tremendous military might and prestige could win the war without invading Japan. The atomic bomb made American power all the more effective. He favored warning the Emperor that the United States had the bomb and would use it against Japan unless she surrendered." McCloy later claimed that his remarks "had appeal," but even at that late date no one in the group would guarantee that the bomb would work.[48]

This was McCloy's recollection of the meeting years later. His recollection in 1947, according to Forrestal, was much different. The use of the atomic bomb was to be subordinated to the mounting of a peace offensive. According to Forrestal's 1947 notes, McCloy recalled saying "that he thought before the final decision to invade Japan was taken *or it was decided to use the atomic bomb* political measures should be taken." Specifically, McCloy recalled to Forrestal proposing on June 18 to tell the Japanese of the new "and terrifyingly destructive weapon" which "we would have to use if they did not surrender." McCloy also proposed giving the Japanese the opportunity to retain the Emperor "and a form of government of their own choosing." According to McCloy, the military chiefs were "somewhat annoyed" at his presumption, but Truman "welcomed it and . . . ordered such a political offensive to be set in motion." In recording McCloy's impressions in 1947, Forrestal added that neither he nor Stimson were present at the time. Since in fact they were, either the Navy Secretary's version of the incident is pure fabrication, or McCloy's remarks to Truman were made in private after the meeting.[49]

That Forrestal's version of McCloy's remarks was not fabricated and that McCloy's ideas did carry weight with Truman is clear from the fact that in the three weeks between June 18 and the President's departure for Potsdam, American officials pursued with varying

[48] McCloy's story is in Hewlett and Anderson, *The New World*, p. 364.
[49] Millis, ed., *Forrestal Diaries*, p. 71, italics added.

intensity and interest all three lines of approach to the problem of a Japanese surrender which had been discussed at the White House.

Planning for the military operations against Kyushu continued, of course. They were supplemented by a psychological offensive designed to break the Japanese will to resist through verbal persuasion. Captain Ellis M. Zacharias had been broadcasting to Tokyo from Washington since May 8 under the auspices of the Office of War Information and with the enthusiastic support of Forrestal, King, and Elmer Davis. His aim was to reach and energize those members of Stimson's "large submerged class in Japan who do not favor the war" and get them started making positive steps toward peace. He had been quickly recognized and heard in Japan, and a weird, elliptical dialogue had ensued with Japanese commentators, who seemed to promise that reasonable conditions of surrender would stimulate cooperation in Tokyo. By the end of June, when Zacharias was joined by Colonel Sidney Mashbir, broadcasting from Manila, the Americans were speaking of "unconditional surrender with its attendant benefits as laid down by the Atlantic Charter." Whether these initiatives in and of themselves might have eventually led to serious negotiation is uncertain. The American and Japanese positions remained defined in tragically vague terms, and very probably the United States did not help its cause by demanding after early July that Tokyo make its position fully known immediately or suffer the consequences.[50]

While the psychological offensive was reaching its peak, the prime military interest shifted to the assurance of Soviet intervention and aid on the Asian mainland. And as Stalin had impressed upon Hopkins, such intervention would not be forthcoming unless a prior Sino-Soviet treaty embodying the Yalta Far Eastern accords had first been concluded. But would such a treaty open a Pandora's box of troubles in postwar Asia? Was Chiang strong enough to resist possible future Kremlin pressures for further and further concessions in Manchuria or outright Soviet aid to the Yenan Communists? These questions continued to haunt certain highly placed officials in the State Department, if not those around the President.

[50] Zacharias, *Secret Missions*, pp. 334–375 *passim*; William Craig, *The Fall of Japan* (New York: Dell Books, 1968), pp. 32–36.

Yet there seemed hope by early summer that at last Chiang
might be pulling his government and country together and that
Stalin's assurances to Hurley and Hopkins might permit the Chinese leader to complete his task. The battle for Burma was practically won, and Chinese troops had been an instrumental force in
the victorious coalition with British and Indian units. In China itself the earlier Japanese thrust toward the south and southeast had
long been dormant, palsied by the increasingly desperate situation
at home. As early as February plans had been laid for a massive
mid-summer Chinese offensive toward the coast to recapture Canton
and Hong Kong. China's war effort in all areas was immensely stimulated by the ever-expanding capacity of the air route over the
Hump and the opening, at last, of the Burma Road.[51]

To be sure, the same gross corruption, the same uncontrollable
inflation, the same unbelievable waste of human and material resources, the same poverty and failure that had so nauseated American sensibilities for so many months continued to exist in China
and to be reported in the American press. But it was now much too
late to let slip the Chungking commitment. Better to remain attached to the image if not the substance of the Kuomintang government and hope that favorable trends could continue to be ex-
ploited by diplomacy.[52]

The chief immediate problem, of course, was inducing Kuomintang concurrence in the Yalta accords as a prelude to later Sino-
Soviet talks which would eventuate in a treaty. On May 10 the ever-
ebullient Patrick J. Hurley held a long talk with Chiang, during
the course of which the Ambassador "discussed the provisions of the
Yalta agreement . . . without identifying them as such." It was
Hurley's impression that Chiang " 'will agree to every one of the
[Yalta] requirements. . . .' " There would be some tough bargaining ahead, nonetheless, Hurley added, because Chiang felt that
" 'preeminent' " Russian interest in the Manchurian railways and
the Soviet " 'lease' " of Port Arthur constituted terms and conditions which infringed upon Chinese sovereignty. But these were
negotiable points—stumbling blocks but not barriers to agree-

[51] Romanus and Sunderland, *Time Runs Out in CBI*, pp. 330–336.
[52] Feis, *China Tangle*, p. 274.

ment.[53] Trouble swiftly emerged from another quarter, however. With military and diplomatic scenes brightening, Chiang felt new resolve to bring his Communist opponents to heel. Ambassador Soong met with Truman on May 14 to discuss Chungking's desperate financial plight and to secure the last two hundred million dollars in gold due on a half billion dollar credit voted China by Congress the previous year. Then discussions turned to political matters and Soong became adamant. According to Grew, Soong "said to the President and myself that the National Government would like to have the Communists join in but could do so only if the Communists recognized that the National Government was in supreme control in China."[54] The Communists were well aware of Chiang's hardening attitude at this time, and their reaction was threatening. Civil war was not improbable.[55] During the final week in May the War Department became seriously alarmed and wrote to Grew urging that " 'some sort of understanding between the Chinese Communists and [Chiang Kai-shek] seems to be in order as of first importance.' "[56]

This was the situation in China, then, at the time of the Hopkins-Stalin talks in Moscow. On June 4, after receipt of Hopkins' cable on his Far Eastern discussions with Stalin, Truman sent an exultant message to Hurley in Chungking: " 'You may expect in the near future instructions to endeavor to obtain approval by Chiang Kai-shek of a military-political matter of the highest importance that, if it is approved, will radically and favorably change the entire military picture in your area.' "[57]

Moving swiftly, the President on June 9 called in Soong and at last broke the news of the Yalta Far Eastern Agreements to the Nationalist Chinese. The session lasted a full hour and the conversation was exhaustive. Throughout Truman made it "clear that he was definitely committed to the agreements reached by President Roosevelt."[58] Soong, in turn, indicated that he would leave Wash-

[53] Romanus and Sunderland, *Time Runs Out in CBI*, pp. 339–340.
[54] Feis, *China Tangle*, pp. 300–302; Truman, *Year of Decisions*, pp. 297–298; Grew, *Turbulent Era*, II: 1450–1451.
[55] Feis, *China Tangle*, p. 290.
[56] Quoted in Grew, *Turbulent Era*, II: 1451.
[57] Quoted in Truman, *Year of Decisions*, p. 298.
[58] Grew, *Turbulent Era*, II: 1465–1466; *Military Situation in the Far East, August 1951, Part 5*, p. 3339.

ington the following week for Chungking to discuss the Yalta accords with Chiang and then would move on to Moscow for negotiations. Following his meeting with Soong, Truman cabled Hurley the gist of Stalin's recent remarks to Hopkins and " 'the conditions for Soviet participation in the war against Japan.' " Truman directed Hurley to " 'take up this matter with Chiang on June fifteenth and to make every effort to obtain his approval.' "[59]

On the fourteenth, the day before Soong's departure, Truman, Soong, and Grew held their major policy discussion. Hopkins had just returned, and Truman began by saying that "after reading the minutes of Mr. Hopkins' conversations in Moscow he was able to tell Dr. Soong that Stalin's assurances with respect to the sovereignty of China in Manchuria and elsewhere had been even more categorical than he had told Dr. Soong the last time he saw him." The President concluded the talks by stating "that his chief interest now was to see the Soviet Union participate in the Far Eastern war in sufficient time to be of help in shortening the war and thus save American and Chinese lives." Truman also told Soong that "just as in Europe," so in the Far East, "the United States desired above all to see these postwar questions settled in such a way as to eliminate any tinderboxes . . . which might cause future trouble and wars."[60]

The implication was clear. Nationalist China was caught between the two paramount American policy goals. One was the determination to get Russia into the Pacific war as soon as possible. The other was to work in conjunction with the Soviets to order worldwide power relationships *before* the end of conflict so as to prevent or eliminate "tinderboxes" in the forthcoming peacetime era. In the face of such pressure Soong could only express his "gratitude." However, he did venture to point out that in several agreements of 1924 the Soviet regime had renounced the Manchurian concessions earlier enjoyed by the czars. If Stalin now wished to see these concessions revived, the matter would have to be negotiated. Echoing Chiang's objections earlier stated to Hurley, Soong expressed special distress at the Russian demands for a lease upon Port Arthur "since after all the suffering in this war the Chinese

[59] Quoted in Truman, *Year of Decisions*, pp. 299–300.
[60] Grew, *Turbulent Era*, II: 1466–1468.

Government and people were very much against the re-establishment of the system of special leased ports in China," with all of its noxious reminders of Western imperial domination. Truman replied that "he would do nothing which would harm the interests of China since China was a friend of the United States in the Far East."[61] Truman's use of the article *a* rather than *the* could only have sounded ominously in Soong's ears. Obviously in American Presidential, if not diplomatic, thinking Russia had now joined China as a major power factor in Asia. So, evidently filled with unease and concern, wishing to be cooperative but seeming fearful of the price, Soong flew off to Chungking to confront Chiang.

Meanwhile ominous developments were brewing in Moscow, in the Chinese capital, and in Washington. On June 13 Hurley told the State Department that on the preceding day the Soviet Ambassador in Chungking had informed the Nationalist Chinese of the conditions upon which Russia would enter the war without, however, making any reference to the assurances of Soviet support for the Kuomintang which Stalin had given Hopkins. Six days later the former Soviet press attaché at Chungking told an American official in a Moscow bar that he was actively working to turn Kremlin policy in China into "more aggressive and expansive" channels. " 'Dr. Soong,' " he added, " 'would not realize his objective' " of a twenty-year Sino-Soviet treaty. Was this Russian official intoxicated and speaking for himself, a dangerous game indeed for a minor bureaucrat to play in Stalin's Moscow? Or was he speaking for his government? Worried American officials could not be certain, but a concerned Harriman dispatched a long memorandum on the conversations to the State Department. When at last, on June 15, Hurley was officially able to inform Chiang of the Yalta agreements, the Chinese leader immediately created new problems, suggesting three modifications in the Crimean accords. First, he asked that the Americans and British become formal parties to whatever Sino-Soviet treaty might emerge from the Yalta accords and the forthcoming Soong negotiations in Moscow. Second, he wished Port Arthur to become a joint four-power base. Finally, he asked that

[61] *Ibid.*

transfer of southern Sakhalin and the Kuriles be discussed by all four powers rather than by China and Russia alone.[62]

Truman and Grew discussed Chiang's modifications on June 16. The two agreed that the United States should continue to stand aloof from the Chungking-Moscow negotiations. "Truman observed in their talk that Chiang Kai-shek and Soong now knew as much as he did about the Yalta Accord, and that while he was committed to it, he was not qualified to expand on its interpretation."[63] Two explanations of Truman's behavior immediately come to mind. First, he was determined that the United States should in no way by its own actions jeopardize Soviet entry into the Pacific war. And second, the President and his Acting Secretary of State seemed determined not to intrude United States power and influence too deeply into the tangled affairs and rivalries of the Asian mainland. The desired American sphere of influence lay in the vast ocean stretches of the Pacific, not on the continent. Stalin had surely seemed accommodating enough in his talks with Hopkins concerning the Far Eastern settlement. This was not the time to allow the Chinese to rock the diplomatic boat with either open or tacit American approval. Truman thus told the Chinese through Hurley "that it seemed very doubtful whether the Soviet Union would consent to the arrangements that Chiang Kai-shek had in mind, since the purpose of the pact with China would be regulating Sino-Soviet relations."[64]

Hurley passed Truman's message on to Chiang and Soong at a meeting on June 22 and pronounced himself encouraged by Chiang's overall eagerness to secure a pact of friendship with, and to carve out a sphere of influence in Northeast Asia contiguous to, the Russians. "'I am convinced,'" Hurley cabled home, "'that the Soviet Union and China will be able to reach an agreement quickly.'"[65]

All seemed promising. Harriman, however, expressed other ideas that ran counter to the Presidential policy of securing swift finali-

---

[62] Feis, *China Tangle*, p. 314; "Memorandum with enclosure, Harriman to State Department," June 19, 1945, Records of the Department of State, decimal file 893.00/6-1945, National Archives.

[63] Feis, *China Tangle*, p. 315.

[64] *Ibid.*

[65] Quoted in *ibid.*

zation of a Sino-Soviet treaty so as to insure the earliest possible Russian intervention. When Soong reached Moscow he immediately told Harriman, who had returned to his post, that the Nationalist Chinese "were anxious to reach an agreement with the Soviet Union." To achieve this, Soong added, China "was prepared to make concessions," which Harriman thought, as he heard them enumerated, "went far beyond the Yalta understanding."[66]

That such concessions might have to be made, however, became obvious rather swiftly. As the negotiations began in the first week of July, a fortnight before Potsdam, Russia asked for controlling rather than joint interest in the Manchurian railways. Stalin also demanded an enlargement of the Dairen and Port Arthur leases to include the entire pre-1904 Russian boundaries on the strategically important Kwantung peninsula. Finally, the Russians demanded that China grant outright independence to Outer Mongolia, a strategic border area between the two countries. An unhappy Soong informed Harriman of these excessive demands, and the Ambassador transmitted the tale to the new Secretary of State, James F. Byrnes. To Harriman, of course, such Russian probes could only serve to rekindle his worst fears of Soviet expansionism. He formally advised Soong and the Chinese government to stand firm on the original Crimean agreements and so, significantly, did Byrnes.[67]

The hardening of Soviet Asian diplomacy on the very eve of the Potsdam Conference surely generated much sober speculation in Washington. Stalin's cordiality to Hopkins, followed by very rigid demands at the negotiating table, confirmed a pattern already observable in Soviet international relations from Tehran to Yalta. Sunny breezes of good will at the summit turned immediately to cold winds of suspicion on the morrow.

Stiffening Soviet attitudes toward the Kuomintang probably came too late, however, to influence significantly American thinking on the other two possible approaches to a Japanese surrender —use of the atomic bomb and modification of unconditional surrender to permit retention of the Emperor. Sino-Soviet negotiations in Moscow, after all, did not commence until the first week in July, and Truman and his party left for Berlin on the sixth. Use of the

[66] *Military Situation in the Far East, August 1951, Part 5*, p. 3339.
[67] *Ibid.*; *China White Paper*, I: 116–117.

bomb and modification of unconditional surrender were explored in an environment largely free of preoccupation with threatening Russian behavior.

Indeed, the overriding preoccupation of government officials and public opinion alike in the final week of June and the first days of July centered around the terrible cost in blood and treasure of the forthcoming invasion of Japan. Commenting on the regular weekly meeting of the Secretaries of State, War, and Navy on June 19, the day after Marshall had outlined plans for the Kyushu campaign which Truman had approved, Stimson recorded "a pretty strong feeling that it would be deplorable if we have to go through with the military program with all its stubborn fighting to a finish. We agreed that it is necessary now to plan and prepare to go through, but it became very evident today in the discussion that we all feel that some way should be found of inducing Japan to yield without a fight."[68]

A week later the three Secretaries registered concern at what was described as a sudden public "deterioration of will to complete the defeat of Japan." With the Okinawa campaign concluded, some sort of initial invasion of Japan was sure to be next. And the American people clearly contemplated the prospect with mounting dread. As late as July 13 Grew wrote to Byrnes in Potsdam of "the growing speculation in this country, as indicated in speeches, editorials, et cetera, as to whether the Japanese Government had or had not made a bona fide peace offer." This trend in public thinking disturbed Grew, for it tended, in his opinion, "to weaken the war morale of the country" even as it created in Japan "the belief that the American people are getting ready for a compromise peace and all the Japanese have to do is to continue to fight."[69]

Clarification of unconditional surrender, which Grew had been pleading for since the end of May, thus seemed imperative by the end of June. During the week June 20–June 26, with Truman out of town on a western trip that took him eventually to San Francisco for the final session of the United Nations Conference, Stimson rested at his Long Island home, Highhold, and pondered the

[68] Stimson Diary, June 19, 1945.
[69] Quoted in *Foreign Relations, 1945; Conference of Berlin*, I: 888, 902.

implications of the atomic bomb and its effects upon the Japanese.[70]
On the twenty-sixth he returned to Washington to confer with his
Navy and State Department counterparts and immediately indicated that Grew had at least partially won him over. "I took up at
once the subject of trying to get Japan to surrender by giving her a
warning *after* she had been sufficiently pounded possibly with S-1."
The old man had brought the draft of a letter to Truman on the
topic and "when we got through, both Forrestal and Grew said that
they approved of the proposed step and the general substance of
the letter."[71] In the letter itself, dated July 2, Stimson said that he
"had prepared a proposed form of proclamation" which, though
discussed with various diplomatic and military officials, "has not
been placed in final form or in any sense approved as a final document by the Secretary of State or the Secretary of Navy, or the Joint
Chiefs of Staff." It had been drafted, Stimson said, "merely to put
on paper something which would give us some idea of how a warning of the character we have in mind might appear." "You will
note," Stimson concluded significantly, "that it is written without
specific relation to the employment of any new weapon. Of course
it would have to be revamped to conform to the efficacy of such a
weapon if the warning were to be delivered, as would almost certainly be the case, in conjunction with its use."[72]

Stimson's words encompassed three critically important assumptions. First was the assumption of reserve when speaking of the
possible use of the atomic bomb. The weapon could not yet be considered a sure thing. Whether and when it would work remained
uncertain. The second assumption was that, should the bomb prove
successful *in combat*, the proposed draft would be "revamped,"
which Stimson presumably defined in terms of significant altera-
tion. The third and most important assumption was that such a
warning would not be delivered earlier than the first use of the
bomb against Japan.

The sense of urgency in these days, the felt need to bring all possible factors to bear in seeking a strong and enduring victory over

[70] Stimson Diary, June 20–25, 1945.
[71] *Ibid.*, June 26, 1945, italics added; *Foreign Relations, 1945; Conference of Berlin*, I: 888.
[72] *Foreign Relations, 1945; Conference of Berlin*, I: 888–889.

Japan short of invasion and a subsequent bloody campaign, was reflected most poignantly in Grew's shifting attitude toward Russian intervention. Deeply fearful of it, as we have seen, as late as mid-May, Grew by June 19 had completely changed his mind. "He is suggesting," Stimson wrote, "an additional sanction to our warning in the shape of entry by the Russians into the war. That would certainly coordinate all the threats possible to Japan."[73]

With his colleagues' support assured by the decision of the State-War-Navy meeting on June 26, Stimson returned to Highhold for further study of the Japanese problem and talks with McCloy.[74] Then, on the morning of July 2, Stimson was ushered into the Oval Office of the White House to see Truman, who had just returned from the West and was about to depart for Europe. Truman, of course, had from the beginning faithfully and consistently followed the hard-line, pro-invasion policy advocated by General Marshall. It would be difficult to deflect him abruptly from this course, but days of quiet thought punctuated by sober conversation seemed to have convinced Stimson that the attempt must be made.

The Secretary began by stressing the full horror attendant upon an outright American assault against the home islands: "the landing may be a very long, costly, and arduous struggle on our part." The terrain was ideally suited to a fanatical defense such as the Americans had already experienced on a much smaller scale, Stimson stressed, on Iwo Jima and Okinawa. "If we once land on one of the main islands and begin a forceful occupation of Japan, we shall probably have cast the die of last ditch resistance. . . . we shall in my opinion have to go through with an even more bitter finish fight than in Germany."[75]

Was there, then, any way of inducing Japan to surrender unconditionally and submit to occupation short of actual invasion? Stimson told Truman that he thought there was. "I believe Japan *is* susceptible to reason in such a crisis to a much greater extent than is indicated by our current press. . . . Japan is not a nation composed wholly of mad fanatics." The Secretary then went on to stress again

[73] Stimson Diary, June 19, 1945.
[74] *Ibid.*, June 30, 1945.
[75] Stimson and Bundy, *On Active Service*, pp. 620–621.

his belief in the presence of "enough liberal leaders" in Japan to work for a negotiated settlement. At the moment these individuals were "submerged by the terrorists," but their energies might be kindled by "a carefully timed warning" to be given by the Allies, including Russia, should she be a belligerent. "The warning must be tendered *before* the actual invasion has occurred," Stimson asserted, "and while the impending destruction, though clear beyond peradventure, has not yet reduced her [Japan] to fanatical despair. If Russia is part of the threat," he continued, "the Russian attack, if actual, must not have progressed too far."[76] Such timing would not exclude use of the atomic bomb, as Stimson indicated in his remarks to Grew and Forrestal on June 26. Moreover, the Secretary had recorded his thoughts on this particular problem with precise clarity in his diary on June 19. "My only fixed date," he wrote, "is the last chance warning that must be given before an actual landing of the ground forces on Japan, and fortunately the plans provide for enough time to bring in the sanctions to our warning in the shape of heavy ordinary bombing attack *and an attack of S-1*."[77]

So much for the timing of the warning. Its content was remarkably free of clarity or generosity despite Stimson's expressed eagerness to find ways of ending the war short of assault. Nowhere did Stimson's proposed warning discuss the future role and position of the Emperor, which to Tokyo was of overriding importance. Insofar as either the Japanese throne or military clique was concerned, Stimson's draft warning simply asserted "the determination of the Allies to destroy permanently all authority and influence of those who have deceived and misled the country into embarking on world conquest." Sullen and suspicious Japanese officials were surely justified in interpreting this sweeping clause to include not only the Emperor, but also various figures in the peace faction. "The disavowal of any attempt to extirpate the Japanese as a race or to destroy them as a nation," American "readiness" to permit Japan to retain light industries and limited access to raw materials and world trade, and, finally, a promised withdrawal of Allied occupation forces once a "peacefully inclined" postwar Japanese government

[76] *Ibid.*, pp. 621, 622–624, italics added.
[77] Stimson Diary, June 19, 1945, italics added.

had been established, could scarcely attract the serious attention of the desperate men in Tokyo. The fact is that Stimson's July 2 proposals did not carry the question of modifying unconditional surrender one step closer to solution.[78]

During the next twenty-four hours, however, the situation changed somewhat. Truman had not had time on the morning of the second to see Stimson at any length, so the two men agreed to meet late in the following afternoon for a long discussion of the problem.[79] Sometime on the third, very possibly before Stimson's second interview with Truman, someone in the State Department telephoned to the War Department a suggested change in Stimson's draft with specific respect to the Emperor. This change incorporated the provision that *after the conclusion of the American occupation* the Japanese might be permitted "a constitutional monarchy under the present dynasty if it be shown to the complete satisfaction of the world that such a government will never again aspire to aggression."[80] This revision, placed at the close of the twelfth paragraph, was accepted by the War Department, apparently accepted by Truman during his second conversation with Stimson on July 3, and was carried on board the cruiser *Augusta* as it prepared to carry Truman and Byrnes to Potsdam on July 7.[81]

But then it was killed. "On the way to Potsdam aboard the *Augusta*, the President and Byrnes made the final decision to eliminate the controversial sentence." At the same time Truman privately re-examined, apparently for the last time, the atomic decision and chose to stick with it. Interviewed years later on the soul-searing nature of his decision, Truman was derisive. " 'Hell no,' " he responded, " 'I made it like'—he snapped his fingers—'that.' "[82]

Too much can be, and has been, made of all the debate surrounding the revised sentences on the Emperor.[83] Truman, and especially Byrnes, appear as villains. The President and the Secretary of State ostensibly had a real instrument of negotiation handed to

---

[78] Stimson and Bundy, *On Active Service*, p. 623.
[79] Stimson Diary, July 2, 1945.
[80] *Foreign Relations, 1945; Conference of Berlin*, I: 893–894.
[81] *Ibid.*, pp. 893–894, 897–899, 900.
[82] Toland, *Rising Sun*, pp. 776, 776n.
[83] *Ibid.*

them by subordinates in the State Department and by Stimson, who agreed to the revision, yet the two men spurned it. But the revision must be placed in its proper context. Paragraph 12, as revised, stipulated that Japan could *not* expect an autonomous constitutional monarchy "under the present dynasty" until *after the completion of the American occupation.* United States occupation of and military governance over Japan was a *sine qua non* of any possible "negotiations." The Emperor—should he be allowed to retain his title, and this was not at all clear in the draft—would definitely be subordinate and responsible to the occupying powers so long as they remained in Japan. This was not at all what Tokyo had in mind! The State Department revision represented in fact no real concession whatsoever, for in truth an Allied occupation in and of itself represented a *de facto* destruction of Japan's traditional national polity—of her *Tennō* system.[84] The Americans remained as determined as ever to exert wholly their will over Japan. In this crucial sense, the opportunity for Japanese-American negotiations to end the Pacific war short of the utter defeat of Nippon was as remote at the time of Potsdam as it had been at the time of Midway or Guadalcanal, Tarawa or the campaign for the Marianas. Despite their anguish over the terrible cost involved in total victory, no person of influence filling a responsible position in Washington during the summer of 1945 could bring himself to consider treating the Japanese other than as a vanquished foe. Within this limited conception all options save an atomic strike or a sudden, unlooked-for, and self-induced Japanese collapse were rigorously precluded as alternatives to a direct and massive invasion of the home islands. America's overriding determination to humble Japan led to an inevitable decision to assault Nippon with all the power that a righteously aroused United States could bring to bear.

On July 4, the day after Stimson's second meeting with Truman regarding the draft warning, the Combined British and American

---

[84] As one of the most perceptive students of modern warfare has stated, "A country that passively accepted the yoke of the occupying state might be acting reasonably (in military terms, the cost of resistance might exceed the 'yield'), but would it not have renounced nationhood?" Raymond Aron, *The Century of Total War* (Boston: The Beacon Press, 1955), p. 41. Or again, in George Kennan's retrospective view: "We had demanded and received unconditional surrender. That was equivalent to demanding and receiving dictatorial power." *Memoirs,* pp. 388–389.

Policy Committee met in Washington to give final and official sanction to the use of the atomic bomb. The question of releasing atomic information to foreign powers, *i.e.*, the Russians, was quickly raised. Stimson stated that there existed two opinions on the matter. The first presupposed that the scientific principles of atomic bomb making would inevitably be known as soon as the weapon was used, "and other countries would understand that one of three or four processes had been employed." The second opinion was simply that "the technical and mechanical difficulties encountered in the production of the weapon and the methods by which they have been overcome need not and should not be disclosed."[85]

Lord Halifax, the ranking British member, argued that the "greater the amount of information which was disclosed to other countries the less inducement there might be for them to agree to measures of international control, should we even desire to suggest them." In response Stimson substantially repeated what he had told Truman the day before. At the White House the Secretary had suggested to the President that "if he found that he thought that Stalin was on good enough terms with him he should . . . simply [tell] him that we were busy with this thing working like the dickens and we knew he was busy with this thing and working like the dickens and that we were pretty nearly ready and we intended to use it against the enemy, Japan; that if it was satisfactory we proposed to then talk it over with Stalin afterwards. . . ."[86] To his British colleagues on July 4 Stimson first admitted that the coming test of the atomic device would probably occur during the Potsdam Conference and that "if nothing was said at this meeting about the T.A. ["Tube Alloy," the British code for S-1 or the atomic bomb] weapon, its subsequent early use might have a serious effect on the relations of frankness between the three great Allies." Therefore, if the atmosphere at Potsdam should prove "real and satisfactory," the President might tell Stalin of American work on "atomic fission for war purposes" and that "an attempt to use the weapon would be made shortly." Should the weapon succeed then

---

[85] A full account of the meeting may be found in *Foreign Relations, 1945; Diplomatic Papers*, II: 12–13.
[86] Stimson Diary, July 3, 1945.

"it would be necessary for discussion to be held on the best method of handling the development in the interests of world peace. . . ." Nothing else of substantive value should be revealed. The British perforce could only accede to the American plan, and the meeting broke up.[87]

Two days later, while American forces mercilessly continued to pound Japan in anticipation of the coming invasion of Kyushu and while plans progressed for the atomic test in the New Mexico desert, Truman left for Potsdam and his first personal meeting with Churchill and Stalin. He took with him a new Secretary of State, James F. Byrnes, whose association with the President and the Presidency was charged with tension. A new and potentially disturbing personality was about to be introduced into American diplomacy.

[87] *Foreign Relations, 1945; Diplomatic Papers,* II: 13.

10

The Emergence of Jimmy Byrnes

On June 27, the day after the close of the San Francisco Conference, Truman formally announced the resignation of Edward R. Stettinius as Secretary of State. Undersecretary Dean Acheson told his daughter of the widespread rumor that Jimmy Byrnes would replace Stettinius, then added: "Archie [MacLeish] says that Ed forced the issue by insisting that he could not go on in this vague way. He must be in or out. And the answer was out."[1]

Some were shocked by what Vandenberg called "the sudden Presidential decapitation of Stettinius." A number of Republican newspapers, especially those in the areas where pre-war isolationist sentiment had been strong and suspicion of the British and Russian allies remained an almost reflexive tradition, were disturbed by the Byrnes appointment and unhappy when Byrnes and Truman subsequently refused to include any ranking member of the G.O.P. in the Potsdam delegation. It is quite possible that this pressure of suspicion from home exerted a marked influence on Byrnes' thinking, if not his conduct, at Berlin. But most Americans were pleased by the

[1] Acheson, *Present at the Creation*, p. 110.

244

change, which appeared to signal a return to the Yalta policy of accommodation. So popular was Truman's decision, in fact, and so pressing the crush of world business, that Byrnes was immediately confirmed by the Senate on July 2 without even a formal hearing.[2]

Stettinius' frustration reflected the long decline in power and influence of the State Department during the Roosevelt years. Throughout the period the department discovered its functional prerogatives and even its administrative integrity increasingly encroached upon by a host of other departments, bureaus, and bureaucrats within the sprawling New Deal and wartime establishments. During the 1930s Secretary Cordell Hull had been forced to surrender a significant portion of influence and decision-making to such Presidential advisers as Raymond Moley and Rexford Tugwell. Only during the cautious years 1934–1939 could Hull claim to have influenced consistently the course of American diplomacy, and even then his innately cautious ideas and plans for the liberalization of international trade were often frustrated by only fitful and half-hearted White House support. Under pressure from bureaus and men charged with overlapping functions, the State Department all too often made survival, not influence, its major goal.[3]

After 1940 State's decision-making role was further eclipsed. It was Harry Hopkins, not Cordell Hull, who at Roosevelt's behest journeyed to Moscow in July of 1941 to lay the groundwork for the Soviet-American wartime alliance. It was Hopkins, not Hull, who throughout the war labored most faithfully to maintain that alliance, becoming in the process the *de facto* chief foreign minister of the Roosevelt administration. And it was Hopkins, understandably enough, who was charged by Truman in the late spring of 1945

[2] Frank McNaughton Report, July 2, 1945, McNaughton Papers, Box 7; Vandenberg and Morris, eds., *Private Papers of Senator Vandenberg*, pp. 224–225; Jay G. Hayden column in *Detroit News*, July 2, 1945, clipping in Vandenberg Papers, Scrapbook Series, Volume 17.

[3] Herbert Feis, *1933; Characters in Crisis* (Boston: Little, Brown & Co., 1966), *passim*; William E. Leuchtenberg, *Franklin D. Roosevelt and the New Deal* (New York: Harper & Row, 1963), pp. 199–205; Robert A. Divine, *The Reluctant Belligerent; American Entry into World War II* (New York: John A. Wiley & Sons, 1965), p. 3; McNeill, *America, Britain, and Russia*, p. 57; Acheson, *Present at the Creation*, Chapter 2; Arthur W. Schatz, "The Anglo-American Trade Agreement and Cordell Hull's Search for Peace, 1936–1938," *Journal of American History*, LVII (June 1970), 85–103.

with the task of arresting the decline in relations between Washington and the Kremlin so as to maintain the wartime coalition intact at least through the defeat of Japan.[4]

At the same time, the necessity to underwrite much of the economic and military effort of the vast Allied coalition brought Henry Morgenthau and the Treasury Department to the center of foreign economic planning and further eroded the State Department's functions and prerogatives. From the inception of lend-lease in 1940 through the long drawn out struggle over the Morgenthau Plan to "pastoralize" Germany, Treasury wielded powerful influence in American foreign policy. Indeed, in the State Department's eyes the incessant debate over Morgenthau's plan prevented the formulation of "a consistent and agreed Allied policy toward Germany." Such a policy never fully emerged until the autumn of 1945 under the spur of Treasury and War, as well as State Department, concern.[5]

Hull, Stettinius, and lesser State Department officials found their roles further reduced during the war by the undeniably necessary intrusion of the military chiefs and the Secretaries of War and Navy into the diplomatic sphere. To a greater or lesser extent, diplomacy and strategy become one during any conflict, and the Second World War was no exception. By 1945 the importance of the military in diplomatic decision-making, both on the day-to-day planning level and at the great international conferences of the Big Three, was fully equal to that of the Department of State. This fact was dramatized by the establishment of a number of interdepartmental committees, of which the Joint State-War-Navy Coordinating Committee was the best known.[6]

The close collaboration between the diplomatic and military services often generated as much heat as light. Stimson, in particu-

[4] Sherwood, *Roosevelt and Hopkins*, I: 270–528; II: *passim*; John L. Snell, *Illusion and Necessity; The Diplomacy of Global War, 1939–1945* (Boston: Houghton, Mifflin Co., 1963), p. 107; McNeill, *America, Britain, and Russia*, pp. 404–405.

[5] Kimball, *The Most Unsordid Act, passim*, esp. p. 34; Smith, *American Diplomacy during the Second World War*, pp. 122–126, 135; Clay, *Decision in Germany*, pp. 4–5, 16–17; Moseley, "Dismemberment of Germany," pp. 131–154.

[6] These developments are thoroughly discussed in Roy S. Cline, *Washington Command Post; The Operations Division* (Washington: Department of the Army, 1951), pp. 322–332.

lar, became increasingly disgusted with Stettinius by the final spring of the war. "Stettinius has not got a firm enough hand on his affairs and with all his pleasantness and briskness does not make his machine go," the old man fumed at one point. Several weeks later he angrily recorded his aggravation "at the way that the State Department is lying down on us in certain matters. It probably cannot be helped because Stettinius is inexperienced and has no background in those matters. Although well intentioned, he is not very firm in his decisions and character, and the result is that we have been called in in several issues in which, while we have some military interest, we are being made to take a very predominating part."[7]

Stettinius had his vociferous supporters, and he did try, amidst the rush of business, to reform and streamline his department.[8] But always he worked, as had Hull, under enormous handicaps of administration and communications.

> Key decisions were taken by the President [Roosevelt] after consultation with a small and varying group of men; and it was more or less a matter of accident whether or not the views of senior officials of the State Department got serious hearing. Moreover, there was no certainty that the State Department would be speedily and officially informed of Presidential decisions after they had been taken. As a result, the State Department frequently found itself competing with other branches of the Government, each with a foreign policy to press on the President.[9]

Frozen out of grand policy-making save in the sphere of United Nations organization and some areas of postwar economic planning, both of which were consistently subordinated to the immediate demands of the Grand Alliance, the department by 1945 had become increasingly demoralized and defensive. As Acheson pungently noted, it frequently "stood breathless and bewildered like an old lady at a busy intersection during rush hour."[10] Uncertain

---

[7] Stimson Diary, April 16, 29, 1945.
[8] Grew, *Turbulent Era*, II: 1385, 1442; Walter Johnson, "Edward R. Stettinius, Jr.", in Norman A. Graebner, ed., *An Uncertain Tradition; American Secretaries of State in the Twentieth Century* (New York: McGraw-Hill Book Co., 1961), p. 221.
[9] McNeill, *America, Britain, and Russia*, p. 58.
[10] Acheson, *Present at the Creation*, pp. 68, 114.

of their power and status, department officials came to define their chief role as being faithful guardians and exponents of the American interpretations of the various Big Three agreements reached at Yalta and before. In particular, the department staunchly defended the Crimean Declaration on Liberated Europe and American prerogatives supposedly guaranteed by the Allied armistice agreements with those Danubian nations—Bulgaria, Rumania, and Hungary—formerly under Nazi control. American representatives on the Control Commissions in Budapest, Bucharest, and Sophia were given department encouragement in their opposition to the unilateral machinations of Soviet officials and local Communists.[11] The deterioration of mutual Soviet-American trust during the early spring of 1945 was thus hastened by State Department initiatives in the countries of Eastern Europe.

Yet this was not at all what Roosevelt had wanted, and Truman made it quite clear in sending Hopkins to Moscow that he did not desire the triumph of such policies either. So once again the State Department would be frustrated. This was made abundantly clear during the first days of June. Toward the end of May ominous developments were perceived in both Bulgaria and Rumania. On the seventeenth the State Department was informed of the recent conclusion of a Soviet-Rumanian economic agreement. This agreement was interpreted by non-Communist Rumanian economists as possessing supreme "political implications as a Russian attempt to monopolize Rumanian markets and to restrict [Rumanian] trade to states in a Soviet-dominated economic zone."[12] At the same time Maynard Barnes, the State Department representative on the Bulgarian Control Commission, reported Russian support for the "tactics" of the Bulgarian Communists "to pulverize the Agrarian" party "and to preserve and dominate" the Fatherland Front established the previous September. By the end of the month these tactics had succeeded. The Agrarian Party leader, Georgi M. Dimi-

---

[11] Cf., for example, Acting Secretary of State (Grew) to U.S. Representative in Bulgaria (Barnes), March 3, 1945, to U.S. Representative in Rumania (Berry), March 29, 1945, *Foreign Relations, 1945; Diplomatic Papers*, IV: 169; V: 525–526.

[12] U.S. Representative in Rumania (Berry) to Secretary of State, May 17, 1945, *ibid.*, V: 544–545.

trov, was driven to seek asylum at Barnes' residence in Sophia, where he remained while Barnes and the State Department sought to use the embarrassment of his predicament to exert concessions from the Russians and the Bulgarian Communists.[13]

In the face of these developments Truman continued to hold his unhappy diplomats at arm's length with an aplomb that Roosevelt would have admired. When Grew and Arthur Bliss Lane, the newly appointed Ambassador to Poland, journeyed to the White House on June 4, Lane urged "that our attitude towards Soviet Russia in connection with the Polish issue should be integrated with the many other issues in Central Europe, particularly the Soviet blackouts in the Balkan states and the states of Central Europe." Truman replied "that he had precisely the same opinion and that this would be the fundamental subject which he intended to discuss at the Big Three meeting." But the President also made it clear that "while Mr. Hopkins is still negotiating in Moscow and while the San Francisco Conference is still going on it would be desirable not to exert too much pressure." Truman promised his intention to "insist" on "the eventual removal of the Soviet blackout in the countries mentioned," and his visitors had to rest content with that vague assurance.[14]

Truman's persistent imperviousness to pressures from the State Department reflected, in fact, a deep Presidential desire to reform thoroughly the department and its leadership even as he was setting in motion significant reorganization of the other Executive departments, such as Labor and Agriculture. And for the implementation of the State Department task he looked to James F. Byrnes. For administrative, diplomatic, and above all, personal reasons, Truman accepted Byrnes from the first as his chief foreign policy adviser.

Jimmy Byrnes was sixty-five at the time of Roosevelt's death. Behind him lay a career of public service unmatched for variety and distinction in his generation. Born in Charleston, South Carolina, in 1879, of immigrant Irish stock, Byrnes was a poor boy who

---

[13] U.S. Representative in Bulgaria (Barnes) to Secretary of State, May 12, 1945, *ibid.*, IV: 212; U.S. Department of State *Bulletin*, XII (June 3, 1945), 1023.
[14] Grew, *Turbulent Era*, II: 1464–1465.

had made good. His father had died two weeks before his birth, and his mother had "slaved and saved" as a seamstress to achieve the respectable status of home ownership. Burdened from an early age by the family's desperate straits, young Jimmy left school at the age of fourteen to work as an office boy in a local law firm at a time when the tradition of reading for the bar in a legal office rather than a college classroom was still strong across the deep South. In 1904, at age twenty-five, he passed his examinations and commenced practice. In 1908 he was elected District Attorney—or Circuit Solicitor, as it was then known in South Carolina. Two years later, in 1910, after narrowly winning "the hottest Congressional race in years" in his district, he entered the House of Representatives in the Democratic surge which presaged the coming of Wilson's "New Freedom."[15] As with Stimson, Cordell Hull, and Joseph C. Grew, but unlike Truman or Forrestal, Byrnes thus entered American public life at the close of the gaslight and buggy era during the "good years" just before World War I. It was the twilight of the gentlemanly, often ambiguous, but still recognizable concert of the pre-eminent Great Powers—France, Britain, and the United States. Domestic politics and foreign affairs were ideally conceived as being guided by certain moral presuppositions which were as widely accepted as they were readily comprehensible after a century of general world peace.[16] In other words, it was an age of security and certitude, parochial and heart-breakingly naive in its assumptions about man and his social conscience. These were the years in which mankind was, for the last moment, blessedly ignorant of what Winston Churchill in after times was to call "the lights of perverted science" as applied to the making of war and the spreading of death.

Byrnes spent a total of fourteen years in the House building up a network of friendships that served him well when, after one electoral failure, he moved to the Senate in 1931. "Small, wiry, neat in appearance, cautious and self-contained in manner, a genial, quiz-

---

[15] James F. Byrnes, *All in One Lifetime* (New York: Harper & Brothers, 1958), pp. 13–21, 23; Richard D. Burns, "James F. Byrnes," in Graebner, *An Uncertain Tradition*, p. 224.

[16] Cf. Henry F. May, *The End of American Innocence* (New York: Alfred A. Knopf, 1959), pp. 3–117.

zical expression nearly always on his face," a gentle persuader, and a southern Senator who pursued a course of "successful independence" during the final stormy years of the New Deal era, a politician who always knew just how far to go in opposition to or support of FDR, Byrnes carved out a brilliant career for himself as one of the leaders of the Democratic moderates in the upper chamber during the 1930s. In 1941, apparently capping a long career of distinguished public service, Byrnes moved on to the permanent security of the Supreme Court. The following year, however, at Roosevelt's request, Byrnes abruptly left the sanctuary of the bench to plunge headlong into the wartime "Battle of Washington." He assumed the awesome responsibility of directing the overall American production effort as Director of the Office of War Mobilization and Reconversion, and in retrospect, performed the job with as much competence as any human being faced with the ceaseless bickering of bureaucratic "czars" and "war lords" could have possibly summoned. As "Assistant President" his reputation as a brilliant legislator was enhanced by his growing stature as a skilled administrator.[17]

Yet the job as Mobilization Director would have been a political graveyard for any man, as Byrnes himself was aware.[18] And while some would claim that he had no enemies, Jimmy Byrnes had inevitably generated a substantial amount of dislike and, above all, mistrust during his long public career. While he could be "genial, humorous and charming," the South Carolinian was also well known by 1945 as a "foxy operator" and a "fixer." "If the cause is about to be lost," one observer wrote, "Byrnes is always ready with a compromise that will save some if not most of it via later interpretations after the opposition is on the dotted line. He is also adept at creating a good press for himself."[19] There is a word to describe the man of professional geniality, adroit operation, and sure instinct for the sources and exercise of power—it is *ambitious*.

[17] Byrnes, *All in One Lifetime*, pp. 52–215, 238–251; Burns, "Byrnes," p. 225; James T. Patterson, *Congressional Conservatism and the New Deal* (Lexington, Ky.: University of Kentucky Press, 1967), pp. 129–130; Janeway, *Struggle for Survival*, pp. 314–316, 336–338, 350–352.

[18] Byrnes, *All in One Lifetime*, p. 219.

[19] "Report—Jimmy Byrnes," September 4, 1945, Box 7, McNaughton Papers; "Mr. Truman Faces It," *Fortune*, XXXIII (January 1946), 235ff.

In 1944 Byrnes' most cherished ambition had received a shattering setback—and, in part at least, at the hands of his long-time Senate colleague, Harry Truman.

In his long public career Byrnes had fulfilled nearly every wish that he could have ever held save one, possession of the Presidency. In 1944 that goal, too, at last seemed within reach. In July of that year the Democratic Party gathered in hot, humid, wartime Chicago to perform the quadrennial coronation of President Franklin Roosevelt for an unprecedented fourth time. Beneath the comfortable sense of victory and power, however, tides of apprehension ebbed and flowed. "The boss" might be at the end of his rope. Later many would publicly admit to being witnesses to a steady decline in Presidential health from at least 1943 on. Jim Farley found Roosevelt's health the subject of endless whispered conjectures in crowded halls and noisy rooms all during convention week. At the Second Quebec Conference two months later the British would be shocked at how "very drawn" Roosevelt looked. What could or should be done, party bosses wondered. Even as the pols prepared to reanoint their king, they pondered his burial.[20]

The Vice-Presidency suddenly became an unprecedentedly important and ardently sought-after prize. The struggle to win it nearly tore that complex and fragile coalition known as the Democratic Party wide open.

By 1944 a dozen years of New Deal policy and Rooseveltian leadership had divided the Democrats into two well-defined and antagonistic interests. On the right lay the conservative old guard. Representing entrenched rural power in the South and the provincial remnants of Bryan's crusade in the West, along with a sprinkling of northern business interests, the old guard had comprised the core of the Democratic Party since the turn of the century. By the early 1930s its leadership included John J. Raskob, a Vice-President of General Motors, some of the "New York investment house crowd," headed by Bernard Baruch, and such Senatorial stalwarts from the South as Carter Glass, Harry Byrd, Joseph Robinson, and

---

[20] *New York Times*, April 13, 1945, p. 9:8; James Farley, *Jim Farley's Story; The Roosevelt Years* (New York: Whittlesey House, 1948), pp. 363–365; Eden, *The Reckoning*, p. 552.

Pat Harrison. By 1937 Jimmy Byrnes could be fairly described as loosely aligned with the latter faction. By 1944 there was no question about his close relations with these "decent" and "not-so-decent conservatives."[21] Often at odds with one another on specific matters, the conservatives nonetheless shared an initial unease and a steadily ripening distaste for the large, noisy, and enthusiastic "dandruff-and-dirty-fingernail" crew of New Deal reformers and pragmatists whom Roosevelt brought or attracted to federal service in and after 1933.

The constantly growing disaffection of the old guard from the New Dealers, which was symbolized by the tightening deadlock between Capitol Hill and the White House after the abortive "purge" of 1938, had not prevented FDR from ramming Henry Wallace down the party's throat in 1940. But by the latter years of war the demands of total mobilization appeared to have sapped much of the New Deal's strength. "Where is the New Deal? Where are the New Dealers?" *Business Week* asked prematurely at the close of 1944. The answer seemed to be that those New Dealers not in subordinate bureaucratic positions had turned their attention and energies to the cause of internationalism and the Grand Alliance. "There is not an old New Dealer at the top level of policy administration or in the President's intimate [domestic] councils," the magazine happily reported. The presence of the conservative Byrnes as "Assistant President" in charge of the O.W.M.R. was especially noted.[22]

This trend was always more apparent than real. A great deal of reformist ferment was still present in both Congress and the Executive branch, as indicated by the presentation and reception of Roosevelt's January 1944 State of the Union message and the developing plans for a postwar program of guaranteed full employment. Nonetheless, the appearance of New Deal exhaustion—often fostered by the ostentatious gloom of New Dealers themselves

[21] Patterson, *Congressional Conservatism*, pp. 128–136; Oscar Handlin, *Al Smith and His America* (Boston: Little, Brown & Co., 1958), pp. 127–128, 149, 152, 154, 156, 179; Harold Ickes, *The Secret Diary of Harold Ickes*, 3 vols. (New York: Simon & Schuster, 1953), II: January 30, 1937 entry, p. 63; *Lilienthal Journals*, pp. 665–666.
[22] *Business Week*, January 6, 1945, pp. 15–16.

—gave encouragement to the old guard. By 1944 its hour seemed to have struck within the Democratic Party,[23] and its chief target was Vice-President Henry Wallace.

In the considered opinion of old guardsmen, Wallace had simply made a fool of himself during the war years by his lack of tact, by his permission of and indeed personal involvement in interdepartmental feuds, and by his general moodiness. And, of course, his radical pronouncements on the century of the common man and the need for sixty million federally guaranteed postwar jobs were only what a sane man might expect from one who had suddenly become fatally smitten with oriental mysticism. Someone with a clearer head, someone who did not alienate business as it pursued the miracle of production, someone who did not infuriate the South, the traditional core of party strength, was absolutely necessary in the Vice-Presidency should the current Presidential heart cease to beat. Conservatives were sure they had the man—Jimmy Byrnes. And on the eve of the Chicago Convention, Byrnes, too, radiated assurance.

On the train to Chicago Byrnes "confided triumphantly" to Tom Connally "that he was going to be Vice President. 'Harry Truman,' he said with a twinkle in his eye, 'will nominate me.' " But it was not to be.[24] The sources of Byrnes' confidence seem to have been Robert Hannegan, the Democratic National Chairman, and Harry Hopkins. In December of 1943 Hopkins had told Byrnes that he was FDR's personal choice. The following June Hannegan urged the South Carolinian to lead the fight against a Wallace renomination. What more could a man demand in the way of proof that

[23] Rauch, ed., *Franklin D. Roosevelt; Speeches, Messages, Press Conferences and Letters*, pp. 338–349; Stephen Kemp Bailey, *Congress Makes A Law; The Story Behind the Full Employment Act of 1946* (New York: Vintage Books, 1964), *passim*. Lilienthal noted as early as March 4 that the national campaign "is already redhot." *Lilienthal Journals*, pp. 561, 625, 629.

[24] The following account of the Vice Presidential battle at Chicago has been pieced together from a number of sources including Phillips, *The Truman Presidency*, pp. 38–47; Daniels, *The Man of Independence*, pp. 237ff.; Connally and Steinberg, *My Name is Tom Connally*, pp. 267–268; Samuel J. Rosenman, *Working with Roosevelt* (New York: Harper & Brothers, 1952), pp. 205, 438–451; Byrnes, *All in One Lifetime*, pp. 219–230; Janeway, *Struggle for Survival*, pp. 348–349; Drury, *Senate Journal*, pp. 214–221; "Transcripts of Sidney Shallet's interviews with Alben Barkley," Box 1, Reel 5, Harry S. Truman Library, Independence, Mo.; and numerous letters and transcripts of conversations dealing with the 1944 Democratic Vice-Presidential nomination in Folder 74, Byrnes Papers.

he was the administration's candidate? The trouble was that while Byrnes may have been the candidate of the administration, he did not enjoy the support of the party bosses and was thus doomed from the start.

On July 11 the Democratic sachems gathered at the White House for a secret strategy conference. Those present included Hannegan, Frank Walker, Ed Flynn, Mayor Kelley of Chicago, Ed Pauley, the California oil man and party money-raiser, George Allen, an inveterate crony to an entire stable of presidents and generals, and Sidney Hillman, head of the C.I.O. Political Action Committee, plus one or two others. "Coldly and calmly" the men ran down a list of possible Vice-Presidential candidates with Roosevelt. Included on the list were Byrnes, House Speaker Sam Rayburn, Senate Majority Leader Alben Barkley, Justice William O. Douglas, and Senator Harry Truman. Byrnes, who had been "very anxious" for the Presidential nomination in 1940 until Roosevelt had decided on a third term, was disqualified early in the discussion. As a southern conservative, whose own state organization had just gone on public record as reconfirming the doctrine of white supremacy in all aspects of South Carolinian political and social life, he was anathema to the newly recruited, carefully nurtured Negro vote.[25] As Director of War Mobilization he was a natural target for organized labor, especially the C.I.O., which chafed under wartime wage, hour, and strike restrictions and was eager to demonstrate its continuing political power through Hillman's Committee. Of equal importance was Byrnes' background as a renegade Catholic, certain to hurt the ticket in the newly acquired party strongholds of the Northeast. Implicit in all this reasoning, of course, was the argument that the party could not throw over a liberal New Dealer merely to embrace a staunch conservative. "Middle-of-the-road" balance, not clear-cut political philosophy, was desired.

So Byrnes, like Wallace, was out. So, too, were the others for one reason or another until the discussion got around to Harry Tru-

[25] Jeff B. Bates, Acting Secretary, South Carolina State Democratic Executive Committee, to President Franklin D. Roosevelt, June 19, 1944, with enclosure; James M. Barnes to Justice James F. Byrnes, with enclosures, June 29, 1944, Folder 181, Byrnes Papers.

man. By now Hannegan was in Truman's corner, eagerly pressing his candidacy. Onetime head of the St. Louis Democratic machine, now party national chairman, a man who owed much of his success to Truman's sponsorship, Hannegan preached Truman's fitness as the ideal available man. He was joined by Pauley, the California oil executive and current party treasurer. The Missouri Senator possessed a good New Deal voting record, the two told their colleagues. Yet Truman had also had the sense and sensitivity to be absent or at least to assume the posture of agonizing deliberation when controversial legislation, especially of a sectional nature, was about to come to a vote. A border state Senator, he had not significantly alienated either North or South, business or labor, during his ten years in the upper chamber. Above all, Truman had shown no marked—and therefore embarrassing—capacity for legislative leadership which would have created enemies as well as admirers. In all his dealings Truman had indeed personified the ancient Senate motto: "If you want to get along, go along."[26]

Truman then it was to be. The bosses ultimately agreed with Hannegan and Pauley that no better—or innocuous—figure could be found to keep the Democratic coalition together in the upcoming fight at Chicago for the second spot on the ticket. Roosevelt might have fought the decision had he so chosen. But, worn out as he was, preoccupied with the final responsibility for running a vast war machine and the even greater problems beginning to loom on the still far distant peacetime horizon, the President acquiesced for the moment.

Within a matter of days, however, Roosevelt appeared ready to repudiate the earlier decision. He first weakly fulfilled an earlier pledge to Wallace and to the more vociferous New Dealers and organized labor, dispatching a tepid telegram of support for the Vice-President's renomination. In fact, the President's "milk and water" statement was so faint-hearted as to be insulting. One reporter called it "perhaps the coolest and cruelest brush-off in all the long Roosevelt career," and both labor and liberal Democrats

---

[26] A brilliant vignette discussing the attractiveness of Truman's availability in 1944 and the effect of his character on the Presidency between 1945 and 1953 may be found in Lubell, *Future of American Politics*, Chapter 2.

felt betrayed.[27] Yet the Wallacites chose to go ahead and make a fight of it. As good political warriors they simply took Roosevelt's message as an endorsement and claimed Presidential support.

Roosevelt next turned on Byrnes. But he did so in such an ambiguous fashion that the South Carolinian believed that his President would not actively oppose his nomination as the avowed candidate of the conservative South. On July 14, the Friday before the convention opened, Byrnes talked with Roosevelt, who told him several times, "I am not favoring anybody. I told them [the party bosses] so. No, I am not favoring anybody."[28]

Roosevelt next confused matters further by apparently inviting Byrnes secretly aboard the Presidential train as it passed through Chicago during the convention.[29] Roosevelt was then on his way to California and Hawaii for talks with MacArthur and Nimitz on future Pacific strategy. His invitation to Byrnes might well have been construed by the South Carolinian, who apparently knew nothing of the July 11 White House meeting, as a probable indication of sudden outright Presidential support. However, soon after Byrnes' quiet departure, Hannegan and his entourage boarded the train and apparently secured Presidential reaffirmation for Truman.

The stage was thus set for bitterness and misunderstanding. Byrnes and Wallace ran all out during the early days at Chicago, splitting the party neatly between the northern liberal and southern conservative wings. The moderate Truman did not run at all —did not even know, in fact, that he was in the running. Having heard vague rumors that he was a possible compromise choice, Truman, before leaving Independence for Chicago, "bowed out, reiterating a statement he has made many times on the Hill, that he does not want the Vice-Presidency."[30] All the available evidence indicates that Truman, Byrnes, and probably even Wallace, were acting in perfect sincerity. No one apparently knew of the July 11 White House meeting or of what had transpired. To everyone the Vice-

[27] Drury, *Senate Journal*, p. 218; *Lilienthal Journals*, pp. 647–649.
[28] "Notes taken down by Mr. Byrnes when he talked with the President on Friday morning before the opening of the Convention," July 14, 1944, Folder 74, Byrnes Papers.
[29] This was what Barkley subsequently learned. "Shallet Transcripts."
[30] Drury, *Senate Journal*, p. 217.

Presidential race seemed to be between Wallace and Byrnes. Arriving in Chicago, Truman fulfilled his pledge to work vigorously and openly for Byrnes. Within a matter of hours the Missourian gradually became aware of the true situation but refused to accept it and continued to work for Byrnes, who thought that the emerging talk for Truman was all a mistake that FDR would soon rectify.

The convention fell into uproar. The party bosses thought they had pinned Roosevelt down to Truman. Byrnes was certain that he enjoyed either covert Presidential support or at the least an overt Presidential neutrality which would permit the ultimate creation of a triumphant Byrnes-Truman, southern-border state coalition to win the Vice-Presidency for South Carolina and Dixie. Wallace, his support slipping, could at least point to a tepid statement of Presidential endorsement publicly read before the convention. No one knew where Roosevelt really stood. Wallacites and Byrnes supporters cried foul at the President and each other. Chaos reigned, and one bemused correspondent observed in the midst of the turmoil that "Few people can hate one another with more cordial enthusiasm than a bunch of Democrats."[31]

Hannegan at last decided that the only way to break the deadlock was to tell Truman personally and get him actively in contention as a rallying point. But at first Truman stoutly resisted the pressure placed upon him. He was supporting Byrnes. Jimmy had the Presidential endorsement, not he. Indeed, the Senator immediately went to Byrnes for advice upon being told by Hannegan of the ostensible Roosevelt decision. Byrnes was initially unmoved and told Truman that Roosevelt would soon "straighten things out."[32] Byrnes was right, but not in the way he anticipated. Hannegan, in order to convince Truman, finally called FDR at San Diego, and the President told Truman in effect to take the nomination he was being offered. A stunned little Senator almost wordlessly acquiesced.

Whatever the reasons for Roosevelt's erratic behavior—whether it simply reflected his well-known penchant for keeping options

---

[31] *Ibid.*, p. 219.
[32] Barkley's statement in "Shallet Transcripts."

open as long as possible, or whether it stemmed directly from mental paralysis attributable to failing health and declining faculties —the result was a deeply wounded James Byrnes. When the South Carolinian was at last informed of the Presidential decision to go with Truman, he immediately called Roosevelt in a fit of righteous anger and cried betrayal. A rather petulant Roosevelt replied that he had made it clear on a number of occasions that Byrnes was critically vulnerable on several counts and implied that the South Carolinian should have anticipated his fate. Byrnes was unappeased, and the embarrassed explanations of Hannegan and others that Truman had been the ideal "available man" from the start only fueled his fury. The South Carolinian quickly "cleared out" of Chicago. Before leaving, however, he revealed the depth of his shame and humiliation. He went to Alben Barkley, who was scheduled to put Roosevelt's name in nomination, and urged the Kentuckian to make the coldest, most perfunctory speech possible. When Barkley demurred on the grounds of party, if not personal, loyalty, "Jimmy left and I never saw him any more for quite a long time."[33]

Whether Byrnes' bitter feelings ever extended to Truman personally, whether he ever suspected the Missourian of possessing inside information and a previously unsuspected capacity for deceit, it is impossible to say at this time. Tom Connally later stated that the 1944 convention marked the beginning of the personal division between the two men, and immediate circumstances would seem to bear out this contention.

Byrnes "returned to the White House from his defeat at the Chicago Convention humiliated and embittered,"[34] while Truman prepared his Vice-Presidential campaign, which proved to be far less than brilliant. In the first place, while FDR ostentatiously courted Byrnes' good opinion in the weeks and months after Chicago and capped his wooing of the Mobilization Director by taking him to Yalta, he just as ostentatiously ignored his Vice-Presidential nominee. In the nine months between the convention and his death, Roosevelt met with Truman only eight times and often merely as

---

[33] *Ibid.*; Byrnes to C. D. Graydon, July 29, 1944; "Memorandum of Telephone Conversation with F.D.R. on Tuesday, July 18, 1944," Folder 74, Byrnes Papers.
[34] Janeway, *Struggle for Survival*, p. 349.

a perfunctory gesture.[35] Ignored to the point of insult, Truman developed a defensive, even hurt and bewildered attitude, which characteristically manifested itself in pugnacious "give 'em hell" oratory. At first the Vice-Presidential nominee had delivered his ghost-written speeches "slowly and mechanically, as if he were translating them from Hindustani as he went along." But as the days passed and his attitude darkened, his speeches became wilder and riddled with blunders. On the eve of election day Truman journeyed into Massachusetts and committed what one administration official gently termed "a *faux pas*" in attacking veteran Democratic Senator David I. Walsh as an isolationist. Not only did his off-the-cuff remarks to reporters put the Bay State's sixteen electoral votes in some jeopardy, they also threatened to lose Walsh's support for the postwar international organization just tentatively framed at Dumbarton Oaks. Roosevelt promptly telephoned Walsh and invited him to ride the Presidential train through the state several days later, and the incident passed.[36] But the impression—even caricature—of Truman as a careless, small-minded loudmouth who might shoot from the hip at any moment was established.

Byrnes' reaction to the Truman campaign and to Roosevelt's disinterest in his Vice-President—save as an object of occasional "hazing" at infrequent Cabinet meetings[37]—may be readily imagined. Even to his friends, and he had many, Truman always seemed terribly vulnerable; his intense desire to be liked often appeared puppy-like in its intensity. An embittered, ambitious, and very capable politician such as Byrnes may well have viewed the Vice-President's character, position, and good fortune with a contempt that was the product of an equal measure of amusement and frustration.

Whatever their personal feelings for one another were on the first day of Truman's Presidency as Byrnes came to call, both men could not have avoided thinking of the past as they sat facing each

---

[35] Daniels, *Man of Independence*, p. 259; Drury, *Senate Journal*, pp. 409–410.

[36] William D. Hassett, *Off the Record with FDR, 1942–1945* (New Brunswick, N.J.: Rutgers University Press, 1958), p. 288; Robert S. Allen and William V. Shannon, *The Truman Merry-Go-Round* (New York: Vanguard Press, 1950), pp. 14–15.

[37] Drury, *Senate Journal*, p. 327.

other in the Oval Office of the White House. Byrnes was for the moment a private citizen, having resigned as Mobilization Director a dozen days earlier. Truman was suddenly President of the United States. Byrnes may have allowed himself the luxury of a moment of sardonic recollection. Truman could not have been comfortable. But there were things to do, and Byrnes immediately began to speak of foreign policy and of Yalta.[38] Doubtless he told Truman of his steadily increasing mistrust of the Russians.

This mistrust had begun in the Crimea and had grown steadily as a result of the early spring crises over Rumania, Poland, and the Eastern European question in general.[39] Byrnes must have impressed Truman with his expertise in foreign affairs, although Yalta was the first real venture into the diplomatic field which the South Carolinian had ever made. Certainly, too, outside pressures in Byrnes' behalf could not have helped but make a strong impression on the new President. In any case, either at this first meeting or several days after Roosevelt's funeral at Hyde Park Truman informed Byrnes that he wished him to become Secretary of State.[40] It seemed a natural decision. Beyond the facts of public pressure for Byrnes' return to the government and his recent exposure to top-level international diplomacy lay his undeniable stature as a brilliant legislator and administrator. What better choice to pull the State Department back on its feet, shake it up and give it direction and purpose, restore it to its rightful place as a policy-making institution, than the energetic and competent South Carolinian. The furtherance of world peace, to say nothing of a smooth, orderly transition from one administration to another within a framework of continuity would be assured. The President made it clear from the start that he wished to concentrate on domestic policies and administration. He was eager to secure Congressional approval for a dramatic and drastic reorganization of the sprawling Executive establishment. He was impatient, as he tirelessly explained in those first days, to plunge into budgetary matters. A man who early

---

[38] Truman discusses this meeting at some length in *Year of Decisions*, pp. 34–35.

[39] Byrnes, *All in One Lifetime*, p. 265; Byrnes, *Speaking Frankly*, pp. 49–60.

[40] Truman, *Year of Decisions*, p. 35; Byrnes, *Speaking Frankly*, p. 49; Acheson, *Present at the Creation*, p. 192.

in his administration indicated that his conception of Presidential power was largely conceived in delegatory terms, Truman obviously felt that he could find no better man than Byrnes to reorganize and run the foreign policy shop while Presidential attention focused on domestic matters.[41]

But Stettinius could not be let go before he completed his United Nations assignment in San Francisco. So Byrnes returned home for a brief time while Truman revealed an underlying unease at his equivocal personal and professional relationship with the South Carolinian. During a press conference on April 17 the President was asked if Byrnes might go to San Francisco in any capacity. Truman testily shot back, "He will not. Mr. Byrnes is going back to South Carolina, and when I need his advice I shall send for him." A fortnight later Truman and Stimson agreed that Byrnes would make an excellent choice as Presidential representative on the Interim Committee, studying the use of the atomic bomb against Japan.[42]

By the time that Byrnes entered the atomic debate, earlier and inconclusive discussions centering around the sharing of the nuclear fission secret with Russia had blended with the problem of the atomic bomb's use at all against the crumbling but still defiant Japanese. The drive to force official reconsideration of the bomb's use, as well as the issue of international control, came from within the "Metallurgical Laboratory" at the University of Chicago. A subcommittee on the social and political consequences of atomic development had been established, headed by James Franck. As the bomb came closer to the test stage in the spring of 1945 the question of its use "became the matter of prime importance" to the subcommittee. Working through laboratory director, Arthur Holly Compton, and overall project director, General Leslie R. Groves, members of the Franck Committee were instrumental in bringing to Stimson's attention the growing concern of many atomic scien-

[41] Harold D. Smith Diary, May 4, 1945; clippings of Marquis Childs column, *Washington Post*, May 26, 1945; clipping: "Truman's Appointments," *Time*, June 4, 1945; clipping: "Schwellenbach Appointment," *United States News*, June 29, 1945, in Schwellenbach Papers, Box 2 (Correspondence), Scrapbook #7; *New York Times*, May 25, 1945, pp. 1:2, 3.
[42] Truman, *Public Papers, 1945*, p. 11; Stimson Diary, May 2, 3, 1945.

tists.[43] Stimson thus suggested the formation of the Interim Committee to study the problem, which brought Byrnes into the atomic picture.

How much did Byrnes know about the bomb at this time? Apparently very little. In later years he would state that Roosevelt had fully informed him of the Manhattan Project as early as 1943. But a letter which Byrnes sent to Roosevelt in early March of 1945, complaining of the two billion dollars expended on the project "with no definite assurance yet of production" to date and urging either its abandonment or curtailment, tends to belie the South Carolinian's later assertions.[44]

The composition of the committee, then, practically foreclosed any possibility that the concerned members of the atomic community would have serious influence over the uses to which their work would be put. Chairing the committee was Stimson himself, who never indicated any doubt that the bomb would be used against the Japanese. His chief deputy on the committee was George L. Harrison, President of the New York Life Insurance Company, who took charge of the meetings in Stimson's absence. Other members included Vannevar Bush, Director of the Office of Scientific Research and Development, who, along with the Manhattan Project's James Conant, continued to press for disclosure of the atomic secret to Russia, while invariably seeming to presume that the bomb would be dropped on Japan. Karl T. Compton of the Manhattan Project and President of M.I.T., Navy Undersecretary Ralph Bard, Assistant Secretary of State Will Clayton, and Byrnes himself completed the committee. Only Bard entertained serious reservations about the bomb's use, and Conant was aware of the essential weakness of the committee as initially constituted. On May 5 he informed Stimson of his concern. The "scientists who had actively been at work in the laboratories" were becoming apprehensive. "Many were deeply concerned about the international impact of the weapon" in relation to both Japan and the Soviet Union. "They feared that soon the United States and the Soviet

[43] Compton, *Atomic Quest*, p. 233.
[44] Typescript Memo, undated, entitled, "White House, 1943, Atomic," Byrnes to Roosevelt, March 3, 1945, both in Folder 596, Byrnes Papers.

Union would be locked in a secret armament race, particularly if the United States should use the bomb in battle before notifying the Russians of its existence."[45]

Urged on by Conant, Stimson decided to form a scientific panel to aid the Interim Committee in its deliberations. Working on the recommendations of Conant and Bush, Stimson appointed Karl Compton's brother, Arthur Holly Compton, Ernest O. Lawrence, Robert Oppenheimer, and Enrico Fermi to serve. Only Compton and Fermi could be said to have been intimately exposed to the concerns of the skeptics among their colleagues, and Compton's sympathy for the Franck faction is open to serious question.[46]

One atomic scientist who sensed that decision-making was drifting into the hands of those who instinctively assumed not only the bomb's employment but also a continued Anglo-American monopoly of its secret was the brilliant Leo Szilard. As early as September of 1942 Szilard had suggested that his colleagues at the Metallurgical Lab give more attention to the political conundrums certain to arise from the perfection of atomic energy. To those who opposed his often blustery tactics, if not his outlook, Szilard was a political adolescent and intellectually erratic. To many others he was a hero.[47]

Szilard did not personally oppose the use of the bomb. But he was convinced of the need for international control of atomic energy, including immediate sharing of the secret with the Russians once the bomb was used. In the spring of 1945 Szilard began a long tenacious campaign to transmute his personal beliefs into public policy. Undaunted by a series of rebuffs at the middle echelons of bureaucracy, Szilard on May 25 called directly at the White House but was unable to see Truman. Matt Connally, the Presidential secretary, shunted Szilard off to see Byrnes, then at home in South Carolina. Byrnes' reaction to Szilard's proposals for sharing the secret and control of atomic energy with the Russians and

[45] Hewlett and Anderson, *The New World*, pp. 337, 344–345.

[46] Cf. Robert C. Batchelder, *The Irreversible Decision, 1939–1950* (New York: The Macmillan Company, 1961), pp. 60–66.

[47] Hewlett and Anderson, *The New World*, p. 342; Stephane Groueff, *Manhattan Project; The Untold Story of the Making of the Atomic Bomb* (New York: Bantam Books, 1968), pp. 24–25.

the rest of the world chilled the Hungarian. "According to Szilard's memory in 1949, the question of using the bomb arose. *Byrnes did not argue that it was necessary for the defeat of Japan;* his concern was the Soviet Union. He thought American possession of the bomb would make Russia more manageable in eastern Europe." The excitable Szilard was appalled, as some scholars have been since, at Byrnes' posture. The Hungarian left South Carolina "convinced that Byrnes did not grasp the true significance of atomic energy."[48] Others have argued from the above remarks that Byrnes really wanted to drop the bomb as a military demonstration against the Russians.[49] Byrnes' recollection of his May 25 conversation with Szilard, while not explicitly denying the comment attributed to him, stresses the fright and oppression which he felt upon hearing more and more about the power of the atom.[50]

In fact, Szilard's recollection and that of Byrnes are not as diametrically opposed as has been assumed. In the first place, and this was the central point at issue, both men assumed that the bomb would be dropped on Japan. Szilard did not represent the views of those atomic scientists who did not wish the bomb used at all. And second, assuming the bomb's initial use against Japan as an act in faithful accordance with the dreadfully total prosecution of the Second World War, might the weapon then not legitimately serve to give the Russians pause? This would be accomplished not by the threat that the United States would use the bomb against the Soviet Union if it stepped beyond prescribed limits set by Washington, but rather by the implication inherent in the bomb's use against Japan that if the Kremlin did not assume a more accommodating attitude toward Western policies, the Americans could refuse to share the atomic secret with Moscow. The bomb, in short, once used, would inevitably become a favorable bargaining counter with the Russians. This was an unavoidable and brute fact. Byrnes may well have been seeking to reassure Szilard that, terrible as the bomb was, something good, namely another means of reducing East-West tensions, might come out of its employment. For months

[48] Hewlett and Anderson, *The New World*, p. 355, italics added.
[49] Alperovitz, *Atomic Diplomacy*, pp. 241–242.
[50] Byrnes, *All in One Lifetime*, p. 285.

Western diplomats had seemingly gone to the Kremlin hat in hand, asking Stalin to "behave" in an "acceptable" manner. All the while they had been uncomfortably aware that with the defeat of Germany the West needed a friendly and cooperative Soviet Union more than the Russians seemed to need the support of London and Washington. Now the atomic bomb might at last reverse this process and force the Russians, for once, to come to the West. Szilard, of course, did not so interpret Byrnes' remarks, and in any case Byrnes was to be proved tragically wrong if this was indeed the way his thoughts were tending. Beyond the formidable moral questions involved in the very use of atomic power against Japan, the immediate future was to reveal that the bomb would be the single most divisive issue between East and West in the early postwar period and the chief, if by no means only, catalyst of the Cold War. The abrupt use of atomic bombs without prior warning to Moscow as well as to Tokyo constituted an irretrievable and inexcusable blunder in American foreign policy. But in May of 1945 the future, as always, was impenetrable and unpredictable.

Byrnes' interest in atomic power as a diplomatic problem fully emerged during the Interim Committee meetings of May 31 and June 1 when he had led the way in the decision to drop the bombs as soon as they were ready and without notice. Byrnes seemed especially impressed by the debate among scientists and engineers as to how long it would take Russia to develop atomic weapons of her own. Bush and Conant guessed three to four years. Groves, however, thought it would take the Soviets at least two decades to duplicate the American achievement. Byrnes, following Arthur Compton's lead, tended to split the difference and assumed that the United States enjoyed a seven to ten year lead in nuclear technology. Further discussion on the subject developed the consensus articulated by Stimson that the United States should keep its industrial atomic plant intact after the war, stockpile atomic materials, and continue atomic research at a rapid pace. As to the sharing of atomic secrets, the scientists were in rough agreement that the United States could not long retain its informational monopoly. The means of developing atomic weaponry would soon be known to scientists in the advanced industrial nations, including Russia.

Marshall for the military and Clayton for the diplomats wanted America to keep the secret as long as possible, though Marshall reiterated his long-standing belief that cooperation with Russia was necessary and probable in the postwar world. The general even suggested inviting two Russian observers to Alamogordo.[51]

But just how unique was the bomb? This question inevitably emerged from the discussions on international sharing and control of the atomic secret. Although in his opening remarks Stimson stressed that the bomb was a potential "menace to civilization" and underscored his and the military's recognition that atomic power created "a new relation of man to the universe," Oppenheimer, the scientific head of the Manhattan Project, presented a distinctly low-key interpretation of what the bomb would do. Its yield would be approximately 10,000 tons of TNT, Oppenheimer hypothesized, and he added that if such a weapon were exploded over a city immediately warned by air raid alert, "some 20,000 people would probably be killed." This incredibly modest projection, far below the effect both in blast and casualties achieved at Hiroshima, reflected the continuing uncertainty and skepticism of the atomic scientists as they pondered the new force coming into their possession. Had they in fact developed a revolutionary new weapons system or not? The answer seemed to be no. As Arthur Compton later wrote in comparing atomic bombing to fire bombing, "an atomic bomb as powerful as 10,000 tons of TNT would be no more destructive than such a combination of conventional weapons."[52] As of June–July 1945, then, the shock power of one, or even several, atomic weapons was conceived to lie not in any unprecedented superiority of explosive force but in the collection of existing explosive forces within a single missile. Only when a nation had achieved a large stockpile of atomic bombs could it possibly be said to have "broken through" to a higher level of weapon superiority.

It was at this point, however, that Byrnes brought his personal influence as Presidential representative to bear on the committee. Whatever the power and uniqueness of the bomb, "He feared that

---

[51] Hewlett and Anderson, *The New World*, pp. 353–354, 356, 357; Byrnes, *Speaking Frankly*, p. 261; Compton, *Atomic Quest*, p. 237.
[52] Compton, *Atomic Quest*, pp. 234, 237.

if the United States gave information to the Russians, even in general terms, Stalin would ask to come into the partnership." When Vannevar Bush countered with the fact that not even the British partner had blueprints of American production plants, Byrnes brushed this aside as irrelevant. He argued that the best policy was to push ahead with production and research to make certain that the United States "stayed ahead." Already in Byrnes' mind—and in the minds of some scientists as well—the idea of an inevitable atomic arms race with the Soviets was beginning to take shape. Byrnes' concluding remark that "he favored making every effort to improve political relations with Russia" did not lessen the force of his earlier outburst, though when Arthur Compton expressed it as the consensus of the meeting that on the atomic question the United States "should seek an understanding with Russia," the Presidential representative said nothing.[53]

He had made his point, as he undoubtedly had in earlier talks, and it was clear enough. He did not share either the basic hopefulness of Stimson and Marshall or the determination of Truman and others regarding good relations with Russia. In outlook closest to Grew and to Harriman at their gloomiest, Byrnes obviously believed that American policy toward the Kremlin must be firm and backed with dry powder. The atomic bomb might represent a decisive breakthrough in weapon technology or it might not. Time and use under combat conditions would tell.[54] Byrnes clearly and unequivocally felt that the bomb had to be used against Japan to end the Pacific war. Beyond that point American possession of the weapon might possibly yield significant diplomatic dividends, particularly in resolving the knotty problem of Eastern Europe, which obviously threatened the continued existence of the Grand Alliance. But no matter what the final outcome of the atomic quest, Byrnes was, as his remarks in the Interim Committee made plain, patently determined to be tougher with the Soviets than either his President or his predecessor at State had been.

[53] Hewlett and Anderson, *The New World*, pp. 357, 358.
[54] Writing two years later, Byrnes recalled being "warned" by the "experts" in May and June "that the static test which was to take place in New Mexico, even if successful, would not be conclusive proof that a bomb would explode when dropped from an airplane." *Speaking Frankly*, p. 261.

Byrnes thus presented a new set of troubles for Harry Truman. The new President had so far kept the State Department zealots at arms length during his first ten weeks in office. But could he continue to face down a State Department now led by Jimmy Byrnes in view of all that had transpired over the past year? Or would the considerable weight of Byrnes and Harriman, Grew and Arthur Bliss Lane, and others wear down the White House and force a reversal of American policy toward Russia just before a Soviet entry into the Pacific war and the invasion of Kyushu? And what role would the atomic bomb eventually play? All these questions awaited answers in the crucible of further Big Three summit diplomacy as Truman and Byrnes left for Potsdam on July 6.

11

Potsdam--The European Issues

The Conference of Berlin proved to be the longest and most complex of the Big Three wartime meetings. Debates seemed to blend and shift, merge and mix and drift in a bewildering variety of patterns. Out of the trials and tedium of grand diplomacy played out nearly every day for a fortnight in the conference room behind the great bay windows of the Cecilienhof Palace, halting progress was begun toward the economic rehabilitation and political reconstruction of Europe. But at what cost to the Grand Alliance? Participants and historians alike, glancing back through the grey fog of cold war and burdened by the knowledge that Potsdam was the last summit meeting for a decade, have almost unanimously declared that the great nonviolent struggle between East and West that has divided the globe in our time began during the final meeting of Truman, Stalin, Churchill, and Attlee.

"Terminal was a bleak ending," Herbert Feis has written. "Potsdam marked in the reality the beginning of the end of [the] 'Big-Three peace.'" Alexander Werth has agreed.[1] The American

---

[1] Feis, *Between War and Peace*, p. 322; Werth, *Russia at War*, p. 924.

participants have been almost unanimous in their support of this gloomy assessment.

Reviewing and expanding his wartime diary entries for publication in 1949, Admiral Leahy remarked that "Potsdam had brought into sharp world focus the struggle of two great ideas—the Anglo-Saxon democratic principles of government and the aggressive and expansionist police-state tactics of Stalinist Russia. It was the beginning of the 'cold war.' "[2] A decade later Byrnes echoed Leahy's comments in the process of reversing his own earlier assertions. In 1947 the former Secretary of State had written that the Potsdam "conference ended in good spirits. . . . Events had shown that agreements reached in conference must be hammered out on the hard anvil of experience. We thought, however, that we had established a basis for maintaining our war-born unity."[3] By 1959 Byrnes had changed his story. He stated at that time that at the close of the Berlin Conference he believed that "Everything depended upon whether the Soviets carried out their agreements and by this time I had little confidence in their pledges."[4]

No such ambiguity has marked President Truman's reminiscences. In an interview with Arthur Krock in February 1950 the President recalled "with what good-will toward the Russian people and their rulers he went to Potsdam. . . . There he planned to offer help for reconstruction, of Russia as well as the rest of the world, on a very large scale. . . . But he found that all Stalin wanted to talk about was the abrupt cessation of lend-lease; hence the atmosphere was unfavorable to what Mr. Truman had in mind." The President revealed a querulous temperament to Krock on the subject. Temporarily cutting off all lend-lease aid in May of 1945 had been a mistake, Truman admitted, but he had been "new" then and "the papers had been prepared for Roosevelt, and represented a Government decision." He had seen no alternative but to sign. And for Stalin to then bait him on the point at Potsdam was unendurable.[5] In his memoirs, published five years after the Krock in-

---

[2] Leahy, *I Was There*, p. 429.
[3] Byrnes, *Speaking Frankly*, p. 86.
[4] Byrnes, *All in One Lifetime*, p. 303.
[5] "An Interview with Truman," *New York Times*, February 15, 1950, reprinted

terview, Truman etched his Potsdam suspicions of Stalin even more sharply. At Berlin

> I had already seen that the Russians were relentless bargainers, forever pressing for every advantage for themselves. . . . It was clear that the Russian foreign policy was based on the conclusion that we were heading for a major depression, and they were already planning to take advantage of our setback.
>
> Anxious as we were to have Russia in the war against Japan, the experience at Potsdam now made me determined that I would not allow the Russians any part in the control of Japan. Our experience with them in Germany and in Bulgaria, Rumania, Hungary, and Poland was such that I decided to take no chances in a joint setup with the Russians. . . .
>
> The persistent way in which Stalin blocked one of the war-preventative measures I had proposed showed how his mind worked and what he was after. I had proposed the internationalization of all the principal waterways. Stalin did not want this. What Stalin wanted was control of the Black Sea straits and the Danube. The Russians were planning world conquest.[6]

While the patent absurdity of the President's final remark may be dismissed as a classic piece of cold war rhetoric a decade after the event,[7] what is striking in both the Krock interview and the memoirs is Truman's sense of insult at Stalin's contemptuous behavior. Personal antagonism rather than sweeping conflicts of ideology or economic and political systems seems to have been the decisive factor if indeed a cold war was generated at Potsdam. Certainly Truman's contentions cannot be wholly ignored, nor can those of Leahy and Byrnes. A number of revisionist historians, of course, have interpreted from the coldest possible perspective the conflicts of interest that were indubitably present throughout the conference.[8] And it is a matter of record that the President and his advisers did prevent Soviet participation in the occupation of

in Arthur Krock, *In the Nation, 1932–1966* (New York: Paperback Library, 1969), pp. 164–165.

[6] Truman, *Year of Decisions*, pp. 454–455.

[7] Robert Murphy, it must be noted, argues in detail and with vigor that Truman was deeply wounded by Stalin's refusal to include the open waters proposal in the final protocol. *Diplomat among Warriors*, pp. 310–312.

[8] Alperovitz, *Atomic Diplomacy*, pp. 127–187; Bernstein, ed., *Politics and Policies of the Truman Administration*, pp. 32–35; David Horowitz, *The Free World Colossus; A Critique of American Foreign Policy in the Cold War*, rev. ed. (New York: Hill and Wang, 1971), pp. 52–53.

Japan, and that Truman never brought up the subject of the six billion dollar credit to Russia.

Nonetheless, close examination of the available record and the various accounts of the Potsdam meeting inevitably induce a sense of profound skepticism. What seems most obvious about the Conference of Berlin is how little it changed existing opinions, both official and personal. Those who were pessimistic before the conference began found their disillusion readily substantiated by Soviet conduct. Within the American delegation unease continued to envelop Byrnes, Leahy, Harriman, and one or two others, while Churchill and Eden, Attlee and Bevin found little to allay their anxieties.[9] Optimists, on the other hand, found their hopes frayed but not destroyed during the contest of wills and interests that raged over a fortnight and more. This was particularly the case with Harry Truman, who doggedly pursued the Rooseveltian policy of accommodation and realism in his own tougher and blunter style. At his first meeting with Stalin on July 17 the President told the Generalissimo, "I am here to be your friend, and to deal directly with you, yes or no; I am no diplomat." Obviously this tactic worked to the satisfaction of both Truman and Stalin. The Russian dictator approvingly said of Truman that " 'Honesty adorns the man.' " Near the close of the conference the President wrote to Henry Wallace that "This is *some* conference. We are getting some good things from it." The following day Truman told Forrestal that "he was being very realistic with the Russians and found Stalin not too difficult to do business with."[10]

How may we account for this discrepancy between retrospection and contemporary impression? The answer, not surprisingly, lies in the terrible influence of the Cold War upon men's minds. Pots-

---

[9] Churchill occasionally fell under Stalin's "spell" at Potsdam. Early on the Prime Minister "kept repeating 'I like that man.' " He was even able to convince himself that Stalin meant what he said about free elections in Eastern Europe. " 'Stalin gave me his word there will be free elections in the countries set free by his armies,' " he told his physician on July 19. " 'You are sceptical, Charles? I don't see why. We must listen to these Russians. They mobilized twelve million men, and nearly half of them were killed or are missing. . . . If they want to be a sea power, why not?' " But the spell quickly vanished under the press of hard negotiation. Quoted in Eden, *The Reckoning*, pp. 631–632; and Moran, *Churchill*, p. 295, cf. also pp. 297, 299; Bryant, *Triumph in the West*, p. 364.

[10] Quotes taken from *Foreign Relations, 1945; Conference of Berlin*, II: 44; Bryant, *Triumph in the West*, p. 365; Millis, ed., *Forrestal Diaries*, p. 78; and Truman to Henry A. Wallace, July 27, 1945, Truman Papers, Office File 27-B.

dam, having failed to settle outstanding differences satisfactorily between East and West, gradually came to assume an importance in the aftertime that it did not have to contemporaries. Running through the reminiscences of the American participants in particular is the implicit and completely erroneous assumption that they went to Berlin determined to obtain far more than in fact they actually expected to get at the time. Potsdam was not viewed by American officials in July of 1945 as TERMINAL, the code name given the conference by Churchill, but rather as prelude to a vast postwar peace conference on the scale of Versailles, which would at last set the seal of world consensus upon the territorial settlements and political rearrangements and rehabilitations that had emerged from or been necessitated by the second global conflict. American objectives at Berlin in the summer of 1945 were thus limited in scope and scale. And they were further compressed by measurable public pressure in the United States to maintain the mediator role, the power broker posture, between Britain and Russia in Europe.

This latter consideration was most forcefully expressed by a group of a dozen Congressmen who at the end of May had written a public letter to the Secretary of State in which they repeatedly expressed their fear "that the United States has begun to lose the position which President Roosevelt struggled to win and maintain for our country, as an independent mediator among the great powers, friendly to all and a partisan to none." They quoted with approval the recent expressions of concern emanating from such sources as the New York *Herald Tribune* and columnist Walter Lippmann, who had asserted "that on the Polish question our 'departure from Roosevelt's position as a mediator has had the most unfortunate consequences. The real issue in [Poland] has been between London and Moscow and it would be very unfortunate indeed if the United States sacrificed its great influence as the mediator. . . . It is not the real interest of Britain or of Europe, and certainly not of the United States, that we should be drawn into this issue as partisans.' " And the Congressmen added their own opinion "that we preserve our more detached role in the Anglo-Saxon difficulties" over Eastern Europe. They closed by asking some blunt questions. Had American diplomacy "become an 'appendage' to

British foreign policy in Eastern Europe?" "Has the United States, through some tacit understanding or through day to day working relations, become *de facto*, part of an Anglo-American 'front' against the Soviet Union?" And finally, "Have old anti-Soviet prejudices, clung to by a group within the State Department despite unity achieved among the Big Three at the Crimean Conference, caused a shift since Roosevelt's death from American friendliness toward our Russian ally?" A month later Joseph C. Grew responded for the department and the administration. Essentially his reply was to invite the Congressmen's attention to the results of the recently concluded Hopkins mission. Grew especially emphasized the bilateral Polish settlement as a reflection not only of current Soviet-American friendship and cooperation but also of the current status of relations between London and Washington.[11]

The tone of the Congressional letter and the nature of Grew's response emphasized the salient features of the Grand Alliance as American officials interpreted them in mid-summer 1945. So acute had the difficulties become between London and Moscow that only Washington could save Big Three unity and only by frequent concessions to the Soviets in Eastern Europe at the expense of the British. A State Department position paper drafted in late June clearly reflected current American policy toward Europe. On that continent Washington's task was conceived as opposing the development of rival British and Soviet spheres of influence which, when fully developed, could generate the tensions necessary for a third world war. The State Department was especially disturbed by the British plan for a Western European economic and political bloc that London wished to establish "As a 'hedge' against the possible failure of Big Three collaboration in the post-war world. . . ." Such a bloc, the State Department argued, would prompt even stronger Soviet countermeasures in Eastern Europe than were already apparent. "The need of the moment," the department asserted, "is to promote understanding between Great Britain and Russia on all matters in dispute. . . . We should direct our best efforts toward smooth-

---

[11] John Coffee, Emanuel Celler, Vito Marcantonio, *et al.*, to Edward R. Stettinius, Jr., May 31, 1945, Acting Secretary of State Joseph C. Grew to John Coffee *et al.*, June 30, 1945, U.S. Department of State *Bulletin*, XIII (July 8, 1945), 49–52.

ing out points of friction between Great Britain and Russia and fostering the tripartite collaboration upon which lasting peace depends."[12]

Brave words. The eagle must maintain the equilibrium within the Grand Alliance between the lion and the bear. But was not the balance already fatally tipped in one direction? "It must be recognized," the paper continued, "that the Russians have already gone far to establish an effective sphere of influence in Eastern Europe." Somehow this must be "discouraged." But the only possible solution that State Department thinkers could imagine was the fostering of a long-term four-power alliance—France, Russia, Britain, and the United States—of encirclement against Germany to insure her military prostration. Such a gambit might induce the Soviets to loosen their grip on Eastern Europe by removing their obsessive and utterly justifiable fear of German military rebirth.[13] Here was a limited goal indeed, coming from the one sector of the American government that had since Yalta arrogated to itself the watchdog role over Soviet conduct in Eastern Europe. Truman's own thinking on the eve of Potsdam was clearly reflected in a brief, single-page memo drafted by three of his most trusted aides on the day of his departure for Europe.

> The following is what we think was the consensus expressed on the boat on July 4th with respect to the important issues to be decided at the forthcoming conference:
>
> 1) The entry of Russia into the Japanese war.
> 2) The economic stabilization of Europe.
>   a) Immediate needs: Coal (especially out of Germany itself), food, transportation and a few raw materials.
>   b) Assistance in long range reconstruction and rehabilitation of the devastated countries.
> 3) Full participation by Great Britain in the Pacific war.
> 4) Policy Toward Germany.
>   a) Demilitarization by reparations and otherwise
>   b) Geographical dismemberment
>   c) Reeducation

[12] State Department Briefing Book Paper: "British Plan for a Western European Bloc, June 28, 1945," *Foreign Relations, 1945; Conference of Berlin,* I: 256–264 *passim.*
[13] *Ibid.*

d) Disbursement of German scientific personnel
e) Proper public relations of the United States toward the German population.
5) Holding the peace conference in the United States.
6) Some military and naval bases, if possible.
In other words, we think that as a well-known Missouri horse trader, the American people expect you to bring something home.
    /s/ JS [John Steelman]
        GA [George Allen]
        SIR [Samuel I. Rosenman][14]

"Something," but definitely not a miracle. Soviet participation and further British aid in the Pacific, rough four-power agreement on the organization of the German occupation, a few other items of less pressing importance—these were the only immediate American objectives at Berlin. There would be no attempts to "roll back" or even to contest Soviet control over Eastern Europe. There would be no efforts by the President and his advisers to control the destinies or the economies of Western Europe for the sake either of American business or military interests. The Truman administration's approach to Potsdam was to be marked by limited, and in many ways strikingly isolationist, goals, sensibly formulated and pursued with restraint.

Truman's position at the conference as well as his own personal self-possession were enormously strengthened at the very first by the realization of three important objectives. At their first meeting on July 17 Stalin informed the President that Soviet forces would intervene in the Far East within the month. The following day at the plenary session the Generalissimo readily agreed with his Western colleague that while Germany would be governed by zonal arrangements, political principles and practices would be "uniform" and free, not "different" and exclusive. The way was thus opened for Big Three agreement on interzonal economic cooperation, which had already been tentatively accepted in the Reparations Commission meetings in Moscow, and was a concern, as we shall see, that preyed heavily on the minds of both the British

[14] "Memorandum for the President, July 6, 1945," in folder entitled "Material Relating to the Potsdam Conf.," Rosenman Papers. This folder had just been received and its contents not yet filed when it was examined.

and the Americans. Finally, both Stalin and Churchill quickly agreed to Truman's first major proposal, namely the establishment of a Council of Foreign Ministers of the Big Three, later to be expanded to include France and China as well. The mandate given the council was as broad as it was simple: preparation of peace treaties with the former Axis nations and satellites.[15]

In part, of course, creation of the council was a triumph for the American view of the interim nature of the Potsdam Conference. Truman repeatedly stressed his belief at Berlin that any agreements reached by the Big Three were tentative, temporary, and subject to renegotiation and finalization by the vast and comprehensive postwar peace conference which he envisioned as convening shortly after the defeat of Japan.[16] The task of the Potsdam meeting and of the ongoing activities of the Foreign Ministers Council created by it was to prepare the diplomatic groundwork for such a conference. Creation of the council seemed to indicate that Stalin and Churchill shared such a view, and it gave to Truman and his advisers a great sense of freedom and maneuverability, because certain unpalatable European settlements could always be brought up for renegotiation at a later date with the excuse that they represented interim agreements and not permanent solutions. In a more immediate sense creation of the council also lent a badly needed sense of stability to the Potsdam discussions themselves. The council served as a safety valve for emotions and helped to govern the rhythm and flow of debate. For whenever controversies involving peace treaties or territorial settlements became too heated among the three heads of state, the matter under discussion could be swiftly shunted off to the foreign ministers for further study and negotiation. Should the foreign ministers forge a solution that was repugnant to one or more of their chiefs, or should the ministers in turn be unable to reach agreement, they were simply told to continue their talks until a resolution could be found at some future date. Thus at Berlin irresponsible pressures to achieve immediate and dramatic agreement on a broad spectrum of problems were greatly eased.

---

[15] *Foreign Relations, 1945; Conference of Berlin,* II: 45, 52, 56–58, 89, 94, 610, 871; Byrnes, *Speaking Frankly,* p. 205; Truman, *Year of Decisions,* p. 380.
[16] Truman, *Year of Decisions,* pp. 380, 447.

Having successfully initiated the establishment of the formal diplomatic machinery necessary to begin the political reconstruction of Europe, Truman wasted no time in informing the British and Russians just what they could expect in the way of a long-term American commitment to the overall rehabilitation of the Continent. United States participation in Europe's political and economic recovery would be as brief as possible. European self-help, defined in both political and economic terms, represented the Truman doctrine of 1945. The army was already leaving, save for a comparatively small occupation force. As soon as practicable American economic support and political tutelege must also be withdrawn. On this point the President, his immediate advisers, and leading members of the American military government for Germany were in complete accord. On the day of Truman's arrival in Berlin Robert Murphy, the chief civilian adviser in the military government, had a long talk with his old friend, Admiral Leahy.

> I explained to Leahy that these various schemes for breaking up Germany were worrying us in Military Government because one of our main problems was how to prevent the occupation from becoming an intolerable financial burden upon the American people. The situation, as we saw it, was that most European countries undoubtedly had legitimate claims for damages against the Nazis, and desperately needed immediate help, but that the war had been prolonged until nearly all of Europe was in ruins and the accumulated capital of generations used up. Since almost every nation was bankrupt except the United States, the American Government might be saddled now with the entire cost of the German occupation, as well as huge reparations for Nazi victims. The Admiral reassured me, "That danger is uppermost in the President's mind, too. I have heard him say that the American people foolishly made big loans to Germany after the First World War, and the money was used to pay reparations. When the loans were defaulted, Americans were left holding the bag. The President says he is determined not to let this happen again."[17]

In early discussions as to the future treatment of Italy, including Soviet reparations demands upon that nation, the President explained his position in simple and forceful terms.

> The United States policy in this matter is that it was trying to bring about a feeling of peace in the world. . . . They were faced with the

[17] Murphy, *Diplomat among Warriors*, p. 302.

situation where the United States must expend enormous sums of money because of countries in Europe. With reference to the question of reparations from Italy, it was necessary to take into consideration that the United States was spending from 750 million to a billion dollars to feed Italy this winter. The United States was rich but it could not forever pour out its resources for the help of others without getting something in return. Unless they were able to get these governments on a self-supporting basis, and there was no prospect of getting them on a self-supporting basis the way things were now going, the United States would not be able to continue indefinitely to maintain them when they should be able to help themselves. They had to try at this meeting to prepare conditions which would bring about a situation in which these countries could help themselves.[18]

The Italian question, in fact, triggered a long series of discussions at Potsdam concerning the future status of former Nazi satellite states in both Eastern and Western Europe. During the course of the conversations the Americans clearly revealed their essential disinterest in the affairs of Eastern Europe and their concurrent desire to rehabilitate the Western European nations as quickly as possible in order to withdraw as greatly as possible from the internal political and economic affairs of the Continent. The problem of the political reconstruction and economic rehabilitation of Italy had been initially raised by Truman at the first plenary session on July 17 and had been placed in tandem with the similar problems of the Danubian countries of Eastern Europe—Bulgaria, Rumania, and Hungary.[19] It was a logical marriage since all four nations had been Axis satellites. The Americans contented themselves at first only with a clear proposition in regard to Italy. Steps should immediately be taken by the Big Three powers to insure "her early political independence and economic recovery, and the right of the Italian people ultimately to choose their own form of government."[20]

[18] *Foreign Relations, 1945; Conference of Berlin,* II: 174. The Soviet record of the daily meetings at Potsdam has recently been published. For the most part it compresses and therefore to a degree inevitably distorts the remarks of the participants. The reader must judge which record of the conference, Russian or American, is the most accurate. The Russian account is in Robert Beitzell, ed., *Tehran, Yalta, Potsdam; The Soviet Protocols* (Hattiesburg, Miss.: The Academic International Press, 1970), pp. 141–355. The Truman statement is on p. 188.
[19] *Foreign Relations, 1945; Conference of Berlin,* II: 53.
[20] *Ibid.*, pp. 1080–1081, 1084–1085.

In response Churchill and Stalin waxed eloquent in their denunciations of all four countries when the subject was first debated among the three heads of state on July 20. But whereas the Prime Minister argued that all four should not be recognized until they had first created responsible democratic governments and then had supported them over a measurable period of time, Stalin shrewdly proposed that the political rehabilitation of the Danubian states proceed almost apace with that of Italy. "The purpose of such a policy," Stalin argued, "was to separate these countries from Germany as a great force. . . . If they started to take revenge against them for the brazen behavior and the losses which they had caused, this was one policy and he was against it." Stalin even went so far as to acknowledge the propriety of Truman's contention that Italy had gone further in expiating her sins than had the Danubian countries—Italy had just declared war on Japan, for example —"but still it was necessary" to broadly rehabilitate all four nations in rough simultaneity. When Churchill persisted in his obstinacy, Truman testily aligned himself with Stalin. "The President pointed out that he had submitted concrete proposals with reference to Italy and that Stalin had submitted proposals with reference to the other satellite states. He suggested that they refer these proposals to the Foreign Ministers." A flustered and isolated Churchill "replied that he could agree here and now to the preparation of a treaty by the Council of Foreign Ministers," and the matter was so referred.[21]

The Americans then proceeded to demonstrate how deep their desire to get out of Europe at an early date really was. When Molotov suggested that Truman wished to "supervise" the coming elections in the Danubian countries, the President immediately interrupted to say "that I had no desire to 'supervise' elections in the liberated countries and that I thought 'observe' would be a better word." Byrnes reiterated this point time and again throughout the conference. He told his Soviet counterparts that "we do not wish to become involved in the elections of any country." To be sure, both the President and his Secretary of State stood firm against Rus-

[21] *Ibid.*, pp. 172–175.

sian suggestions that the Danubian countries be recognized immediately without being first "reorganized."[22] The Americans would have their perfunctory consultative and advisory rights east of the Elbe as guaranteed by the Declaration on Liberated Europe fully respected. But Truman and Byrnes had first been careful to make their point: They were wholly averse to assuming an important role in the affairs of Eastern Europe.[23] There was no practicable way to avoid the unpleasant fact raised by the State Department's briefing book paper. Russia already had a sphere of influence in that area insured by the presence of the Red Army. If any part of Europe should escape entanglement in a sphere of influence, it would have to be the western half. In the diplomatic game of spheres of influence only Britain could lose as the United States pursued its policy—clearly revealed in the case of Italy—of rapid political and economic rehabilitation in each country before disengagement. Before she left the Continent America would to the best of her ability—always conceived in limited terms—guarantee the autonomy and independence of each state west and south of the Rhine. She could not and would not do the same for the regions further to the east.[24]

[22] Truman, *Year of Decisions*, p. 400; Byrnes, *Speaking Frankly*, p. 73; *Foreign Relations, 1945; Conference of Berlin*, II: 207, 228–231, 239.

[23] When on July 23 the Three briefly returned to the question of preparing peace treaties with Italy and the Eastern European nations, Truman and Byrnes said little as Stalin and Churchill resumed their debates. According to the Soviet record Truman spoke most strongly when pressed by Stalin. The President said at one point that he wanted the Eastern European governments "reorganized, and we shall give them our recognition when they become more responsible and democratic." But he then subsided as Churchill resumed the offensive. When the Prime Minister spoke of the difficulties encountered by British members of the Allied Control Commissions in Eastern Europe, Truman seconded him weakly, adding, "But we should not like to speak of that here." When Churchill asserted that the foreign ministers could not meet at London in September to prepare Eastern European peace treaties because the governments would not be reorganized, Truman again openly sided with Stalin, this time by simply evading the issue. The President agreed with the Generalissimo that this would not necessarily be true, and he urged that the issue be returned to the foreign ministers, where a change of wording involving preparation of peace treaties "for" rather than "with" the countries in question resolved the dispute. The more fulsome Soviet record of these exchanges strongly implies that over Churchill's impassioned rhetoric Truman and Stalin were signalling to one another the mutual desire not to allow this issue to wreck or impede the other work of the conference. Beitzell, *Tehran, Yalta, Potsdam*, pp. 237–245; *Foreign Relations, 1945; Conference of Berlin*, II: 357–365, 370–372.

[24] This point was brought out most clearly in a conversation between Will Clayton and Stanislaw Mikolajczyk at Potsdam on July 25. Mikolajczyk was probing

The broad Soviet-American rapprochement over Italy and the Danubian countries reached on July 20 did not wholly dispose of the problems surrounding the rehabilitation of these states, for the Russians continued to press reparations claims upon Italy, despite the repeated warnings of Byrnes and Clayton "in the best spirit . . . that the United States does not intend to make [financial] advances to any country in order that reparations may be paid, . . ."[25] and in the face of Truman's renunciation of American reparations claims. However, Stalin was finally forced to realize how important the American disinterest in Eastern Europe was to Soviet designs, and he wisely decided not to dun the Italians and their American allies on this point.

The occasion of his awakening was the arrival in Potsdam on July 28 of the formerly quiescent Clement Attlee and Ernest Bevin, now at the helm of British foreign policy as the result of their shocking upset win in the general election. Prior to Churchill's departure the British and Soviet delegations had been at loggerheads for days over a United States request that the three powers "support the entry of Italy into the United Nations Organization," as a part of the American plan for the rapid political revitalization of that country. What had happened was that the British delegation had asked for the inclusion of several wartime neutral nations in the proposal, and the Americans had at first agreed. But the Russians had insistently demanded that Franco's Spain be excluded and indeed be censured as an outlaw nation by the Big Three. Truman had supported Stalin over Churchill's vehement protests that this was tantamount to interference in the internal affairs of another state. Then, to the Prime Minister's utter dismay, the Soviets had asked that Rumania, Hungary, Bulgaria, and Finland also be supported for United Nations membership; and Truman and Byrnes had agreed to that also. The result was a stalemate that lasted until the departure of Churchill and the return of Attlee and Bevin. For if the United States "agreed with the Soviet Delegation, the British

the prospects of an American loan. In reply Clayton indicated that "urgent cases" had been presented by Norway and Denmark among others, and "He concluded by stating that the United States recognizes the reconstruction needs of Poland and wants to be helpful, and by asking that the Poles remember that we have calls for materials and credits from all sides." *Foreign Relations, 1945, Conference of Berlin,* II: 405–406.

[25] *Ibid.,* pp. 148–149, 209.

Delegation did not agree; if we agreed with the British Delegation, the Soviet Delegation disagreed." So, Byrnes said, "It was now up to the Soviet and British Delegations to see if they could get together."[26]

They could not. After Stalin pointed out to Attlee and Bevin that the proposal "did not provide for the establishment of full diplomatic relations" between the Danubian states and the United Nations "but only that they consider the question," and that "He did not understand" the British "distinction made between Italy and the other" former Nazi "satellites" in the Danube Valley, Bevin roughly suggested that the difference was that "they [the British] knew about the Italian Government but that they did not know anything about the other governments." When Stalin then pointed to the fact that the Russians had not been invited to learn much about the post-Mussolini Italian government before being asked to recognize it and that the proposal in question did not constitute recognition in any case, Attlee responded with asperity that it was his opinion that this was precisely what the proposal would do and that an American suggestion for a minor change of words "did not alter the substance of the matter. One question in Parliament would bring out the real difficulty."[27]

Then the two British officials began to grill Stalin about the extent and nature of Soviet reparations demands upon Italy. At one point "Bevin observed that it was difficult to tell what the Russians would take away or to define the effect that removal of equipment might have on the economic life of a nation."[28]

Stalin had never been so indelicately handled by Churchill on so comparatively minor a point. Moreover, the new British negotiating team was unpredictable since it seemed to look with greater favor and sympathy upon the present Italian regime than had Churchill and Eden. The Russians needed help and time to assess the change in British policy. When, therefore, Truman "said he thought they were not far apart" on the "principle" of Italian reparations and that he "fully sympathized" with Soviet desires to

26 *Ibid.*, pp. 123–127, 462; Moran, *Churchill*, p. 296.
27 *Foreign Relations, 1945; Conference of Berlin*, II: 462–463.
28 *Ibid.*, pp. 464–465; Truman, *Year of Decisions*, pp. 439–440.

use reparations to rebuild a shattered homeland, Stalin gratefully "agreed" that the Three were in closer agreement than it seemed, adding "that the Russians did not want to touch the advances the United States was making to Italy."[29] Better by far for the Russians to protect American friendship and insure continuing American disinterest in Eastern Europe than to have Attlee and Bevin once again tear open the whole question of the reconstruction of the former Axis states over the issue of Italian reparations.

Italian reparations payments to Russia thus remained in limbo as the conference closed. In the protocol the three heads of state agreed that the preparation of an Italian peace treaty should be "first among the immediate important tasks to be undertaken by the new Council of Foreign Ministers," with the Rumanian, Bulgarian, and Hungarian peace treaties to follow as soon as the political reorganization of the countries was completed. American diplomacy had achieved as much as it ever could or ever wished in this regard.[30] As for Big Three support for the admission of the four former Axis satellites into the United Nations, this was finally agreed to as part of the large, American-sponsored, package proposal revolving around the German settlement which ended the conference. And finally, British interests suffered in the protocol to the extent that Franco's Spain was harshly condemned for her Fascist leanings during the late war, and her exclusion from the world organization was earnestly recommended.[31] Very possibly Attlee and Bevin did not share the sensitive regard for Spain's integrity which agitated Churchill and Eden, but traditional British diplomatic objectives received a setback even if those of the new team did not.

The negotiations over the rehabilitation of the former Axis satellite states strikingly revealed both the limited goals and the resulting flexibility of American diplomacy. Seeking nothing substantial in the way of political or economic influence and concessions east of the Elbe, desirous of remaining in western and central Eu-

[29] *Foreign Relations, 1945; Conference of Berlin*, II: 464–465; Beitzell, *Tehran, Yalta, Potsdam*, p. 263; Truman, *Year of Decisions*, pp. 439–440.

[30] *Foreign Relations, 1945; Conference of Berlin*, II: 1492.

[31] Byrnes, *Speaking Frankly*, p. 86; *Foreign Relations, 1945; Conference of Berlin*, II: 1493.

rope only so long as and to the extent that was necessary to mini-
mally revitalize the various nations struggling to survive there, and
determined to preserve friendship with the Russians at least through
the end of the Pacific war and hopefully well beyond, Truman
and the other American officials were able to continue Washington's traditional role as mediator between London and the Kremlin.

This fact became fully apparent as the Big Three struggled to un-
tangle the many strands of interest that made up the German problem and to weave them into some sort of coherent policy. At the
last moment only the broker diplomacy practiced by Byrnes and
supported by Truman was able to fashion an acceptable and surprisingly workable general compromise that saved the conference
from collapse.

Germany in mid-summer 1945 was a land in ruins. While waiting for Stalin's arrival, members of the American and British delegations toured nearby Berlin and returned shaken by their impressions of utter devastation and destitution.[32] Perhaps this fact alone
stiffened Allied—and particularly American—resolve to rehabilitate Germany as rapidly as possible. Certainly the extent of destruction seemed to deal a body blow to the United States resolve to
bind up Europe's wounds as swiftly and economically as possible
and then withdraw. Could Germany ever recover?

Possessed by these gloomy thoughts, Western leaders confronted
a Stalin who was determined to get his full share of what remained
of the German naval and merchant fleets, to obtain the largest
amount of reparations possible from the ruins of the Reich, and to
place the Poles in full administrative charge of the large area between the eastern and western forks of the Neisse River. The prospects for a favorable resolution of these issues was not bright as the
preliminary skirmish on July 19 over the disposition of the German
fleet revealed. For Stalin was obdurately determined that the Russians should claim that portion of the remaining German war fleet
that had fallen into their hands, not as reparations but as war

---

[32] Truman, *Year of Decisions*, pp. 377–378; Churchill, *Triumph and Tragedy*,
p. 538; Leahy, *I Was There*, pp. 395–396; Moran, *Churchill*, pp. 288–289; Stimson
Diary, July 17, 1945.

booty. They also demanded as reparations one-third of the German merchant navy, most of which lay in British hands. Churchill immediately contested Stalin's proposal. The Prime Minister's formal argument in plenary session was that the Royal Navy had suffered a disastrous loss of power during World War II. It would never again be mistress of the seas, all the more reason why Britain should have her fair one-third share of what remained of the German naval as well as merchant fleet.

The real motive behind the British refusal to accede to Russian demands had already been cogently set forth by Eden. Britain did not "have . . . many cards in our hand" to contest Russian "aggrandisement" in Eastern Europe and even in China. One of the cards London did have, however, was possession of the German fleet. "We must not, I am sure, yield a single German ship in our possession until we have obtained satisfaction for our interests, which the Russians are treating with contempt," Eden had written to his chief on July 15. But after Churchill's remarks Truman interjected the American view at this moment, which was simply that the whole question should be held in abeyance until victory was achieved in the Pacific and sufficient relief was dispensed to Europe, including the Soviet Union, to insure the economic recovery of the entire area. Until such time as Japan laid down her arms and Europe was on the road to prosperity, all German vessels should be placed in a shipping pool for use by all the Allied participants in the Pacific war and all the hungry nations of the Continent.[33]

The President had raised a delicate point concerning the Japanese war, as Russia had not yet committed her arms and men to the Far Eastern struggle. The ever-suspicious Stalin instantly probed for duplicity. "Are not the Russians to wage war against Japan?" he queried. Truman "replied that when Russia was ready to fight Japan, she would be taken in the shipping pool the same as the others. He added that we wanted them in the pool." The President also informed his colleagues that after the war the United States would make available for sale both surplus naval and merchant vessels. But all that lay in the future. A maximum effort at sea, as in the air

[33] Eden, *The Reckoning*, pp. 632–633; *Foreign Relations, 1945; Conference of Berlin*, II: 118–122.

and on the ground, must first be exerted against the Japanese. Beyond that "we must use these ships for the . . . relief for liberated areas and the carrying of goods to our Russian Ally." The topic emerged here and there throughout the rest of the conference, though the President thought he had settled the matter in the course of the first discussions. In the protocol the Allies finally agreed on a three-way division of both the German naval and merchant fleets, with disposition of the former to commence no later than the following August 15, while division of the latter "shall take place as soon as practicable after the end of the war against Japan." Tripartite naval and marine commissions were created to handle the chore of bestowing specific vessels to one country or the other.[34]

The three-way contests over the Polish border and reparations were of far greater importance, of course, involving as they did the long-term future of Germany.[35] And on these issues the fact that both Truman and Churchill were dealing from felt positions of weakness made them the more determined to resist Stalin's will.

Poland had died as a political issue by the time of Potsdam. Truman and Hopkins had seen to that the previous month, and not even Churchill was disposed to resurrect the issue. Indeed, the Prime Minister did not even wish to discuss it at length—save to protect Polish fighting forces in the West from forcible repatriation—or to see any Poles at all of whatever stripe and persuasion.[36] But the matter of the postwar Polish border in the West was another issue entirely. As Churchill was later to write:

> The Soviet-dominated Government of Poland had also pressed forward, not to the Eastern Neisse, but to the Western. Much of this territory was inhabited by Germans, and although several millions had fled many had stayed behind. What was to be done with them? Moving three or four million Poles [from beyond the Curzon Line in eastern Poland, now claimed and occupied by the Russians] was bad

---

[34] *Foreign Relations, 1945; Conference of Berlin*, II: 118–122, 131–133, 382, 1487–1488.
[35] Ellen Clayton Garwood oral history interview with Will Clayton, 1947 (n.d.), Garwood Papers, Box 1, p. 19.
[36] *Foreign Relations, 1945; Conference of Berlin*, II: 91–94; Moran, *Churchill*, p. 304.

enough. Were we to move more than eight million Germans as well? Even if such a transfer could be contemplated, there was not enough food for them in what was left of Germany. Much of Germany's grain came from the very land which the Poles had seized, and if this was denied us the Western Allies would be left with wrecked industrial zones and a starved and swollen population.[37]

This was a hideous prospect for the economically prostrate and exhausted British, who now might be forced to feed the "swollen" and "starving" multitude of their former enemy from their own dwindling stocks at home. It was also upsetting to the Americans, who by now had come to feel that in zonal occupation terms the other powers "got something worthwhile and the United States got the scenery."[38] If the American zone of occupation were to survive and prosper without constant effusions of agricultural and industrial aid from the United States, then American policy-makers felt a system of balanced interzonal trade, hopefully based upon the 1937 borders of Germany, would have to be worked up with the British, French, and Russians. Stalin's early commitment to "uniform" political practices, following earlier agreements in the Reparations Commission at Moscow to treat Germany as an economic unit, seemed to promise great hope of reaching such an agreement. But the reparations tangle threatened to undo this promising start.

From the American side reparations policy was still somewhat unclear down to the eve of Potsdam, for it remained entwined with the question of the totality of the defeat to be imposed upon Germany. The long fight within the United States government in 1944 over the Morgenthau Plan had centered around this very issue, of course, but to many Morgenthau's defeat seemed more apparent than real. Officially American policy by early 1945 was that Nazism must die but Germany must live and even eventually prosper. The mere word that Morgenthau was going to Potsdam to lobby his views, however, set aflutter the pulses of his opponents within the Truman administration. They had some cause for concern. Ostensibly the Morgenthau Plan was dead, and Truman, Byrnes, Clay-

---

[37] Churchill, *Triumph and Tragedy*, p. 554.
[38] John Gimbel, *The American Occupation of Germany, 1945–1949* (Stanford, Calif.: Stanford University Press, 1968), p. 13.

ton, and the military were all set upon the eventual reestablishment of a self-sufficient Germany. As Clayton explained to the Russians in the Economic Subcommittee meetings at Potsdam, "The American people will not again, as they did after the last war, finance Germany" either to support her reparations payments or to underwrite her prosperity.[39] Truman's doctrine of the most rapid political and economic self-help seemed to apply as much to Germany as to Italy.

But, understandably enough, American planners could never precisely determine at what point healthy and necessary economic recovery in Germany might create the essential industrial base for a swift military revival. Prior to mid-May American officials had been able to evade the problem, while the British and Russians bickered steadily over the composition of the Reparations Commission, which was to meet in Moscow to negotiate a coherent policy.

As early as mid-March Britain had pressed the Americans and Soviets for French inclusion in the reparations negotiations since the French had been granted an occupation zone in Germany by the Big Three at Yalta. The Russians had countered with a demand of their own. If France should be included so should Poland and Yugoslavia. Stalin rightly observed that the two East European countries had surely suffered as much, if not far more, at German hands as had the French. They should therefore be entitled to equal representation and an equal say on the Reparations Commission. For weeks the Russians remained obstinate, until at last their Western Allies caved in and announced on May 17 that they were prepared to begin discussions on the original tripartite basis.[40]

In his instructions to Reparations Commission representative Edwin Pauley, Truman wrote that "fundamental United States policy" demanded "that Germany's war potential be destroyed, and its resurgence as far as possible be prevented, by removal or de-

---

[39] Stimson Diary, July 4, 1945; *Foreign Relations, 1945; Conference of Berlin,* II: 142; Ellen Clayton Garwood interview with Will Clayton, 1947 (n. d.) Garwood Papers, Box 1, pp. 19–22.

[40] British Aide-Mémoire to State Department, March 16, 1945; Undersecretary of State Grew to Ambassador Harriman, March 27, 1945; Harriman to Secretary of State, April 1, 3, 10, 1945; Grew to Chargé Kennan, May 17, 1945, *Foreign Relations, 1945; Diplomatic Papers,* III: 1177–1178, 1185–1186, 1194–1195, 1220.

struction of German plants, equipment and other property." At the same time "This Government opposes any reparation plan based upon the assumption that the United States or any other country will finance directly or indirectly any reconstruction in Germany or reparation by Germany." "The Reparation Plan should not maintain or foster dependence of other countries upon the German economy."[41] Here was confusion indeed, for what constituted "war potential" or "dependence of other countries upon the German economy"? Just what was to be the future configuration of the German economy? Exactly how were reparations and other punitive policies to fit into that configuration?

Despite the ambiguous American position, the Reparations Commission at Moscow had shaped some significant agreements about the economic treatment of postwar Germany, the most important from the American and British perspective, of course, being the tripartite decision to treat Germany as a unit. But then at the last moment, in the words of one State Department official, "the Russians threw in a definition of war booty—or war trophies as they call it—which included everything. The outcome of that was a general scrapping of what had gone before," and the problem was thrown directly into the laps of the Big Three and their Foreign Ministers at Potsdam.[42]

Meanwhile throughout May and June the Russians had been systematically looting as much of Germany as they could reach of everything that could be carried away by hand, cart, truck, locomotive, and any other conveyance. All of this material was defined, of course, as war booty or "trophies." So vociferous had British and American indignation become by the time of Potsdam that Stalin claimed that "the Americans had charged the Russians with taking everything." The Western Allies remained unmoved, whereupon Molotov pressed the issue by again raising the question, which had remained unresolved since Yalta, concerning the proper reparations total to be assessed the Germans. The Soviets charged that twenty billion dollars, half of it to go to Russia, had been the figure agreed to at the Crimea and that the Americans and British

[41] *Ibid.*, pp. 1222–1223.
[42] *Foreign Relations, 1945; Conference of Berlin,* II: 871.

were now reneging on their pledge. In response Byrnes tirelessly reiterated that there had been no such pledge. The Americans had simply agreed that the twenty billion dollar figure "would be accepted as a basis for discussion" to be referred to the Reparations Commission and no more. The records of the Yalta Conference would seem to indicate that the Soviet assertion more closely approximated the truth. But by the time of Potsdam the American determination not to underwrite desired German recovery any more than necessary had become unshakeable.[43]

And now the Russians were complicating the problem of German economic recovery even further by their demand that Poland be given the western Neisse line and hence a large and agriculturally productive area of what had been prewar Germany. Truman originally resisted any such proposal. With an economically weak zone to occupy, the President wished interzonal trade within Germany to reach as wide an area as possible. He therefore demanded that the political and economic treatment of postwar Germany be based upon its 1937 territorial limits. Stalin, however, insistently demanded that the new Polish border be recognized by adding the words "minus what [Germany] lost in 1945."[44]

Total impasse seemed to have been reached. The Russians had begun to strip their zone and had defined their loot as "booty." They then demanded that their beaten enemies assume a further and impossibly high reparations burden which, if accepted, might have kept Germany prostrate for decades, the welfare of her western zones wholly in the hands of America and Britain. The Soviets had then proposed to weaken the country still more through dismemberment. And all this in the face of repeated American assertions that the United States would not be party to a rape of Germany which in the end would place the bill in the hands of the American taxpayer. The chasm between Soviet and Anglo-American plans for postwar Germany seemed impossible to bridge.

Truman and Byrnes set about the chore nonetheless. And their greater sense of flexibility, their conviction that any Potsdam agree-

---

[43] Byrnes, *Speaking Frankly*, pp. 81–82; Millis, ed., *Forrestal Diaries*, p. 79; *Foreign Relations, 1945; Conference of Berlin*, II: 296, 428–432, 514; Diane Shaver Clemens, *Yalta* (New York: Oxford University Press, 1970), pp. 165, 169.
[44] *Foreign Relations, 1945; Conference of Berlin*, II: 90, 96.

ments were of an interim nature and not a permanent solution, permitted them to explore the areas of possible compromise more thoroughly and comfortably than either their Soviet or British compatriots. The first faint signs of a break came in the course of an otherwise acrimonious debate over the Polish border on July 25, the last meeting that Churchill attended. Truman expressed his "sympathy with the Poles and with Marshal Stalin in regard to the difficulties they were up against." There were then four zones of occupation. The President now began speaking of the area between the eastern and western Neisse as a possible Polish zone. And "If the Poles were to have a zone, they were responsible to the Soviet Union for it." In other words, if Stalin was determined to dismember a part of eastern Germany, fully within the current Soviet occupation zone, and give it to Poland, Truman would not object. But the Poles should behave responsibly and contribute, as the Russians had already promised to do, their fair share to the interzonal trading pattern, which would help maintain the economically weak American zone and the industrially prostrate British area in the West. And it was Stalin's ultimate responsibility to see that the Poles did behave. If these conditions were met, the President was hinting, Poland could remain in the disputed area until the postwar peace conference, at which time, he firmly stipulated, her "frontier should be fixed" permanently.[45]

Here was a solution to one segment of the problem. Stalin promptly, if tacitly, offered a proposal to begin resolution of the other segment when he observed "that coal and steel were much more important than food in the question of supplies for Germany. 90 per cent of Germany's metal came from the Ruhr and 80 per cent of its coal." Stalin had hit upon a crucial point. Save for Silesia, the Soviets—and their Polish colleagues—had got "the feeding grounds" of Germany but not its industrial heartland, which lay in the Ruhr.[46] If the Soviets could be promised some sort of reparations matériel from the Ruhr, they might well relax their other demands. It was worth consideration, and Byrnes promptly set to work.

[45] *Ibid.*, pp. 384, 389.
[46] *Ibid.*, pp. 385, 386.

He was greatly aided after July 28 by the appearance of Attlee and Bevin, whose rough behavior toward the Russians was not confined to the issue of Italy and recognition of the Danubian nations. Bevin wasted no time in bluntly telling Stalin and Molotov that on the issue of the Polish border "his instructions were to hold out for the Eastern Neisse."[47] If Stalin were to have his way on the Polish border issue while obtaining some further substantial reparations awards, especially from the Ruhr, he would need American aid.

Byrnes, in consultation with Clayton, Pauley, and, significantly, Joseph E. Davies, had already decided that the reparations problem had become so entangled with related questions of war booty, interzonal exchange, and the like, that the only solution was to have each country take reparations from its own zone.[48] He first proposed this solution to Molotov at a private meeting on July 23. The Secretary commenced by again stating in "very plain" language "that the United States did not intend to pay out money to finance imports to Germany and thus repeat the experience after the last war when in fact United States funds had been used to pay reparations to others." Molotov's response was conciliatory and understanding. Byrnes was thus encouraged to make his proposal, during the course of which he pointed out that according to American estimates "about 50% of the existing wealth of Germany was in the Soviet zone." Byrnes stressed that while his proposal obviously denied the agreed principle of unitary political and economic treatment of Germany, the compromise embodied in it would be confined to reparations alone. "In other matters such as currency, transport, etc. Germany" would continue to be treated "as an economic whole." Molotov replied positively and even hinted that the Russians might be willing to reduce their rigid reparations figure of $20 billion somewhat. On this positive note the interview ended, and in what was becoming a distressingly predictable pattern, there followed four days of silence while the Polish border question raged on and Molotov returned to his defense of the Soviet reparations figure.[49]

[47] Truman, *Year of Decisions*, p. 447; Byrnes, *Speaking Frankly*, p. 79.
[48] Byrnes, *Speaking Frankly*, p. 83.
[49] *Foreign Relations, 1945; Conference of Berlin*, II: 274–275, 871; Byrnes, *Speaking Frankly*, pp. 83–84.

On the twenty-seventh, the day before the arrival of Attlee and Bevin, Byrnes came to the problem again. Following up Stalin's hint about the Ruhr delivered at the plenary session two days earlier, Byrnes presented a modification of his earlier proposal as a sweetener to the Soviets. While "in substance" he continued to press for the independent zonal handling of reparations, he also "had in mind working out arrangements for the exchange of needed products between the zones." As an example, Byrnes said, there might be a possibility that with British agreement the Soviets could remove "machinery and equipment" from the most industrially saturated and sophisticated area of Western Europe—the Ruhr Valley. This could be done in exchange "for goods—food and coal—in the Soviet zone." Throughout the discussion the Secretary of State persistently stressed the need to secure Attlee's acquiescence.[50] Presumably Byrnes by this time was thinking of the "Soviet zone" as including the Polish area between the eastern and western Neisse. Molotov said nothing at this point, but discussions were resumed on the twenty-ninth. With the British conspicuously absent, Byrnes and Truman revealed a bit more of their emerging package solution. "The Secretary said that if we were able to get an agreement on reparations along the lines of his proposals to Mr. Molotov that the United States was prepared to go further to meet the Soviet wishes in regard to the Polish western frontier. . . ."[51] The President's earlier hint had now become a solid bargaining counter.

But then an eager and inexperienced President nearly wrecked his Secretary's careful efforts. For Truman suddenly told Molotov "that what they were trying to do here was to fix a workable plan for reparations and that he desired to see the Soviet Union receive 50% of the total" German reparations from the Ruhr! Since Molotov had only mentioned a figure of twenty-five percent and Byrnes had steadfastly refused so far to set any percentage figure whatsoever, Truman's concession was a real blunder, for it could only encourage those Soviet appetites which Byrnes had delicately sought to awaken only to control. Not surprisingly "Mr. Molotov expressed his appreciation at the President's statement," and the following day the Russian stepped up Soviet pressure to get into the Ruhr

[50] *Foreign Relations, 1945; Conference of Berlin,* II: 450–452.
[51] *Ibid.,* p. 472.

by proposing the establishment of a separate four-power Allied Control Commission for the region.[52]

Fortunately for Byrnes, the Soviets had not yet obtained a suitable settlement of the Polish border dispute nor a possible Big Three recommendation that the Balkan states as well as Italy be admitted to UN membership. Attlee and Bevin meanwhile continued to view all Russian objectives with suspicion. Mutual need still bound Soviet and American negotiators together.

On July 31, therefore, Byrnes finally completed his package proposal designed to end all immediately outstanding Big Three differences over Europe. First, the United States would recognize Polish occupation and administration of the area up to the western Neisse line, as Stalin and Warsaw had persistently demanded. Bevin furiously interjected at this point, charging that "according to the United States proposal, the territory would be under the Polish state and not part of the Soviet zone of occupation. . . ." Truman did not dispute this contention. Rather he said, as he had all along, that the United States was willing to make such a concession only until the postwar Judgment Day when the great peace conference would convene and all previous territorial and political arrangements would be renegotiated and completed.[53]

The second part of Byrnes' proposal stipulated that not only Italy, but also the Danubian countries, would be recommended for United Nations membership by the Potsdam Conference, contingent upon their acceptance of the peace treaties to be immediately drawn up by the Foreign Ministers Council. Such recommendation, however, did not imply immediate Western recognition of the East European states. Such recommendation could only come after the governments of Bulgaria, Rumania, and Hungary were suitably "reorganized."

And finally, reparations: They would be handled by each power in its respective zone, but there would also be provisions made for interzonal reparations exchanges as Byrnes had suggested. The Russians balked at Byrnes' specific provision as to the amount, however. Stalin had already indicated that he wanted twenty-five per-

[52] *Ibid.*, pp. 473–474, 482; Truman, *Year of Decisions*, p. 442.
[53] Truman, *Year of Decisions*, p. 447.

cent of the surplus industrial—or "capital"—equipment of the Ruhr without payment or exchange of any kind. Byrnes had agreed to this, whereupon the Russians, taking advantage of Truman's blundering good will, had indicated that they wanted yet an additional fifteen percent. Western negotiators had countered with various offers that the Russians could have a bit more of the Ruhr equipment as *gratis* reparations but that the rest must be paid for by exchange from the Soviet zone. The total percentage figure mentioned varied from about seven and one-half to twelve and one-half. Now, at the plenary session on July 31, Stalin began to bargain the percentage amount once more. At last the Generalissimo, in Byrnes' words, "proposed that the amount of capital equipment to be removed from the western zone [Ruhr] in return for products such as food, coal, timber, and so on, be increased from 12 per cent to 15 per cent. I said if he would withdraw his other demands and agree to the other two proposals in dispute," regarding the Polish border and Italian and Balkan admission to the United Nations, "we would agree to the 15 per cent. He agreed. . . ." Nothing more was heard from the Russians about joint control of the Ruhr. "Agreement quickly followed on such matters as the economic principles to govern the occupation of Germany, including the compact to treat the country as an economic unit; the orderly transfer of German population" from the area between the eastern and western forks of the Neisse River; "and the revision of the Allied Control Council procedure" in the Balkan countries to meet American and British demands for greater rights of consultation.[54]

And so the great European compromise was reached. It had been forged and carried through by American negotiators, led by Byrnes, with Truman's obvious prodding and backing. At Berlin the President clearly mastered whatever immediate desires his new Secretary of State might have entertained to force American diplomacy onto a new and narrower track. Maintenance of the Grand Alliance in some semblance of unity and amity remained a necessary and worthy objective of United States foreign policy at Potsdam,

[54] *Foreign Relations, 1945; Conference of Berlin,* II: 511–572; Byrnes, *Speaking Frankly,* p. 85; Gimbel, *American Occupation of Germany,* p. 15; Ellen Clayton Garwood Interview with Will Clayton, 1947 (n. d.), Garwood Papers, Box 1, p. 22.

especially where questions of European reconstruction and rehabilitation were concerned. Such an objective not only forced American officials to accept at least the temporary reality of an existing Soviet sphere of influence in Eastern Europe; it also forced them to blunt any British initiatives designed to question or contest this reality. Whatever frustrations the Americans may have felt in the negotiations over Europe were largely appeased by the belief—which must have been especially attractive to the opportunist, Byrnes—that all or part of the agreements reached at Potsdam could be severely modified if not completely undone on Judgment Day, that moment when the great postwar peace conference would at last convene.

And, of course, over the short run the German agreements reached at Potsdam were quite favorable to the Americans. Burdened by the possession of an occupation zone that was almost completely dependent upon imports for whatever future prosperity it might achieve, the United States had gotten the British and Russians to agree to the principle of German economic unity and the establishment of "an interzonal trade balance that would reduce or eliminate" the necessity for direct imports from the United States "to feed Germans and to prime German industry." Moreover, "the Byrnes compromise on reparations avoided setting a specific reparations amount"—such as the $20 billion figure bandied about by the Russians at Yalta and in the Reparations Committee discussions at Moscow. Since it was finally agreed that "reparations were linked to the study and calculation of excess capital equipment," which seemed fairly evenly distributed at least between the British, French, and Russian zones,[55] the "compromise seemed to forestall" any future "imbalance within the German economy as a whole."[56] The most important and heartening fact was that Byrnes' great compromise created the conditions necessary to get the Allied Control Commission for Germany started as an effective, working body. The rehabilitation of the German people, economy, and political system, upon which the Americans pinned so much hope for an early

---

[55] The Russian and Polish zones, of course, included the industrial region of Silesia.

[56] Gimbel, *American Occupation of Germany*, pp. 14–15.

withdrawal from Europe, could now begin.[57] With these substantial, if temporary, European compromises achieved and with the Council of Foreign Ministers established, Truman and his colleagues had every right to feel cautiously satisfied. Available contemporary evidence, as previously mentioned, strongly indicates that this was indeed their state of mind.

There emerged at Potsdam, however, a number of peripheral irritations that warned of gathering storms on the diplomatic horizon. The issue of a Soviet United Nations trusteeship over one or more of the Italian North African colonies fronting the Mediterranean was one of these. The possible expansion of Russian power into the Dardanelles was another. Both issues deeply affected Britain, for they represented flagrant Soviet probes toward the traditional imperial lifeline running from Gibraltar to Suez and thence east to India, Singapore, and Hong Kong. Control of the Dardanelles would permit a Soviet fleet abrupt access to the eastern Mediterranean; control of the former Italian colonies would give such a fleet a permanent base of operations.

It will be recalled that in the flush of comradeship and elation at the close of the San Francisco Conference Stettinius had rashly pledged his government to support any subsequent Russian trusteeship bid. At Potsdam three weeks later Molotov and Stalin quickly raised the issue with Truman and Byrnes during their first brief meeting on July 17. Three days later Molotov formally submitted his government's proposals on trusteeships over the Italian African colonies, and the matter went on to the heads of state for discussion. To Stalin's evident displeasure, Churchill first sought to dismiss the question as of minor importance, to be discussed either at the postwar peace conference or possibly at some future date by the foreign ministers. Truman was non-committal, saying only that the United States did not wish to exercise any such mandate over the Italian colonies in Africa. "We had enough poor Italians to feed," the President characteristically complained. The matter was only fitfully discussed throughout the rest of the conference and no firm decision was taken. Russian remarks and proposals, however,

[57] Clay, *Decision in Germany*, p. 48; Truman, *Year of Decisions*, p. 381.

seemed to indicate that when the foreign ministers came to work up the peace treaties, Molotov would raise the question as to whether Italy should be relieved of her African possessions, some of which might be placed under Soviet trusteeship.[58]

Churchill opened the discussion on possible revision of existing treaty relationships in the Dardanelles Straits in plenary session on July 22 with the admission that the Montreux Convention should be revised. But he reminded his Russian colleagues that Turkey was understandably alarmed at the current concentration of Russian and Bulgarian troops on Bulgarian soil. What was the Russian position, he asked. Molotov in response circulated a paper in which the Soviets asked that henceforth Russia and Turkey jointly control the Dardanelles, that Russia be allowed to build bases along the Straits, and that Turkey and Russia jointly be permitted to prevent "by their common facilities in the Straits the use of the Straits by the other countries for . . . purposes inimical to the Black Sea powers."[59]

Churchill's reply was subdued but clear enough: Britain, traditionally the guarantor of Turkish rights as befitted her pre-eminent Mediterranean interests, demanded the right to join with Stalin and the Turks in any treaty revision respecting the Dardanelles and the Black Sea. Truman initially offered no opinion, but within several days he circulated his famous proposal that many of the waterways of Europe and the world, including the Rhine, the Danube, and the Straits, be internationalized. In a supporting statement that summed up much of his thinking about European affairs throughout the conference, the President said: "I do not want to fight another war in twenty years because of a quarrel on the Danube. We want a prosperous, self-supporting Europe. A bankrupt Europe is of no advantage to any country, or to the peace of the world." Stalin became obstinate; he wished the issue of the Straits considered separately. "I am afraid we won't reach an agreement on the Straits," he told the President. "Our ideas differ widely."[60] And so they did.

Truman had offered his proposal for a number of reasons. First, it was in line with the "open world" policy of free trade and rep-

---

[58] *Foreign Relations, 1945; Conference of Berlin,* II: 44, 47, 160, 254, 550–551, 604.
[59] *Ibid.,* pp. 256–257, 1427–1428.
[60] *Ibid.,* pp. 258, 313, 372.

resentative governments formally embraced, if not always practically pursued, by both the President and his State Department. Second, the proposal might become a means of appeasing Soviet maritime appetites. And finally, the President obviously viewed his plan as a solution to what he simplistically believed was a basic source of European warfare over the previous two centuries. "I had come to the conclusion," he told Churchill and Stalin,

> after a long study of history, that all the wars of the last two hundred years had originated in the area from the Black Sea to the Baltic and from the eastern frontier of France to the western frontier of Russia. In the last two instances the peace of the whole world had been overturned—by Austria in World War I and by Germany in this war. I thought it should be the business of this conference and of the coming peace conference to see that this did not happen again.
>
> I announced that I was presenting a paper proposing free access to all the seas of the world by Russia and by all other countries. I was offering as a solution of the straits problem the suggestion that the Kiel Canal in Germany, the Rhine-Danube waterway . . . the Black Sea Straits, the Suez Canal, and the Panama Canal be made free waterways. . . .
>
> I went on to say that we did not want the world to engage in another war in twenty-five years over the straits or the Danube. I said that our only ambition was to have a Europe that was sound economically and that could support itself. I wanted to see a Europe that would make Russia, England, France, and all other countries in it secure, prosperous, and happy, and with which the United States could trade and be happy as well as prosperous.[61]

Sincere as were Truman's pleas, the plan simply ran up against Soviet interests and suspicions. Soviet control of the Straits was seen as essential by the Kremlin if Russia were to protect her southern Black Sea flank from future aggression. The President's plan was thus doomed from the beginning, although Churchill vigorously supported it "in contrast to that of a [Russian] base in the straits in close proximity to Constantinople." In the Potsdam protocol the three governments merely agreed to hold further discussion with Turkey looking to an unspecified "revision" of the existing Montreux Convention, and the subject was temporarily dropped.[62]

[61] Truman, *Year of Decisions*, p. 415.
[62] *Ibid.*, p. 416; *Foreign Relations, 1945; Conference of Berlin*, II: 1496–1497.

One other issue briefly emerged at Potsdam which would steadily grow in intensity and concern in the coming months. This was the question of Allied troop withdrawal from Iran. Soviet, British, and some American troops had been in the country since 1942 to protect the supply corridor to Russia from German arms. Since the necessity for their presence had clearly lapsed, Churchill proposed their early withdrawal.[63] Stalin disagreed, saying that the Allied occupation should not be terminated prior to the end of the Pacific war. Stalin was evidently working on the assumption that since lend-lease supplies to Russia would continue with the Russian declaration of war on Japan, the Iranian corridor would remain operative. Truman, however, expressed indifference. Although the State Department was alarmed at the "progressive deterioration of Iranian internal affairs, which is being hastened by intense Soviet-British rivalry in Iran," the President told Churchill and Stalin that the United States was proceeding swiftly with its own withdrawal from the country "because we needed our troops in the Far East. I estimated that we could be out of Iran in sixty days." Stalin, doubtless mindful of State and War Department determination to maintain a measure of influence in Iran in the form of several advisory missions, hid whatever amusement he may have felt and blandly promised to protect United States interests there. Truman thanked him, while his diplomatic advisers doubtless shuddered, and the matter was dropped without Churchill's proposal for immediate withdrawal being pressed to a conclusion.[64]

The effect of these peripheral issues upon official American thinking is difficult to assess. What is clear in retrospect must have been equally apparent at the time. Soviet initiatives with respect to the Straits, the African trusteeships, and the continued presence of Russian troops in Iran all seemed to indicate that the Kremlin, its Eastern European borderlands at last substantially secure, was now probing the Middle East and Mediterranean for new areas of influence. However, the State Department's mounting concern with the

---

[63] *Foreign Relations, 1945; Conference of Berlin*, II: 237, 309. The importance of Iran to the three Allied powers during World War II and the story of their presence there is told well enough in Motter, *The Persian Corridor*.

[64] *Foreign Relations, 1945; Conference of Berlin*, II: 1389; Truman, *Year of Decisions*, pp. 418–419.

situation in Iran was not wholly confined to Russian behavior. For the Iranian government informed the American Ambassador during the Potsdam Conference that it feared the British presence as much as it did that of the Red Army. It was the continuing joint "Anglo-Soviet intervention in Iran," and not just the Kremlin itself, that generated anxieties at Tehran.[65] In any case, Truman obviously did not share whatever concern agitated his diplomatic advisers. He may well have been piqued, as he later maintained, by Stalin's unwillingness to commit himself to the open waterways proposal, but if his letter to Wallace and his remarks to Forrestal are recalled, his unhappiness seems to have been submerged by his respect for Stalin and his continuing faith that hard and persistent negotiation over a period of time could yield mutually beneficial results.

Did Potsdam mark the beginnings of the Cold War between the United States and Soviet Russia? Certainly not with respect to European affairs. As in the past, Washington's European policy at the Conference of Berlin was marked by a sense of limited aims and infused with a determined sense of conciliation—if not outright appeasement—of Kremlin demands. If any interests were bartered away in the European discussions at Potsdam, they were those of Great Britain. The existing pattern of Big Three wartime relations was thus not broken at Potsdam; it was maintained. American compromises mitigated the many clashes between London and Moscow and thus kept the Grand Alliance intact. As the conference drew to a close Truman revealed his attitude toward the Soviets and summit diplomacy in general to his mother and sister in Missouri. "You never saw such pig-headed people as are the Russians," he wrote. "I hope I never have to hold another conference with them—*but, of course, I will.*"[66] Potsdam—and especially the European issues argued out there—surely deepened the pessimism of many American officials, generated real suspicions of Russian ambition among a number of others, and clearly frayed Truman's determined policy of patient good will. But it was no watershed marking off wartime cooperation and wary amity from cold war an-

---

[65] Ambassador in Iran (Murray) to Acting Secretary of State, July 20, 1945, *Foreign Relations, 1945; Conference of Berlin*, II: 1390–1391.
[66] Truman, *Year of Decisions*, p. 444. Italics added.

tagonisms. Truman and Byrnes obviously meant to meet and to negotiate with their Soviet counterparts again as they left the ruined German capital. For nowhere across the entire spectrum of European problems had the President allowed important national goals to become confused with vital national interests. European political and economic recovery simply was not at the top of the American list of priorities at this juncture. The swift rehabilitation and reconstruction of the Continent remained an important American objective. But vital American interests lay to the west—in East Asia and across the vast, watery expanses of Oceania. At Potsdam, in the words of one veteran diplomat who was there, "Truman was more concerned with the possible effect of the atom bomb on the war in the Pacific than with the squabbling aftermath of the war in Europe."[67] Whether this preoccupation with the bomb and the Japanese war resulted in any dramatic changes in our Asian policies toward the Kremlin at Berlin remains to be explored.

[67] Murphy, *Diplomat among Warriors*, p. 312.

12

Potsdam--The Atomic Bomb and the Far East

It began as a pinprick of brilliant bluish light on the dark and silent floor of the remote New Mexico desert. Within milliseconds the light became a fireball that struck the ground, flattening at the base and acquiring a skirt of molten black dust. The ground was suddenly bleached a ghastly white. With horrendous rapidity and terrible force the fireball then inflated to a half-mile in diameter and leaped from the ground in a great mushroom-shaped geyser that clawed thousands of feet into the nighttime sky. Then came the terrible shockwave of the unprecedented explosion: "the blast across the desert was like a thunderclap of doom. . . ." On a hill not too far away "silent silhouettes of a minute ago . . . cheering and stomping the earth in a festival of joy" repeated over and over again to each other, "It worked, my God, the damn thing worked." It was 5:30 a.m., Mountain War Time, July 16, 1945. After years of secret, frantic effort and the expenditure of vast treasure, the Americans had at last conjured up the curse of atomic power. "We share a feeling," one excited scientist immediately wrote, "that we have this day crossed a great milestone in human progress." One horrified, high-ranking military observer (not General Groves) demurred. Recalling that a recent betting pool among the scientists on the expected TNT yield of the blast had been quite conservative (Oppenheimer had guessed three hundred tons, a bit larger than the biggest existing "block-buster" bombs), the general took one look at the frightening fireball and concluded that "the long-hairs had let it get away from them."[1]

News of the Alamogordo explosion was immediately flashed to Berlin, and in the following days, as more complete reports were received, the successful test became the subject of intense interest and lively speculation among and within the British and United States delegations. But did incipient possession of the atomic bomb change Anglo-American diplomatic thinking and reshape United States military and political policy? Certainly not in the case of Europe, where, as we have just seen, Truman and Byrnes labored to carry on the essentially aloof and detached, if far from disinterested, posture inherited from Roosevelt. What, then, of the Far East? Tantalizing hints of such a change do emerge from the extant records of and reminiscences about the Potsdam Conference, and it will be well at first to note them carefully.

From the beginning Winston Churchill was tremendously excited over the diplomatic possibilities of the atomic bomb. When, after lunch on July 17, Stimson took the occasion of a brief private walk with the Prime Minister to inform him of the success at Alamogordo, the Secretary of War found the British leader to be "intensely interested and greatly cheered up." Churchill was also "strongly inclined against any disclosure" of the news to the Russians. "I argued against this to some length," Stimson recorded that evening.[2]

As more and more information about the test filtered into Potsdam, Churchill's interest grew. Soviet entry into the Pacific war

[1] The most dramatic re-creation of the Alamogordo blast is in Lansing Lamont, *Day of Trinity* (New York: Atheneum Press, 1965), pp. 235–240. The immediate aftermath reports of Manhattan Project Chief Major General Leslie R. Groves and of scientist Ernest O. Lawrence are republished in *Foreign Relations, 1945; Conference of Berlin*, II: 1360–1370. The comment on the "long-hairs" is from a retrospective story by William L. Laurence, "Atom Bomb Designers Bet in '45 It Would 'Fizzle,'" *New York Times*, June 29, 1951, clipping in Folder 596, Byrnes Papers.
[2] Stimson Diary, July 17, 1945.

was now no longer mandatory; "the new explosion alone was sufficient to settle the matter. Furthermore, we now had something in our hands which would redress the balance with the Russians. The secret of this explosive and the power to use it would completely alter the diplomatic equilibrium which was adrift since the defeat of Germany." Churchill "had at once painted a wonderful picture of himself as the sole possessor of these bombs," Lord Alanbrooke gloomily recorded, "and capable of dumping them where he wished, thus all-powerful and capable of dictating to Stalin!"[3] " 'It has just come in time to save the world,' " the Prime Minister told his physician. "I asked what would happen if the Russians got the idea and caught up. The P.M. replied that it was possible, but they wouldn't be able to do it for three years, and we must fix things up in that time."[4]

Churchill's reaction, however, must be gauged in the context of the time. He and his colleagues came to Potsdam desperately weary men—exhausted by the burdens of over five years of unremitting wartime leadership and wholly aware that their American allies were willing to sacrifice England's interests in Eastern Europe to perpetuate the Grand Alliance. It would have taken a neurologically sound and utterly rational British leader to have placed Alamogordo in its proper context at Berlin and to have fully appreciated Truman's dogged determination to get along with the Russians at least until the end of the war in the Pacific. And Churchill was neither mentally vigorous nor physically healthy at the time. "The P.M.'s health has so far deteriorated," his personal physician wrote on July 23, "that he has no energy left to seize his opportunities. Bridges and Leslie Rowan tell me that a great deal depends here on Anthony [Eden], because the P.M. is not mastering his brief. He is too tired to prepare anything; he just deals with things as they come up."[5] Alanbrooke, who did not share his chief's enthusiasm for the bomb, wrote as early as June 6, 1945, that "I feel very, very weary." Six weeks later, on the day of his return from

---

[3] Bryant, *Triumph in the West*, pp. 363–364. Eight years later Churchill candidly repeated these sentiments in his own recollections. Cf. *Triumph and Tragedy*, p. 545.

[4] Moran, *Churchill*, p. 301.

[5] *Ibid.*, p. 300.

Potsdam, he spoke again of his mental prostration: "It all feels flat and empty. I am feeling very, very tired and worn out. . . . I find my brain quite exhausted nowadays and have to read each paper two or three times to make any sense out of it."[6] The results of the General Election at home also preyed heavily on the minds of British statesmen at Berlin, frequently irritating and distracting them from the business at hand.[7]

But what of the Americans, most of whom possessed minds and physiques indisputably fresher for having been so recently thrust into positions of national leadership? Among them, also, one discerns certain disquieting evidence of a strong temptation to reverse certain policies and commitments *vis-à-vis* the Soviets and East Asia in the wake of the New Mexico explosion.

Stimson continuously fed Truman and Byrnes every scrap of information available about the atomic test in the days immediately following Alamogordo. On the eighteenth the aged Secretary of War wrote that "Harrison's second message came giving a few of the far-reaching details of the test. I at once took it to the President who was highly delighted." Three days later Major General Groves' on-the-spot report at last reached Berlin by courier, and Stimson immediately showed it to Marshall. "I then went to the 'Little White House' and saw President Truman. I asked him to call in Secretary Byrnes and then I read the report in its entirety and we then discussed it. They were immensely pleased. The President was tremendously pepped up by it and spoke to me of it again and again when I saw him. He said it gave him an entirely new feeling of confidence and he thanked me for having come to the Conference and being present to help him in this way." Churchill's comments to Stimson the following morning were interesting in the extreme.

> He told me that he had noticed at the meeting of the Three yesterday that Truman was evidently much fortified by something that had happened and that he stood up to the Russians in a most emphatic and decisive manner, telling them as to certain demands that they absolutely could not have and that the United States was entirely against them.

[6] Bryant, *Triumph in the West*, pp. 359, 365.
[7] Moran, *Churchill*, pp. 276, 292, 300, 304; Murphy, *Diplomat among Warriors*, pp. 306–307.

He said "Now I know what happened to Truman yesterday. I couldn't understand it. When he got to the meeting after having read [Groves'] report he was a changed man. He told the Russians just where they got on and off and generally bossed the whole meeting." Churchill said he now understood how this pepping up had taken place and he felt the same way.[8]

The next day, July 23, Truman told Stimson point-blank "that he was very anxious to know whether Marshall felt that we needed the Russians in the war or whether we could get along without them." The Secretary had just come from a gloomy session with Harriman, who had reported on the previous day's plenary session, in which Stalin first introduced the question of Soviet influence in the Dardanelles and a possible Russian trusteeship over one or more of the former Italian colonies in North Africa. "They are throwing aside all their previous restraint as to being only a continental power and not interested in any further acquisitions, and are now apparently seeking to branch in all directions," Stimson noted.[9] As we shall see, such apprehensions did not inspire Truman's query, but the President was clearly under some pressure from his advisers throughout the conference to rethink the traditional American approach to the Russian problem.

This pressure was probably applied most powerfully by Byrnes and Admiral Leahy and stemmed from their mounting concern over Soviet behavior in both Europe and Asia. On July 28 Byrnes told Forrestal quite frankly that he hoped that the war against Japan could be concluded before the Red Army marched into Manchuria "with particular reference to Dairen and Port Arthur. Once in there, he felt, it would not be easy to get them out." Leahy has indicated in his memoirs that he entertained the same hopes and fears.[10] Senior members of the American delegation were becoming appalled by Soviet demands and activities with respect to reparations. "All hands disturbed by Russian negotiations on reparations," Forrestal wrote on July 29, after talks with Harriman, Clay,

[8] Stimson Diary, July 19, 21, 22, 1945; cf. also Murphy, *Diplomat among Warriors*, p. 306.
[9] Stimson Diary, July 23, 1945.
[10] Millis, ed., *Forrestal Diaries*, p. 78; Leahy, *I Was There*, p. 419.

Pauley, and Bohlen. The Russians "are stripping every area they are in of all movable goods, and at the same time asking reparations and designating the goods they take as war booty. They are shooting and impressing Germans out of the American district. . . . Averell said this did not represent persecutions particularly, but rather reflected the Russians' indifference to life." "Averell was very gloomy about the influx of Russia into Europe," Forrestal added. "He said Russia was a vacuum into which all movable goods would be sucked. He said the greatest crime of Hitler was that his actions had resulted in opening the gates of Eastern Europe to Asia."[11]

Disturbing as were all these trends, concern within the American delegation at Potsdam centered around Stalin's increased demands upon the Nationalist Chinese for concessions in the Far East that went beyond the bounds of the Yalta accords. Stimson, who had invited himself to Berlin, tried to impart his anxieties to the President as early as July 15, the day that the American delegation arrived in Potsdam. The Secretary of War feared that "the Russians had in mind to monopolize trade in Manchuria," and he spoke to Truman about

> the conflict between the supposed plans of Russia as to Dairen in Manchuria and our Open Door policy and went over them with him carefully, again and again warning him to be absolutely sure that the Russians did not block off our trade by their control over the Chinese Eastern Railway. I pointed out that an open port would be useless if our trade could be smothered by railroad control behind that, and that was what it looked as if the Russians were trying to do.[12]

Truman was characteristically impressed without being panicked. He and Byrnes briefly raised the Open Door question with Stalin at the first meeting between the two heads of state on July 17, and the Soviet leader evidently soothed whatever apprehensions the President might have entertained. After the talks Truman told Stimson that "he thought that he had clinched the Open Door

---

[11] Millis, ed., *Forrestal Diaries*, pp. 79–80.
[12] Stimson Diary, July 4, 15, 1945. Cf. also Stimson memorandum to Truman, July 16, 1945, *Foreign Relations, 1945; Conference of Berlin*, II: 1223–1224.

in Manchuria." Two days later, after first hearing reports about the successful Alamogordo test, "The President once again repeated that he was confident of sustaining the Open Door policy." Was this confidence due to the apparent American possession of atomic power? It is hardly likely, for Stimson reacted to Truman's comments with continued concern. The aged Secretary emphasized "to him that the matter must be examined detail by detail. . . ." In other words, it should be brought up in both plenary session and at the foreign ministers level.[13]

This was never done. Truman had said that he had clinched the Open Door with Stalin, and he evidently continued to believe through all the trials and tedium of the conference that he had. His chief diplomatic aides, however, continued working to stiffen resistance at Chungking to Stalin's demands. Their first opportunity came on July 20, when Chiang indicated to Truman that he would be willing to modify the Yalta accords somewhat in order to appease the Russians.

In his note Chiang said that he had just informed the Soviet Ambassador that while China could not accept Kremlin demands for the independence of Outer Mongolia and would insist that the President of the Manchurian railways be Chinese, nonetheless China would accept Soviet military control over Port Arthur and the creation of a Russian military zone between Port Arthur and Dairen.[14] State Department officials viewed these dispensations as unwarranted—stretching the Yalta accords completely out of shape—and they reacted quickly. The same day Byrnes' Special Assistant, Donald Russell, wrote a memo to his chief as a reminder that "the concessions already made by us to the Russians at Yalta represent, to some extent at least, a compromise of the traditional American policy with reference to China. It was in the maintenance of that policy that our country became embroiled in the Japanese war. Any compensation beyond the Yalta agreement would seriously weaken the prestige of the President in the international field at the very beginning of his term."

[13] *Foreign Relations, 1945; Conference of Berlin*, II: 45–46; Stimson Diary, July 17, 19, 1945.
[14] *Foreign Relations, 1945; Conference of Berlin*, II: 1225–1227.

Russell then added some suggestions of his own.

> If Russia does not bring the Chinese negotiations up [at Potsdam], we should do so and emphasize our firm position. So far as possible, we should avoid any developments in China such as have occurred in Poland. Accordingly, we should, in advance of any entrance by Russia into the Japanese war, make clear what our position is and shall be with reference to the territorial integrity of China and the maintenance of our traditional "open-door" policy there, without special privileges to any nation.[15]

Russell had touched the heart of American concern over Soviet demands upon China. China was America's Poland. We had been lured or forced or dragged, or had stumbled deliberately or otherwise, into war in the Pacific by our traditional defense of China's political and territorial integrity. The possibility now of a direct, Poland-like showdown with Stalin, in which American interests were as deeply and directly engaged as Churchill's had been in contesting the legitimacy of the Lublin Poles, was too terrible to contemplate. The only solution was to stiffen the Chinese without publicly assuming their defense. So Byrnes apparently believed, at any rate, and the President doubtless saw no harm in reinforcing Stalin's commitment to the Open Door by demanding a show of Chinese firmness. On July 23, therefore, at the same time that he queried Stimson about the bomb's possible impact upon a Soviet entry into the Far Eastern conflict, Truman cabled Chiang direct, requesting the Kuomintang leader not to "make any concession in excess" of the Yalta accords. The President closed by saying: "I hope you will arrange for Soong to return to Moscow and continue your efforts to reach complete understanding." Byrnes sent a similar message to Soong via Ambassador Hurley five days later, and by return wire Soong promised an early return to Moscow after Stalin's arrival there.[16]

The Americans had thus done all that they could while at Potsdam to compress the Sino-Soviet negotiations over Northeast Asia

---

[15] *Ibid.*, p. 1227.

[16] President to Ambassador in China, July 23, 1945; Secretary of State to Ambassador in China, July 28, 1945; Ambassador in China to Secretary of State, July 29, 1945, *ibid.*, pp. 1241, 1245.

into the framework of the Crimean accords. The real decisions would now be reached at Moscow between Soong and Stalin. If the Chinese negotiator chose to make concessions anyway, knowing as he did so that he risked American disapproval, then there was nothing more that Truman or Byrnes or Stimson could do about it unless the war with Japan ended with shocking abruptness. This wistful hope was obviously at the front of Byrnes' thinking when he spoke to Forrestal on July 28 about the Russians in Manchuria. Certainly he had the atomic bomb in mind as a possible agent of such a swift denouement. But whether this was a realistic hope, or even a hope at all in Byrnes' mind, remains to be explored.

Truman's apparent change of attitude toward the Russians upon receipt of the full report of the Alamogordo test, his subsequent query as to whether the bomb might preclude any need for Soviet intervention in the Pacific war, and Stalin's ominously expanding demands upon China, all seem to offer powerful suggestive evidence that American policy-makers might have begun to practice, or at least have been tempted to practice, a covert form of "atomic diplomacy" *vis-à-vis* the Russians at Potsdam. Two other incidents at Berlin, both concerning the Japanese war, also tend to lend superficial credence to such a supposition.

The first in order of time and importance was the Potsdam Declaration itself. In final form it retained all of the worst ambiguities, all of the tragic vagueness, of prior American debate over retention of the Emperor. Unconditional surrender remained the uncompromising American goal. Paragraph 12, to be sure, still promised the Japanese people the right to freely express their will in the establishment of "a peacefully inclined and responsible government," once the American occupation had done its work in establishing a new democratic order. Presumably this held out the promise of an interrupted continuation of the imperial institution as a constitutional monarchy at some future date. But this faint promise was totally compromised by the proclamation's silence concerning the Allied conception of the Emperor's role in Japan's recent history. Did the British, Americans, and Chinese define Hirohito and the royal family as active or passive partners of the military clique that had plotted and waged war against the Western powers? If not, then Paragraph 12 held the key to vague hopes for a resumption of Japan's "national polity" at a future date. But if so, then it was logical for Japan to assume that the Allies meant to destroy the imperial system and national polity, and thus the Japanese might as well fight to the end. Since the declaration ringingly stated that "There must be eliminated for all time the authority and influence of those who have deceived and misled the people of Japan into embarking on world conquest, for we insist that a new order of peace, security and justice will be impossible until irresponsible militarism is driven from the world," Tokyo was certainly justified in asking itself whether the Allies considered the Emperor an "irresponsible militarist" who must be "forever" driven from public life. "We do not intend that the Japanese shall be enslaved as a race or destroyed as a nation," the declaration added, "but stern justice shall be meted out to all war criminals, including those who have visited cruelties upon our prisoners."[17] Was the Emperor a "war criminal"? Tokyo could not be at all certain.

Was this Allied deception deliberate or unintentional? And if deliberate, did it reflect a deep psychic urging in official American souls to keep Japan fighting until the unimaginable force of the atom could be used against her and as a warning to the Russians to keep their commitments in Europe and Asia? Here is another insistent and haunting hypothesis that demands exploration.

The last incident which occurred at Berlin to suggest an intimate connection between the atomic bomb and changing relations between the Americans and Russians was directly related to the formal Soviet entry into the war against Japan. Stalin was indisposed on the second Sunday of the conference, July 29, and so there was no plenary session. But Molotov came over to the "Little White House" for some unofficial talk about outstanding business. After roving over the Polish border and reparations problems which were moving toward their package solution under Byrnes' skillful guidance, Molotov begged leave to "take up one final matter with us in behalf of Premier Stalin." The Soviet government, it soon emerged, was asking the United States, Britain, and China "to address a formal request to the Soviet government for its entry into

---

[17] *Ibid.*, pp. 1474–1476.

the [Pacific] war." This was three days after the issuance of the Potsdam Declaration, which, of course, had not been signed by the Russians. Stalin therefore argued that the formal Allied request to the Soviet Union "could be based on the refusal of the Japanese to accept the recent ultimatum to surrender and could be made on the basis of shortening the war and saving lives."[18] This was a momentous proposal, because if the British and Americans should agree to it, they would explicitly admit that Soviet help was not just an important, but an essential ingredient of victory in the Pacific. The Soviet demands upon China and defeated Japan that could be expected to flow from such an Allied admission would be limitless.[19]

According to Leahy "the President did not indicate what action he would take. I talked with the Chief Executive at length and told him I did not believe he should place us under a permanent obligation that would be attached to such a request, and I did not think he should even consider complying. The British and ourselves were fully capable of defeating Japan without assistance."[20] Here, in fact, was the perfect opportunity for the Americans to tell the Russians that they were no longer needed or wanted. Byrnes had said that he feared the Soviets in Manchuria. Very well, why not insist to them that they come in on American terms—including strict adherence to the Yalta accords in their negotiations with the Chinese—or either not come in at all or risk going it alone without United States aid and supplies if they did decide to fight Japan? Byrnes himself wrote in 1947 "that in view of what we knew of Soviet actions in eastern Germany and the violations of the Yalta agreements in Poland" and elsewhere in Eastern Europe, "I would have been satisfied had the Russians determined not to enter the war. Notwithstanding Japan's persistent refusal to surrender unconditionally, I believed the atomic bomb would be successful and would force the Japanese to accept surrender on our terms. I feared what would happen when the Red Army entered Manchuria."[21] Moreover, it had been nearly a week since Stalin had been told that

[18] Truman, *Year of Decisions*, p. 443; Byrnes, *Speaking Frankly*, p. 207.
[19] "I did not like this proposal for one important reason. I saw in it a cynical diplomatic move to make Russia's entry at this time appear to be the decisive factor to bring about victory." Truman, *Year of Decisions*, p. 444.
[20] Leahy, *I Was There*, p. 422.
[21] Byrnes, *Speaking Frankly*, p. 208.

the Americans had acquired a powerful new weapon. The Generalissimo very probably realized that it was an atomic bomb, given the activities of Klaus Fuchs and others at Alamogordo.[22] Now would have been a splendid time to employ the atom's power in pursuit of diplomatic objectives.

But instead of provoking a showdown with the Soviets, using America's superiority in conventional military and naval power in the Far East as the bargaining counter, to say nothing of the atomic bomb, Byrnes successfully sought to outmaneuver the Soviets diplomatically. He and Benjamin Cohen, the State Department's legal adviser, "spent hours" alone and with Truman trying to develop a proper reply to Stalin's proposal that would, in effect, force Russia and not the United States formally to initiate and justify Soviet entry into the Far Eastern conflict. The President has indicated that he spoke at some length with Attlee and with other of his advisers besides Leahy and Byrnes on the subject, though Stimson had already left for home.[23]

Out of these rounds of discussion came the decision to inform the Russians that in fact they had already obligated themselves to fight Japan through the Moscow Declaration of 1943 and Article 103 of the United Nations Charter. Moscow had agreed in both of these documents to "cooperate" with the world's other great powers in "joint action on behalf of the community of nations to maintain peace and security." Now was the proper time to redeem the pledge, Truman wrote Stalin on July 31.[24]

Byrnes has said that Stalin expressed appreciation for the President's letter, since it provided him with the excuse he had been looking for to enter the war. The Generalissimo's sincerity may be

[22] For American knowledge of Soviet spy activities within the Manhattan Project prior to Alamogordo, cf. Hewlett and Anderson, *The New World*, pp. 334–335. The activities of Allan Nunn May and others in Canada who handed over atomic secrets to the Russians prior to Potsdam are detailed in *The Report of the Royal Commission to Investigate the Facts Relating to and the Circumstances Surrounding the Communications by Public Officials and Other Persons in Positions of Trust of Secret and Confidential Information to Agents of a Foreign Power* (Ottawa: 1946), *passim*, esp. pp. 447, 615. The activities of David Greenglass and the Rosenbergs as well as of Fuchs are discussed in Lamont, *Day of Trinity*, pp. 8, 38, 66, 78–81, 111–115, 135, 272–290.

[23] Byrnes, *Speaking Frankly*, p. 208; Truman, *Year of Decisions*, p. 444.

[24] Truman, *Year of Decisions*, pp. 444–446; Byrnes, *Speaking Frankly*, pp. 208–209; *Foreign Relations, 1945; Conference of Berlin*, II: 1333–1334.

legitimately doubted since neither before nor after did he often seek legal justification for his actions. More likely his thanks were an acknowledgement that he had been adroitly outmaneuvered in this instance. At any rate, Truman left Potsdam confident that he and Byrnes had secured and protected the major objective that had brought them to Germany and this without severe damage to American interests in either Europe or the Pacific war. Indeed, the Presidential sense of success at Potsdam must be given central consideration in any assessment of American attitudes and diplomacy during and just after the Conference of Berlin. Harry Truman left Europe in early August of 1945 with a lively sense of accomplishment. As he told Eisenhower on his departure from Potsdam, "he had achieved his objectives and was going home."[25]

Some ambiguous evidence does exist suggesting that Truman may have modified his enthusiasm over Potsdam while permitting himself to wax more enthusiastic over the possibilities of the atomic bomb during the leisurely trip home abroad the *Augusta*. Byrnes' press secretary and confidant, Walter Brown, noted in his diary for August 3 that during a dinner conversation, devoted in part to the possibility of an early Japanese surrender, the President remarked that he feared Tokyo would sue for peace through Russia rather than Switzerland. Two nights later, over the evening meal in the wardroom, Truman was asked by one of the ship's officers what he thought of Stalin. " 'I thought he was an S.O.B.,' " the President replied, adding that no " 'deal' " had been made at Potsdam to bring the Russians into the Pacific war. "And even if the Russians had been somewhat difficult at Potsdam," Truman continued, "it did not matter so far as the war in the Pacific was concerned, because the United States had developed an entirely new weapon of such force and nature that we did not need the Russians—or any other nation."[26] While these comments suggest that Truman may have finally moved in the direction of Byrnes' hope that the Japanese war could be ended before a Russian intervention, they do not

[25] Byrnes, *Speaking Frankly*, p. 209; Millis, ed., *Forrestal Diaries*, pp. 78–79; handwritten note, "Potsdam," dated 1958, Folder 636, Byrnes Papers.
[26] "W.B.'s book," August 3, 1945, Folder 602, Byrnes Papers; Fletcher Knebel and Charles W. Bailey, II, *No High Ground* (New York: Bantam Books, 1961), pp. 1–2.

prove or even suggest that the President practiced a covert form of nuclear diplomacy at Potsdam, for the final atomic decision had been made long before Truman returned to the United States on the *Augusta*.

The American refusal to practice atomic diplomacy when the opportunity arose near the close of the Potsdam Conference inevitably calls into question the importance to be ascribed to the other incidents in which the bomb seemed to play a predominant role in shaping United States foreign policies and international attitudes toward Japan and East Asia. In fact, the behavior of Truman and Byrnes at the Berlin Conference was fairly straightforward. Their objectives were always what they said they were. The Secretary of State's crucial role in shaping a compromise settlement on the outstanding Polish border and reparations issues should be recalled immediately. That settlement satisfied the Americans, gave the Russians pretty much what they wanted, and subverted only the interests of the British—interests which the Americans were showing an increasing willingness to barter away for the sake of continued Russian cooperation.

Beyond this crucial fact lay another and more vital consideration. Demonstrably eager as Byrnes was to see the Pacific war end before the Russians intervened, he was never willing to compromise or sacrifice the transcendent objective of an unconditional Japanese surrender to this subsidiary aim. Throughout the conference, it is true, the Secretary repeatedly voiced the hope that Japan would collapse before the Red Army began its massive move into Manchuria. Even before the formal meetings of "the Three" began, the ever-suspicious Byrnes was certain that Stalin "is playing his cards for all he can get out of them." After the first round of meetings and several telegrams from Chungking regarding Sino-Soviet negotiations, Byrnes' fear of Soviet designs on China grew appreciably stronger. "JFB determined to out maneuver [*sic*] Stalin on China," the Secretary's press aide noted on July 20. "Hopes Soong will stand firm and then Russians will not go in war. Then he feels Japan will surrender before Russia goes to war and this will save China. If Russia goes in the war, he knows Stalin will take over and China will suffer." Two days later this same source noted gloomily: "It is becoming more apparent that Russians have gone imperialistic and are out to extend their sphere of influence in all directions and wherever possible." Finally, on the twenty-fourth, Byrnes specifically linked the still uncertain and untried bomb to his hopes for a restraint of Soviet expansion in East Asia. "JFB still hoping for time, believing after atomic bomb Japan will surrender and Russia will not get in so much on the kill, thereby being in a position to press claims on China."[27]

Yet when the bomb subsequently did work and Tokyo duly sued for peace, Byrnes suddenly revealed his overriding concern to assure Japan's unconditional surrender above all else. Tokyo's initial response of August 10 to the Potsdam Declaration blandly assumed that Japan would surrender with the imperial prerogatives and sovereignty intact. Truman, Stimson, and Leahy were immediately inclined to accept on the grounds that the incipient American occupation of Nippon would be eternally disrupted by fanatics if the Emperor were not retained in full sovereignty. Informed of the President's mood, an incensed Byrnes rushed to the White House. The American people would "crucify" their President, Byrnes told Truman, if unconditional surrender was to be practically renounced. "At Potsdam, the big-3 said 'unconditional surrender,'" the angry Secretary reminded his President. "Then there was no atomic bomb and no Russia in the war. I cannot understand why now we should go further than we were willing to go at Potsdam" in placating the Japanese. It hardly needs to be stressed that this was strange behavior indeed for a man who ostensibly was more concerned with the origins of a cold war than the end of a warm one. At that moment the Red Army was expanding its control over Manchuria at an hourly rate. If this fact had preoccupied Byrnes to the exclusion of all other considerations, then surely he too would have immediately opted for the conditional surrender terms offered by Tokyo. Instead the Secretary stubbornly held his

---

[27] "W.B.'s book," July 16, 20, 22, 24, 1945, Folder 602, Byrnes Papers. In later years Byrnes never tried to disguise the fact that at Potsdam he hoped somehow that events would conspire to keep the Russians out of the Pacific war. Cf. "Was A-Bomb on Japan a Mistake?" *U. S. News & World Report*, XLIX (August 15, 1960), 66. What Byrnes did obscure was the transcendent determination of Truman, himself, and all other Americans at Potsdam to defeat Japan unconditionally.

ground, while a flurry of subsequent telegrams passed between Washington and Tokyo and the Soviets steadily expanded into Manchuria and northern Korea. Not until the Japanese agreed to subvert the Emperor—and thus their national polity—to control by a Supreme Allied Commander did Byrnes express the satisfaction necessary to bring the Second World War to a close.[28]

As for Truman, it is worthwhile to look into his conduct at Berlin a bit more closely, for it consistently conformed to his initial objectives and strongly suggests that his remark to Eisenhower that he had achieved his objectives at Potsdam faithfully reflected his thinking as the conference adjourned. As a starting point, we may do well to briefly reexamine Churchill's own assumptions about the atomic bomb's impact upon American policy-making. "Here, at Potsdam, it was soon plain that Roosevelt's death had changed everything. Truman is very blunt; he means business," Lord Moran optimistically observed as he prepared to return to London with his celebrated patient to discover the will of the British people. And he tells us of Churchill's sigh, " 'If only this had happened at Yalta.' "[29] But in fact the British Conservatives refused to see or to fully assess the evidence about Truman accumulating before them. To be sure, during the plenary session of July 21 the President *was* firm and even blunt, as the British quickly perceived, in rejecting Soviet demands for an immediate settlement of the Polish border along the Oder-Neisse line. But even then, as the British refused to see, the President couched his own demands in the most careful and minimal terms. "I made it clear that I was very friendly toward the Polish provisional government, and I felt that full agreement could probably be reached on what the Soviet government desired, but I wanted to be consulted."[30]

[28] "W.B.'s book," August 10, 1945, Folder 602, Byrnes Papers; George Curry, *James F. Byrnes*, Vol. XIV of *The American Secretaries of State and their Diplomacy* (New York: Cooper Square Publishers, Inc., 1965), pp. 126–127.

[29] Moran, *Churchill*, p. 306.

[30] Truman, *Year of Decisions*, pp. 404–405. Truman's real concern about the Oder-Neisse issue seems to have fixed upon the spectre of massive and continuing American economic aid to Germany in the postwar era, and not upon the immediate fact of Soviet territorial expansion. According to the Russian record of the Potsdam discussions the President stated at one point during the July 21 session, "It seems to be a *fait accompli* that a considerable part of Germany has been handed over to Poland for occupation." The President added at the close of debate that day, "I want to

In other words, to take the most extreme view of the situation, with the atomic bomb "on his hip" the President only pressed for traditional consultative, not supervisory rights in Eastern Europe. What in fact plainly annoyed Truman on this day—and others— was not so much Soviet demands as the endless bickering between Stalin and Churchill. "I was becoming very impatient," he later recalled of this particular session, "and on a number of occasions I felt like blowing the roof off the palace."[31] But his annoyance was obviously directed as much at the Prime Minister as the Generalissimo. If the President "bossed the whole meeting" that particular session, Churchill as well as Stalin was the subject of his determined direction. The fatigued and apprehensive Prime Minister initially refused to believe that this was the thrust of Presidential thinking. At the following plenary session on July 22, however, Truman swiftly stripped him of his illusion. " 'I prayed the Americans on my knees not to hand over to the Russians such a great chunk of Germany, at least until after the Conference,' " the Prime Minister bitterly told Moran that evening. " 'It would have been a bargaining counter. But they would not listen. The President dug in.' " Political defeat and bodily rest restored perspective to Churchill's restless mind after July, and he sadly observed in early August that " 'After I left Potsdam, Joe did what he liked.' "[32] It was an inaccurate analysis in some ways, yet far closer to the mark than was Churchill's understanding of the Americans and their policy positions during the conference.

In truth the American delegation at Potsdam, for all the restlessly expressed yearnings of some for a change in official attitude and posture toward the Soviets, remained locked into decisions and policies taken weeks and even months and years before. If Soviet behavior had become alarming in Europe and potentially disturbing

---

say frankly what I think on this question. I cannot agree to the alienation of the eastern part of 1937 Germany *in as far as it bears upon settling the reparations question and supplies of food and coal for the whole German population.*" Here was yet another Presidential signal to the Russians to help find an acceptable compromise reparations formula for Germany before the territorial issue could be considered settled. When that formula was at last discovered and accepted, American objections to the Oder-Neisse line evaporated. Beitzell, *Tehran, Yalta, Potsdam,* pp. 206–208; italics added.

31 Truman, *Year of Decisions,* p. 408.
32 Quoted in Moran, *Churchill,* pp. 299–300, 310.

in the Far East, countervailing considerations of overwhelming weight and overriding magnitude continued to thrust American policy toward continuing efforts at accommodation and cooperation with the Russians.

Four differing but interrelated realities were never far from the surface of American thinking and planning at Potsdam: first, the uncertainty of early victory in the Pacific; second, the uncertainty of the atomic bomb as a fully efficient combat weapon; third, the certainty that the United States could not keep the Soviet Union from expanding in Northeast Asia short of war; and fourth, the actual willingness of American policy-makers to accept such an expansion on limited terms. The most important of these considerations was the unslackening determination of the Japanese government to resist an American victory to the bitter end. Tokyo's fanaticism was most forcibly expressed in a fascinating dialogue between Foreign Minister Togo and his Ambassador in Moscow, Naotake Sato, just before and during the Potsdam Conference.

It will be recalled that on June 22 the Emperor had at last been induced by members of the so-called "peace faction" within the government to express a personal wish to see the war end. At no time prior to the Hiroshima and Nagasaki strikes and Soviet entry into the war, however, did Hirohito suggest termination on American terms. His minions responded to the imperial mandate of mid-June, therefore, in a characteristically unimaginative fashion. They decided to have another go at bribing the Russians to intervene as mediators in behalf of the retention of Japanese sovereignty. With their own military figuratively holding a gun at the head of anyone foolhardy enough to seek peace on broader terms than these, we may well ask with some sympathy what else they could have done.

Foreign Minister Togo opened the newest Japanese diplomatic offensive on July 11 with a cable to Sato asking that the U.S.S.R. be sounded out as a medium "in connection with the termination of the war." The ludicrous bribe, apparently offered in all sincerity, followed: "The Soviet Union should be interested in, and probably will greet with much satisfaction, an abandonment of our fishery rights as an amendment to the Treaty of Portsmouth." Later that

day Togo supplemented his earlier message with a further statement of Japanese intent: "We have no intention of annexing or
taking possession of the areas which we have been occupying as
a result of the war."[33] Sato was bombarded with yet a third wire
the following evening elaborating current Japanese diplomatic
thinking. The crux of the message was unmistakable: "it is His
Majesty's heart's desire to see the swift termination of the war. In
the Greater East Asia War, however, as long as America and England insist on unconditional surrender, our country has no alternative but to see it through in an all-out effort for the sake of survival
and the honor of the homeland."[34]

Sato responded in a lengthy cable filed near midnight on July 12.
His reply was that of a great spirit and a supreme realist faced with
the task of correcting the preposterous misconceptions of superiors
steeped in folly. Profound despair permeated his every thought.

> I believe it no exaggeration to say that the possibility of getting the So-
> viet Union to join our side and go along with our reasoning is next to
> nothing. That would run directly counter to the foreign policy of this
> country as explained in my frequent telegrams to you. . . .
>
> Moreover, the manner of your explanation in your telegram No.
> 891—"We consider the maintenance of peace in Asia as one aspect of
> maintaining world peace"—is nothing but academic theory. For En-
> gland and America are planning to take the right of maintaining peace
> in East Asia away from Japan, and the actual situation is now such
> that the mainland of Japan itself is in peril. Japan is no longer in a po-
> sition to be responsible for the maintenance of peace in all of East Asia,
> no matter how you look at it.
>
> Although the Empire and its commanders have said, "We have no
> intention of annexing or taking possession of the areas which we have
> been occupying," what kind of reaction can we expect when in fact
> we have already lost or are about to lose Burma, the Philippines, and
> even a portion of our mainland in the form of Okinawa?
>
> As you already know, the thinking of the Soviet authorities is realis-
> tic. It is difficult to move them with abstractions, to say nothing about
> the futility of trying to get them to consent to persuasion with phrases
> beautiful but somewhat remote from the facts and empty in content.[35]

[33] *Foreign Relations, 1945; Conference of Berlin,* I: 874–875.
[34] *Ibid.,* p. 876.
[35] *Ibid.,* p. 877.

Tokyo was unmoved by such devastating frankness. The following evening Sato was instructed to inform the Kremlin that the Emperor wished to dispatch Prince Konoye to Moscow "as special envoy, carrying with him the personal letter of His Majesty stating the Imperial wish to end the war." However, Molotov immediately sent Sato the chilling reply "that he was simply not able to accommodate my request." Sato was shunted off to one of Molotov's underlings, Lozovsky, who promised to try to expedite the Japanese request. Sato had already learned, as had Tokyo, that Stalin and his foreign minister were about to depart for Berlin, and so he asked Lozovsky "that in the event that an answer was not possible prior to Molotov's departure, we would like" Lozovsky "to establish communications directly with Berlin by telephone or other means for their answer."[36]

All of Japanese officialdom was frozen in continual anxiety, of course, by the fear of an early and abrupt Soviet declaration of war, and Sato repeatedly warned his superiors that their entire approach to the Russians was hopelessly unrealistic. "Even if we are overawed by the fact that the dispatch of a special envoy is the Imperial wish," he wrote on July 13, "if the Japanese Government's proposal brought by him is limited to an enumeration of previous abstractions, lacking in concreteness, you would not only be disappointing the authorities of this country [the Soviet Union] and causing a feeling of great dissatisfaction with the insincere attitude of Japan but would also be provoking trouble for the Imperial Household. I have great apprehensions on this point."[37]

It was all to no avail. Togo summarily dismissed Sato's anguished cries that Japan was not yet prepared for serious negotiations. Winning the Soviets over in the present circumstances "is difficult. This was clear from the outset," Togo cabled on July 17, "but in view of the demands of the times it is essential to accomplish this boldly." Therefore, "the Soviet reply concerning the dispatch of the special envoy should be obtained as soon as possible."[38]

Sato continued to chafe. At last on July 20 he burst out again in a remarkable telegram. It was no secret in Moscow by this time that

[36] *Ibid.*, pp. 879–880.
[37] *Ibid.*, p. 881.
[38] *Ibid.*, II: 1249.

Japan was being systematically laid waste from one end to the other by the United States Navy and Army Air Force. And the American enemy

> must also have a thorough knowledge of how great an influence the present autumn harvest will have on our fighting strength; . . .
>
> If we lose our autumn harvest, our situation will be absolutely critical and we will be in no position to continue the war. Our Empire, which has already lost command of the skies, can do nothing to combat the above circumstances; we are at the mercy of the enemy and committed to whatever the enemy should will.
>
> As I have already urged . . . continuing the war after our fighting strength has been destroyed should be considered impossible. It goes without saying that the Imperial Army and the populace as a whole will not surrender to the enemy as long as there is no Imperial command to do so; they will literally not throw away their spears until the last man.

Given these terrible realities,

> Our country is literally standing at the crossroads of destiny. If we were to continue the war under the present circumstances the citizens would die with the satisfaction of having truly served their country loyally and patriotically, but the country itself would be on the verge of ruin. . . .
>
> Since the Manchurian incident Japan has pursued a policy of authoritarian rule. In the Greater East Asia War she finally plunged into a war beyond her means. As a result, we are confronted with the danger of having even our mainland trampled upon. Since there is no longer any real chance of success, I believe that it is the duty of the statesmen to save the nation by coming quickly to a decision to lay down our arms.

Sato closed with a point-blank attack upon his superiors and his country: "The scorn for diplomacy and the indifference to international relations, even before the Manchurian incident, were the cause which brought about our present misfortune."[39]

The Ambassador's intelligence and eloquence made no demonstrable impression upon Tokyo. He was instructed to continue to press the Konoye mission on the ominously silent Soviets. As for an earlier suggestion of Sato's that unconditional surrender was pre-

[39] *Ibid.*, pp. 1253, 1255.

ferable to national suicide, Togo continued firm in his assertion that insofar as the Japanese government was concerned, the two were inseparable. "We cannot accept unconditional surrender . . . in any situation," Togo wrote on July 21. "Although it is apparent that there will be more casualties on both sides in case the war is prolonged, we will stand united as one nation against the enemy if the enemy forcibly demands our unconditional surrender."[40] There might have been some grounds for accommodation in Togo's carefully phrased reservation concerning a "forcible" United States demand for unconditional surrender. There was the lurking implication that if the Americans withdrew their forces from the skies above and the seas surrounding Japan, direct or indirect negotiations might commence looking toward a firm definition of surrender terms with respect to the Emperor. But Sato surely knew—and Togo should have—that this was a chimerical aspiration indeed.

United States intelligence officers had long since broken the Japanese code and had eavesdropped on the agonizing debate between Tokyo and Moscow. The problem was that the Americans not only knew of Togo's initiative but also of Sato's justifiably bitter criticisms of its utter lack of realism. This latter point has been frequently ignored or overlooked by scholars who argue that Washington knew of Tokyo's readiness to surrender in July of 1945 yet did nothing to encourage it. The fact is that there was nothing substantial to encourage.

Forrestal in Washington quickly pounced on the translations. Japan "was thoroughly and completely defeated," he wrote on the eve of Potsdam. Washington had known it; now Sato had indicated that he knew it. But did Tokyo know it—or knowing it, would Tokyo ever acknowledge the fact short of a blood bath in the home islands? Forrestal noted Sato's anguished cry that Togo's "proposals were quite unrealistic." On July 24, just before departing, uninvited, to Berlin, Forrestal recorded in his diary that the Japanese Cabinet "had weighed all the considerations which he [Sato] had raised and that their final judgment and decision was that the war

[40] *Ibid.*, p. 1258.

must be fought with all the vigor and bitterness of which the nation was capable so long as the only alternative was the unconditional surrender."[41] This notation was in apparent reference to a much earlier Togo-Sato exchange, probably during the first week of that month. But Togo's cable of July 21, of course, showed no weakening in Japan's resolve to fight on.

Nor did Stalin, Churchill, or Truman detect any significant change in Japanese attitude during the course of the Potsdam Conference. At the beginning Stalin first informed Churchill privately —and fully—of the Togo messages of July 11–13. The Soviet Premier informed his British counterpart "that as the message[s] contained no definite proposals the Soviet Government could take no action." Stalin explained to Churchill that he did not wish to inform Truman directly lest the President think the Soviets were trying to force the United States toward a modification of unconditional surrender. Churchill promptly relayed these sentiments to Truman with Stalin's approval.[42]

Shortly thereafter Stalin spoke directly—and again accurately— to Truman of Togo's message of July 13 proposing the Konoye mission. On July 28, two days after the issuance of the Potsdam Declaration and twenty-four hours before Molotov's proposal that the Anglo-Americans formally request Soviet intervention, Stalin brought Truman up to date on further messages from Tokyo which indicated a firmer Japanese desire for Russian mediation to end the war. According to Truman, "After the interpreter finished reading the Japanese message to Russia," which Washington, of course, had also intercepted, "Stalin declared that there was nothing new in it except that it was more definite than the previous approach and that it would receive a more definite answer than was the case the last time. The answer would be in the negative, he said." During these desultory Soviet-American discussions of Japanese peace feelers, Stalin made it clear that he continued to adhere to the position that he had first outlined to Hopkins at Moscow six weeks before. In response to a direct query from Byrnes on July 18 the Gen-

---

[41] Entries of July 13, 15, 24, 1945, Millis, ed., *Forrestal Diaries*, pp. 74–76.
[42] Churchill, *Triumph and Tragedy*, p. 548; Ehrman, *Grand Strategy*, p. 302.

eralissimo stated that there was "no change" in his thinking about the need to subdue Japan unconditionally.[43]

Stalin and Sato were thus in substantial agreement regarding the vagueness of the Japanese initiative, for Tokyo's Ambassador in Moscow warned as late as July 27 that his government's request for mediation "does not even indicate an outline" of what Japan hoped to achieve through the Konoye mission.[44] And Stalin was certainly not about to facilitate Japanese diplomacy. Any threat to an early Soviet intervention in the Pacific war was a threat to Soviet expansionist designs in Northeast Asia as legitimized by Roosevelt at Yalta. Also, the Russians may well have sensed from the attitude of Truman or other members of the American delegation at Potsdam that the United States had broken the Japanese code. It behooved the Soviets to act with strict correctness in passing on news of any Japanese initiative. It was to Russian advantage to stress rejection of such initiatives.

This, then, was the background in which the Potsdam Declaration was issued and the Truman policy of attracting Soviet intervention in the Far East was carried out. Tokyo simply seemed to remain too bellicose, too unrepentant, too bitterly fanatical in its will to resist, to consider seriously a significant modification of unconditional surrender. Thus Stimson's last forlorn attempt at Potsdam to influence the President and his Secretary of State to move in just that direction was doomed from the start.

It was on July 17 that Stimson first approached Byrnes about the subject of "a prompt and early warning to Japan" in light of the Alamogordo test. But the Secretary of State was opposed to such a plan. Instead "he outlined a timetable on the subject warning which apparently had been agreed to by the President, so I pressed it no further." Byrnes was determined, insofar as he was able, to exclude his fellow Secretaries as much as possible from foreign policy-making at Potsdam, and he largely succeeded. "He gives me the impression that he is hugging matters in this Conference pretty close to his bosom," Stimson wrote several days later, "and that my as-

---

[43] Truman, *Year of Decisions*, p. 437; "W.B.'s book," July 18, 24, 28, 1945, Folder 602, Byrnes Papers.
[44] *Foreign Relations, 1945; Conference of Berlin*, II: 1291.

sistance, while generally welcome, was strictly limited in the matters in which it should be given."[45]

Still the Secretary of War was determined to use his key position in the atomic project as leverage to influence Presidential decision-making. He therefore made one last—and futile—attempt to modify the emerging Potsdam Proclamation in favor of an explicit promise to the Japanese that the Emperor might be retained. On July 20 he began by reading a memo to the President urging that the phrase "unconditional capitulation" in the Declaration draft be revised to read "until Japan ceased to resist."[46] Before Stimson could follow up on his initiative, however, George Harrison, his liaison man with the Manhattan Project, reported on July 21 that an atomic strike against Japan might be mounted earlier than expected. On the morning of the twenty-third Byrnes telephoned Stimson "asking me as to the timing of the S-1 program," and Stimson passed along Harrison's messages. The Declaration was rapidly taking final shape. Later that morning, when the Secretary of War saw Truman, the President said "that he had the warning message which we prepared [on July 2] on his desk and had accepted our most recent change in it, and that he proposed to shoot it out as soon as he heard the definite day of the operation." This last remark is of crucial importance, for it indicates that the President had already either overtly or tacitly given the order for the bomb to be used. In fact, Stimson had already spoken to Air Force Chief General "Hap" Arnold on July 12 and had shown him Harrison's messages. Arnold had responded "that it would take considerable hard work to organize the operations now that it was to move forward." It may be confidently assumed that this was the moment at which the "final order" was given and that the formal directive of July 24 to General Spaatz, later quoted by Truman, simply represented the next initiative down the chain of command. As for the President's 1952 letter to Professors Craven and Cate, it would appear that Truman honestly confused the timing of the final atomic decision, for, as has been noted, he made that decision

---

[45] Stimson Diary, July 17, 1945.
[46] *Foreign Relations, 1945; Conference of Berlin,* II: 1271–1272.

on board the *Augusta* on his way to and not, as he said in 1952, on his return from Berlin.[47]

With the strike thus set, the Potsdam Declaration ready to be issued, and his own suggested modifications on the Presidential desk if not in the Presidential mind, Stimson again discussed modification of unconditional surrender in the course of a long conversation with Truman on the morning of July 24.

> I . . . spoke of the importance which I attributed to the reassurance of the Japanese on the continuance of their dynasty, and I had felt that the insertion of that in the final warning was important and might be just the thing that would make or mar their acceptance, but that I had heard from Byrnes that they preferred not to put it in, and that now such a change was made impossible by the sending of the [Potsdam Declaration] to Chiang [for his concurrence]. I hoped that the President would watch carefully so that the Japanese might be reassured verbally through diplomatic channels if it was found that they were hanging fire on that one point. He said that he had that in mind and that he would take care of it.[48]

The President had already confided his true feelings to the British, however. On July 18, at lunch with the President, Churchill himself obliquely brought up the subject of a liberal revision of surrender terms.

> I dwelt upon the tremendous cost in American and to a smaller extent in British life if we enforced "unconditional surrender" upon the Japanese. It was for him to consider whether this might not be expressed in some other way, so that we got all the essentials for future peace and security and yet left them some show of saving their military honour and some assurance of their national existence. . . . The President replied bluntly that he did not think the Japanese had any military honour after Pearl Harbour. I contented myself with saying that at any rate they had something for which they were ready to face certain death in very large numbers, and this might not be so important to us as it was to them. He then became quite sympathetic, and spoke, as had Mr. Stimson, of the terrible responsibilities that rested upon him for the unlimited effusion of American blood. I left it at that. It was obviously in their minds, and they are thinking a good deal about it.[49]

[47] Stimson Diary, July 21, 22, 23, 1945; Truman, *Year of Decisions*, pp. 463–464; Craven and Cate, *Matterhorn to Nagasaki*, pp. 712–713.
[48] Stimson Diary, July 24, 1945.
[49] Churchill, *Triumph and Tragedy*, p. 548; Moran, *Churchill*, pp. 293–294.

Yet, of course, nothing was done to reshape the Declaration along the lines that Churchill suggested and Stimson had urged. Truman and Byrnes held firm to the decision they had reached on the way to Potsdam to eliminate that sentence in paragraph 12 which held out the promise of a possible restoration of the imperial institution at the close of the American occupation. In this they seem to have been swayed not only by their own prejudices but also by the vociferous arguments of high State Department aides in Washington whose influence proved to be decisive.

On July 6, the day that Truman and Byrnes left for Europe, Assistant Secretary of State Archibald MacLeish had penned a long memorandum to Byrnes entitled "Interpretation of Japanese Unconditional Surrender." "What has made Japan dangerous in the past and will make her dangerous in the future, if we permit it," MacLeish wrote,

> is, in large part, the Japanese cult of emperor worship which gives the ruling groups in Japan—the *Gumbatsu*—the current coalition of militarists, industrialists, large land owners and office holders—their control over the Japanese people. As Mr. Acheson pointed out in the Staff Committee, the institution of the throne is an anachronistic, feudal institution, perfectly adapted to the manipulation and use of anachronistic, feudal-minded groups within the country. To leave that institution intact is to run the grave risk that it will be used in the future as it has been used in the past.[50]

The following day MacLeish discussed his memorandum to the Secretary of State in the regular Secretary's staff meeting, chaired in Byrnes' absence by Joseph Grew. With the President and Secretary in Berlin, the State Department felt as though it were "left in a fog of rumor and ignorance about the war in the Pacific,"[51] and Acheson and MacLeish were determined that this situation should not be used to slip into any possible negotiations with Japan the promise of future imperial retention.

Grew opened the meeting with a forceful defense of his long-held position. The draft proclamation which Byrnes had taken aboard the *Augusta* providing for the possibility of imperial resur-

---

[50] *Foreign Relations, 1945; Conference of Berlin*, I: 895–897.
[51] Acheson, *Present at the Creation*, pp. 112–113.

gence at the conclusion of American occupation had been approved by Stimson, Forrestal, Admiral King, "and probably General Marshall," Grew reminded his colleagues. The Acting Secretary then restated his arguments in favor of ultimate imperial retention "including his belief that it is absolutely impossible to abolish the institution; that it is the military element and not the Emperor which has been responsible for the war; and that what is most important is to eliminate the military machine and the big industrial families of Japan." MacLeish was completely unmoved and repeated the arguments he had previously incorporated into his memorandum to Byrnes. Acheson next asked why the Japanese military was so determined to retain the Emperor if he had no role in his nation's war-making capacity. After further animated discussion, Green Hackworth's suggestion of a simple statement of American determination to purge Japan of military control and permit the Japanese ultimately to form a government of their own choosing was tentatively adopted to replace the controversial sentence in Paragraph 12 referring to imperial retention. Assistant Secretary James Dunn apparently took the revised statement to Potsdam several days later as the formal policy statement of the Department, including Grew. Dovetailing neatly with Byrnes' own thinking, it was incorporated into the Declaration that was formally issued on the twenty-sixth.[52]

In the meantime, on July 16, the day of Trinity at Alamogordo and twenty-four hours before Byrnes rejected Stimson's proposal of an ultimate return to imperial rule in Japan, former Secretary Cordell Hull decisively threw his own powerful influence in the State Department onto the scale in behalf of the MacLeish-Acheson faction. Hull and Byrnes had already talked for some twenty minutes on July 6—just before Byrnes' departure for Europe—on matters likely to dominate the Berlin meeting. Very possibly Hull had then alerted Byrnes to the perils involved in any modification of unconditional surrender. And ten days later, in a direct cable to Byrnes, Hull made his position crystal clear. The former Secretary weighed both sides of the argument and then stressed the dread-

---

[52] *Foreign Relations, 1945; Conference of Berlin,* I: 900–901.

ful uncertainties involved in imperial retention: "The militarists would try hard to interfere." Also, should an Allied invasion fail after the Japanese had first rejected a previous American agreement to modify unconditional surrender, "terrible political repercussions would follow in the U.S. Would it not be well first to await the climax of allied bombing and Russia's entry into the war?" Hull concluded.[53] Here was a powerful rationale for deferral, for a drift in policy down familiar corridors of hard-line thought until Japan's utter defeat should no longer be in question by anyone, Tokyo included. Then, and only then, should the problem be explored. This was precisely the turn events took after Hiroshima and Nagasaki.

By the time that Dunn and Hull's cable reached Potsdam, it had become impossible to defer a decision on the subject any longer, and State Department pressure triumphed in the minds of Byrnes and Truman over the arguments of Churchill and Stimson. And why not? Byrnes could not afford to alienate his own department so early in his stewardship, and the astute South Carolinian did not do so. Very early on July 17, before he saw Stimson, Byrnes cabled Washington and told Grew that he fully accepted Hull's suggestion of delay until further heavy attacks should be mounted against Japan.[54] The President, in turn, had indicated from the beginning deep interest in a sweeping reorganization of the Executive Branch, which would, among other things, reestablish and reimpose traditional, but long-forgotten, lines of authority and responsibility. Foreign affairs was the task of the State Department. Its recommendations should, to the greatest degree possible, be translated into policy and should surely take precedence, save in extreme cases, over the blandishments of the Secretary of War and the British Prime Minister. This was particularly the case when such recommendations fitted in so smoothly with Presidential prejudices and thinking. As we have seen, Truman had been under growing pressure for weeks to make some sort of public statement defining unconditional surrender. The President had already decided that the Potsdam Conference would provide the perfect forum.[55]

---

[53] *Ibid.*, II: 1267; "W.B.'s book," July 6, 1945, Folder 602, Byrnes Papers.
[54] *Foreign Relations, 1945; Conference of Berlin*, II: 1268.
[55] Truman, *Year of Decisions*, pp. 459–460.

And so all the elements of a vague pronouncement flowed smoothly together, and tragedy was the result. Tokyo's initial reaction was correct: The Potsdam Declaration was "an order to surrender, not an invitation to negotiate." Japan's equally vague response was hammered out after agitated debate between hawks and doves and susceptible to several interpretations, most of which were pejorative. Such a response was only to be expected given Tokyo's grim mood, the paltry nature of the American initiative, and the completely unrealistic hopes of the Japanese for real progress in negotiations through Moscow.[56] Never was the ancient truth that war generates its own momentum better illustrated than at this melancholy moment. And in the atmosphere of mounting dread in America over the prospect of a massive death-list in the forthcoming Battle of Japan, Senator Alexander Wiley of Wisconsin on July 25 spoke up on the floor of the upper chamber about the role that Russia must play in this vast drama.

> In millions of American homes, mothers, fathers and sweethearts are awaiting with anxiety for news of Russia's intentions. Countless American lives are at stake in Russia's decisions. . . . Why should we follow the lead of the "nice Nellies" of our State Department who have been more concerned with diplomatic niceties than with the preservation of American interests and lives? Let no one say that we are meddling in Russia's business when we tell them we want them to carry their load in the Far East. . . . We will not easily forget Russia's contribution in the Far East if she pitches in with us and will not easily forgive her shirking of her responsibility if she remains on the sidelines.[57]

Neither the speech nor its implications in the sphere of American foreign policy-making need extended comment here save to note in passing that Wiley was, of course, not privy to the tightly

---

[56] The fullest and most scholarly discussion of Suzuki's famous—or infamous —"*Mokuratsu*" response of July 28 is in Butow, *Japan's Decision to Surrender*, pp. 142–149. Cf. also Craig, *The Fall of Japan*, pp. 58–59; and Alperovitz, *Atomic Diplomacy*, p. 185, which characteristically employs hindsight evaluation as contemporary thought and motivation in order to create a distorted and inaccurate historical climate of behavior. The official American translation of Suzuki's remarks is in *Foreign Relations, 1945; Conference of Berlin*, II: 1293.

[57] Quoted in Richard H. Rovere and Arthur Schlesinger, Jr., *The MacArthur Controversy and American Foreign Policy* (New York: Farrar, Straus and Giroux, 1965), p. 207 (first published in 1951 as *The General and the President*).

held atomic secret. Even those who were in the know at Potsdam were well aware that the Alamogordo test had not yet guaranteed the United States a workable, combat-ready atomic bomb. This was the second great consideration which Truman and his advisers constantly had to keep in mind as they assessed developments in the Far East and on the Pacific battlefront.

Years later Anthony Eden recalled that even after the New Mexico explosion "there was still some uncertainty about the bomb's effectiveness" among the Americans at Berlin. In particular "Admiral Leahy continued frank in his doubts." Byrnes too was later to admit that, despite his strongly expressed hopes at Potsdam that the weapon might bring the war to an unexpectedly swift end, "the experts advised us that the [Alamogordo] experiment did not offer conclusive proof that a bomb would of a certainty explode when dropped from a plane."[58] Most importantly, the Manhattan Project Director, General Leslie R. Groves, himself remained skeptical about the bomb's combat worthiness after the New Mexico test. "The Alamogordo test had not set aside all doubts about the bomb," he has written.

> It proved merely that one implosion type, plutonium bomb had worked; it did not prove that another would or that a uranium bomb of the gun type would. We had made every possible component test we could think of. We were reasonably sure of each one. We knew we could bring the U-235 portions of the bomb together in such a way that, if the theories of atomic energy were correct and U-235 behaved as plutonium had, the bomb should go off. *But still no test had been made of the complete bomb.* Nevertheless, the indications for success were strong enough so that no one urged us to change our plans of dropping the first gun-type bomb in combat without prior test.[59]

Groves' deep concern as to whether the uranium bomb would work as well as the plutonium device static-tested at Alamogordo was not a reflection of mere academic quibbling. The untested uranium bomb would be dropped over Hiroshima, the plutonium weapon—"fat man"—over Nagasaki. Both had to work flawlessly,

[58] Eden, *The Reckoning*, p. 634; undated typescript memorandum, "White House, 1943, Atomic," Folder 596, Byrnes Papers.
[59] Groves, *Now It Can Be Told*, p. 305. Italics added.

it was firmly believed, if the maximum psychological "shock" value was to be attained. From the beginning American strategists planned on delivering two successful strikes in the quickest possible succession. "Admiral Purnell [who oversaw Groves' performance on behalf of Roosevelt, Truman, and Stimson] and I had often discussed the importance of having the second blow follow the first one quickly so that the Japanese would not have time to recover their balance. It was Purnell who had first advanced the belief that two bombs would end the war." General Marshall was convinced of the soundness of this argument by the time of Potsdam. Stopping off to visit Patton's troops in Bavaria on his early departure home, the Army Chief of Staff told Maxwell Taylor on July 28 that "it will only take two" bombs to force Japan to surrender. But should Hiroshima be a success and Nagasaki a "dud," or vice-versa, the Japanese government and High Command might have sufficient time to rally their people to withstand atomic strikes. This eventuality seems ludicrous in the aftertime only because we know what the bombs did. But in late July of 1945 the effects of an atomic strike upon a city—indeed the predictability of atomic power itself—was still unknown. Only two bombs existed in "combat readiness" at the time of the Hiroshima raid.[60] They had to work, or the shock value of the sudden American atomic monopoly might be dissipated.

Yet there was no assurance that both weapons would perform under combat conditions. Byrnes could write with the luxury of hindsight in 1947 and again in 1959 that he was sure they would, and one observer at Alamogordo impulsively wrote to Potsdam that "As to the present war, there was a feeling that no matter what else might happen, we now had the means to insure its speedy conclusion and save thousands of American lives." Groves, however, wrote at the time cautioning Stimson and Truman that "We are all fully conscious that our real goal is still before us. The battle test is what counts in the war with Japan."[61]

---

[60] *Ibid.*, p. 342; General Maxwell D. Taylor, *The Uncertain Trumpet* (New York: Harper & Brothers, 1960), p. 3; Craven and Cate, *Matterhorn to Nagasaki*, p. 748.

[61] *Foreign Relations, 1945; Conference of Berlin*, II: 1366, 1368.

It was what obviously counted with Truman and Leahy, with Marshall and the rest of the Joint Chiefs at Potsdam. "We reviewed our military strategy in the light of this revolutionary development," Truman has said. "We were not ready [at the time of Potsdam] to make use of this weapon against the Japanese, although we did not know as yet what effect the new weapon might have, physically or psychologically, when used against the enemy. For that reason the military advised that we go ahead with the existing military plans for the invasion of the Japanese home islands."[62] Harriman later recalled that "At Potsdam . . . the Joint Chiefs of Staff were still planning the invasion of the Japanese home islands and still considered Soviet participation in the Pacific war essential. . . . The Combined [British and American] Chiefs of Staff also stated: 'the invasion of Japan and operations directly connected therewith are the supreme operations in the war against Japan.' "[63]

What is heartrending in retrospect is the total failure of the American military at Potsdam to fully appreciate the devastating reduction of Japan's power to resist as a result of the massive July poundings of the home islands by the Allied air forces and navies. The fanatical determination of the militarists in Tokyo to continue resistance was becoming an increasingly irrelevant factor in the continuing Battle of Japan. To be sure, there is some indication that American leaders appreciated the desperate straits to which the Japanese had been reduced. Truman, for example, on July 18 agreed with Churchill that "the war might come to a speedy end." And Admiral King's autobiography notes that:

> In order that the commanders in the field might not be unaware of the possibility of the end approaching more rapidly than had been expected, the Joint Chiefs on 21 July sent a dispatch from Potsdam to MacArthur and Nimitz, informing them that it was believed that the Russian entry into the war might take place on 15 August, and that there were increasing indications that it might prove necessary within the near future to take action on the basis of Japanese capitulation, possibly even before the Russian entry into the war.[64]

[62] Truman, *Year of Decisions*, p. 458.
[63] *Military Situation in the Far East, August 1951, Part 5*, pp. 3338–3339.
[64] King, *A Naval Record*, p. 611.

Five days later, in conjunction with the Potsdam Declaration, "the Joint Chiefs of Staff informed the Pacific commanders that the 'coordination of plans for the procedure to be followed in the event of Japanese governmental surrender is now a pressing necessity.' Outlines of the plans to both commanders were available on July 27." The significance of these warnings should not be overrated, however. As early as the autumn of 1943, for instance, Allied strategists in Europe had laid plans in "the event of German collapse that fall" under the impact of the first great Soviet offensive in the East and the Allied aerial offensive in the West against German cities and industries. Such plans had, of course, been swiftly abandoned. Moreover, the formal Anglo-American report of July 24, 1945, continued to postulate "15 November 1946" as the planning date for the end of organized resistance in Japan, and the report further stressed as a major objective: "Encourage Russian entry into the war against Japan."[65] Comparatively isolated in Berlin, immersed in an unprecedented spectrum of worldwide strategic problems, and above all skeptical and ignorant of the enormous potential and revolutionary nature of the atomic bomb, the Joint Chiefs became in their quiet and professional way almost as much a "fanatical hierarchy"—to use Churchill's phrase[66]—as their opposites in Tokyo. They obviously believed that the atomic bomb first would have to prove itself as a revolutionary agent of warfare before strategic planning would be revised or reversed.

Only once did Truman himself, as we have noted, seriously consider the atomic bomb sufficiently close to an existing reality as to ask for an assessment of its impact upon Russian entry into the Japanese war. This was on July 23, when he asked Stimson to sound Marshall out on the question. What were the President's motives in making this query?

Stimson had just come from a gloomy session with Harriman when he saw his President that day. Harriman had spoken of the previous day's plenary session, during which Stalin first introduced

---

[65] Bradley, *A Soldier's Story*, pp. 198–199; *Entry of the Soviet Union into the War Against Japan*, p. 106; *Foreign Relations, 1945; Conference of Berlin*, II: 1463, 1467.

[66] Churchill, *Triumph and Tragedy*, p. 547.

the issue of Soviet influence in the Dardanelles and a possible trusteeship in North Africa, and he had successfully transferred some of his anxieties to the older man. When Stimson met Truman the two thus spoke briefly of Harriman's concern, and the President "told me that the United States was standing firm." Stimson added that Truman "was apparently relying greatly upon the information as to S-1," but this was the interpretation of a man obsessed with a particular subject around which all other realities revolved and were assessed. The President's next remarks were very revealing and completely in character with his consistently low-key and realistic approach to the conference and the problem of Soviet demands. "He evidently thinks," Stimson wrote that evening, that "a good deal of the new claims of the Russians are bluff, and told me what he thought the real claims were confined to."[67] Stimson elaborated no further, but it is obvious that Truman sensed in Soviet behavior no great or immediate threat to United States interests. The President evidently assumed that Stalin was pursuing a diplomatic tactic which, applied in politics, war, or sport, is summed up in the maxim that the best defense is a good offense. In order to protect Soviet hegemony over Eastern Europe, the President thought Stalin would for a time press claims elsewhere which would keep his Western Allies, especially the British, preoccupied.

Above all others the factor which seems to have prompted the Presidential query was a simple desire to go home. So far Russian military leaders had dragged their feet about meeting their American counterparts to coordinate activities in Asia. "The President was frank about his desire to close the conference and get away," Stimson noted on the twenty-fourth. Marshall had also been chafing with impatience. The problems of coordination with the British were "practically all settled now," and Marshall understandably wished to return to Washington to oversee the buildup for the OLYMPIC operation against Kyushu.[68] If the Russians would not meet on the Asia issue, possibly the Americans could go their own way.

[67] Stimson Diary, July 23, 1945.
[68] *Ibid.*, July 23, 24, 1945.

Truman's flash of temper and Marshall's impatience to get going with final plans for the end of the Pacific war were monentary aberrations of burdened men. There appeared to be no realistic chance or hope to do without Russian aid, and Marshall quickly struck down the idea that there was when he and Stimson took up the Truman query on the afternoon of the twenty-third. The general simply repeated again the observation he had made as early as April 23. He "pointed out that even if we went ahead in the war without the Russians and compelled the Japanese to surrender on our terms, that would not prevent the Russians from marching into Manchuria anyhow and striking, thus permitting them to get virtually what they wanted in surrender terms."[69] A successful demonstration of the bomb and even the invasion of Japan itself were simply not factors of sufficient weight and force to keep the Russians out of Northeast Asia. Here was the third great consideration in Far Eastern affairs that faced the Americans at Potsdam.

And there was a fourth and almost equally important factor as well, Byrnes' remarks to Forrestal and others at Potsdam about the Russian menace in the Far East notwithstanding: Namely that in the view of many policy-makers in Washington the overall objectives of the United States in Asia and the Pacific were not inimical to a limited expansion of Soviet influence in the region. These people vigorously argued that the establishment of a workable postwar security arrangement in the Far East depended far more upon the slow but steady and ultimately drastic reduction of British and French colonial power in the area than upon the restriction of Soviet influence there.

"When V day comes in the Far East and the Pacific it will be the result in largest measure of the military might and sacrifices of the United States," the State Department asserted in a position paper prepared for the Potsdam Conference near the end of June.

> In return the American people ask for a reasonable assurance of peace and security in this great area and economic welfare. Peace and security, and economic welfare, however, depend on a number of condi-

---

[69] *Ibid.* Byrnes and Forrestal were fully aware of this potentiality. Recalling Potsdam in a personal memorandum of 1958, Byrnes wrote of his July 28 meeting with Forrestal: "Forrestal thought it would take an army to keep Stalin out of the war and I agreed with him." Handwritten note, "Potsdam," Folder 636, Byrnes Papers.

tions. One of these conditions is the right of all peoples to choose the form of Government under which they will live. . . .

Aside from the traditional American belief in the right of all peoples to independence, the largest possible measure of political freedom for the countries of Asia consistent with their ability to assume the responsibility thereof is probably necessary in order to achieve the chief objective of the United States in the Far East and the Pacific: continuing peace and security.[70]

Elaborating on these basic points, State Department planners noted that "After the unconditional surrender or total defeat of Japan," East Asia would be in chaos.

China will probably be disunited. The Soviet Union . . . may be in military occupation of Manchuria, and, possibly, of Korea and parts of north China. Soviet ideology will be a rising force throughout the entire Far East. . . . the great dependencies, especially India and Burma, will be demanding a greater measure of self-government, and will be receiving the moral support of the United States, China, and probably the Soviet Union, while the colonial powers will be attempting to satisfy these demands by such minimum concessions as will not threaten the loss of these imperial possessions.

The great task of American diplomacy in the area in the coming years would be to steer a delicate middle course in which the colonial powers would be forced to grant concessions to native aspirations faster than they would have wished, while the Asian colonial peoples would be restrained from rushing into such precipitate adventures in sovereignty and self-government as would perpetuate or re-create the political, social, economic, and moral chaos of the immediate postwar period. "The United States," the State Department paper continued, "is prepared to do its utmost to bring about the adoption of forward-looking programs and to see that they are not merely hollow promises but are calculated to bring results."[71]

In formulating such a Far Eastern policy "The Soviet Union offers the most perplexing problem. *It is not certain to what extent, if at all, United States and Soviet objectives in the Far East are in*

[70] "An Estimate of Conditions in Asia and the Pacific at the Close of the War in the Far East and the Objectives and Policies of the United States," Policy Paper Prepared in the Department of State, June 22, 1945, *Foreign Relations, 1945; Diplomatic Papers*, VI: 556–557.

[71] *Ibid.*, pp. 577–578.

conflict. The future Soviet course of action can only be surmised."[72]
Should the Russians seek to use their entry into the war against
Japan as the pretext to aid the Chinese Communists, then "the most
hopeful course for the United States Government would be to attempt to reach an agreement with the Soviets by which the Soviet
Union would promise *inter alia* to respect the integrity and independence of China and to refrain from any intervention in China's
internal affairs." But the mere threat of Soviet expansion at China's
expense was viewed with decidedly mixed emotions by the State
Department planners, for such a threat in and of itself might provide the one salutary means by which Chiang Kai-shek and his Kuomintang colleagues could at last be forced to acknowledge and to
deal with the terrible set of crises facing their country. "The attitude
of the Soviets and the action which they take in regard to China
may depend in large measure on the character and conduct of the
Chinese National Government. If it should become genuinely representative of the Chinese people and should adopt liberal policies,
especially in economic matters [an obvious reference to the then
ruinous inflation raging inside that country], the chief cause—or
excuse—for possible Soviet interference would no longer exist."
Implicit in this analysis was growing American exasperation with
Chiang and an emerging sentiment that if Russia *did* endanger
traditional Chinese rights and territory, the Kuomintang would itself be largely to blame because of its years of irresponsible governance. Patience with the Chinese Nationalists was wearing thin
indeed in official Washington circles, and the State Department
paper urged continuing American pressure on Chungking "to adopt
essential reforms, in order to remove any occasion for Soviet intervention. . . ."[73]

Viewed in light of the above policy proposals, Byrnes' and Truman's response to Stalin's expanded demands upon China is drained
of much of whatever sinister qualities might be superficially attributed to it by those who have postulated aggressive American designs against Russia at Potsdam. The President and his Secretary
were obviously and properly concerned about the possibility of the

[72] *Ibid.*, italics added.
[73] *Ibid.*, pp. 578–579.

bear in the China shop, but they were not alarmed. Soviet pressure on China, as well as Soviet intervention in the Pacific war, should if possible be manipulated in such a way as to maximize American policy objectives. Stalin's demands served as a perfect pretext for the United States to demand that the Chinese Nationalists assume their total governmental responsibilities as representatives of a sovereign state. Byrnes' comment to Forrestal on July 28 concerning his fears of a Russian thrust to Dairen and Port Arthur may well have reflected as much an anxiety that the Chinese Nationalists were not capable of meeting their responsibilities as it did a concern with Soviet conduct *per se*. It cannot be doubted that Byrnes, Leahy, and Forrestal—and possibly Stimson as well—went to Potsdam profoundly skeptical of Soviet motives throughout the world. And it is also undeniably true that observed Russian behavior at Potsdam and in Germany as a whole further deepened this skepticism. But, as in Europe, the Soviet problem in Asia was not consistently viewed by these men, Byrnes, Harriman, and Kennan excepted, as the supreme or even invariably the major problem facing the United States in the coming years. French and British aspirations in both Europe and Asia, Chinese weakness in the Far East, and the numerous clamors for independence and self-government from colonial peoples all around the periphery of the Eurasian land mass were frequently sources of equal concern to American policy-makers and the subjects of much worried study and scrutiny. And, as in the case of East Asia, Russian appetites were often viewed as a potentially healthy adjunct to American diplomacy as late as Potsdam. Friction between Moscow and Washington had clearly increased at a number of points since Yalta. The Cold War, however, had not yet begun.

In Asia, indeed, the great opponent—though certainly no enemy—of American diplomacy was conceived by many to be Britain, not Russia. "British policy in the Far East," the State Department paper of late June asserted,

is in harmony with United States policies in many respects, but in certain other respects it is at variance. In regard to China and Japan, the British Government will in general probably go along with the United

States, although the emphasis of their policy will be different. British sentiment against Japan is neither so unanimous nor so strong as is American opinion. *The British Government, although anxious to avoid friction with the Soviet Union, supports the Chinese National Government and opposes the Chinese Communists more unreservedly than does the United States. The apparent unwillingness of the British Government to grant to its dependencies as early and as adequate an increase of self-government as is favored by American opinion presents the major issue with the United States.* Great Britain will not support Australia and New Zealand in all of their ambitions as expressed in the Anzac Pact. As to a number of small islands in the central Pacific, British and American claims conflict. *Above all, the chief problems for the British Empire and the United States, in view of their global entente, especially for the maintenance of mutual security and world peace, is to reach some understanding in regard to the issue of dependencies in the Far East.*[74]

Britain thus represented the chief obstacle to the realization of American diplomatic objectives in the postwar Far East. France, however, was not far behind. "French policy in the Far East presents a similar problem to the United States: to harmonize support of France in Europe with support of a greater measure of self-government in Indo-China." However, time and the shifting balance of power across Oceania and upon its western coastal rim favored the United States in its quest for an influential role. "Australia and New Zealand will seek to play a major role in the settlement of general Pacific questions. Canada, while always desirous of exerting a moderating influence in any conflict of policy between the United States and the United Kingdom, is likely in the last analysis to accept the American view of any major issue because of its dependence on the United States for security."[75]

As in the American response to the Sino-Soviet negotiations, so in Allied military planning at Potsdam for the final assaults upon Japan, the ideas expressed in the State Department position paper were translated into policy. Soviet intervention was encouraged and welcomed by the Joint Chiefs, while British and French participation, though not discouraged, was most certainly subverted to United States efforts. OLYMPIC and the later CORONET inva-

[74] *Ibid.*, p. 579, italics added.
[75] *Ibid.*, p. 580.

sion of the Tokyo Plain would definitely be preponderantly American "shows."

Serious British planning for the invasion of Japan had begun in April of 1945, and the first report appeared in early May. But it was unacceptable to Churchill because of its modesty in assuming a British role in the assault. London at this time was determined that "If the Japanese Home Islands were to be invaded over the next ten months, it was important for political reasons that the British should play a part in the operations." A modest British task force had been operating with the American fleet since March, and a portion of the R.A.F.'s Bomber Command was already moving toward Okinawa to aid the United States Army Air Force in its attacks upon Japan, despite a "cool" reception in both Washington and the Pacific. But this did not satisfy British designs. "Naval and air support of the invasion, accompanied by 'mopping-up' operations far away"—British and Commonwealth forces under Mountbatten had long assumed responsibility for the recapture of Malaya and adjacent areas in Southeast Asia and the Southwest Pacific— "were not considered enough. Land forces must participate, on whatever scale, in the invasion itself."[76]

On June 8 British planners went back to work and on June 30 "tabled" their revised report to Churchill. Because of commitments in the Southwest Pacific, there was no hope of gaining a foothold for British troops in the Kyushu operation. As for CORONET, in the spring of 1946 only three and two-thirds divisions, one or two of them British and one probably a mixture of Indian and New Zealand troops, would be offered to the Americans. Though moved to the invasion beaches by British and Commonwealth shipping, "The whole force would depend for its subsequent supply," after the initial landings, "on American 'rear services.'" Churchill approved the report on July 4 and it was forwarded to the American Joint Chiefs.[77]

The Joint Chiefs responded in rather chilly fashion on the seventeenth. Employment of Indian troops would be " 'doubtful' " because of " 'language complications and the necessity for prior ac-

---

[76] Ehrman, *Grand Strategy*, pp. 263–264; King, *A Naval Record*, p. 611.
[77] Ehrman, *Grand Strategy*, pp. 265, 267; Bryant, *Triumph in the West*, pp. 353–354.

climatisation.' " Any thought of including Canadians within the Commonwealth division was scotched because Washington had already made arrangements to " 'organise and equip along United States lines one Canadian Division, to operate as a part of a United States Corps.' " The British offer of further tactical air units to aid in CORONET was also summarily dismissed; they were not needed; American air power would be adequate.[78] The following day MacArthur in Manila further dampened British enthusiasm.

> he . . . drew attention to the difficulties in allocating a separate national sector to the Commonwealth, and to the dangers of introducing a new force, unaccustomed to the practice of the rest, into a complex operation. He therefore preferred to limit the Commonwealth troops definitely to three divisions—one British, one Canadian, one Australian —who should be concentrated by 1st December 1945 in Borneo or the United States and moved to the operational area by 10th March [1946], should be trained in American methods, lifted by British assault shipping but equipped and supplied by the Americans, and should function, as a Corps within a U.S. Army, as part of the assault *reserve*.[79]

The British glumly examined MacArthur's proposals during the rest of the month. They were in no position politically or militarily to argue the point effectively. On July 31, with a sigh, they gave in. " 'We consider,' they stated, 'that the views of the Supreme Commander concerned should be accepted wherever possible.' "[80] Not only were the British forced to acquiesce in the views of the American Supreme Commander; they were even barred from his headquarters in any meaningful sense. For in their message of July 17, the American Joint Chiefs bluntly told their British counterparts "that the role of the Combined Chiefs of Staff in the European war cannot appropriately be applied to the Pacific war." As the Americans viewed and stated the matter, there were two distinct military theaters of operations in the Far East. Mountbatten headed the Southeast Asian-Southwest Pacific theater, which constituted "an area of British Empire responsibility associated with the

[78] Quoted in Ehrman, *Grand Strategy*, pp. 267–268.
[79] *Ibid.*, p. 269, italics added. Cf. also *Foreign Relations, 1945; Conference of Berlin*, II: 1336–1337.
[80] Quoted in Ehrman, *Grand Strategy*, p. 269.

Portuguese, the Dutch, and perhaps eventually the French." On the other hand, "The Pacific area is devoted to the main effort, is organized under a command and control set-up peculiar to the United States, and has forces and resources overwhelmingly United States unless the Chinese, and possibly Russian, contribution is considered."[81] If anyone was to take the major credit for ending Japanese tyranny in Asia and the Pacific, it was, as Admiral Leahy has so forcefully reminded us, to be the United States. British—and French, Dutch, and Portuguese—aid was to be kept strictly peripheral. Despite a number of attempts at Potsdam, the British failed to break the resolve of their American allies. Lend-lease aid was to be minimal, and there was to be no significant British share in control of Pacific strategy. As Marshall put it to Alanbrooke, the Americans "would be prepared to discuss strategy but final decisions must rest with them."[82]

And even these minimal American concessions to British hopes for participation in the final Battle of Japan were withdrawn on August 10, after Hiroshima and Nagasaki. Washington, as we shall see, was still uncertain at this late date as to whether the atomic strikes and Soviet entry into Manchuria would be of sufficient weight to force Japan into surrender. Invasion plans were still going forward, and London was informed that American thinking " 'has proceeded to a point where the United States Chiefs of Staff question very seriously the feasibility of utilising any British forces . . . in an assault role.' " As the chief British military historian of these events has written: "Much debate must have lain ahead before British troops could have waded ashore onto the beaches of Honshu."[83]

In contrast, Soviet-American military talks at Potsdam were almost completely free of friction. Both countries had obtained for themselves over the months a large measure of strategic independence: Russia would handle the Japanese army on the Northeast Asian mainland for an already agreed-upon price. The Americans,

[81] *Foreign Relations, 1945; Conference of Berlin*, II: 1314.
[82] Leahy, *I Was There*, pp. 409–411; Bryant, *Triumph in the West*, pp. 361–362.
[83] Ehrman, *Grand Strategy*, p. 271.

true to their own self-conceived sphere of influence and interest over Oceania, would handle the invasion of Japan. Rivalry and conflict between the two nations was nonexistent when their military staffs, along with those of the British, at last got together on July 24. As Leahy later remarked, "The entire meeting was very friendly and none of the suspicion that so often frustrated our military mission in Moscow was apparent."[84]

At this first session on the twenty-fourth the Soviets made an important and explicit pledge, though one that Byrnes obviously took with a grain of salt if his remark to Forrestal four days later is correct. General Antonov categorically stated "that after the defeat of Japan, in combination with Allied armies, 'it is the intention of the Soviet Union to withdraw its troops from Manchuria.' "[85] A list of operational questions was submitted to Antonov and Kuznetzov, the ranking Soviet military chiefs, and two days later, at a second meeting at which the British were conspicuously absent (having returned home to learn of the General Election results), the Soviets replied in terms quite satisfactory to the Americans. Operational boundaries were established, the Russians agreed to establish radio and weather observation stations in Siberia to inform the Americans of climatic developments, and the formation of liaison groups between American and Soviet commanders in the Far East "beginning with military operations of the Soviet Union against Japan" was agreed to. All of this highly pleased Marshall and the Americans. But their greatest source of pleasure lay in the quick Soviet agreement "to select ports and airfields for [American and British] ships and planes in need of repairs and to make available, as far as possible, repair facilities and medical assistance to the personnel of the above-mentioned ships and planes."

At only one point did the Russians antagonize their American counterparts. When Antonov emphasized that the Siberian radio and weather stations must be manned by Soviet and not American personnel, "a deep red flush appeared above Admiral King's collar and soon spread to his face and head. I could see that he was a bit irate, but he restrained himself admirably and simply expressed

[84] Leahy, *I Was There*, p. 416.
[85] *Ibid.*, p. 415.

his disappointment." The Soviets then relented to the extent of permitting American liaison and observation teams into the weather stations. Marshall next turned aside a Soviet query about opening up the straits between Kyushu and Honshu as a supply corridor to Russian ports with the observation that Kyushu would first have to be secured by American forces. After the Joint Chiefs reported to the Russians on recent American operations and plans, the second and final meeting broke up in an atmosphere of general cordiality. "The military meeting at Potsdam thus ended in complete accord," General Deane later recalled. "Not only were the Russian military leaders amenable to our proposals, but for the first time they were punctilious in carrying them out. . . . when the Japanese surrendered on August 14, our [weather station] parties were ready to leave Seattle."[86]

Only one point remained obscure, and it may well have played a role—though how important a role is highly conjectural—in the American decision to use the bomb as soon as it was ready. The Russians on July 24 and 26 gave their American colleagues the distinct impression that they would not strike at Manchuria before "late August," a point that Stalin had apparently already made at a Big Three dinner on July 18.[87] The August 8 date, to which Stalin had committed himself in his May-June talks with Hopkins in Moscow and which he had reaffirmed to Truman on July 17, now seemed to be reversed. The Russians were surely coming in; Marshall made that point very clear to Stimson, it will be recalled, on July 23, and we must assume that Marshall's emphatic assumption was based as much or more upon army intelligence reports as upon instinct or purely personal analysis of existing conditions. But if the Soviets delayed until the end of August, this might give Tokyo the impression that its Moscow initiative was about to work, despite Sato's vigorous and informed denials that it would not and despite a total absence of any such evidence available to us now. Such a reckless Soviet gamble as would be entailed in selling out its powerful—and

---

[86] *Entry of the Soviet Union into the War Against Japan*, pp. 91–102; *Foreign Relations, 1945; Conference of Berlin*, II: 408–417; Deane, *The Strange Alliance*, pp. 273–275.
[87] Leahy, *I Was There*, p. 415; Ehrman, *Grand Strategy*, p. 303.

wealthy—United States ally for the sake of aiding or allying with a ruined Japan is beyond contemplation or comprehension. It would have flown against every known instinct that Stalin possessed as a cold, ruthless, patient, and very careful practitioner of *Realpolitik*. More likely, the Soviets were carefully marshalling their forces for an attack that would be as powerful, and above all, penetrating, as possible.

Whatever the reason for the possible Russian delay, American officials may well have derived increased justification for a swift test of the atomic bomb under combat conditions from Stalin's remarks of July 18 and the comments of his military chiefs a week later. Japan must be kept reeling. The absolute hopelessness of her military position must be driven home to her in the most powerful and sustained manner possible. If the force of a Soviet intervention could not be immediately utilized for this purpose, then the shock of an abrupt and successful atomic strike must be. In a little-known passage from one of his several memoirs, President Truman has added some validity to this hypothesis. In 1960 he wrote that at Potsdam Stalin told him that a Soviet intervention would not take place until three *months* after the conference.[88] This would place the time of the Manchurian operation in rough simultaneity with the American invasion of Kyushu. If Truman either heard something from Stalin in private—and he could have at the numerous parties—or if he simply misunderstood a poor translation of the Generalissimo's words, then it was logical for him to assume that the options available for possibly shocking Japan into a quick surrender short of invasion were closed save for a series of American atomic strikes. Truman's 1960 assertion must be approached with caution. He had not made this statement in his formal memoirs, there is no other available information to substantiate it, and the criticism he endured for his atomic decision over the years may well have swayed his pen toward exaggeration. But if his memory was correct, then his final decision at Potsdam on July 20 or 21 to use the bombs as soon as they were ready is more understandable, if still inexcusable.

[88] Harry S. Truman, *Mr. Citizen* (New York: Bernard Geis Associates, 1960), p. 269.

For it was not only the advisability and morality of the American use of the bombs against Japan that must be judged in the aftertime but also the American approach to the Russians on the subject. Truman's handling of the problem at Potsdam and thereafter was lamentably confused and inept. And in this failure the seeds of immeasurable tragedy were sown.

It will be recalled that in early July Stimson had at last, after much personal soul-searching, advised his President to give the Russians at Potsdam at least some inkling of the atomic project and incipient Anglo-American success therein. News from Alamogordo two weeks later made a decision on the matter imperative. Churchill was initially "strongly inclined against any disclosure" to the Russians about the atomic project or its possible fruits. But with the receipt of General Groves' full report on July 22 the Prime Minister changed his mind. After first telling Stimson, who had been the one to bring him the successive scraps of atomic information, of the tremendous "pepping up" that had taken place in Truman with the news of Alamogordo, Churchill said "that he felt the same way. . . . He now not only was not worried about giving the Russians information on the matter but was rather inclined to use it as an argument in our favor in the negotiations." The British delegation's attitude in general "was unanimous in thinking that it was advisable to tell the Russians at least that we were working on that subject and intended to use it if and when it was successful."[89]

Truman and Byrnes, meanwhile, "had given the matter their careful thought." Churchill was consulted, and as has already been noted, Stimson was listened to, by the President at least, with full attention and sympathy. The traditional assumption has been that the President and his Secretary "decided to inform Stalin as casually and briefly as possible" and that Truman played his part in a "low key" fashion. Strolling around the conference table without even his interpreter, Charles Bohlen, Truman at the close of the plenary session on July 24 "simply reported" to Stalin "that the United States had a new weapon of unusual destructive force. Stalin showed no special interest, saying only that he was glad to hear it and hoped

---

[89] "W.B.'s book" July 15, 1945, Folder 602, Byrnes Papers; Stimson Diary, July 18, 22, 1945.

the Americans would make 'good use of it against the Japanese.' "
Moments later Churchill asked the President, " 'How did it go?' "
" 'He never asked a question,' " Truman responded. "Truman had
taken the minimum step necessary to warn Russia of the advent of
the bomb."[90]

So he had, but had he meant to? Or did he mean to do more and
drew back at the last moment? We in fact have no one's word,
other than Truman's, as to just what the President told Stalin. Churchill observed from across the room. But what was in Truman's
mind as he approached Stalin? Feis argues that it was deception,
that "What had been feared did not come to pass. Stalin had not
tried to find out what the nature of the new weapon was, or how it
was made. He had not suggested that Soviet officers or technicians
be allowed to examine or witness its use." Feis further speculates
that this may have been because Stalin already knew about the bomb
from his own spies. Tantalizing evidence exists to suggest, however, that Truman may well have been prepared to say much more,
but did not. In a note from Potsdam to the War Cabinet on July 18,
Churchill wrote that Truman "seemed determined" to tell Stalin
and the Russians about the bomb. On the twenty-third Churchill
told Lord Moran that " 'We thought it would be indecent to use
it [the bomb] in Japan without telling the Russians, so they are
to be told today.' "[91] Since Stalin was not told for another twenty-
four hours, Truman may well have reconsidered. Equally plausible
is Feis' hypothesis that the President assumed that Stalin already
knew about the bomb and much if not all its technology from his
own spy network. Stimson's admonition of July 3 to the President,
namely to say to Stalin "that we were busy with this thing, working
like the dickens and we knew he was busy with this thing and working like the dickens . . ."[92] becomes a potentially very important
element in Presidential thinking with regard to the July 24 disclosure.[93]

[90] Hewlett and Anderson, *The New World*, pp. 393–394; Truman, *Year of Decisions*, p. 458; Churchill, *Triumph and Tragedy*, pp. 572–573; Eden, *The Reckoning*, pp. 634–635; Craven and Cate, *From Matterhorn to Nagasaki*, p. 712; Feis, *Between War and Peace*, p. 177.
[91] Feis, *Between War and Peace*, p. 178; Churchill, *Triumph and Tragedy*, p. 547; Moran, *Churchill*, p. 301.
[92] Stimson Diary, July 3, 1945.
[93] In this connection it should be noted that when Truman told Byrnes later in

But when conjecture is exhausted the simplest explanation appears to be the best. Truman was temperamentally incapable of taking the multitude of risks involved in offering to share the atomic secret with the Soviets at Potsdam or at any subsequent date. Years later he casually remarked: "My position on secrecy in connection with the military application of atomic power has always been the same. I have been uncompromisingly opposed to sharing or yielding atomic military secrets to any other government." At the time of the Berlin Conference, Britain and Canada had already been brought into the atomic quest by Roosevelt; there was no possibility of exclusion there. But it is evident that Truman firmly believed that no one else should know and that even those who did know should not be permitted to know more. Ten months after Potsdam, in the spring of 1946, the President adamantly opposed Attlee's assertion that "until such a time as U.N. control might become effective, the British should either have atomic weapons made available to them or at least be supplied with the data necessary to start their own production."[94] In atomic matters Harry S. Truman remained determined that he and his country should hold the power and bear the responsibility.

But Truman's failure at Potsdam to at least make a tentative gesture toward atomic cooperation with the Russians was, *in the context of that moment*, a major blunder. The President need not have immediately made good on any promise to share. Indeed he could not have done so, because there were no Americans at Potsdam sufficiently conversant in atomic technology to make such an offer feasible, nor were there any Russians present with the requisite atomic knowledge to exploit it. In failing to make some minimal gesture of trust and cooperation to an ally whose aid in the Japa-

---

the day of Stalin's quiet and apparently disinterested response, Byrnes, according to one account, "was surprised. He did not expect such a lack of interest." The Secretary "guessed that when Stalin got back to his headquarters it would dawn on him that he had missed a great opportunity, and so he would return the following day with a list of questions for the President to answer. Truman agreed that this was probable." That night Truman and Byrnes "spoke at length about how to answer the aggressive inquiries from Stalin which, of course, never came." Joseph I. Lieberman, *The Scorpion and the Tarantula; The Struggle to Control Atomic Weapons, 1945–1949* (Boston: Houghton Mifflin Co., 1970), p. 106. This account is fully supported by the contemporary observations of Byrnes' personal press aide, Walter Brown. Cf. "W.B.'s book," July 24, 1945, Folder 602, Byrnes Papers.

[94] Truman, *Years of Trial and Hope*, pp. 25–30, 344–346.

nese war had, after all, been ardently sought, was to invite the profoundest suspicion and recrimination should the atomic bombs
work. The fact that the British had been privy to the atomic secret
right along—and indeed had made substantial contributions to the
atomic project from the start—only made the situation all the worse.
For Hiroshima would give the Soviets the perfect pretext for charging that an abrupt change had come in Soviet-American relations,
that the Americans were now joining the British in a nuclear club
whose aim was to "gang up on the Russians." Had the President
made the merest gesture at Potsdam toward the promise of a future sharing of atomic knowledge with the Kremlin, the Soviets
might have been held in line for some months, and various behavioral and political concessions might have been wrung out of them
in exchange for their participation in a postwar atomic partnership
with London and Washington. The risk would have been grave,
to be sure. But certainly not any greater than was the policy of exclusion which was ultimately followed and which led directly to
the Cold War.

The Cold War had not yet begun at Potsdam. In the first place,
de facto Soviet and American spheres of influence in Eastern Europe, Latin America, and the Pacific did not clash. The only point
of *potential* conflict lay in Northeast Asia, and it was not at all certain that that potentiality would ever materialize. Moreover, American diplomacy had under Truman's overall direction handled the
Soviet problem since Roosevelt's death with great delicacy, skill, and
care. It had faithfully reflected much of articulate and emotional
American public opinion, which continued to demand that we do
all in our power to maintain the policy of "getting along with the
Russians" in peace as in war. Where interests had to be sacrificed
to maintain either the myth or reality of Soviet-American friendship, the interests were almost invariably those of virtually power-
less Britain. Britain, indeed, had long served a useful purpose as a
buffer between Stalin, Roosevelt, and Truman. So long as those
three could barter or nibble away at London's interests across the
world there was no reason for a direct clash between Kremlin and
White House, eagle and bear. Finally, the atomic bomb, despite
its *potential* attractiveness to some as a diplomatic "master card," re-

mained an untried and uncertain weapon of war as late as the end of the Berlin Conference.

But now the bomb—if successful—would at last inescapably create a direct diplomatic problem, a direct source of immediate friction, between America and Russia. A daring, courageous, calculated risk on Truman's part at Potsdam on July 24, 1945, to move swiftly to give the Russians at least the promise of joining Britain and the United States in a joint nuclear club, should the bombs do their work in Japan, was the only way to stave off the sudden disaster in East-West relations. But Truman, for whatever reason, was not equal to this particular task of statesmanship. He allowed the supreme moment to pass. And then, with the war at an end, the President handed over the custodianship of American foreign policy to the one man initially ready and eager to use the bomb aggressively as a powerful diplomatic tool—Secretary of State Byrnes. Truman's administration, the people it led, and those across the planet whom it ultimately opposed, would thus pay heavily and suffer long in the coming years for the President's singular failure of nerve and vision at Potsdam.

13

Hiroshima

And so the vile acts were carried out. Hiroshima and Nagasaki disintegrated in a second under the atomic blows. The massive global hemorrhage known as World War II closed on an unspeakably sordid note. At a stroke the military balance, not only within the Grand Alliance, but across the world, tipped decisively in America's favor. So much that Truman and Stimson and Hopkins—and even Byrnes—had worked for at Potsdam and before literally went up in the smoke of the mushroom clouds over Japan.

Stimson, "rushing back to Washington" from Berlin in the last days of July, waited impatiently for the atomic raids to begin. He whiled away the time until the bombs were dropped, gathering together suitable material on the Manhattan Project and nuclear energy, which was to be released in the form of the Smyth Report once news of successful attacks became known.[1] On August 1 Groves brought to Stimson's office the latest product of Leo Szilard's incessant campaign to force a policy of restraint in the use of atomic weaponry. The document was—and remains—an eloquent

[1] Hewlett and Anderson, *The New World*, pp. 398–400.

testimonial to rationality and foresight. First pointing to the fact that "Until recently we have had to fear that the United States might be attacked by atomic bombs during this war and that her only defense might lie in a counterattack by the same means," Szilard and his sixty-six co-signers noted that "Today, with the defeat of Germany, this danger is averted." The use of atomic weapons against Japan might well bring an abrupt end to the war, the scientists admitted, but the price of such a speedy victory was certain to be prohibitive in terms of future national and global stability.

> The development of atomic power will provide the nations with new means of destruction. The atomic bombs at our disposal represent only the first step in this direction and there is almost no limit to the destructive power which will become available in the course of their future development. Thus a nation which sets the precedent of using these newly liberated forces of nature for purposes of destruction may have to bear the responsibility for opening the door to an era of devastation on an unimaginable scale.
>
> If after the war a situation is allowed to develop in the world which permits rival powers to be in uncontrolled possession of these new means of destruction, the cities of the United States as well as the cities of other nations will be in continuous danger of sudden annihilation. All the resources of the United States, moral and material, may have to be mobilized to prevent the advent of such a world situation. Its prevention is at present the solemn responsibility of the United States—singled out by virtue of her lead in the field of atomic power.
>
> The added material strength which this lead gives to the United States brings with it the obligation of restraint and if we were to violate this obligation our moral position would be weakened in the eyes of the world and in our own eyes. . . .[2]

The warning was to no avail. Alamogordo had made a great "change" in Stimson's "psychology." "Added 'pep' " now flowed through the old man as he realized that the means to bring World War II to a sudden close now lay in his own hands and those of the President. "Nothing could have seemed more irrelevant to Stimson and Harrison on August 1 than further expositions of scien-

[2] Matthew J. Connelly, Secretary to the President, Personal and Confidential Memo (with enclosures to James F. Byrnes), September 6, 1945, "Correspondence of Harry S. Truman Not Part of the White House Files, 1945–1953," Truman Papers, Box 1.

tific opinion."[3] The looming atomic strike now dominated all of Stimson's thoughts. First scheduled for the night of August 3, the Hiroshima raid was delayed by adverse weather, then postponed once more while Stimson's irritability palpably mounted.[4]

On the afternoon of August 5 Hanson Baldwin, the preeminent military analyst, who wrote for the *New York Times*, predicted "a major crisis in the Pacific war" within "the next one to three months —quite possibly within the next thirty days." For Japan was being subjected to unprecedented military blows from sea and sky and "Blows against Japan, far, far heavier than any yet delivered are in the making and may shake the Empire to its foundations. Bombings and bombardments that will surpass in fury and intensity anything hitherto known, a tighter and tighter blockade, attacks upon enemy communications and upon regions hitherto untouched will be the keystone of the approaching crisis." Then, too, an early Russian entry into the war could not be discounted simply because such a commitment had not been publicly expressed at Potsdam. And, finally, "a careful campaign" of political and psychological warfare, now clearly underway from Washington, San Francisco, and Manila, might well further erode the Japanese will to resist. Yet "No one can predict the outcome," Baldwin concluded:

> and we would be unwise, first, if we depended upon, or hoped too much, for Russian help, and second, if we did not prepare mentally and physically for a hard-fought invasion and a long war. Many observers believe Japan will not be able to "take it," but those with longer knowledge of the enemy's fanaticism and greater experience in the imponderables of war believe that quick collapse without invasion is possible but not probable.[5]

Even as these words reached print that evening the bulk of Hiroshima's population slept its last. In the early morning darkness of August 6, 1945, the *Enola Gay* at last rose ponderously from her airfield on Tinian and six hours later carried out the ghastly assassination from the clean blue sky above Japan. Once more, as at

---

[3] Hewlett and Anderson, *The New World*, pp. 399–400.
[4] Stimson Diary, August 2, 3, 4, 1945.
[5] *New York Times*, August 6, 1945, pp. 3:3, 4.

Alamogordo, "the damned thing worked." In an instant tens of thousands of human souls were vaporized. They were the fortunate ones. The real hell of living death was reserved for the survivors.

At his Long Island estate Stimson awoke to "a very rainy day" and the triumphant news from Marshall "that the S-1 operation was successful."[6] Swiftly the news was relayed to the Presidential party nearing the Virginia coast on board the cruiser *Augusta*. Truman and Byrnes had awaited news of a successful atomic strike with no less eager anticipation than Stimson. Just four days before the President and his Secretary of State had paused briefly at Plymouth to lunch with King George before resuming their journey home. Throughout the meal Byrnes was "a chatterbox," according to one witness. At one point "Byrnes began discussing in front of the waiters the impending release of the atomic bomb. As this was top secret, the King was horrified. 'I think Mr. Byrnes,' he said, 'that we should discuss this interesting subject over our coffee.' "[7]

But now the need for security had vanished, and the President, "jubilant," "smiling," and "buoyantly happy," according to those present, raced through the ship to tell everyone, officers and enlisted men alike, the good news. "The President was cheered loudly after each announcement. . . . 'Send some more of 'em over Japan and we'll all go home,' seemed to be the most universal comment" from the *Augusta*'s crew. "The President afterward said he had never been happier about any announcement he had ever made."[8]

Despite Presidential jubilation much of Washington remained far from certain that the atomic strike against Hiroshima or the abrupt Soviet entry into the Pacific war two days later—as per Stalin's assurances to Hopkins in June—would be sufficient in themselves to induce a Japanese surrender. On August 9, the day of the second successful atomic assault against Nagasaki, Undersecretary of War Robert Patterson cautioned Presidential adviser Samuel I. Rosenman that "under the circumstances our armed forces and in-

[6] Stimson Diary, August 6, 1945.

[7] Nigel Nicolson, ed., *Diaries and Letters of Harold Nicolson*, 3 vols. (New York: Atheneum Press, 1966–1968), Vol. III: *The Later Years, 1945–1962*, pp. 31–32.

[8] Flysheet, *U.S.S. Augusta Evening Press*, 6 August 1945, in folder: "Material Relating to Potsdam Conf.," Rosenman Papers.

dustry must be prepared for either an unconditional surrender of Japan within the immediate future or for a long, bitter last ditch struggle to abolish Japanese military power."[9] Several days later Groves, who, in his own words, "had become convinced that the war would end just as soon as the Japanese could surrender," induced Marshall to hold up delivery to the Pacific of fissionable material for a third bomb. Japan would have "until the thirteenth" to decide. "Then, if there was no surrender, shipments would be resumed."[10] The remorseless American determination to conquer had not diminished.

As the world waited for Japan to resolve her agony in the tense days following Hiroshima, the Allied world pondered the meaning of its achievement. For the Grand Alliance the end of World War II yielded only dubious victory. For all three partners the taste of triumph soon turned bitter. Britain had literally exhausted herself in the struggle for survival and had seen her position as a world power irretrievably eroded in the process. For America and Russia the crux of frustration was the atomic bomb.

Insofar as the Russians were concerned, Stalin and his Kremlin colleagues had fallen victim to one of the supreme ironies of our time. In his talks with Hopkins the Russian dictator had clearly indicated his wish that his American allies fight the Pacific war to a conclusive finish. They had done so, but in a terrifying fashion, apparently completely unforseen by the men in Moscow.

It swiftly became evident that the use of the atomic bomb had struck great fear into the hearts of the Russian people and government alike. Although the Soviet press played down the Hiroshima raid and did not even mention Nagasaki, "the bomb was one thing everybody in Russia . . . talked about" that entire first day of the atomic age. According to one Western journalist who walked the streets of Moscow then, "The news had an acutely depressing effect on everybody. It was clearly realised that this was a New Fact in the world's power politics, that the bomb constituted a threat to Russia. . . ." All of the popular Russian suspicions of Western intentions that had bubbled to the surface in 1942 and 1943, when the

---

[9] Patterson to Rosenman, August 9, 1945, *ibid.*, Box 3.
[10] Groves, *Now It Can Be Told*, pp. 352–353.

Red Army had held off the Nazis almost alone, now reemerged. "Some Russian pessimists I talked to that day dismally remarked that Russia's desperately hard victory over Germany was now 'as good as wasted,' " Alexander Werth later recalled. One Western diplomat, in casual conversation with a Red Army lieutenant, asked him what he thought of the atomic bomb. It is " 'a revolutionary technical discovery,' " the lieutenant shot back, " 'nevertheless we shall hold Manchuria.' "[11]

Twenty-four hours after Hiroshima Stalin abruptly summoned five of the leading Soviet nuclear scientists to the Kremlin "and ordered them to catch up with the United States in the minimum of time, regardless of cost."[12] Three and a half months later, just prior to the climactic East-West atomic discussions in Moscow, Sir Archibald Clark Kerr poignantly recalled the frightened reaction of the Russians to the sudden dawning of the atomic age. The British Ambassador was a man of remarkable wisdom and profound compassion. His lengthy message deserves extended quotation because of the intense light that it casts upon the whole post-Hiroshima atomic dilemma between East and West. Clark Kerr commenced his assessment by reminding his superiors in London that

> Nearly all of those who now govern Russia and mould opinion have led hunted lives since their early manhood when they were chased from pillar to post by the Tsarist police. Then came the immense and dangerous gamble of the Revolution followed by the perils and ups and downs of intervention and civil war. Independence and even ostracism may have brought some passing relief to their country but not to the survival of their system or to their bodies whose safety remained as precarious as ever. Witness the prolonged and internecine struggle that came after the death of Lenin and the years of the purges when their system was wobbling and no one knew today whether he would be alive tomorrow. . . . and it may be said that through all these years they trembled for the safety of their country and their system as they trembled for their own. Meanwhile, they worked feverishly and by means of a kind of terror till they dragooned an idle and slipshod people without regard for its suffering into building up a machine that

[11] Werth, *Russia at War*, p. 934; Ambassador Harriman to American Embassy, Chungking, August 12, 1945, Records of the Department of State, Record Group 84, Foreign Service Post File (Chungking), 710 Series, National Archives.
[12] Werth, *Russia at War*, p. 935.

might promise the kind of security they rightly felt they needed. The German invasion caught them still unready and swept them to what looked like the brink of defeat. Then came the turn of the tide and with it first the hope and then a growing belief that the immense benison of national security was at last within their reach. As the Red Army moved westward belief became confidence and the final defeat of Germany made confidence conviction.

There was a great exaltation. Russia could be made safe at last. She could put her house in order and more than this from behind her matchless three hundred divisions she could stretch out her hand and take most of what she needed and perhaps more. It was an exquisite moment. . . .

I have reviewed all this in order to recall to you the uncommon, and at times almost unbearable, tension that has strained these people's lives (it explains perhaps some of their abnormalities); and has hung over the whole history of the movement they have led, and in order also to suggest that the measure of relief that must have come to them with the end of Nazism would be hard to overestimate.

Then plump came the Atomic Bomb. At a blow the balance which had now seemed set and steady was rudely shaken. Russia was balked by the west when everything seemed to be within her grasp. The three hundred divisions were shorn of much of their value. About all this the Kremlin was silent but such was the common talk of the people. . . .[13]

For the Americans, too, victory proved to be a bittersweet experience. A sense of bemused horror spread through much of the American public as it impatiently awaited the news of Japan's formal capitulation. The bewildered nation sought to grasp the enormity of what had been done in its name. Millions viewed the horrors of Hiroshima as an acceptable price of triumph; millions more were stunned by the cost. "Yesterday we clinched victory in the Pacific, but we sowed the whirlwind," a shaken Hanson Baldwin wrote on the morrow of Hiroshima. The "frantic and intensive work in secret American laboratories" had culminated in "God-like power under men's imperfect control. . . . We face a frightful responsibility."[14] Others were not so restrained. The Secretary of the Federal Council of the Churches of Christ wired the President on

[13] British Ambassador in U.S.S.R. (Clark Kerr) to British Secretary of State for Foreign Affairs (Bevin), from Moscow, December 3, 1945, *Foreign Relations, 1945; Diplomatic Papers*, II: 82–84.

[14] *New York Times*, August 7, 1945, p. 10:2, 3.

August 9 that "Many Christians [are] deeply disturbed over use of atomic bombs against Japanese cities because of the necessarily indiscriminate destructive effects and because their use sets [an] extremely dangerous precedent for [the] future of mankind. . . ."[15] "I am impelled to write to you now and tell you how stunned and sick at heart I am over what our country has just done to Japan and her people—thousands of them innocent," wrote one professional woman from New York. "I think it is a disgrace that America should be involved in such a diabolical thing. America that was to give example to the rest of the world. . . . I had hoped and prayed that America under your leadership would be a good example to the rest of the world. I don't know what to think now."[16]

Near panic gripped some. To the Portland, Oregon, Rotary Club the coming of the bomb instantly called into question every existing political institution, foreign and domestic. A resolution was promptly passed urging Truman to convene immediately the nascent United Nations Organization "in order to guarantee to the little peoples of all the earth the right of the free flow of information—the right of knowing the incalculable power which science, for good or ill, holds over them."[17]

The administration was initially unmoved by the public outcry. Truman told one correspondent that "Nobody is more disturbed over the use of Atomic bombs than I am but I was greatly disturbed by the unwarranted attack by the Japanese on Pearl Harbor and their murder of our prisoners of war. The only language they seem to understand is the one we have been using to bombard them." And the President concluded: "When you deal with a beast you have to treat him as a beast. It is most regrettable but nevertheless true." Nor did the President disdain to say publicly what he wrote privately. In his August 9 radio report to the American people on the Potsdam Conference, Truman said:

Having found the bomb we have used it. We have used it against those who have attacked us without warning at Pearl Harbor, against those

[15] Samuel McCrea Cavert to Truman, August 9, 1945, Truman Papers, Office File 92-A.

[16] Anne Ford to Truman, August 9, 1945, *ibid.*

[17] A. Palmer Hoyt to Charles Ross, with enclosures, August 20, 1945, *ibid.*

who have starved and beaten and executed American prisoners of war, against those who have abandoned all pretense of obeying international laws of warfare. We have used it in order to shorten the agony of war, . . .

We shall continue to use it until we completely destroy Japan's power to make war. Only a Japanese surrender will stop us.[18]

As early as August 10, however, key administration officials began experiencing misgivings. At the Cabinet meeting that day Stimson "made the suggestion that we should now cease sending our bombers over Japan; he cited the growing feeling of apprehension and misgiving as to the effect of the atomic bomb even in our own country." Forrestal concurred, adding "that we must remember that this nation would have to bear the focus of the hatred by the Japanese."[19] Most revealing of all was the reaction of the American government to Tokyo's formal protests against the Hiroshima raid. For months the Japanese government had protested the indiscriminate massacre of large numbers of "innocent civilians" by aerial bombardment, first on Okinawa and then in the home cities. Silence had been Washington's only reply. On August 11 the Swiss Legation in Washington passed on to the State Department a formal Japanese protest over the Hiroshima raid. In their message the Japanese defined Hiroshima as "a provincial town without any protection or special military installations of any kind. . . ." Not until August 29 did Byrnes routinely acknowledge to the Swiss that he had received the message. But on September 5, with vocal dismay over the atomic attacks unabated, the Special War Problems Division of the State-War-Navy Coordinating Committee raised the question as to whether or not a formal and public reply should be given to the Japanese note. The conclusion reached was "that no publicity whatsoever be given to the receipt of this protest from the Japanese Government." On October 24 the Swiss were again briefly informed of American receipt of the Japanese protest of August 11, and there the matter died.[20] Whatever burden of guilt

[18] Truman to Samuel McCrea Cavert, August 11, 1945, *ibid.*; Truman, *Public Papers, 1945*, pp. 212–213.
[19] Millis, ed., *Forrestal Diaries*, p. 83.
[20] *Foreign Relations, 1945; Diplomatic Papers*, VI: 469–474.

some of the American people may have chosen to assume for their government's act, that government itself was determined to brazen through.

The atomic bomb did more than simply create a sudden imbalance of military and diplomatic power between East and West in the late summer of 1945. It abruptly propelled its progenitors to an unchallengeable position of dominance in world affairs. However reluctant the American government and people might have been to assume such a role, however mistrustful or ignorant they were of the many forces battering the planet, however much they might yearn for a cooperative and balanced postwar world order, they could not evade the brute fact in August 1945 of their sudden acquisition of overwhelming global power and influence through their singular possession of atomic weaponry. Nor could they dismiss the frightening possibility that their newly acquired position might soon draw upon themselves and their actions all of the suspicions and malice that a torn and bleeding and exhausted world could bring to bear.

But in the final analysis the Americans had no one but themselves to blame for the awful predicament in which they were fixed at the close of the Second World War. Filled with the wrathful conviction that Japan must be humbled and the pathetic hope that the Russians could somehow be induced to conform, Truman and those he led pursued a policy of such demonic ferocity toward the former that they inevitably frightened and alienated the latter. At heart the Americans of 1945 believed—as they all too frequently have since—that peace can be bought by force, that stability can be achieved through violence, and that the democratic millenium, surely one of the noblest aspirations of the human spirit, can be imposed through the enormous expenditure of blood and treasure.

Across the gulf of a quarter century we can see what those at the time refused to accept. Japan was clearly defeated in every way save formal surrender by the end of July 1945, if not a month earlier. Continually bombed and blockaded as she was, she simply could not have continued the war beyond mid-autumn. There was no need for an invasion. There was no need to drop the atomic bombs. But in its passionate quest for victory the American government refused to rise above wartime emotionalism and the momentum of unrestrained militarism to consider realistically or humanely the plight of Japan. The burden of moral stigma which the United States has had to bear for this failure has been immense.

With respect to Russia, the tragedy of the atomic decision was even more profound. Truman and Stimson, Hopkins and Marshall —the four who most truly shaped American foreign policy in the months between Roosevelt's death and the end of the war—sacrificed so much in their determined quest for peace, and it all went for naught. To preserve formal Soviet allegiance, if not warm Russian good will, they had with fair consistency pursued a policy of enlightened self-restraint. In the process they practically surrendered all of what American influence there might have been in Eastern Europe and opened the way for a substantial expansion of Moscow's power in Northeast Asia. At all times they were prepared to sacrifice British interests upon the altar of Soviet-American friendship.

Prior to Hiroshima, it can be argued, this policy was not only workable, but legitimate. The glittering promise of a peaceful and rapidly rebuilding postwar world, stabilized and protected by the harmonious alliance of the Red Army and the United States Navy and Air Force, was—and remains—an alluring image. But whatever faint hope existed for such a development—and exist it did on August 5, 1945—was shattered by the atomic bomb. For not only was the bomb in itself a terrible weapon of horrifying dimensions, but its sudden use revealed a disturbing trait in the American character. The United States would seemingly throw self-restraint to the winds and would employ unlimited power in an unrestrained fashion to achieve its primary objectives. Throughout the spring and summer of 1945 those objectives had always centered around the defeat of Japan. But with victory achieved, where else might America's vital national interests become fixed? These were the fearful questions which Moscow's apprehensive citizenry and the ruthless men in the Kremlin dared not ignore in the first days and weeks of the atomic age.

There are some who contend that while the American leadership capitulated to the attractions of unlimited power in August of 1945, the American people did not. They remained, after all, ignorant of the atomic secret until the dreadful genie was let out of the bottle over Japan. And ignorance, it is implied, is the essence of innocence.[21] But in retrospect it is impossible to succumb to what Samuel Lubell years ago called "the myth of the blameless public."[22] Even the most cursory examination of popular attitudes in the United States during World War II indicates how faithfully those in power acted as the agents of those whom they led. It may well be that substantial segments of the population were able to maintain a quiet balance of outlook. Very possibly there were many thousands who, despite Pearl Harbor, the Bataan death march, and the flood of wartime propaganda, stubbornly refused to believe that all Japanese of whatever age or sex were barbarians or similarly that all or any Russians were filled with vibrant democratic impulses simply because Hitler had also turned on them. But the fact remains that these people did not raise their voices in substantial numbers, did not seek to create an alternative and rational mode of thinking to what can only be described as wartime hysteria. That hysteria was at the very least accepted and at the very most ardently embraced. It became the formal national creed, and it culminated in an act of nearly unimaginable monstrosity. It should not be forgotten that the Americans who in August of 1945 expressed sudden revulsion over Hiroshima and Nagasaki had not spoken out in appreciable numbers against the equally hideous fire bomb raids upon Tokyo and other Japanese cities which had been fully reported in the press. The historian may be permitted to wonder whether the fierce reaction to Hiroshima on the part of many was not due in large measure to the dimly perceived possibility that the bomb might some day be employed against the United States. Certainly in

[21] Cf. for example, Gar Alperovitz, "Perspective and Prospect," in *Cold War Essays* (New York: Anchor Books, 1970), pp. 75–121, and, in the same vein, Gabriel Kolko's remark that "In the conduct of wartime grand diplomacy the people of all the major nations were the objects of worried attention, manipulation and, in many cases, physical restraint, but nowhere were they consulted on the contours of the policy of any state" (*Politics of War*, p. vii). While it is true that no national referenda were held on foreign policy in the United States, public opinion definitely defined the limits in which statesmen and diplomats worked and acted, as the evidence in the preceding pages amply testifies.

[22] Samuel Lubell, *The Revolt of the Moderates* (New York: Harper & Brothers, 1956), p. 15.

his first, fiercely exultant reaction to Hiroshima Harry Truman was in many ways more honest than many of those he led.

It was not immediately clear in August of 1945 that the atomic bomb would soon create an almost unbridgeable chasm between East and West. As Clark Kerr noted in his dispatch, the "disappointment" of the Russian people at the time "was tempered by the belief inspired by such echoes of the foreign press as were allowed to reach them that their Western comrades in arms would surely share the bomb with them. That some such expectation as this was shared by the Kremlin became evident in due course."[23]

But such was not to be. It was not in the mind of Harry Truman nor in the tradition and temperament of the mistrustful and divided people whom he governed to share or surrender real power. "Power must remain in the hands of those who hate power," Forrestal had sententiously remarked to the American United Nations delegation at San Francisco, and for once the Navy Secretary bespoke the sentiments of nearly all of his fellow citizens. But did the Americans in 1945 possess the requisite knowledge, maturity, and generosity to use their newly found power wisely or well? Could they heal their own internal divisions and resolve the problems of their own economic and emotional reconversion from war to peace with sufficient equanimity as to face the international problems of the early postwar period—including the atom—with a decent sense of purpose? The history of the Republic during the first increasingly unhappy months of peace provided only discouraging answers. But that is a melancholy tale whose telling awaits another time and another place.

[23] *Foreign Relations, 1945; Diplomatic Papers*, III: 84.

★

_____

A Note on Sources

Having already indulged myself in what Carl Briden-
baugh once aptly called "a paroxysm of citation," I shall not tax
the reader's indulgence further with an extended bibliographic essay. The following comments are intended for those who may wish
to know the major sources from which this study was written.

In all some thirty manuscript collections were consulted, in addition to the extensive published records of the State Department
for this period, supplemented by the memoirs and published private papers of leading participants. The manuscript collections
which provide the closest illumination of the day-to-day unfolding
of policy-making in the early Truman administration are: the Harry
S. Truman Papers, both the Office and Personal Papers files plus
the small but vitally important collection entitled "Harry S. Truman Papers Not Part of the White House File," the papers of Will
Clayton, Ellen Clayton Garwood, George M. Elsey, Frank Mc-
Naughton, and Samuel I. Rosenman, all in the Harry S. Truman
Library in Independence, Missouri. Less important but still significant collections for this period which may be found at the Truman
Library include the papers of Clinton P. Anderson, John W. Gibson, and the Sidney Shallet-Alben Barkley Oral History papers.

Collections at other libraries which yielded factual and interpretive data of the greatest importance include the Henry L. Stimson Papers at the Sterling Memorial Library, Yale University; the Harold D. Smith Papers, housed in the Franklin D. Roosevelt Library; the Arthur M. Vandenberg Papers at the William L. Clements Library, University of Michigan; the Lewis Schwellenbach, Tom Connally, and William D. Leahy Papers, all of which are in the Library of Congress; and the Kenneth S. Wherry Papers at the Nebraska State Historical Society, Lincoln. The James F. Byrnes Papers of the Robert Muldrow Cooper Library, Clemson University, have been greatly augmented by the May 1970 release by Mr. Byrnes of thousands of documents dealing with his public career during the nineteen-forties. This collection has thus become a prime source for the study of the war and immediate postwar period both at home and abroad.

On January 21, 1972, the State Department formally declassified all of its records for the year 1945, thus closely following similar action taken by the British government in declassifying all of its World War II documents (State Department Press Release number 19, January 21, 1972). Historians now have free access to immense and richly detailed diplomatic manuscripts residing in the National Archives. These collections are of indispensible aid to the diligent scholar of the war and immediate postwar period. I make no pretense of having examined all of the existing files, but I have gone through the most important of them with, I hope, sufficient care.

The single most important collection of cables, messages, and conversations dealing with American views of the Grand Alliance and its efforts to forge a lasting peace in the final year of the war are to be found in Lot File F-96, comprising the Moscow Embassy Collection. Here may be found, in addition to all of the cables to and from the Department in Washington, most of which have been published, a number of messages between the British Foreign Office and its embassies in Eastern Europe, which were subsequently passed on to the American government, plus valuable summaries of the current Soviet press. This file also contains the complete American minutes of the ill-fated Polish Commission meetings during the spring of 1945, as well as a number of messages of minor importance which were understandably excluded from the *Foreign Relations* series.

The China (Chungking) Diplomatic Post Records, Record Group 84, also contain some unpublished materials of great value covering Sino-Soviet relations during the last nine months of the war (710 Series) and also American observations of and reactions to Chinese Nationalist-Chinese Communist relations during the same period (800 Series).

Among the more valuable Decimal Files which yielded some pertinent information across the entire spectrum of Allied relations during this period are the 740 E.W. and Control Series, dealing with European reparations problems, surrender procedures, and postwar occupation policies in Germany, Italy, and Eastern Europe; the 840.24 Series, dealing with equipment and supply problems among the European Allies, including some material on lend-lease; the 711.51 and 711.61 Files, covering certain aspects of Franco-American and Soviet-American relations, respectively; and the 861.24 File, which contains documents relating to American aid to Russia. For the Far East, I have consulted the 893.00 File (Internal Political Affairs, China), which contains many of the same documents found in the China Diplomatic Post Records; and the 893.20 File (Internal Military Affairs, China), in which may be found a few valuable documents which have not been published.

The overwhelming majority of important American diplomatic documents for 1945 have, of course, now been published in the recently completed *Foreign Relations* series for that year, compiled by Historical Office of the Department of State. This series, comprising in all twelve, heavy volumes, contains nearly all of the primary materials necessary for any reasoned exploration and judgment of American diplomacy at the end of World War II, and the responsible scholar can begin his researches into the period with this series, confident in the knowledge that subsequent digging in the State Department's unpublished manuscripts will be supplementary and will yield at best tangentially important information.

The United States Department of State *Bulletin*, released weekly by the Department since the nineteen-thirties, is also an extremely valuable source of published contemporary information on the history of American foreign policy at any given moment over the past four decades. It often contains important studies of current problems, plus correspondence between ranking members of the Department and leading public officials and private citizens, in addition to official Department press releases and the formal texts of important treaties and agreements.

Finally, four published government documents which are of central importance in any study of this period are: U.S. Department of Defense, *The Entry of the Soviet Union into the War Against Japan; Military Plans, 1941–45* (Washington, 1955), a mimeographed copy of which may be found in the Harry S. Truman Library; the United States Senate, Committees on Armed Services and Foreign Relations, *Hearings; Military Situation in the Far East*, May, June, August, 1951; the United States Strategic Bombing Survey, *Japan's Struggle to End the War* (Washington, July 1, 1946); and *Public Papers of the President of the United States; Harry S. Truman, April 12–December 31, 1945* (Washington: U.S. Government Printing Office, 1961).

The several hundred books and articles containing primary and secondary materials which I have used and which often shed strong, if not always clear, light on this era are well known to most interested students of the period and many laymen as well. Their citation and frequence of utilization in the text is, I think, sufficient recognition of their worth.

Index

Acheson, Sec. of State Dean G., 15, 331-32; quoted, 247
Adriatic Sea, 120, 152
AEF, 86
Agrarian Party, 248
Alamogordo, N.M., 217, 267, 306-308, 311, 313, 316, 332, 335-36, 351, 357, 359
Alanbrooke, Lord, 307
Alexander, Field Marshal Sir Harold R.L.G. (Supreme Allied Commander in Mediterranean), 116, 120-23, 125
Allen, George, 255
Allies, 16, 119, 246, 248, 314-15; and problems in France, 2; and conflict with Tito, 120-26; and occupation of Japan, 201; and German fleets, 288; and warning to Japanese, 239; and troop withdrawal from Iran, 302; concept of Emperor's role, 313
Allied Military Command, 114-15
Allied Control Commission, 296-98
Alperovitz, Dr. Gar, 185-215
Amalgamated Clothing Workers, 38
American Embassy in Spaso House, 94
America First Party, 61-62

American Friends of Polish Democracy, 52
Amoy, 222
Amur River, 133-34; B-29 base project, abandonment of, 140
Anami, War Minister, 210
Anderson, Sherwood, 43
Anglo-American International Petroleum Commission, 81
Anglo-American oil agreement (1944), 81
Anglo-American-Soviet Control Commissions, 106
Anti-imperialism in U.S., 62, 64-65, 69, 82
Antonov, Gen., 140; and Soviet pledge to withdraw troops from Manchuria, 348
Anzac Pact, 344
Arabian-American Oil Company, 80
Ardennes, 221
Argentina, 171-72; demands for inclusion of in U.N., 178-79
Ariake Wan, 223
Arnold, General Henry H. "Hap," 212, 225, 329

Article VII, 68-69
Asia: and American interests, 12
Atlantic Charter, 44, 61, 68, 108, 229
Atomic bomb, 140, 142-45, 149, 158, 159, 160, 187-88, 215, 235-36, 237, 239, 329, 359; use of, 152, 214-15, 242, 262-63, 334-36, 365-66; control of, 147; and East-West relations, 157, 368; military and diplomatic implications of, 159, 218, 306, perfection and use of, 162; and Japanese decision to end war, 206; and Japanese strategic thinking, 210; and foreign policy, 214, 355; and bargaining with Stalin, 216; and Russian spying on, 217; workability of, 217, 322, 335, 355; and Kyushu invasion, 228; and effects on Japanese, 237; and Truman's decision to use, 240-41, 403, 318, 329; test of, 243, 305, 308, 350; and impact on Soviets, 263-69, 313, 316, 360-61; international impact of, 263-64; and possible armament race, 263-64, 268; and disclosure of to Soviets, 263, 306, 351, 353-54; and estimates of destructive power, 267, 338; and TNT yield, 306; and dates for strike, 347; and disclosure of to Stalin, 351-52; and Britain's knowledge of, 354; and plans for third drop, 360; and public opinion in U.S.S.R., 360-62; in America, 362-64
"Atomic diplomacy," 142, 158-59, 217; atomic monopoly, x
Atlee, Prime Minister Clement Richard: at Potsdam, 270, 273, 283-84, 294-95, 316; wins in British general election, 283; and Spain, 285; and suspicions of Russian objectives at Potsdam, 296; and sharing of atomic secrets, 353
Augusta, 317-18, 330-31, 359
Automotive Council, 39
Australia, 175; and Anzac Pact, 344
Austria, 168; English occupation zone in, 120
Axis, 280

B-29's, 212
Balance of power, 5
Baldwin, Hanson: quoted, 358, 362

Baltic Republic, 7; and Russian occupation, 13
Bancor, 70
Bard, Ralph, 263
Barkley, Vice-President Alben W., 216, 255, 259
Barnes, Maynard, 248, 249
Bataan, 139, 227, 367; and demands for retribution for, 221
Bavaria, 167
Battle of Britain, 3
Battle of Japan, 334, 337, 347
Balkans, 30, 173, 249; and Britain's renunciation of influence in, 11; political problems in, 121-23; and secondary Western thrust in Europe, 166; and admission to U.N., 296, 297
Beaverbrook, Lord William M.A., 4
Belgrade, 124
Berne: American mission in, 9
Beveridge plan, 3
Bevin, Foreign Minister Ernest, 284; at Potsdam, 273, 283, 284, 295; wins in British general election, 283; compared to Churchill, 284; and Spain, 285; and issue of Polish border, 294; and Potsdam, 296
Berlin, 1, 6, 10, 166-67, 169, 220, 244, 306; and Soviet offensive against, 167; and control over, 169; devastation of, 286
Berlin Conference. *See* Potsdam Conference.
Bidault, Foreign Minister Georges, 114-17, 119
Big Three Alliance, 12, 35, 163, 166, 169, 171, 180, 216, 246, 270, 277, 280, 283, 290-91, 296, 319, 349; and separate peace agreement, 92-93; and French occupation zone, 114; Churchill's plea for early meeting of, 183; and unity in Pacific War, 200; agreements of, 248; meeting of, 249; and end of peace in, 270-71; at Yalta, 275; wartime relations, 303
Black Sea, 300-301
Bohlen, Charles E., 100, 151, 182-86, 193, 310, 351
Bohr, Niels, 148
Bradley, Gen. Omar, 221
Brenner Pass, 125

Bretton Woods Conference, 68-70, 216; and IMF, 74

Bridges, Mr., 307

Britain, 250; postwar economy of, 3, 60, 68; decline in power of, 3, 360; and naval power, 4; morale after W.W. II, 4; refusal to recognize Soviet occupation, 8; and Elbe, 20; and aspirations in Europe and Asia, 20, 343; U.S. postwar association with, 48; and trade with China, 54; oil holdings in Middle East, 62-63, 80; postwar aid to, 70; and debts to U.S., 71; and imperialism, 82; and recognition of Syrian and Lebanese independence, 118; army of, 118-19; in Middle East, 120; and Lend-Lease, 189, 192, 347; and deteriorating position in Grand Alliance, 199; and atomic secret, 242-43, 353; and Polish issue, 274; and Four Power Alliance, 276; and occupation of Germany, 298; fears U.S.S.R. power expansion, 299; and troops in Iran, 302; and sacrifice of interests in Eastern Europe, 307; and colonial power in Far East, 340; foreign policy in China, 343-44; and opposition to Chinese Communists, 344; and support of Chinese National govt., 344; as obstacle to American diplomatic objectives in Far East, 344; and Pacific War strategy, 345, 347; interests of, 366

Brown, Walter, 317

Bryan, William Jennings, 252

Bulgaria, 106, 280, 296; Soviet-dominated gov't in, 199; allied armistice agreement with, 248; and U.N. membership, 283

Bulgarian Control Commission, 248

British Empire, 48, 63, 344; and American resentment of, 60-61

Bucharest: Control Commission in, 248

Budapest, Control Commission in, 248

Bundy, Harvey, 145, 147, 148

Burgess, Randolph, 74

Burma, 230

Burma Road, 230

Bush, Vannevar, 147, 148, 263-64, 266, 268

Business Week: quoted, 253

Butow, Prof., 152-53

Byelorussia, 171

Byrd, Harry, 252

Byrnes, Secretary of State James F., 38, 85, 89-90, 215, 271-73; and relations with Truman, 182-83, 249, 252, 269; and Soviet demands on China, 235; and relations with Grew, 236; at Potsdam, 240, 243, 269, 281-83, 289, 292-93, 294-98, 304, 306, 308-12, 315-19, 327-29, 331-33, 340, 342-43, 348, 351, 356; and replacement of Stettinius, 244-45; biographical sketch of, 249-63; and relations with FDR, 256-57, 263; and mistrust of Soviets, 261; and atomic bomb, 263-67, 269, 335-36, 351, 355, 359; broker diplomacy of, 286; and question of German reparations, 292-93; relations with Davies, 294; relations with Molotov, 294; relations with Stalin, 295; and China, 313; and Potsdam Declaration, 329-31; and relations with Stimson, 329; and relations with MacLeish, 332; and fears of Russian thrust into China, 343; and Soviet pledge to withdraw troops from Manchuria, 348; and Japan's formal protest of Hiroshima raid, 364

Cadogan, Sir Alexander, 165

Caffery, Ambassador, 115, 117

Cairo Conference, 55

Canada, 344; living standard in during W.W.II, 3; and relationship to U.S. and Britain, 4-5; deployment of troops of, 346; and atomic secret, 353

Canton, 230

Capitalism, American, 63-65

Casablanca Conference, 9, 59

Casualties (of W.W.II): in Europe, 1; in Britain, 3; of U.S.S.R., 5; of projected Japanese mainland invasion, 25; American, 25; in Pacific War, 209; of Japan, 212; in Kyushu operation, 225; at Okinawa, 225

Cate, Prof., 329

Cecilienhof Palace, 270

C.E.D. *See* Committee for Economic Development.

Chapultepec Conference, 172

Chiang, Madame, 55-56

Chiang Kai-shek, 26-27, 34, 56-57, 128-

31, 133, 342; forced off mainland, 55; and Soviet break with, 132; and Chinese unification, 157; and Stalin's support of, 200; and Manchuria, 229-30; and Yalta agreements, 230, 232, 233, 234; and relations with Chinese Communists, 231; and relations with Truman, 311, 312

Chicago Convention of 1944, 256-58, 259

China, 34, 149, 175, 341; and Japanese pilot losses, 21; army of, 21, 26, 129; and American policy toward, 25-26, 53, 56, 83, 150, 159; control of, 26-27; military ability of, 26; inflation in, 27; Shensi province, 27; government corruption in, 27; efforts at reconciliation, 27-28; conflict between Kuomintang and Communist forces, 28; and trade relations with U.S., 53-54; public opinion toward, 55, 57, 60; U.S. response to, 127-28, 129; possibility of civil war in, 128, 129; coalition government in, 128, 129; and domination by Japan, 132; unification of, 133, 157; and American interests in, 134, 312, 313; and question of military aid to, 161; and U.N. trusteeships, 177-78; and Soviet intentions in, 182; and Yalta proposals, 200; and U.S. economic aid to, 200; invasion of, 222; war in, 230; and relations with U.S.S.R., 233-35; and Soviet demands on, 312, 315, 318-19, 342-43; and Soviet intervention in, 342; weakness of, 343

"China myth," 55-56

Chinese Communists, 57, 127-31, 139, 231; and U.S.S.R., 132, 342; and British opposition to, 344

Chinese Nationalist government, 342-43; and British support of, 344

Chou En-lai, 27

Chungking, China, 26, 129-31, 230-33, 311, 318

Churchill, Sir Winston, 5, 8, 9, 14-15, 33, 250, 337-38; and response to Beveridge Plan, 3; and talks with Molotov, 7; and relations with Stalin, 11, 34, 108-109, 287; at Second Quebec Conf., 17-18, 189; and Declaration on Liberated Europe, 30-31; at Yalta, 66, 153; and reaction to Truman's suc-

cession to the presidency, 85; and separate peace agreement, 92-93; and Polish issue, 96, 195-96; and sphere of influence in Eastern Europe, 108; and relations with Truman, 108-109, 113-14, 119-20, 166, 180, 195-96, 243, 330; and attitude toward de Gaulle, 113-14; and Val d'Aosta problem, 116; and Middle Eastern crisis with France, 118-19; conflict with Tito and Venezia Giulia situation, 121-23, 124, 125, 126; and support of U.S. China policy, 131; and briefing from Eden, 142-43; relations with Roosevelt, 143; and attempts to counter Soviet expansion in Europe, 164; and concern over Balkans, 165-67, 281; at Potsdam, 169, 192, 270, 273-74, 278, 281, 283, 288, 299, 300-302, 306-309, 321, 327, 330, 333, 351-52; and plea for early meeting of Big Three, 183; and relations with Davies, 183, 192-93, 197-99; and tough line against Russians, 186; compared to Bevin, 284; quoted, 288-89; and Dardanelles control, 300; and withdrawal of Allied troops from Iran, 302; and diplomatic possibilities of A-bomb, 306, 307; and relations with Stimson, 306; quoted, 308-309; and Lublin Poles, 312; and report to, 345; and invasion of Japan, 345; and disclosure of A-bomb secret to Russians, 351

Ciechanowski, Jan, 197

C.I.O., 39

C.I.O.: Political Atcion Committee of, 38, 255; demands at end of war, 40; and confrontation with big business, 40

Curzon Line, 7, 10-11, 97

Civil War (U.S.), 220

Clay, Mr. 309

Clayton, William L., 48-49, 54, 64, 67, 95, 263; and post-war planning, 76-78; opposition to U.S.S.R. loan, 77; and Congress, 78; and A-bomb secret, 267; at Potsdam, 283, 289-90; and relations with Byrnes, 294

Cohen, Benjamin, 316

Cold War, ix, x, 79, 141-42, 272-73, 319; efforts to prevent, 95; beginnings of, 271; and Potsdam, 303; and policy

of excluding Russians from A-bomb knowledge, 354

Colonialism: crumbling in Africa and Asia, xii; British, in Far East, 340; French, in Far East, 340, 343, 344

Combined British and American Policy Committee, 241-42

Combined Chiefs of Staff, responsibility of, 346

COMECON, 174

Comintern, 49

Committee for Economic Development, 67, 75n

Committee of National Liberation (Lublin Provisional Government), 10-11

Commonwealth: troops of, 346

Communism, 61; in China, 27

Communist Party, 109

Communists: forcing Chiang Kai-shek off mainland, 55; takeover in Rumania, 91-92; in Japan, 153-55, 206; curbing influence of in Far East, 156; in Hungary, Rumania, and Bulgaria, 248; in Bulgaria, 248, 249

Compton, Arthur Holly, 262, 264, 266-68

Compton, Karl T., 263-64

Conant, James, 147, 263-64, 266

Confederate Army, 220

Conference of Berlin. See Potsdam Conference.

Connally, Matt, 264

Connally, U.S. Senator Tom, 59, 89, 254, 259; and oil control treaty, 81, 82; discusses Truman's legislative record, 87

Constantinople, 301

Cooke, Vice Admiral, 150

Coolidge, President Calvin, 85

Corregidor, 139, 176, 221

Coward, Noel, 17

Council of Foreign Ministers, 278

Craven, Prof., 329

Crowley, Leo: and lend-lease policy, 188, 190

Czechoslovakia, 168; and penetration by Patton's army, 165; and Churchill's hopes for liberation, 166; and American drive into, 167

Dairen, 34, 217, 235, 309, 310; and Soviet military control over, 311; and Byrne's fear of Soviet thrust to, 343

Danube, 165, 300

Danube Valley, 164, 167

Danubian nations, 280-82, 284, 294; Soviet-American rapprochement over, 283

Dardanelles, 300, 302; and Soviet influence, 299, 309, 339

Darlan, 113

Davis, Elmer, 229

Davies, John, 129

Davies, Ambassador Joseph E., 46; and mission to London, 161; and discussion with Truman on Soviet-American relations, 183; and relations with Churchill, 183, 185, 188, 192-93, 197-99; and relations with Byrnes, 294

Deane, Maj. Gen. John, 93, 94, 102, 134-36, 139, 140, 148, 349; on Russia's entering Pacific War, 104; on need for U.S.S.R. military aid, 104

Declaration on Liberated Europe, 30, 32, 282; weaknesses of, 31; and violation of by U.S.S.R., 91

Deficit spending, 74-75

DeGaulle, Gen. Charles A.J.M., 2; difficulties in dealing with, 113; and relationship with FDR, 113; and treatment of by Anglo-Americans, 114; and exclusion from Yalta, 114; and possible annexation of Val d'Aosta, 115; and relationship with Truman, 117; and special rights in Syria and Lebanon, 118; and Middle Eastern crisis, 118-19

"Demaree Bess," 62, 63

Demilitarization of Germany, 14-19; of Japan, 60

Deming, Barbara, 43

Democracy, 43

Democratic National Committee, 47, 52

Democratic Party, 51, 254; and labor influences within, 38-39; divisions within, 41; makeup of, 252-53

Democrats, Southern, 38

De Tassigny, Gen., 114

Dimitrov, Georgi M., 248-49

Diplomacy: setback to, 285; American flexibility, 285-86; U.S. narrowing of after Potsdam, 297; and A-bomb, 306; American, in Far East, 341; and

China, 343, 344; with Soviets, 354, 355
Divine, Robert, 44
Doenitz, Adm. Karl, 170
Dollar gap, 71
Dominion Conference, 62
Duclos, Jacques, 109
Douglas, William O., 255
Dulles, John Foster, 61
Dumbarton Oaks, 158, 179, 260; and outlines for new League of Nations, 171, 172
Dunn, James, 332, 333
Dutch East Indies, 175

Eaker, Gen. Ira C., 224, 225
East Asia, 211; British power in, 64; Truman's policy toward, 26; and American interests in, 304
Eastern Europe, 7, 182, 268, 280, 310, 354; and American disinterest in, 12, 13, 283; and foreign policy regarding, 90; Churchill-Stalin agreement on, 107; and Soviet conduct in, 113, 188; as a base to expand Russian power, 151; and American penetration into, 167; and withdrawal of American forces from, 169; and Truman's refusal to maintain troops in, 180; American influence in, 184; Truman's attitude toward, 199; U.S. interests in, 215, 366; crises in, 261; and U.S. foreign policy, 274-75; and Soviet influence, 276-77, 298; American involvement in, 282; and Italian reparations negotiations, 285; British interests in, 307; and Soviet interests in, 339
East Prussia, 16, 19
East-West relations, 134, 141, 142, 171, 355; deterioration in, 134; and A-bomb, 157, 365, 368; reduction of tension in, 180, 265; and conflict over Poland, 187; and Potsdam Conf., 274
Economic policy: of Clayton, 76-78
Economy: British postwar, 62-63; U.S. postwar, 67-69
Eden, Prime Minister (Robert) Anthony, 98, 101, 284; 1941 visit to Moscow, 7; and Cairo Conference, 55; and talks with Mikolajczyk, 96-97; and Molotov, 107; and attitude toward Tito, 125; supports U.S. China policy, 131; briefed by Marshall, 142; relationship with Churchill, 142-43; and liberation of Prague, 165-66; and Hopkins mission, 192-93; relations with Davies, 193; and relations with Stimson, 217; and Russian reparations, 287; attitude towards A-bomb, 335
Edwards, Adm., 150
Eisenhower, Gen. Dwight D., 244; and evacuation of Stuttgart, 114-15; in European campaign, 165, 221; relationship with Stalin, 167; and E. European penetration, 168; transportation of command, 212-13; and military tradition, 220; and Truman, 317
Elbe region: and British-U.S.S.R. relations, 20
Elbe River, 14, 199, 282
Emperor of Japan. *See* Hirohito.
Enola Gay, 358
Europe, revived economy of, xi; war destruction in, 1; mood of, 2; balance of power in, 5; and Yalta Conference, 30; American occupation of, 32; war in, 44; disturbing events in, 113; victory in, 164; invasion of, 201; American interests in, 317; Soviet behavior in, 321; British and French aspirations in, 343
European Advisory Commission, 14
European Advisory Committee, 15
Evatt, Dr., 179

Far East, 35, 58; and Soviet intervention in, 25, 151, 277; war in, 59; Yalta agreements on, 88, 133; settlement in, 234; and Soviet demands for concessions in, 310, 311; and colonial influence in, 340; and British and French aspirations in, 343; British and American policy in, 343-44
Farley, James A., 252
Fatherland Front, 248
FDR. *See* Roosevelt, President Franklin D.
Feis, Herbert, 80; quoted, 270; and Truman's A-bomb warning to Stalin, 352
Fermi, Enrico, 264

Filipinos, 58
Films: and wartime emotionalism, 43-44
Finland, 7; and U.N. membership, 283
Fire bombing: against Japan, 21, 22, 187
Fleming, Lamar: quoted, 48-49
Flynn, Ed, 255
Foreign aid, postwar, 65
Foreign policy, American, during W.W. II, xii, 65; American toward Japan, 60; U.S. toward Britain, 60-61; U.S. against imperialism, 62-63; toward U.S.S.R., 96, 133, 308; in Middle East, 119; toward China, 130-31, 150, 311, 343-44; and Lend-Lease, 190-91; and E. Europe, 274-75; toward postwar Germany, 290-91; toward East Asia, 308; and Far East, 150-51, 340-42; and A-bomb, 355
Foreign trade, 65, 67
Forrestal, Secretary of the Navy James V., 90, 95, 102-103, 137, 144, 157, 162, 202, 222, 229, 250, 273, 303, 313, 326-27, 340; and suspicions about U.S.S.R., 149; and conference with Harriman, 150; and Soviet entry into Pacific War, 161; and skepticism over trusteeship approach, 175-76; and plans for invasion of Japan, 226-27, 237, 239; and relationship with Byrnes, 309; quoted, 310, 368; at Potsdam, 343
Fortune, 46; quoted, 58-60
France, 21, 70, 221, 250; mood of after W.W.II, 2; and Saar Valley, 16; army of, 21, 115, 117; and trade with China, 54; influence of, 114; and occupation of Germany, 114, 290, 298; and passive resistance to American troops, 115; and Anglo-American relations with, 116; demands on Germany, 116; and Val d'Aosta, 116; and secondary Western thrust in, 166; and treaty with U.S.S.R., 174; and U.N. trusteeships, 177; and Four Power Alliance, 276; and colonial power in Far East, 340; and aspirations in Europe and Asia, 343; and foreign policy in Far East, 344
Franck Committee, 262
Franck, James, 262, 264
Franco, 283

"Free French" forces, 113
Fuchs, Klaus, 316

Garwood, Ellen: quoted, 76
Gauss, Ambassador, 128
Germany, 1; defeat of, 5, 20-21; 206, 220, 286; withdrawal from Poland, 11; and reparations, 14, 18, 66-67, 286-88, 291; control of economy, 15; European Advisory Committee's postwar plans for, 15; Morgenthau's postwar plan for, 16-17; Yalta Conference plans for, 19; public opinion against, 44, 59, 83; and trade with China, 54; surrender of 92, 188; operations against, 115; French demands on, 116; and Russian advances into, 139; and Eisenhower's strategy for victory over, 166; and Lend-Lease, 188; and counteroffensive in the Ardennes, 221; postwar plans for, 246; and demilitarization of, 276; problem over, 286; rehabilitation of, 286, 299; navy of, divided as reparations, 287-88; borders of, 289; and postwar recovery, 289-90, 292; and U.S. postwar policy toward, 290-91; postwar treatment of, 291-93; economic recovery of, 292; and U.S. postwar policy toward, 290-91; postwar treatment of, 291-93; economic recovery of, 292; and Soviet reparation demands, 294-95; Soviet actions in, 315; war strategy against, 338
Germany, occupation of, 15, 30, 164, 180, 277, 289, 298; by U.S.S.R., x, 295-96, 298; by France, 290, 298; by Poland, 290, 296; by Yugoslavia, 290
Gibraltar: and Soviet probe toward, 299
Glass, Carter, 252
G.O.P. *See* Republican Party.
Grand Alliance, xii, 2, 4, 12, 21, 36, 52-53, 216, 268, 270, 275-76, 303, 356, 360; dissension in, 7, 10, 91, 121; and deteriorating position of Britain, 199; and Japanese efforts to destroy, 207, 211; survival of, 221; demands of, 247; perpetuation of, 297, 307
Grant, Gen. U.S., 220

Great Depression, 37, 40-42, 65
Great Oil Scare, 79
"Great War," 86
Greece, 30; Communist roles in, 11;
  Churchill-Stalin meeting and agreement on, 107; as bargaining point on
  Poland, 108
Grew, Joseph C., 59-60, 115, 119, 121-
  24, 148-49, 158-59, 225, 167, 186,
  199, 250; report to Truman, 106;
  submits memorandum on Bulgaria,
  107; and alarm at Soviet actions since
  Yalta, 151; and Soviet entry into Pacific War, 156-57, 161, 238; and skepticism of Soviets, 162; and Soviet
  relations, 182, 268-69, 275; and Big
  Three meeting, 185; and Lend-Lease,
  188, 190-91; and Polish issue, 197-
  98, 249; and modification of unconditional surrender of Japan, 214, 226,
  236; and Chinese relations, 231-32,
  234; and relations with Byrnes, 236,
  333; and plans for invasion of Japan,
  237, 239; and Potsdam Declaration,
  331-32
Gromyko, Andrei A., 174; and trusteeship program, 178
Groves, Gen. Leslie R., 144, 262, 266,
  308, 336, 351, 356; and report on
  Manhattan Project, 145-46; and combat worthiness of A-bomb, 335;
  quoted, 335, 336, 360
Groza, Petru, 91
Guadacanal, 241

Hackworth, Green, 332
Halifax, Lord, 242
Halsey, Adm. William F., 211
Hannegan, Robert, 254-59
Harriman, W. Averell, 9, 12, 30*n*, 50,
  64, 101, 132, 136, 158-59, 183-84,
  202, 233, 309-10, 343; and U.S.S.R.
  aid in the Pacific, 28; and relations
  with U.S.S.R., 29, 162, 268-69; and
  issue of separate peace agreements,
  93; and Polish issue, 94-95, 97-98,
  104; and views on Yalta Conference,
  98*n*; and Truman, 100, 104, 185-87,
  192-93, 199; attitude toward Soviet
  control of E. Europe, 100; and fear
  of Soviet intentions in China, 130,
  182; and warning to State Dept., 139;

and conference with Forrestal, 150;
  and demand for statement on Far East
  policy, 150-51; and memorandum
  from Grew, 151; and American aims
  in Asia, 155; concern over Soviet
  policies, 157; and China settlement,
  234-35; at Potsdam, 273, 338-39
Harrison, George L., 147-48, 263, 308,
  329, 357
Harrison, Pat, 253
Helsinki: American mission in, 9
Highhold, 236, 238
Hillman, Sidney, 38, 255
Hiroshima, xi, 142, 152, 322, 333, 347,
  360-62, 364, 366-68; atomic strike
  on, 335-36, 356, 359, 360; delay of
  raid on, 358; Tokyo's formal protest
  of raid, 364
Hirohito, 23, 152-53, 154, 155, 156,
  205-207, 210-11, 235, 239, 324, 332;
  retention of, 240-41, 319, 329; and
  role in Japan, 313, 314; and end of
  war, 323
Hirota, 207
Hitler, Adolf, 3, 16, 19, 220, 310, 367
Hodge, Gen., 149
Hoffman, Paul, 67
Hong Kong, 151, 230, 299
Honshu, 208, 210, 222, 225, 347, 349
Hoover, Pres. Herbert H., 129
Hopkins, Harry L., 4, 20, 35, 88, 90,
  97, 254, 356, 366; and relations with
  Stalin, 157, 221, 229-32, 234-35, 359-
  60; and Moscow mission, 180-88,
  191-202, 217, 245-46, 249, 275, 327,
  349; and relations with Truman, 231-
  32
House Banking Committee, 66; and
  IMF, 75
Hull, Secretary of State Cordell, 18,
  25-26, 50, 61, 183, 245, 247, 250;
  and discussion with Stalin, 29; and
  negotiations over IMF, 88; and reduction of role in gov't decisions,
  246; and Potsdam Declaration, 332,
  333
"Hundred Million Die Together," 154
Hungary, 280, 296; Soviet-dominated
  gov't in, 199; and Allied Armistice
  agreement with, 248; and U.N. membership, 283
Hurley, Ambassador Patrick J., 28*n*,

129-33, 232, 312; and China policy, 28, 234; and relations with Stalin, 140, 230
Hyde Park, 182, 261

Ibn Saud, 80
IBRD. *See* International Bank for Reconstruction and Development.
Ickes, Harold, 80
IMF. *See* International Monetary Fund.
Imperialism: moral imperialism, 44; British, 60-62; USSR charged with, 156
India, 299; deployment of troops of, 345-46
Indo-China, xi, 159; and self-government of, 344
Infantry Journal, 223-24; quoted, 224
Inflation, 27
Interim Committee, 263, 264, 268
International Bank for Reconstruction and Development (IBRD), 75, 75*n*
International central bank, 70
International Clearing Union, 70-71, 72; voting rights in, 71-72; U.S. reaction to, 72; cf. to IMF, 78
International Monetary Fund, 66, 72-73; organization of, 72-73; assessment of, 73-74; Congress distrust of, 76; compared to Int'l Clearing Union, 78; Hull's queries about, 88
International trade, 73; in U.S. postwar economy, 76
Inouye, Masutaro, 155, 156
Iran, 79; troops withdrawn from, 302
Isaacs, Harold R., 27
Isolationism, 48
Istrian region. *See* Venezia Giulia
Italy, 70, 284, 285, 294; government of, 115; and Yugoslav territorial conflicts, 116; French forces in, 117; and dispute over Venezia Giulia, 120; and Soviet reparations demands, 279-80, 284; postwar treatment of, 281; and rehabilitation of, 282; entry into U.N., 283, 296, 297; Soviet-American rapprochement over, 283; Stalin's attitude toward, 284
Italian North African colonies, 299, 309, 339
Italian peace treaty, 285

Iwo Jima, 135, 209, 238; U.S. capture of, 21

Japan, atomic attack on, x, 143-47, 148, 149, 218, 241-42, 314-15, 334-36, 356-59, 365-66; revived economy of, xi; war casualties of, 21, 212; army of, 21, 138, 204-205, 207, 209, 222-23; civilian life in, 22; fire-bombing raids against, 22, 187; attitude toward continuation of war, 22-23; police state nature of, 23; attitude of Japanese militarists, 23; and control of China, 26-27, 34, 53, 132; surrender of, 33, 149, 235, 359, 364; war against, 35, 59, 134, 168, 188-89, 211-12; public opinion toward, 44, 57-60, 82-83; and trade with China, 54; peace with, 59-60, 151-53, 201, 210, 236; occupation of, 60, 219, 272-73, 332; and war in China, 128; blockade of, 137, 222; invasion of, 138, 140, 149, 158, 162, 204-43, 345; and aid to Third Reich, 138; air force of, 139, 222; navy of, 139, 154, 211-12, 221-22; strength of, 139, 213, 221-22; and unconditional surrender, 150, 153, 222, 236-37, 313, 315, 326-27, 329, 332, 360; attitude toward U.S.S.R., 153, 157; and war with U.S.S.R., 158; and postwar U.S. sphere of military influence, 175; defeat of, 202-203, 246; and efforts to bribe U.S.S.R., 206-207, 211; and attempts to destroy Grand Alliance, 207; preparations to meet American assault, 208-10; bombing of, 209, 212; and diplomacy with U.S.S.R., 222, 322-24, 325-27, 328, 334; warning to, 238-41; and U.S.S.R.'s demands on, 315; war damage of, 324-25
Jewish Council, 47
Jews: and pro-Soviet movement, 47
Joint Chiefs of Staff, 29, 136, 138, 139, 140, 141, 142, 218, 222, 237, 337, 338, 349; and consideration of E. European penetration, 167; and Kyushu operation, 227; and response to Churchill's report, 345-46
Joint State-War-Navy Coordinating Committee, 246

Juin, Gen., 117
JCS 1067, 19

Kagoshima, 223
Kamikazes, 139; and Okinawa invasion, 24
Karlsbad, 165
Katyn Forest massacre, 52
Kelly, Mayor (of Chicago), 255
Kennan, George F., 131-33, 343; memo on Stalin-Hurley conversations, 140; fears Soviet intentions in China, 182
Kerr, Sir Archibald Clark: quoted, 361-62, 368
Kesselring, Marshal, 93
Keynes, Lord John Maynard, 70-71, 74; plan for postwar reconstruction, 70-72
Kido, Marquis, 210, 211
King, Adm. Ernest J., 225, 229, 348-49; quoted, 337
King, George, 359
Kirk, Ambassador: on troop withdrawal from Europe. 109-10
Kolko, Gabriel, 63
Komsomolsk-Nikolaevsk region, 133
Konoye, Prince, 153-54, 155, 156, 211; and proposed mission to Moscow, 324-25, 327, 328
Korea, xi, 222, 223, 341; American invasion of, 138; and U.N. trusteeship, 157, 200
Korean War, x
Kremlin, 46, 64, 129
Krock, Arthur: Truman's interview with, 271, 272
Kuomintang National Government, 26, 56, 57, 128, 129, 131, 133, 230, 235, 312, 342; U.S. attitude toward, 27; and reconciliation with Mao Tse-tung, 27-28
Kuomintang China: near collapse of, 127. *See also* China.
Kuomintang government, 129
Kurile Islands, 34, 35, 157, 234
Kuwait, 80
Kuznetzov, 348
Kwantung Army, 141
Kyushu, 139, 140, 155, 222, 349; invasion of, 140, 208, 213, 214, 219, 222-23, 224, 225, 226, 227, 228, 229, 236, 339, 345

Kyushu operations: reasons for decision about, 140-42; American casualties in, 225

Labor, 38; and influence within the Democratic Party, 39; militancy of, 40
Lane, Arthur Bliss, 249, 269
Latin America, x, 171, 172, 254
Latin Americans: postwar treaty with, 173; inclusion of Argentina in U.N., 178-79
Laval, Pierre, 113
Lawrence, Ernest O., 264
Leahy, Adm. William D., 32, 35, 102, 117, 123, 132, 165, 185, 186, 193, 225, 227, 272-73, 279, 309, 315, 316, 319, 337, 346; attitude toward peacetime Lend-Lease, 76; and impressions of Yalta Conference, 103; on Polish question, 105; and A-bomb project, 187, 217, 335; and occupation of Japan, 219; quoted, 271, 348; and Potsdam, 343
Lebanon, crisis in, 118
Lee, Gen. Robert E., 220
Leipzig, 167
Le May, Gen. Curtis, 212
Lend-Lease, to U.S.S.R., 6, 192; agreements on, 68, 69; peace-time use of, 75-76; and curtailment of after V-E Day, 188; to Britain, 189, 192, 347; statement of U.S. policy, 191; cessation of, 271
Lenin, 361
Levantine area, 118-19
Light industry, of Japan, 22
Lilienthal, David, 48, 85, 89, 162; and Truman, 112
Lippman, Walter, quoted, 25n, 274
Lewis, John L., 39
Leyte, 211
Life magazine, 56
Lincoln, Gen. George A., 136
Lindley, Ernest K., 60
London Poles, 10, 12, 96-97, 194, 197
Low countries, 21
Lozovsky, 324
Lubell, Samuel: quoted, 367
Lublin government, 31-32, 52, 94, 96, 97, 100, 195, 312; agreement with U.S.S.R., 105; and San Francisco Conference, 105; Stalin's support of, 107

Luzon, 225
Lyons, Eugene, 51

MacArthur, Gen. Douglas, 222, 337; and views concerning Soviet entry into Pacific War, 136, 137; and Pacific strategy, 138, 139; and FDR, 257; reacts to British plans, 346
MacLeish, Archibald, 24, 244; quoted, 331
Malaya: and Mountbatten's responsibility for, 345
Malik, Ambassador Jacob, 207
Manchuria, 28, 132, 159, 217, 229-30, 309-10, 313; Japanese forces in, 34, 137, 223; and Soviet entry into, 135, 141, 347, 350; return of, to China, 157; Cezar's concessions in, 232; and Soviet interest in, 235; and Open Door Policy, 310-11; and U.S.S.R. in, 315, 318-19, 340-41; and Soviet pledge to withdraw troops from, 348
Manila, 58, 137, 227, 229
Mao Tse-tung, 27, 128, 129
Marianas, 135, 209, 212, 241
Manhattan Project, 145, 263, 329, 335, 356
Marshall, Gen. George C., 117, 124-26, 136, 138-39, 142-43, 144, 158, 162, 165, 366; on need for U.S.S.R. military aid, 104; and invasion of Japan, 160, 219, 221-22, 224, 236, 238; and question of E. European penetration, 168; and memo to Stimson, 202; and A-bomb, 267-68, 308-309, 336-37, 359; quoted, 340; at Potsdam, 348-49
Marshall Plan of 1947, x, xi, 76
Master Race, 14, 18
McCloy, Assistant Secretary of War John J., 117, 159, 176, 180, 222, 238; and relations with Stimson, 173; and Kyushu invasion, 226; and suggested use of A-bomb, 228
Mashbir, Colonel Sidney: and broadcasts frrm Manila, 229
Massachusetts Institute of Technology (M.I.T.), 263
Mediterranean: and Soviet interest in, 302
Metallurgical Laboratory, 262, 264
Middle East: Britain's oil holdings in,

62-63; and U.S. policy, 79; and American oil companies, 80; and oil, 81; disturbing events in, 113; crisis between U.S. and deGaulle, 118; and Soviet interest in, 302
Midway, 241
Mikolajczyk, Premier Stanislaw, 11, 12, 96-97, 101, 194-96; unacceptable to Lublin Poles, 97; mental flexibility of, 97; influenced by Churchill, 99
Mikoyan, Anastas I., 50
Military aid: from U.S.S.R., 25-26
Military power: of U.S., x, xi
Military strategy: in Pacific War, 142
Missionaries: American in China, 55, 57
"Mission to Moscow," 46
Miyazaki, 223
Molotov, Vyacheslav, 7, 9, 12, 14, 50, 101, 104, 107, 179; and Soviet charge of separate peace agreements, 92-93; and Polish question, 94, 107; and U.N., 99, 171; and Soviet treatment of Polish underground members, 106; and Truman, 111, 221; and Yenan forces, 129; and attitude toward Nationalist China, 131; at San Francisco Conference, 156; replacement of, 174; and discussions with Hopkins, 184; at Potsdam, 281, 291, 295, 299, 314; and relations with Byrnes, 294; and Soviet trusteeship over Italian African colonies, 299, 300; and relations with Japan, 324
Moley, Raymond, 245
Monroe Doctrine, 172
Montgomery Field Marshall (Bernard Law): and capture of Denmark and Western Baltic ports, 167
Montreux Convention, 300-301
Moran, Lord, 352
Morgenthau, Treasury Secretary Henry, Jr., 15, 16, 18, 68-69, 70, 75, 149, 246, 289; advocacy of reconstruction plan, 19-20; diary of, 88
Morgenthau Plan, 16-17, 246, 289
Moscow Declaration of 1943, 316
Mosely, Philip, 15
Mountbatten, Admiral Louis, 345; command responsibility of, 346
Muhammed Riza, Shah, 63

Munich, 8
Murphy, Robert, 279-80

Nagasaki, 152, 322, 333, 347, 367; atomic attack on, 335-36, 356, 359, 360
Nationalist China, 129, 139, 230; army of, 27; collapse of, 57; and Soviet attitudes toward, 131; and resistance to Yalta accords, 141; and American policy goals, 232-33; and Stalin's demands upon, 310-11
National Committee of Americans of Polish Descent, 52
National Labor Relations Board, 40
National War Labor Board, 39
NATO: formation of, 174
Navy Day, 59
Nazis, 47, 59, 248
Nazism: collapse of, 62, 141, 164, 289
Nazi Germany, 8, 69, 114; government of, 17; surrender of, 148-49; destruction of, 224; sattelite states of, 280-84. See also Germany.
Nazi occupation, 2
Near East, Soviet threat to, 151
Negro vote, 255
Neisse River, 286, 293, 295, 297
Neisse line, 296; Western Poland and, 292
Nelson, Donald M., 48-49; quoted, 50
New Deal 38, 46, 87, 245, 250, 252, 253, 255-56; "anti-business" legislation, 40; Truman's attitude toward, 112-13
"New Freedom," 250
New Mexico: and A-bomb test, 210, 305, 308, 335
New York Federal Reserve Bank, 74
New York Herald Tribune, 274
New York Life Insurance Company, 263
New York Times, 90; quoted, 84, 138
New Zealand: deployment of troops of, 121-22, 345; and Anzac Pact, 344
Nicolson, Harold, 85
Nimitz, Adm. Chester W., 138, 139, 222, 337; and FDR, 257
Nine Power Treaty on China, 53
Nippon, 152, 201, 213, 241; American occupation of, 319
Normandy, 21, 224
North Africa, 9
North China, 132, 159

Northeast Asia, 366
Nuclear arms race, 148

Occupation, by Nazis, 2; of Austria, 164; of Germany, 164, 277, 289
—by Britain, 298
—by France, 290, 298
—by Poland, 290, 293, 296
—by U.S.S.R., 164, 293, 295-96, 298, 341
—by U.S., 60, 322; of Iran, 302
—by Yugoslavia, 290; of Japan, 219, 272-73
Occupation zones, 180
Oder Line, 97
Office of Price Administration (O.P.A.), 112
Office of Production Management, 38
Office of Scientific Research and Development, 263
Office of War Information, 46, 229
Office of War Mobilization and Reconversion, 251
Oil: British holdings, 62-63, 81; in Middle East, 78, 80; oil interests and Roosevelt, 79; regulation of, 81; in Oklahoma and Texas, 81
Okinawa, 135, 138, 139, 210-12, 226, 236, 238, 345, 364; U.S. invasion of, 21, 23-34; and U.S. sphere of influence, 175; fall of, 213; casualties at, 225
Okinawa Campaign, 21
Oklahoma, 81
Olympic, 222. See also Kyushu operation.
Open Door Policy, 310, 311, 312
Oppenheimer, J. Robert, 264, 267, 306
Organization of American States, 174
Orthodox churches, 49
OSS, 152, 155
Outer Mongolia, 34, 311

P-47 raids, 212
P-61 raids, 212
PAC. See Political Action Committee.
Pacific: war in, 44, 59; oil supply in, 80; U.S. control of, 177, 178
Pacific War, and Soviet entry into, 34, 104, 128, 132-33, 150, 162, 277, 306-307, 312-19, 321, 327-28, 337-38, 340, 342-43, 349, 353-54, 358-59; victory in, 57, 322; American

policy toward, 127; 134-35; and strategy of, 136, 138, 142, 257, 347; and Siberian project, 140; U.S. interventions in, 152; operations in, 158; and Big Three unity, 200; and U.S. peace initiatives, 205; and American casualties, 209; end of, 241, 340; and German reparations negotiations, 287; American interests in, 317; responsibility for, 346-47

Pasvolsky, Leo, 15

Patterson, Robert, 358-59

Patton, Gen. George S., 164, 336

Pauley, Edwin, 255-56, 290, 294, 310

Peace treaties: Hungarian, 285; Bulgarian, 285; Rumanian, 285; Italian, 285

Pearl Harbor, 44, 55, 57-58, 87-88, 175-76, 226, 330, 363, 367; retribution for, 221

Peffer, Nathaniel: quoted, 55-56

Pendergast, Jim, 86, 87, 88

Pentagon, 221

Pershing: quoted, 219-20

Persian Gulf: and American oil holdings, 80

Pétain, Henri Philippe O., 113

Petroleum: U.S. reserves of, 79-80. *See also* Oil.

Philippines, 21, 138, 175-76; U.S. sphere of influence, 175

Pilsen, Czechoslovakia, 165

Pogue, Forrest C., 30*n*

Point Four, xi

Poland, 16, 127, 312; and Soviet demands for, 7, 292; Britain's refusal to abandon, 10; U.S.-Soviet relationships, 94; border of, 97, 292-94, 296-97, 318; importance to U.S.S.R. security, 108; and problems of East-West relations, 171; and Yalta agreements on, 195; and resolution of issue in, 195-98, 275, 295; and Stalin's victory, 196-97; and reparations, 288; as a political issue at Potsdam, 288; and occupation of Germany, 290, 296. *See also* Polish question.

Polish border: and contests over, 288

Poland Fights, 52

Polish question, 94, 181-82, 193-96, 249, 261, 274-75; Churchill's position on, 108-109; and Stalin, 107; as viewed by Stimson, 104; U.S. policy on, 104-105; as viewed by Leahy, 105;

U.S.S.R. arrests members of Polish underground, 109

Polish-Americans: and anti-Soviet feelings, 52

Polish Declaration, 32

Polish Government Information Center, 52

Polish Labor Group, 52

Polish Review, 52

Polish underground, 11, 105-106; Russian treatment of, 106; members arrested in U.S.S.R., 109

Political Action Committee of CIO, 38; and New Deal proposals, 38

Port Arthur, 34, 159, 217, 230-33, 235, 309; Soviet military control over, 311; and Byrne's fear of Soviet thrust to, 343

Potsdam Conference, 4, 77, 79, 113, 192, 215, 228, 235-36, 241-43, 269, 270, 317, 347; and Soviet aspirations, 20; achievements of, 200; and U.S. delegation to, 244; and Big Three peace, 270-71; and European issues, 270-304; close of, 271; and Truman's memo for, 276-77; and beginning of Cold War, 303; and Far Eastern issues, 305-55; and A-bomb, 305-55

Potsdam Declaration, 315, 319, 327, 329-32, 334, 338

Potsdam Proclamation, 329

Prague, 165-66; and fall to Soviets, 169

Public opinion: on German war settlement, 17; against wartime labor strikes, 39; and diplomatic decision-making, 43, 44, 65; toward U.S.S.R., 45-47, 51, 57, 60; and anti-U.S.S.R. sentiment among Polish Americans, 52; toward China, 53, 56-57, 60; toward Japan, 57-60, 82, 221; against Germany, 59; and British imperialism, 60-62, 82; and oil regulation, 81, 82; and shock over Russian behavior in Rumania, 92; and crisis in Syria, 116; and French refusal to leave Val d'Aosta, 116; on A-bomb in Russia, 360-62; in U.S., 362-64; U.S., during W.W.II, 367

Purnell, Adm., 336

R.A.F. Bomber Command, 345

Raskob, John J., 252

Rayburn, U.S. Congressman Sam, 255
Realpolitik, 350
Reciprocal Trade Agreement Bill, 66
Reciprocal Trade Program, 67
Reconstruction, postwar, 71; postwar economic, 82
Red Army, 6-8, 10, 11, 135, 201, 282, 303, 309, 362, 366; in Manchuria, 315, 318, 319; and Nazis, 361
Red Star: Tito's interview with, 121
Regional pacts, 173-75, 180-81
Reparations, 285, 318; German, 66-67, 286-87, 291-92, 298; U.S.S.R. demands for Italy, 284; and German navy, 287-88; and Poland, 288; and Soviet claims for, 291-92, 294, 295
Reparations Commission, 277, 289-92, 298
Reparation Plan, 291
Republican Party, 144
Rhine, 300
Rickenbacker, Edward V. "Eddie," 48
Robinson, Joseph, 252
Roman Catholic Church, 51
Romney, George, 39-40
Roosevelt, Eleanor: and succession of HST to Presidency, 84
Roosevelt, President Franklin D., 2, 9, 15, 16, 20, 30, 32, 33, 46, 47, 49, 50, 98, 101, 129, 161, 249, 251, 253-59, 274, 306, 336; and restoration of Polish state, 11-13; and second Quebec Conference, 17, 18; at Yalta, 19, 29, 66, 88, 153, 231, 328; death of, 23, 47, 83-85, 99, 138, 144, 261, 354, 366; and Stalin, 34, 35; last days of presidency, 36; and hints for guaranteed annual wage, 40; and fear of Polish-American anti-Soviet feeling, 52; and U.N., 55; and attitude toward British Empire, 61; and oil interests, 79-81; policies and personality of, 83; and Truman, 85, 259-60; relationship with Hopkins, 88; and foreign policy, 88; succeeded by Truman, 89; and Rumania, 92; and denial of separate peace agreement, 92-94; and policy toward U.S.S.R., 96; policies of, followed by Truman, 105; and plan for policy with Tito, 122; and relations with Churchill, 143, 166; and U.N. trusteeship, 175; and Lend-Lease, 188,

271; and decline of State Dept's influence, 245; health of, 252; and Byrnes, 256-57, 258-59, 263; and atomic secret, 353
Roosevelt Revolution, 38
Roseman, Samuel I., 359
Rowan, Leslie, 307
Ruhr, 16, 19, 166, 293, 295; and Stalin's demand for, 295-97
Rumania: and Soviet claims to, 7; and Communist-imposed gov't, 91, 199; Soviet intervention in, 106-107; and Allied armistice agreement with, 245; crisis over, 261; and U.N. membership, 283
Russell, Donald: and Soviet demands on China, 311; quoted, 312
Russian Liberation and Polish resistance, 11
Russian War Relief, Inc., 47
Ryukyus. *See* Okinawa.

S-1. *See* Atomic bomb.
Saar Valley, 16
Sakhalin, 207, 234; Russian reoccupation of, 34
San Francisco United Nations Conference, 59, 90, 109, 119, 142, 145, 147, 163, 171-72, 175, 178-81, 183, 199-200, 236, 244, 249, 262, 299, 368; and Polish Lublin government, 105; and trusteeship issue, 176, 181
Sato, Naotake, 28, 322; and relations with Molotov, 324; quoted, 325; and relations with Stalin, 328
Sattelite states: in E. Europe, 7
Saturday Evening Post, 62
Saudi-Arabia: and American oil interests in, 80
Second Front, 8, 9
Second Quebec Conference, 16-17, 189
Senate. *See* U.S. Senate.
Service, John, 129
Shantung peninsula, 138
Shensi province, 27
Shigemitsu, Foreign Minister, 207
Shipping pool, 287-88
Shuri Line: on Okinawa, 24
Siberia, 133-34; and U.S.S.R. military bases, 25; and radio and weather stations in, 348-49
Silesia, 16, 19, 293

Singapore, 299

Sino-Soviet relations, 312-13, 318, 344

Sino-Soviet Treaty, 229-30, 235; in Yalta agreements, 34

Smith, Harold, 112-13; and Lend-Lease, 189-90

Smyth Report, 356

Sophia, Control Commission in, 248, 249

Soong, T. V., 160-61, 312-13, 318; and relations with Soviets, 200, 213, 235; and relations with Truman, 231-34

Soviet-American relations, 20, 133, 145, 178, 182, 186, 275, 366; strain in, 92, 144, 184; and nuclear arms race, 148; and impact of A-bomb, 160-61; and lessening of tensions in at San Francisco, 180; following German surrender, 191; and military talks at Potsdam, 347; and Hiroshima, 354

Spaatz, Gen. Carl, 329

Spaso House, 94-95, 135

Spain, 283; Attlee's attitude toward, 285; Bevin's attitude toward, 285; condemnation of, 285

Stabilization: as U.S. goal, 20

Stalin, xii, 7-12, 15, 30, 33, 52, 156, 180, 192, 307; and Yalta, 14, 66, 88, 130, 153; and American romanticism of, 45, 83; purges of, 46; and rebuilding U.S.S.R., 49; and talks with Nelson, 50; and separate peace agreement, 92; and charges of violations of Yalta Polish agreement, 95-96; and Warsaw uprising, 95; and Polish question, 97, 99, 107, 194-95, 198-99; and support of Lublin government, 105, 107; and U.S. interpretation of Yalta Agreement, 107; difficulties in dealing with, 113; and Venezia Giulia situation, 125; and Yenan forces, 129; and Far Eastern concessions to, 130; and Nationalist China, 131; and Kennan's charges against, 132; and support of Chinese Communists, 139; and relations with Hurley, 140, 230; and relations with Truman, 162, 193-94, 196-97, 201-202, 243, 273, 281, 327; and trusteeship compromise, 178; and relations with Hopkins, 181, 183-84, 187, 191, 193-97, 199-202, 221, 229-32, 234-35, 349, 359-

60; and reaction to lend-lease policy, 191; and American sattelites, 199; and relations with Soong, 200, 313; and support of Chiang Kai-Shek, 200; and influence on American strategic planning, 202, 221; and demands on China, 235, 312-13, 342-43; and A-bomb, 268, 351-52, 361; at Potsdam, 270-71, 273, 277-78, 281, 283-84, 288, 291-97, 299-303, 309-18, 327-28, 338-39, 342-43, 350; and Soviet intervention in Far East, 277; questioned by Bevin, 284; on U.N. proposal, 284; confronted on reparations, 286-87; and occupation of Germany, 293; and demands for Ruhr, 295-97; and issue of Dardanelles, 300-301, 309; and withdrawal of troops from Iran, 302; and commitment to Open Door Policy, 312; and relations with Sato, 328

Stanton, E. F., 132

Stassen, Commander Harold, quoted on trusteeship issue, 177

State Department (U.S.), 15, 18, 50-51, 53, 78, 106, 121, 133, 158, 172, 177, 180, 183, 229, 231, 241, 246-49, 261, 275-76, 282, 316, 333; attitude toward U.S.S.R., 20; and attitude toward Kuomintong, 27; sentiments toward China, 27; and Declaration on Liberated Europe, 30-31; and Roosevelt's foreign policy, 80; and U.N., 101; and Middle Eastern crisis with France, 119; and Hopkins mission, 185-87; and Lend-Lease, 190; decline in power and influence of, 245; and Potsdam Declaration, 331-33; and position paper on Far East for Potsdam Conf., 340-42; and paper on British policy in Far East, 343-44; and official Japanese protest on Hiroshima, 364

State-War-Navy Coordinating Committee, 364

Steinbeck, John, 42

Stettinius, Edward R., 90, 98, 101, 109, 131-32, 144, 167, 174, 178, 180, 245-47; and policy toward U.S.S.R., 90; and Molotov, 107, 109; and distrust of Stalin, 130; and statement of Lend-Lease policy, 191; resignation of,

244; replacement of, 262; at San Francisco Conf., 299

Stilwell, Gen. Joseph W., 58, 128-29

St. Lô, 221

Stimson, Secretary of War Henry L., 15, 116, 117, 122-24, 126, 133, 136, 144-45, 157-58, 162, 173, 180, 202, 217, 222, 229, 250, 313, 316, 319, 333, 336, 338, 340, 349, 366; and objections to Morgenthau Plan, 18; views on Eastern Europe problem, 103; and relations with Truman, 145, 176, 214, 217-18, 225-26, 228, 238-42, 262, 309-12, 316, 351-52; and A-bomb, 145, 148, 188, 214-15, 217, 236-37, 262-64, 266, 268, 308, 351-52, 357-59; and fading hopes for U.N., 146, 147; and plans for attack on Japan, 159-60, 213, 225-26, 228, 236-42; and view on Soviet entry into Pacific War, 161; and Soviet-American relations, 161; and skepticism of trusteeship approach, 175-76; and Russian Lend-Lease, 190; quoted, 217, 339; and disgust with Stettinius, 247; and relations with Churchill, 306; quoted, 308-309; and Potsdam Declaration, 328-32; and relations with Byrnes, 329; at Potsdam, 343, 356; and cessation of bombing raids over Japan, 364

Stockholm: American mission in, 9

Stuttgart, 114-15

Suez: and Soviet probe toward, 299

Suicide missions: Japaneses, 208-209, 210

Sultan of Morocco, 62

Supreme Court (U.S.), 251

Suzuki, Adm. Baron Kantaro, 205-206

Swiss legation: and Japan's protest of Hiroshima raid, 364

Switzerland, 317; exploratory talks in, 92

Syria, crisis in, 116, 118

Szilard, Leo, 264-66; and atomic weaponry, 356-57

T.A. (Tube Alloy), 242. See also "S-1" atomic bomb.

Taft, Sen. Robert A., and lend-lease, 75

Tanham, James, 39

Tarawa, 209, 241

Taylor, Gen. Maxwell D., 336

Tehran Conference, 12, 15, 29, 46, 50, 52, 79

Tennessee Valley Authority (TVA), 112

Tennō system, 152, 154, 241

Terminal, 274. *See also* Potsdam Conf., 274

Texas, 81

"Three Russian Girls," 45

Third Reich, 138

Time magazine, 66; quoted, 216

Tinian, 358

Tito, difficulties in dealing with, 113; dealings with Truman, 116; and Anglo-American relations, 120; and Venezia Giulia, 120-23, 124, 125, 182

Togo, Foreign Minister Shigenori, 322-24, 326-27

Tokyo, 151, 204; and U.S. fire-bomb raids, 22

Tokyo Plain, 149, 155; invasion of, 214, 223, 227, 344, 345, 346

Trade relations, 53-54

Treasury Department, U.S., 72, 78, 246

Trieste, 120-21, 123-26; crisis in, 199

Truman Committee, 88

Truman, President Harry S., xi, 47, 107, 215, 222, 250, 255-56, 264, 284-85, 336-37, 349; and comment made on V-E Day, 59; accession to presidency, 84-85, 88-89, 94, 99, 139; biographical sketch of, 85-90; entry into politics, 86; Senate service of, 87-89; foreign policy of, 89; and Polish question, 99-100, 196-97, 293; advised by Harriman, 100; reaction to Russian demands, 101-102; and Eastern Europe, 102-103, 167-68, 199; and relations with Molotov, 104, 221; and relations with Churchill, 108-109, 113-14, 166, 180, 193, 195-96, 199, 243, 330; on presidency, 111; compared with Roosevelt, 111; and U.N., 111; domestic goals of, 112; and efforts to reorganize Executive Dept., 112; at Potsdam, 113, 216, 242-43, 269-70, 273, 275-84, 293, 295, 297, 300-304, 306, 308-313, 316-19, 327-31, 333, 339-40, 342, 350-56; and relations with deGaulle, 114-16, 119; and Val d'Aosta problem, 116; and view toward U.S.S.R., 120; and Venezia Giulia situation, 121-26; and East Asian diplomacy, 126; and China, 133, 232-34, 313, 315; and plans to use A-bomb, 143-44, 214, 335, 338; and relations with Stimson, 145, 176, 218, 225-26, 238-42, 262, 309-12, 330, 351; and decision to drop A-bomb, 146, 240-41, 318, 329, 350-51; and statement on domestic transportation, 149; relations with Hopkins, 157, 182-88, 191, 193-200, 245-46; and meeting with Stalin and Churchill, 159; and Soviet-American relations, 161, 182; relationship with Grew, 162; and view on Soviet entry into Pacific War, 162; and ebb of interest in European affairs, 169; and U.S. withdrawal of forces from E. Europe, 169; and postwar treaty with Latin Americans, 173; and lend-lease, 189-90, 192, 271; and relations with Stalin, 193-94, 196-97, 199, 215-16, 242-43, 273, 281, 327; and postponing of Potsdam Conf., 215; and approval of Kyushu operation, 226-27; and talks with Soong, 231; and San Francisco Conf., 236; and warning to Japanese, 241-42; and relations with Byrnes, 244-45, 249, 269; and resignation of Stettinius, 244; and relations with Barnes, 249; supported for vice-presidential nomination, 256-58; and FDR, 259-60; and reminiscences of Potsdam, 271; quoted, 272, 337; and memo for Potsdam Conf., 276-77; and renunciation of American reparations claims, 293; on German reparations, 287; and blunder over Ruhr negotiation, 295-97; and European waterways, 300-301; on troops in Iran, 302; and Open Door Policy, 310-11; and relations with Chiang, 311-12; and Eisenhower, 317; and Potsdam Declaration, 329-31; and unconditional surrender, 333; and disclosure of A-bomb secret to Stalin, 351, 353; and reaction to Hiroshima, 359, 368; and reaction to public outcry on bomb, 363-64; and report on Potsdam Conf. (quoted), 363-64;

and effects of decision to drop A-bomb, 366
Truman Doctrine, xi, 279, 290
Tugwell, Rexford, 245
Turkey and Dardanelles, 300-301

U-235, 335
Ukraine, 171
United Mine Workers, 39
United Nations Charter, 145, 316
United Nations Conference, 170-71, 236
United Nations Organization, 30, 44, 55, 100, 147, 283, 363; American sentiment on, 101; and Truman, 111; and French rights in Lebanon and Syria, 119; and lack of ability to restrain Soviets, 151; and trusteeships, of Korea, 157, 200; and organization problems of, 171, 172; Security Council of, 172, 179; structure of, 174; and trusteeships, 175-78, 181; and San Francisco Conf., 262; and U.S.S.R.-British relations, 284; and membership of Balkan States and Italy, 285, 296, 297; and trusteeships of U.S.S.R. over Italian N. African colonies, 299, 309, 339; American delegation to, 368
United Nations Relief and Rehabilitation Agency, 66, 71
UNRRA. *See* United Nations Relief and Rehabilitation Agency.
U.S.S.R., 28; U.S. proposed loan to, x, xi, 6, 49-50, 77, 156, 191-92; effects of W.W.II on, 2, 5; and balance of power, 4, 5; and W.W.II casualties, 5; military power of, 6, 163; and rebuilding its economy, 6, 14; purges in, 6; industrial system in, 6; and control of E. Europe, 7, 91-92, 113, 151, 169, 188, 199, 248, 276-77, 298, 339; and desire for physical security, 8, 49, 108, 174; and war with Nazi Germany, 8, 14, 139, 361-62; State Dept.'s attitude toward, 20; and Elbe, 20; military bases, 25; and entry into Pacific War, 28, 34, 132-33, 138-41, 148-50, 162, 214, 229, 234, 277, 306-307, 312-19, 321, 327-28, 337-38, 340, 342-43, 349, 353-54, 358-59; and war against Japan, 29, 33, 104, 134, 158; and reoccupation of

Sakhalin, 34; agreements on China with Churchill and Roosevelt, 34-35; as great Pacific naval power, 35; public opinion toward, 44-47, 57, 60, 83; and strengthening of American economy, 50; and Polish question, 52, 171; and trade with China, 54; and postwar credits, 64; and postwar economic policies, 68; and interest in Middle East, 80, 302; and relations with U.S., 82, 94, 144, 245-46; and violation of Declaration of Liberated Europe, 91; and charges of separate peace agreement, 92-93; and misinterpretation of U.S. actions, 95; and American foreign policy toward, 95, 102; and recognition of Syrian and Lebanese independence, 118; and support of Tito, 123; and Venezia Giulia situation, 123; and Chinese Communists, 128-29, 132, 342; and recognition of Kuomintang gov't, 129; and intentions in China, 130, 182, 230-31, 315, 319; and China, attitude toward Nationalist China, 131; and feared break with Chiang Kai-shek, 132; and violation of Yalta agreements, 135; non-renewal of Neutrality Pact with Japan, 138, 206, 208; and expansion in Northeast Asia, 140, 322, 366; and A-bomb secret, 147-48, 263-69, 306, 351, 353-54, 366; and China, unification of, 157; and occupation of Japan, 164, 272-73; of Germany, 293-96, 298; and anger with Latin Americans, 172; and interest in autonomous regional security, 174; and treaty with France, 174; and U.N. trusteeship, 177, 178; and demands for inclusion of Argentina in U.N., 178-79; and conflict with U.S. at San Francisco, 179; and Hopkin's mission to, 182-203; and Japan's attempt to bribe, 206-207, 211; and Marshall's attempt to involve U.S.S.R. in Manchuria, 223; and China, 233-35; and Four Power Alliance, 276; and pledges at Potsdam, 271; and intervention in Far East, 277; and claims for reparations, 284, 291-92, 294-95; and postwar plans for Germany, 292-

94; and access to Eastern Mediterranean, 299; and trusteeship over Italian N. African colonies, 299, 309, 339; and control of Dardanelles, 299-301, 339; and troops in Iran, 302; and demands for concessions in Far East, 310-11; in Manchuria, 313, 315, 340-41, 347-49; and demands on Japan, 315; and China, intervention in, 342

U.S., and policies affecting Cold War, ix; and balance of power, ix, 4, 5; and military might, xi, x, 4; living standard during W.W.II, 3, 37; anti-imperialist sentiment in, 5, 79; reparations policy on Germany, 14-15, 289, 292-93; and proposed loan to U.S.S.R., 19, 156; and attack of Japan, 21, 136, 213; and capture of Iwo Jima, 21; economy of at end of W.W.II, 37; wartime mood of, 37, 43-44; and attitude toward U.S.S.R., 47-48; and penetration of Eastern European market, 50; and loans to U.S. business in China, 54; and China, 55, 131; and pledge of resources to World Bank, 69; and Mideast policy, 79; and attitude toward postwar reconstruction, 83; reliance upon U.S.S.R. aid, 101; and recognition of Syrian and Lebanese independence, 118; and China, attitude toward Russian influence, 128; and Soviet plans for assault against Japanese, 134; and air and naval blockade of Japan, 137; and relations with France over Indochina, 151; and relations with British over Hong Kong, 151; and China, market in, 155; and relations with Latin America, 173-74; and U.N. trusteeship question, 176-77; and control of Pacific, 177, 178, 180; and conflict with Soviets at San Francisco, 179; and postwar loans to Britain, 189; and lend-lease policy, 191; and relations with U.S.S.R., 245-46; and possible armament race in U.S.S.R., 263-64; and Four Power Alliance, 276; as mediator between U.K. and U.S.S.R., 286; and occupation of Germany, 289; and troops in Iran, 302; and occupation of Japan, 332

U.S. Army, 114, 120, 149, 164; in France, 115; and Brenner Pass, 124-25

U.S. Army Air Force, 149, 212-13, 366; and fire-bomb raids against Japan, 21-22; in Marianas, 22; and Okinawa invasion, 23-24; and attack on Japan, 345

U.S. Navy, 366; and Okinawa invasion, 23-24; and Middle Eastern crisis with France, 120

U.S. Senate: Manpower Investigating Committee, 39; Foreign Relations Committee, 59, 81-82; and Lublin government, 100

U.S. Strategic Bombing Survey, 213

University of Chicago, 262

V-2 attacks, 4

Val d'Aosta, 115, 116, 117; crisis in, 199

Vandenberg, U.S. Sen. Arthur H., 85, 179, 180; quoted, 65-66; and Lend-Lease funds, 75; and Polish question, 197-98; and replacement of Stettinius, 244

Van Schuyler, Gen., 107

V-E Day, 59, 166; and curtailment of lend-lease, 188

Venezia Giulia, 120-21, 122-25; and Tito's movement in, 182

Versailles, 20, 274

Vichy government, 113

Vienna, 169

Vietnam, xi

Vistula, 10

Volga, 1

Vyshinski, Andrei, 91, 92

Walker, Frank, 255

Wallace, Henry, 85, 128, 253, 254, 255, 256, 257, 258, 273, 303

Walsh, U.S. Sen. David I., 260

War correspondents, 58, 59

War Department, 240

Warsaw, 11

Warsaw Pact, 174

Wartime contracts, 88

Wehrmacht, 8, 165, 166

Welles, Secretary of the Navy Sumner, 55

Werth, Alexander, 270, 361

Western Europe: and revival of trade in, 54; operations in, 115

White, Harry Dexter, 15; and U.S. post-war finance plan, 72-73

White, Theodore H., 57

Whitehall, 221

Wiley, U.S. Sen. Alexander: quoted, 334

Wilkie, Wendell: quoted, 65

Wilson, President Woodrow, 250

Winant, Ambassador, 165

World Bank, 69

W.W. I, 18, 66, 250

W.W. II, 43; Cold war after, ix; American foreign policy during, xii, 65; casualties of in Europe, 1; mood of Europe after, 2; casualties of in Britain, 4; and European balance of power, 5; in Europe, 36; American entry into, 55; American mood throughout, 82; end of, 139, 142, 158, 187, 356, 357, 360, 365; power relations between U.S. and U.S.S.R. created by, 181; casualties of U.S. in Pacific, 209; and diplomacy and strategy, 246

Yalta Conference, 14, 17, 19, 29, 30, 32, 34, 47, 52, 66, 91, 93, 94, 95, 97, 130, 152, 153, 219, 245, 248, 259, 261, 275, 276, 290, 291; and Polish question, 13, 94, 96, 104, 195; objectives of, 29; and agreements on Europe, 30; and U.N., 30; agreements presented to French government, 31; Far Eastern accords, 33, 187, 229, 231, 232, 235, 310-11, 313, 315, 327; "spirit of," 36, 90, 180; agreement on Poland, 96, 97, 195; and Mikolajczyk, 99; Declaration on Liberated Europe, 106, 248; vagueness of, 108; and exclusion of de-Gaulle, 113, 114; and Russian attitude toward Nationalist China, 129; Stalin-Roosevelt agreements at, 133; and Soviet attitudes, 134; and Soviet violations of agreements of, 135; and possible modification of Far Eastern accords, 140-41, 157; and Nationalist China's resistance to, 141; Soviet actions after, 151; and concessions to

Russia at, 161, 164, 206-207, 312; and agreements on German and Austrian occupation of, 164; and occupational zones, 168; and Truman's adherence to, 169; and outlines for new League of Nations, 171; and veto power agreement, 179; and proposals on China, 200; U.S.S.R. commitment to enter Pacific War, 200; and reparations, 291, 292, 298; U.S.-U.S.S.R. friction after, 343

Yalta Declaration on Liberated Europe, status of, 107-108. *See also* Declaration on Liberated Europe.

Yen, Y. C. James: quoted, 56-57

Yenan, 133; forces of, 129; Communists, 229

Yugoslavia, 107, 127, 167; government of, 96; and dispute over Venezia Giulia, 120-22; and proposed occupation of Germany, 290

Yugoslavs: and territorial conflicts with, 116

Zacharias, Capt. Ellis M., 229